DIVINE MYSTERIES
OF THE
MOST HOLY ROSARY

Taken verbatim from the "City of God" (4 Volumes). Complete, inspiring, beautiful, a help for all who wish to understand the spiritual depth and meaning of The Rosary and the important events that it represents in the Life of Our Lord and His Most Holy Mother.

Imparting a full knowledge of its Mysteries, you will realize, possibly for the first time, what a treasure the Mother of God gave us about 750 years ago thru St. Dominic.

Because it has so often in the past revitalized the spirituality of people from every walk of life, clergy, religious, laity— young, middle aged, elderly, many are now turning again to Our Lady for help through it.

Yes, because of it, everyone's faith becomes more vital, alive and fruitful. Thru the promotion of it all can make their spare time invaluable to help save Souls, our Youth, Country and Church.

With a history replete with victory after victory, and now in our times, Austria, Brazil and Chile, should we then have anything but full trust and confidence in it. Also starting today, make a sincere, honest, Yes, even heroic effort so this "Heaven sent," most powerful weapon for saving souls and to obtain peace can become known to all sincere Christians everywhere. Can you think of anything that you could do that would be more important!!!

PUBLISHED In gratitude
To Our Lord for giving us and the world thru His Most Holy Mother and Mary of Agreda the following interesting and enlightening details of His Life.

The narrations are historic, authentic and in a terminology unique yet simple.

Once committed to memory, many of these important and intimate details will have a flash back each time you pray with devotion the various fifteen decades composing the complete Rosary.

You may also wish to remember that the Rosary is a gift from the World's Greatest Mother, the Person who knew Our Lord better than anyone who ever lived on earth.

It will be a treasure to you now, and until you are safe in your heavenly home for all eternity; there to enjoy the beatific vision of Our Lord Himself, His Holy Mother and the Saints forever and ever and ever.

You will also have the satisfaction of knowing that you are contributing in an important way each day and with each Rosary you say to the Security of Our Church and Country as well as the Peace of the World. Remember the Promise of Our Lady of Fatima, 1917, "WHEN ENOUGH PEOPLE WILL PRAY THE ROSARY EVERYDAY, RUSSIA WILL BE CONVERTED AND AN ERA OF PEACE GRANTED TO THE WORLD," is still in effect. She is only awaiting the cooperation of each and everyone of us.

DIVINE MYSTERIES
OF THE
MOST HOLY ROSARY

FIRST PRINTING, FEBRUARY, 1973
SECOND PRINTING, MAY, 1974
THIRD PRINTING, JUNE, 1976

Compiled, edited and published by
J.M.J. BOOK COMPANY
P.O. Box 15
Necedah, Wis. 54646

Printed in the United States of America

THE SUBLIME MISSION OF THE ROSARY

The "MISSION" of the Rosary is to bring us to a realization of the purpose of our existence and of the importance of applying the TRUTHS of the Gospel in our daily life and conduct. If, up until now, the praying of the Rosary has not produced these results, is it not because we have not been properly informed in its correct use, nor told of its purpose? In consequence of this lack of sufficient knowledge, then, we have not been praying the Rosary with due understanding and devotion.

Our Blessed Mother once complained: My little children are not taught the true meaning of the Rosary.

"When the Rosary is said properly, My POWER is behind it. Say it with My Divine Son and Me in mind, and *ask Me* to *bring about* the *true value of this Devotion;* then each bead said well can conquer a host of men."

The great St. Bernard, Doctor of the Church, gives us the correct method of praying the Rosary and if adopted, surprising results will follow. He states in his writing on the subject: "While your lips pronounce the words let your mind 'picture' the Mystery—not as an event which took place centuries ago, but as events taking place NOW in your presence. In each mental picture thus formed, see also yourself there *in* the scene, *studying* the scene. St. Bernard warns not to change the mental 'picture' but let it remain unchanged. He states that if the 'picture' is recalled without change, it will become more life-like.

A clearer mental picture of each mystery of the Rosary will be attained if only one meditation on a mystery is read a day. Perhaps better effects still would result, if some one would read aloud each of the meditations on the different mysteries while the others of the family listen. After several weeks, the various members of the family should take turns at reading the meditations so that all may share alike the opportunity to profit from the Scriptural promise: *"Faith* comes through *hearing."*

DEDICATION

To the "Queen of the Holy Rosary and Queen of the Powerful Scapular of Carmel." Also to "The Woman" (Mary, the Mother of Christ), referred to in Genesis, Chapter 3 verse 15: "I will put enmities between thee and the Woman, and thy seed and Her seed: She shall crush thy head, and thou shalt lie in wait for Her heel."

The Apocalypse, Chapter 12: "And a great sign appeared in the heaven: a Woman clothed with the sun, and the moon and stars under Her feet, and upon Her head a crown with twelve stars."

St. Peter Damian says of Mary that She is "The Mother of True Peace." For centuries the whole Church has designated Her Scapular the Signum Pacis, Sign of Peace. Hence, in our days when peace among nations is so precarious, the Scapular takes on a fresh value in our eyes, i.e., a value Mary has placed there appears in new brilliance. That Sign commandeers the prayers of the Mediatrix of All Grace and since Peace is effected solely by the disposition of hearts, something Grace alone can effect, the Scapular can be said to be indeed a most powerful Sign of Peace.

It is to be remembered that absence of conflict is not a state of Peace. When a strong man bullies a weak one to quiet submission, although there is no conflict there is no peace. Only one thing can bring about World Peace, and that is Prayer. World conferences which are convened to forestall the crazed thirst of a dictator only feed his ego. Only God, Who alone has power over human wills, can prevent war.

CONTENTS

PREFACE

Taken from the City of God and given by The Blessed Virgin Mary to Venerable Mary of Agreda, these Meditations are reprinted to help all sincere Christians to better understand and appreciate the beauty and depth of the intimate details of the Life, Death and Resurrection of Our Lord as only His Most Holy Mother could give them. Therefore, it is both vocal and mental prayer. The mental prayer consisting of the Meditations, while the vocal is made up of the Our Father, the perfect prayer, the Hail Mary, the Angels salutation to Mary as He informed Her that She was chosen to be the Mother of God, and the "Glory Be" in which the Blessed Trinity is recognized and honored.

Speaking to Blessed Alan one day, Our Lord said, "If only these poor wretched sinners would say My Rosary, they would share in the Merits of My Passion and I would be their Advocate and would appease My Father's Justice."

On another occasion Our Lady revealed to Blessed Alan, "that after the Holy Sacrifice of the Mass, which is the most important as well as the Living Memorial of Our Blessed Lord's Passion there could not be a finer devotion or one of greater merit than that of the Rosary."

Naturally, it will be of interest to those who sincerely hope and strive to go to Heaven as soon as possible after their death, that Our Blessed Mother said, "I want you to know that, although there are numerous indulgences already attached to the recitation of My Rosary, I shall add many more to every fifty Hail Marys (each group of five decades) for those who say them devoutly, on their knees, being of course, free from mortal sin. And whosoever shall persevere in the devotion of the Holy Rosary, saying these prayers and meditations, shall be rewarded for it; I shall obtain for them full remission of the penalty and of the guilt of all his sins at the end of his life. Do not be unbelieving, as though this is impossible. It is easy for Me to do because I am the Mother of the King of Heaven, and He calls Me 'Full of Grace.' And being 'Full of Grace,' I am able to dispense Grace freely to My dear children."

The Rosary is the "Root and the storehouse of many blessings. Through it: sinners are forgiven, souls that are fettered have their bonds broken, those who weep find happiness, those who are tempted find peace, the poor find help, religious are reformed, those who are ignorant are instructed, the living learn to overcome pride, the dead (the Holy Souls) have their pains eased by prayer and sacrifice."

For far too long, sincere good Christians, clergy and laity, have not given full consideration to the outstanding and beautiful promise by the Mother of God at Fatima 1917 when She said, "When enough people will pray the Rosary every day, Russia will be converted and an Era of Peace granted to the World."

Considering the threat of a Nuclear War and the even more devastating holocaust of Divine Chastisement, that apparently is very close, should not every Christian start now, today, to say at least five or whenever possible the full fifteen decades.

For proof in our time of the "Power of the Rosary," see Brazil's Victory over Communism, "The Country that Saved Itself," Reader's Digest, Nov. 1964. Also The Victory in Chile 1973.

What the Universities of Europe, the Religious Orders and Learned Men Say of the "City of God"

Forty years after the first appearance of the "City of God" the great universities of Europe were called upon to give their opinion about this great work. All the faculties, except the Jansenistic members of the Sorbonne at Paris, published highest recommendations. At the same time the learned men and teachers of each religious order that maintained institutions of learning in Europe, were asked to contribute their opinions. The following religious orders complied: The Augustinians, Benedictines, Carmelites, Dominicans, Jesuits, Cistercians, Basilians, Trinitarians, Mercedarians, Minims, Hieronymites, Premonstratensians, Reformed Augustinians, Theatines, Minors of the Regular Clergy, all unanimously endorsing the favorable decision previously published by the University of Salamanca. To the approbation of nearly all the Universities and Religious Orders, were then added the high eulogiums of other learned men, Great Divines, Bishops and Princes of the Church and of the Popes and the Roman Congregations. As a sample of what these witnesses said concerning the wonderful "City of God," we here select the official approbation of the University of Louvain, one of the great Universities of Europe. After pointing out that God's power of giving private revelations to whom He chooses, must not be circumscribed, and after referring to some general rules in regard to private revelations, the document proceeds to say:

1

Now, while abiding the decision of the Church concerning the revelations, which are given us under the title of The City of God, we, having read the whole work, say and are of the opinion, that the faithful can read it without danger to their faith and without damage to the purity of morals; for there is not found anything within it, which could lead to relaxation or to indiscreet rigor; but on the contrary, we have come to the conclusion that it will be most useful for enlivening and augmenting the piety of the faithful, the veneration of the Most Holy Virgin, and the respect for the Sacred Mysteries."

"The strong and the weak, the wise and the ignorant, and in fine, all the world will gather richest fruit from the reading of these books: for they contain what is most sublime in theology and in a style so simple, easy and perspicuous that, in order to enter deeply into an understanding of the Holy Mysteries, no more is necessary than to read them with sound judgment."

"Combined with this simplicity are found many doctrines and valid proofs, free from contradictions and not easily found in other writings. This History explains more than a thousand difficulties in Holy Scripture, in a manner equally natural and wonderful. At every step are encountered exquisite interpretations, until now unknown, and which had been hidden beneath the mere letter, but are laid open in these writings and brought to the light. In short, the whole work is a beautiful web of Scripture passages which, though spun from its different books, are directly and specially woven into a whole for the purpose intended by the Venerable Mother."

"In addition thereto the instructions given by the Most Holy Virgin at the end of each chapter contain the purest morality, instruct, entertain, and at the same time sweetly inculcate the love of virtue and abhorrence of vice, painting them in the most vivid and natural colours. They do not only convince the intellect, but they contain such a special unction, that they enkindle a sacred ardor in the soul. In meditating upon them one certainly will experience a delight not met with in ordinary writings; and the more they are read the greater is the delight experienced. Finally, the whole work contains something so unwonted and attractive that, once begun, the reading of it can scarcely be relinquished."

"The novelty and variety found in these writings delight and recreate the reader beyond all that is pleasant in the world, at the same time instructing him and inspiring him with new fervor. All can easily persuade themselves that, if the interior life of Christ Our Lord and of the Most Holy Virgin was not just as described in these books, it could certainly have been like it; and that it would have been well worthy of Them, if it was as it is there depicted. All that is there said is befitting the majesty and humility of Christ, and in correspondence with the holiness of the Virgin and the dignity of the Mother; since there is found nothing in the whole work which was not worthy of both One and the Other.

"Notwithstanding all this, we should not at all wonder if the book met with men who are disposed to be critical; for what book is there which can hope to escape the opposition of the people of our times? God has not even provided that the Sacred Scriptures should be free from such attack among the greater part of the learned of this world. The whole philosophy of the pagans causes them to join the number of those who are opposed to the Cross of Christ Crucified; and among that number are also the libertines of our day."

"Of course there are certain points in this work which might give rise to apparent difficulties, and some of them occurred, and do occur, to us. But, in accordance with what we have said of the excellence and usefulness of this work, we have come to the conclusion that these few passages must not hinder us from giving it the commendation already given; besides, we must confess that we might possibly be ourselves mistaken in making these objections."

"This seemed to us the most reasonable course, since in this book there is something more than human. Anything so excellent and sublime cannot be ascribed to an over-excited imagination, since the whole work is consistent throughout. Nor can it be believed to be the work of a perverted mind, for, with a constant equanimity, it treats of the most deeply hidden and abstruse matters without involving itself in any contradictions; though often also it descends to innumerable minute and particular circumstances."

"There are contained in this work such noble, such devout circumstantial and pertinent discourses, as cannot be the result of mere discursive thought. Nor can it be attributed to the demon; for, from beginning to end, it suggests and breathes nothing but humility, patience and endurance of hardships."

"Therefore, just as "City of God" must without a doubt be attributed to the venerable Mother of Agreda, who is

3

claimed as its author, so she cannot have composed it without particular help from on high. Our conclusive opinion is, that the City of God, for the good of the public, and for the advantages to be derived therefrom, should be brought forth to the light. This is our judgment, which we submit entirely to the supreme decision of the Holy See, to whom alone belongs the right of finally judging such writings."

Louvain, 20th of July 1715.

(Signed) HERMAN DAMEN
    Doctor, Professor Ordinary and Regent of the Theological Faculty, Don of Saint Peter, President of the College of Arras, Censor of Books, etc.

Anton Parmentier,
    Doctor, Professor Ordinary, Regent of the Theological Faculty, President of the Great College of Theologians, etc.

APPROBATIONS

The first Pope officially to take notice of "City of God" was Pope Innocent XI, who, on July 3, 1686, in response to a series of virulent attacks and machinations of some members of the Sorbonne, known to be Jansenists, issued a breve permitting the publication and reading of the "City of God." Similar decrees were afterward issued by Popes Alexander VIII, Clement IX and Benedict XIII. These decrees were followed by two decrees of the Congregation of Rites, approved by Benedict XIV and Clement XIV, in which the authenticity of "City of God" as extant and written by the Venerable Servant of God, Mary of Jesus, is officially established. The great Pope Benedict XIII, when he was Archbishop of Benevent, used these revelations as material for a series of sermons on the Blessed Virgin. On Sept. 26, 1713, the bishop of Ceneda, Italy, objecting to the publication of the "City of God," was peremptorily ordered by the Holy Office to withdraw his objections as interfering with the decree of Pope Innocent XI for the Universal Church.

The process of canonization of Mary of Agreda was promoted by the Spanish Bishops and other eminent men of the Church soon after her death by 1666. It has resulted so far in securing her the title of Venerabilis, thus clearing the way to her beatification, for which, let us hope, God will soon raise a promoter among the many pious and eminent men who hold in esteem her writings and have learned of her holy life and of the miracles wrought at her tomb.

The Redemptorist Fathers published a new German translation in 1885, which was approved and highly recommended by the Bishop of Ratisbon in the following terms:

We take pleasure in giving our Episcopal approbation to the annotated translation of the Spanish original "City of God" of Mary of Jesus and recommend this book, which will

5

surely edify all readers and be the occasion of great spiritual blessings."

Ratisbon, September 29, 1885.

✠IGNATIUS, Bishop of Ratisbon.

Notable is the high recommendation of the Prince-Archbishop of Salzburg, Apost. Legate, Primate of Germany, etc.

"According to the decrees of Pope Innocent XI and Clement XI the book known as "City of God" written by the Venerable Servant of God, Maria de Jesus, may be read by all the faithful."

"A number of Episcopal approbations, the recommendations of four renowned Universities, namely, of Toulouse, Salamanca, Alcala and Louvain, and of prominent members of different orders, coincide in extolling the above-named work. The learned and pious Cardinal D'Aguirre says that he considers all the studies of fifty years of his previous life as of small consequence in comparison with the doctrines he found in this book, which in all things are in harmony with the Holy Scriptures, the Holy Fathers and Councils of the Church. The Venerable Superior-General of St. Sulpice, Abbé Emery, adds: "Only since I read the revelations of Mary of Agreda do I properly know Jesus and his Holy Mother."

"We therefore do not hesitate—in granting our Episcopal approbation to—"City of God"—and wish to recommend it to the faithful and especially to our clergy."

✠FRANZ ALBERT,
Archbishop.

Archiepiscopal Chancery, Salzburg.
September 12, 1885.

A more recent Official approbation of "City of God" is from the Bishop of Tarazona, prefacing the new edition of 1911-1912.

"We, Dr. James Ozoidi y Udave, by the grace of God and of the Apostolic See, Bishop of Tarazona, Administrator Apostolic of the Diocese of Tudela, etc., etc.

Having charged the priest Don Eduardo Royo, chaplain and confessor at the convent of the Immaculate Conception of Agreda, carefully and exactly to compare the

6

manuscript which is to serve as copy for the printing of the new edition of the "City of God" now about to be published by the religious of the above-named convent, with the authenticated autograph manuscript of that work there preserved,—and having ascertained by a personal revision of a great part of the manuscript that the said priest has diligently and faithfully fulfilled this charge imposed upon him by us:

We now therefore certify that this present edition of "City of God," with the exception of a few more orthographic modifications, is entirely conformable to the autograph of that work as composed and written by the Venerable Mother Mary of Jesus of Agreda.

Tarazona, April 7, 1911.

[Diocesan Seal] ✠JAMES, Bishop of Tarazona.

Finally follows the Official approbation of the Right Reverend Bishop of the Fort Wayne Diocese, where this English translation is published.

Rome City, Ind., Aug. 24, 1912.

The Rev. George J. Blatter,

Dear Rev. Father:—

My Imprimatur is herewith granted to your English translation of the work entitled "City of God." Wishing you every blessing, I remain,

Devotedly in Domino,

✠H. J. ALERDING, Bishop of Fort Wayne.

City of God is divided into four volumes, the author judged it best to head these divisions as follows:

THE CONCEPTION, Books 1 and 2.
THE INCARNATION, Books 3 and 4.
THE TRANSFIXION, Books 5 and 6.
THE CORONATION, Books 7 and 8.

A Novena of Meditations

The power of effectiveness of this Novena, when offered for the Poor Souls, have already been tested. A Priest in a neighboring state has suggested this Novena to many hundreds of people, from all walks of life, who seek his advice and aid. Many favors have been granted —peace restored in the home; health recovered; employment found; relatives returned to their religious duties; property sold; success attained in business and professional life; an intensified spiritual life granted—all these, and many others have been granted in response to the NOVENA OF MEDITATIONS based upon the "City of God."

Read several pages a day and meditate upon the minute and authentic account of each event in the life of our Blessed Lord and in that of His Mother. In so doing you will participate in those helps and graces attached to the contemplation of those events; you will begin to glimpse the tremendous and mysterious power of Her who is Queen of Angels and Mediatrix of all graces; you will begin to comprehend the joy and sweetness of actually trying to fashion your life along the pattern set by Christ and His Mother.

Every meditation is a thought but every thought is not a meditation. We often have thoughts which have no aim or intention at all but are simply musing . . . and however attentive this kind of thought may be it cannot be called meditation. Sometimes we think attentively about something in order to understand its causes, effects, qualities; and this thinking is called study. But when we think about the things of God, not to learn, but to kindle our love, that is called meditating. ("Treatise on the Love of God", VI.2 St. Francis de Sales)

PRAYER TO THE HOLY GHOST

Come Holy Ghost, fill the hearts of Thy faithful and kindle in them the fire of Thy love. Send forth Thy Spirit and they shall be created and You shall renew the face of the earth. LET US PRAY: O God, Who by the light of the Holy Ghost does instruct the hearts of the faithful, grant us by the same Holy Spirit to know what is right, and ever to rejoice in His consolation, through Jesus Christ Our Lord. Amen.

THE FIVE JOYFUL MYSTERIES

THE ANNUNCIATION

THE INCARNATION OF THE SON OF GOD.

THE BLESSED TRINITY SENDS THE ARCHANGEL GABRIEL AS A MESSENGER TO ANNOUNCE TO MOST HOLY MARY THAT SHE IS CHOSEN AS THE MOTHER OF GOD

For infinite ages had been appointed the convenient hour and time, in which the great mystery of piety (1 Tim. 3, 16), which was approved by the Spirit, prophesied to men, foretold to the angels, and expected in the world, was to be drawn from the hidden recesses of the Divine Wisdom in order to be appropriately manifested in the flesh. The plentitude of time (Gal. 4, 4) had arrived, that which until then, although filled with prophecies and promises, was nevertheless void and empty. For it wanted the fullness of the Most Holy Mary by whose will and consent all the ages were to receive their complement, namely the Eternal Word made Flesh, capable of suffering and redeeming man. Before all ages this mystery was prearranged in such a way, that it should be fulfilled through the mediation of This Heavenly Maiden. Since now She existed in the World, the redemption of man and the coming of the Only begotten of the Father was not longer to be delayed.

At the bidding of the Divine Will the Holy Gabriel presented himself at the foot of the throne intent upon the immutable essence of the Most High. His Majesty then expressly charged him with the message, which he was to bring to the Most Holy Mary and instructed him in the very words with which he was to salute and address her. Thus the first Author of the message was God Himself, who formed the exact

9

words in His Divine Mind, and revealed them to the holy Archangel for transmission to the Most Pure Mary.

Thereupon His Majesty announced to all the other angels that the time of the Redemption had come and that He had commanded it to be brought to the World without delay; for already, in their own presence, the Most Holy Mary had been prepared and adorned to be His Mother, and had been exalted to the Supreme Dignity. The heavenly spirits heard the voice of Their Creator, and with incomparable joy and thanksgiving for the fulfillment of His eternal and perfect will, they intoned new canticles of praise, repeating therein that hymn of Sion: "Holy, holy, holy art thou, God and Lord Sabaoth (Is. 6, 3). Just and powerful art Thou, Lord our God, who livest in the highest (Ps. 112, 5) and lookest upon the lowly of the earth. Admirable are all Thy works, most high and exalted in Thy designs."

The supernal prince Gabriel, obeying with singular delight the divine command and accompanied by many thousands of most beautiful angels in visible forms, descended from the highest heaven. The appearance of the great prince and legate was that of a most handsome youth of rarest beauty; his face emitted resplendent rays of light, his bearing was grave and majestic, his advance measured, his motions composed, his words weighty and powerful, his whole presence displayed a pleasing, kindly gravity and more of Godlike qualities than all the other angels until then seen in visible form by the Heavenly Mistress. He wore a diadem of exquisite splendor and his vestments glowed in various colors full of refulgent beauty. Enchased on his breast, he bore a most beautiful cross, disclosing the mystery of the Incarnation, which He had come to announce. All these circumstances were calculated to rivet the affectionate attention of the Most Prudent Queen.

The whole of this celestial army with their princely leader Holy Gabriel directed their flight to Nazareth, a town of the province of Galilee, to the dwelling place of Most Holy Mary. This was a humble cottage and her chamber was a narrow room, bare of all those furnishings which are wont to be used by the world in order to hide its own meanness and want of all higher goods. The Heavenly Mistress was at this time fourteen years, six months and seventeen days of age; for Her birthday anniversary fell on the eighth of September and six months seventeen days has passed since that date, when this greatest of all mysteries ever performed by God in this World, was enacted in Her.

The bodily shape of the Heavenly Queen was well proportioned and taller than is usual with other maidens of Her age; yet extremely elegant and perfect in all its parts. Her face was rather more oblong than round, gracious and beautiful, without leanness or grossness; its complexion clear, yet of a slightly brownish hue; Her forehead spacious yet symmetrical; Her eyebrows perfectly arched; Her eyes large and serious, of incredible and ineffable beauty and dovelike sweetness, dark in color with a mixture tending toward green; Her nose straight and well shaped; Her mouth small, with red-colored lips, neither too thin nor too thick. All the gifts of nature in Her were so symmetrical and beautiful, that no other human being ever had the like. To look upon Her caused feelings at the same time of joy and seriousness, love and reverential fear. She attracted the heart and yet restrained it in sweet reverence; Her beauty impelled the tongue to sound Her praise, and yet Her grandeur and Her overwhelming perfections and graces hushed it to silence. In all that approached Her, She caused divine effects not easily explained; She filled the heart with heavenly influences and divine operations, tending toward the Divinity.

Her garments were humble and poor, yet clean, of a dark silvery hue, somewhat like the color of ashes, and they were arranged and worn without pretense, but with the greatest modesty and propriety. At the time when, without Her noticing it, the Embassy of Heaven drew nigh unto Her, She was engaged in the highest contemplation concerning the mysteries which the Lord had renewed in Her by so many favors during the nine preceding days. And since, as we have said above, the Lord Himself had assured Her that His Only-Begotten would soon descend to assume human form, this Great Queen was full of fervent and joyful affection in the expectation of its execution and inflamed with humble love, She spoke in Her heart: "Is it possible that the blessed time has arrived, in which the Word of the Eternal Father is to be born and to converse with men? (Brauch 10, 38). That the World should possess Him? That men are to see Him in the flesh? (Is. 40, 5). That His inaccessible light is to shine forth to illumine those who sit in darkness? (Is. 9, 2). O, who shall be worthy to see and know Him! O, who shall be allowed to kiss the earth touched by His feet!"

"Rejoice, ye heavens, and console thyself, O earth (Ps. 95, 11); let all things bless and extol Him, since already His Eternal happiness is nigh! O children of Adam, afflicted with sin, and yet creatures of My Beloved, now shall you raise your heads and throw off the yoke of your ancient servitude! (Is. 14, 25). O, ye ancient Forefathers and Prophets, and all ye just, that are detained in limbo and are waiting in the bosom of Abraham, now shall you be consoled and your much desired and long promised Redeemer shall tarry no longer! (Agg. 2, 8). Let us all magnify Him and sing to Him hymns of praise! O who shall be the slave of Her, whom Isaias points out as his Mother (Is. 7, 4); O Emmanuel, True God and Man! O Key of David, who art to unlock Heaven! (Is. 22, 22). O Eternal Wisdom! O Law giver of the new Church! Come, come to us, O Lord, and end the captivity of Thy people; let all flesh see Thy salvation!" (Is. 40, 5).

In these petitions and aspirations, and in many more too deep for my tongue to explain, the Most Holy Mary was engaged at the hour, when the Holy Angel Gabriel arrived. She was most pure in soul, most perfect in body, most noble in Her sentiments, most exalted in sanctity, full of grace, and so pleasing to the sight of God, that She was fit to be His Mother and an instrument adapted for drawing Him from the bosom of the Father to Her virginal womb. She was the powerful means of Our Redemption and to Her we owe it on many accounts. And therefore it is just, that all generations shall bless and forever extoll Her (Luke 1, 48).

I saw that The Eternal Word had awaited and chosen as the most opportune time and hour for His descent from the Bosom of the Father, the midnight of mortal perversion (Wis. 18, 14), when the whole posterity of Adam was buried and absorbed in the sleep of forgetfulness and ignorance of Their True God, and when there was no one to open his mouth in confessing and blessing Him, except some chosen souls among His people. All the rest of the world was lost in silent darkness, having passed a protracted night of five thousand and about two hundred years. Age had succeeded age, and generation followed upon generation, each one in the time predestined and decreed by the Eternal Wisdom, each also having an opportunity to know and find Him, Its Creator; for all had Him so nigh to them, that He gave them life, movement, and existence within their own selves (Acts 17, 28). But as the clear day of inaccessible light had not arrived, though some of the mortals, like the blind, came nigh to Him and touched Him in His creatures, yet they did not attain to the Divinity (Rom. 1, 23) and in failing to recognize Him, they cast themselves upon the sensible and vile things of the earth.

The day then had arrived in which the Most High, setting aside the long ages of this dark ignorance, resolved to manifest Himself to men and begin the Redemption of the human race by assuming their nature in the womb of the Most Holy Mary, now prepared for this event.

In order that the mystery of the Most High might be fulfilled, the Holy Archangel Gabriel, in the shape described in the preceding chapter and accompanied by innumerable angels in visible human forms and resplendent with incomparable beauty, entered into the chamber, where Most Holy Mary was praying. It was on a Thursday at six o'clock in the evening and at the approach of night. The great modesty and restraint of the Princess of Heaven did not permit Her to look at him more than was necessary to recognize him as an angel of the Lord. Recognizing him as such, She, in Her usual humility, wished to do him reverence; the Holy Princes would not allow it; on the contrary he himself bowed profoundly as before his Queen and Mistress, in whom he adored the heavenly mysteries of his Creator. At the same time he understood that from that day on the ancient times and the custom of old whereby men should worship angels, as Abraham had done (Gen. 28, 2), were changed. For as human nature was raised to the dignity of God Himself in the Person of the Word, men now held the position of adopted children, of companions and brethren of the angels, as the angel said to Evangelist Saint John, when he refused to be worshipped (Apoc. 19, 10).

The holy archangel saluted our and his Queen and said: "Ave gratia plena, Dominus tecum, benedicta tu in mulieribus" (Luke 1, 28). Hearing this new salutation of the angel, this most humble of all creatures was disturbed, but not confused in mind (Luke 1, 29). This disturbance arose from two causes: first, from Her humility, for She thought Herself the lowest of the creatures and thus in Her humility, was taken unawares at hearing Herself saluted and called the "Blessed among Women;" secondly, when She heard this salute and began to consider within Herself how She should receive it, She was interiorly made to understand by the

Lord, that He chose Her for His Mother, and this caused a still greater perturbance, having such an humble opinion of Herself. On account of this perturbance the angel proceeded to explain to Her the decree of the Lord, saying: "Do not fear, Mary, for Thou hast found grace before the Lord (Luke 1, 30); behold Thou shalt conceive a Son in Thy womb, and Thou shalt give birth to Him, and Thou shalt name Him Jesus; He shall be great, and He shall be called Son of the Most High," and the rest as recorded of the holy archangel.

Our most prudent and humble Queen alone, among all the creatures, was sufficiently intelligent and magnanimous to estimate at its true value such a new and unheard of sacrament; and in proportion as She realized its greatness, so She was also moved with admiration. But She raised Her humble heart to the Lord, Who could not refuse Her any petition, and in the secret of Her spirit She asked new light and assistance by which to govern Herself in such an arduous transaction; for, as we have said in the preceding chapter, the Most High, in order to permit Her to act in this mystery solely in faith, hope and charity, left Her in the common state and suspended all other kinds of favors and interior elevations, which She so frequently or continually enjoyed. In this disposition She replied and said to Holy Gabriel, what is written in Saint Luke: "How shall this happen, that I conceive and bear; since I know not, nor can know, man?" At the same time, She interiorly represented to the Lord the vow of chastity, which She had made and the espousal, which His Majesty had celebrated with Her.

The Holy Prince Gabriel replied (Luke 1, 24): "Lady, it is easy for the Divine Power to make Thee a Mother without the co-operation of man; the Holy Spirit shall remain with Thee by a new presence and the virtue of the Most High shall overshadow Thee, so that the Holy of Holies can be born of Thee, who shall Himself be called the Son of God. And behold, Thy cousin Elisabeth has likewise conceived a son in her sterile years and this is the sixth month of her conception; for nothing is impossible with God. He that can make her conceive, who was sterile, can bring it about, that Thou, Lady, be His Mother, still preserving Thy virginity and enhancing Thy purity. "To the Son Whom Thou shalt bear, God will give the throne of His Father David and His reign shall be everlasting in the house of Jacob. Thou are not

14

ignorant, O Lady, of the prophecy of Isaias (Is. 7, 14), that a Virgin shall conceive and shall bear a Son, whose name shall be Emmanuel, God with us. This prophecy is infallible and it shall be fulfilled in Thy Person. Thou knowest also of the great mystery of the bush, which Moses saw burning without its being consumed by the fire (Exod. 3, 2). This signified that the two natures, divine and human, are to be united in such a way, that the latter is not consumed by the Divine, and that the Mother of the Messias shall conceive and give birth without violation of Her Virginal Purity. Remember also, Lady, the promise of the Eternal God to the Patriarch Abraham, that after the captivity of His posterity for four generations, they should return to this land; the mysterious signification of which was, that in this, the fourth generation, the incarnate God is to rescue the whole race of Adam through Thy co-operation from the oppression of the devil (Gen. 15, 16). And the ladder, which Jacob saw in his sleep (Gen. 28, 12), was an express figure of the royal way, which the Word was to open up and by which the mortals are to ascend to heaven and the angels to descend to earth. To this earth the Only-Begotten of the Father shall lower Himself in order to converse with men and communicate to them the treasure of His Divinity, imparting them His virtues and His immutable and Eternal perfections."

With these and many other words the ambassador of heaven instructed the Most Holy Mary, in order that, by the remembrance of the ancient promises and prophecies of Holy Writ, by the reliance and trust in them and in the infinite power of the Most High, She might overcome Her hesitancy at the heavenly message. But as the Lady Herself exceeded the angels in wisdom, prudence and in all sanctity, She withheld Her answer, in order to be able to give it in accordance with the Divine Will and that it might be worthy of the greatest of all the mysteries and sacraments of the Divine Power. She reflected that upon Her answer depended the pledge of the Most Blessed Trinity, the fulfillment of His promises and prophecies, the most pleasing and acceptable of all sacrifices, the opening of the gates of paradise, the victory and triumph over hell, the Redemption of all the human race the satisfaction of the Divine Justice, the foundation of the new law of grace, the glorification of men, the rejoicing of the angels, and whatever was connected with the Incarnation of the Only-Begotten of the Father and His assuming the form of servant in Her virginal womb (Philip 2, 7).

A great wonder, indeed, and worthy of our admiration, that all these mysteries and whatever others they included, should be intrusted by the Almighty to a humble Maiden and made dependent upon Her fiat. But befittingly and securely He left them to the wise and strong decision of this courageous Woman (Prov. 31, 11), since She would consider them with such magnanimity and nobility, that perforce His confidence in Her was not misplaced. The operations, which proceed within the Divine Essence, depend not on the co-operation of creatures, for they have no part in them and God could not expect such co-operations for executing the works *ad intra;* but in the works *ad extra* and such as were contingent, among which that of becoming man was the most exalted, He could not proceed without the co-operation of Most Holy Mary and without Her free consent. For He wished to reach this acme of all the works outside Himself in Her and through Her and He wished that we should owe this benefit to this Mother of Wisdom and Our Reparatrix.

Therefore this great Lady considered and inspected profoundly this spacious field of the dignity of Mother of God (Prov. 21, 16) in order to purchase it by Her *fiat;* She clothed Herself in fortitude more than human, and She tasted and saw how profitable was this enterprise and commerce with the Divinity. She comprehended the ways of His hidden benevolence and adorned Herself with fortitude and beauty. And having conferred with Herself and with the heavenly messenger Gabriel about the grandeur of these high and divine sacraments, and finding Herself in excellent condition to receive the message sent to Her, Her Purest Soul was absorbed and elevated in admiration, reverence and highest intensity of divine love. By the intensity of these movements and supernal affections, Her most pure heart, as it were by natural consequence, was contracted and compressed with such force, that it distilled three drops of Her most pure blood, and these, finding their way to the natural place for the act of conception, were formed by the power of the Divine and Holy Spirit, into the Body of Christ Our Lord. Thus the matter, from which the Most Holy Humanity of the Word for our Redemption is composed, was furnished and administered by the most pure heart of Mary and through the sheer force of Her true love. At the same moment, with

16

a humility never sufficiently to be extolled, inclining slightly Her head and joining Her hands, She pronounced these words, which were the beginning of our salvation: "Fiat mihi secundum verbum tuum" (Luke 1, 31).

At the pronouncing of this "fiat," so sweet to the hearing of God and so fortunate for us, in one instant, four things happened. First, the Most Holy Body of Christ Our Lord was formed from the three drops of blood furnished by the heart of Most Holy Mary. Secondly, the Most Holy Soul of the same Lord was created, just as the other souls. Thirdly, the soul and the body united in order to compose His perfect humanity. Fourthly, the Divinity united Itself in the Person of the Word with the humanity, which together became one composite being in hypostatical union; and thus was formed Christ True God and Man, our Lord and Redeemer. This happened in springtime on the twenty-fifth of March, at break or dawning of the day, in the same hour, in which Our First Father Adam was made and in the year of the creation of the world 5199, which agrees also with the count of the Roman Church in her Martyrology under the guidance of the Holy Ghost. This reckoning is the true and certain one, as was told me, when I inquired at command of my superiors. Conformable to this the world was created in the month of March, which corresponds to the beginning of Creation. And as the works of the Most High are perfect and complete (Deut. 32, 4), the plants and trees come forth from the hands of His Majesty bearing fruit, and they would have borne them continually without intermission, if sin had not changed the whole nature. The Divine Child began to grow in the natural manner in the recess of the womb, being nourished by the substance and the blood of its Most Holy Mother, just as other men; yet it was more free and exempt from the imperfections, to which other children of Adam are subject in that place and period. For from some of these, namely those that are accidental and unnecessary to the substance of the act of generation, being merely effects of sin, the Empress of Heaven was free. She was also free from the superfluities caused by sin, which in other women are common and happen naturally in the formation sustenance and growth of their children. For the necessary matter, which is proper to the infected nature of the descendants of Eve and which was wanting in Her, was supplied and administered in Her by the exercise of heroic acts of virtue and

17

especially by charity. By the fervor of Her soul and Her loving affections the blood and humors of Her body were changed and thereby Divine Providence provided for the sustenance of the Divine Child. Thus in a natural manner the humanity of Our Redeemer was nourished, while His Divinity was recreated and pleased with Her heroic virtues. Most Holy Mary furnished to the Holy Ghost, for the formation of this body, pure and limpid blood, free from sin and all its tendencies. And whatever impure and imperfect matter is supplied by other mothers for the growth of their children was administered by the Queen of Heaven most pure and delicate in substance. For it was built up and supplied by the power of Her loving affections and Her other virtues. In a like manner was purified whatever served as food for the Heavenly Queen. For, as She knew that Her nourishment was at the same time to sustain and nourish the Son of God, She partook of it with such heroic acts of virtue, that the angelic spirits wondered how such common human actions could be connected with such supernal heights of merit and perfection in the sight of God.

In order to understand what were the first acts of the Most Holy Soul of Christ Our Lord, we must refer to that which has been said in the preceding chapter, namely, that all that substantially belonged to this Divine Mystery, the formation of the body, the creation and the infusion of the soul, and the union of the individual humanity with the Person of the Word, happened and was completed in one act or instant; so that we cannot say that in any moment of time Christ our highest Good was only man. For from the first instant He was Man and True God; as soon as His humanity arrived at being man, He was also God; therefore He could not at any time be called a mere man, not for one instant; but from the very beginning He was Godman or Man God.

Thus adorned and deified by the Divinity and its gifts, the Most Holy Soul of Christ Our Lord proceeded in its operations in the following order: immediately it began to see and know the Divinity intuitively as It is in Itself and as It is united to His Most Holy Humanity, loving It with the highest beatific love and perceiving the inferiority of the human nature in comparison with the essence of God. The Soul of Christ humiliated Itself profoundly, and in this humility it gave thanks to the immutable being of God for having created it and for the benefit of the hypostatic union, by

18

which, though remaining human, it was raised to the essence of God. It also recognized that His Most Holy Humanity was made capable of suffering, and was adapted for attaining the end of the Redemption. In his knowledge It offered Itself as the Redeemer in sacrifice for the human race (Ps. 39, 8), accepting the state of suffering and giving thanks in His own name and in the name of mankind to the Eternal Father. He recognized the composition of His Most Holy Humanity, the substance of which it was made, and how Most Holy Mary by the force of Her charity and of Her heroic virtues, furnished its substance. He took possession of this holy tabernacle and dwelling; rejoicing in its most exquisite beauty, and, well pleased, reserved as His own property the Soul of this most perfect and most pure Creature for all eternity. He praised the Eternal Father for having created Her and endowed Her with such vast graces and gifts; for having exempted Her and freed Her from the common law of sin, as His Daughter, while all the other descendants of Adam have incurred its guilt (Rom. 5, 18). He prayed for the Most Pure Lady and for Saint Joseph, asking Eternal Salvation for them. All these acts, and many others, were most exalted and proceeded from Him as True God and Man. Not taking into account those that pertain to the beatific vision and love, these acts and each one by itself, were of such merit that they alone would have sufficed to redeem infinite worlds, if such could exist.

Even the act of obedience alone, by which the Most Holy Humanity of the Word subjected Itself to suffering and prevented the glory of His Soul from being communicated to His Body, was abundantly sufficient for our salvation. But although this sufficed for our salvation, nothing would satisfy His immense love for men except the full limit of effective love (John 13, 1); for this was the purpose of His Life, that He should consume it in demonstrations and tokens of such intense love, that neither the understanding of men nor of angels was able to comprehend it. And if in the first instant of His entrance into the world He enriched it so immeasurably, what treasures, what riches of merits must He have stored up for it, when He left it by his Passion and Death on the Cross after thirty-three years of labor and activity all Divine! O Immense Love! O Charity without limit! O Mercy without measure! O Most Generous Kindness, and, on the other hand, O ingratitude and base forgetfulness of mortals in the face of such unheard of and such vast benefaction! What would have become of us without Him? How much less could we do for this Our Redeemer and Lord, even if He had conferred on us but small favors, while now we are scarcely moved and obliged by His doing for us all that He could? If we do not wish to treat as a Redeemer Him, who has given us Eternal Life and liberty, let us at least hear Him as Our Teacher, let us follow Him as Our Leader, as Our Guiding Light, which shows us the way to our true happiness.

These operations of Christ Our Lord in the first instant of His conception were followed, in another essential instant, by the beatific vision of the Divinity, which we have mentioned in the preceding chapter (No. 139); for in one instant of time many instants of essence can take place. In this vision the Heavenly Lady perceived with clearness and distinction the mystery of the hypostatic union of the divine and the human natures in the person of the Eternal Word, and the Most Holy Trinity confirmed Her in the title and the rights of Mother of God. This in all rigor of truth She was, since She was the natural Mother of a Son, who was Eternal God with the same certainty and truth as He was man. Although this Great Lady did not directly cooperate in the union of the Divinity with the humanity, She did not on this account lose Her right to be called the Mother of the True God; for She concurred by administering the material and by exerting Her faculties, as far as it pertained to a True Mother; and to a greater extent than to ordinary mothers, since in Her the conception and the generation took place without the aid of a man. Just as in other generations the agents, which bring them about in the natural course, are called father and mother, each furnishing that which is necessary, without however concurring directly in the Creation of the Soul, nor in its infusion into the body of the child; so also, and with greater reason, Most Holy Mary must be called, and did call Herself, Mother of God; for She alone concurred in the generation of Christ, True God and Man, as a Mother, to the exclusion of any other natural cause; and only through this concurrence of Mary in the generation, Christ, the Man-God, was born.

But She was especially persistent and fervent in Her prayer to obtain guidance of the Almighty for the worthy fulfillment of Her office as Mother of the Only-Begotten of the Father. For this, before all other graces, Her humble heart urged Her to desire, and this was especially the subject of Her solicitude, that She might be guided in all Her actions as becomes the Mother of God. The Almighty answered Her: "My Dove, do not fear, for I will assist Thee and guide Thee, directing Thee in all things necessary for the service of My Only-Begotten Son." With this promise She came to Herself and issued from Her ecstasy, in which all that I have said had happened, and which was the most wonderful She ever had. Restored to Her faculties, Her first action was to prostrate Herself on the earth and adore Her Holiest Son, God and Man, conceived in Her Virginal Womb; for this She had not yet done with Her external and bodily senses and faculties. Nothing that She could do in the service of Her Creator, did this most prudent Mother leave undone. From that time on She was conscious of feeling new and divine effects in Her Holiest Soul and in Her exterior and interior faculties. And although the whole tenor of Her life had been most noble both as regards Her body as Her soul; yet on this day of the Incarnation of the Word it rose to still greater nobility of spirit and was made more Godlike by still higher reaches of grace and indescribable gifts.

WORDS OF THE QUEEN.

My Dearest Daughter, many times I have confided and manifested to Thee the love burning within My Bosom: for I wish that it should be ardently re-enkindled within Thy own, and that Thou profit from the instruction, which I give Thee. Happy is the Soul, to which the Most High manifests His Holy and Perfect Will; but more happy and blessed is he, who puts into execution, what he has learned. In many ways God shows to mortals the highways and pathways of Eternal Life: by the Gospels and the Holy Scriptures, by the Sacraments and the laws of the Holy Church, by the writings and examples of the saints, and especially, by the obedience due to the guidings of its ministers, of whom His Majesty said: "Whoever hears you, hears Me;" for obeying them is the same as obeying the Lord Himself. Whenever by any of these means thou hast come to the knowledge of the Will of God, I desire thee to assume the wings of humility and

21

obedience, and, as if in ethereal flight or like the quickest sunbeam, hasten to execute it and thereby fulfill the divine pleasure.

Besides these means of instruction, the Most High has still others in order to direct the Soul; namely, He intimates His Perfect Will to them in a supernatural manner, and reveals to them many sacraments. This kind of instruction is of many and different degrees; not all of them are common or ordinary to all Souls; for the Lord dispenses His light in measure and weight (Wis. 11, 21). Sometimes He speaks to the heart and the interior feelings in commands; at others, in correction, advising or instructing: sometimes He moves the heart to ask Him; at other times He proposes clearly what He desires, in order that the Soul may be moved to fulfill it; again He manifests, as in a clear mirror, great mysteries, in order that they may be seen and recognized by the intellect and loved by the will. But this Great and Infinite Good is always sweet in commanding, powerful in giving the necessary help for obedience, just in His commands, quick in disposing circumstances so that He can be obeyed, notwithstanding all the impediments which hinder the fulfillment of His Most Holy Will.

In receiving this Divine Light, My Daugher, I wish to see Thee very attentive, and very quick and diligent in following it up in deed. In order to hear this most delicate and Spiritual Voice of the Lord it is necessary, that the faculties of the soul be purged from earthly grossness and that the creature live entirely according to the spirit; for the animal man does not perceive the elevated things of the Divinity (I Cor. 2, 14). Be attentive then to His secrets (Is. 34, 16) and forget all that is of the outside; listen, My Daughter, and incline Thy ear; free Thyself from all visible things (Ps. 44, 11). And in order that thou mayest be diligent, cultivate love; for love is a fire, which does not have its effect until the material is prepared; therefore let Thy heart always be disposed and prepared. Whenever the Most High bids Thee or communicates to Thee anything for the welfare of Souls, or especially for their Eternal Salvation, devote Thyself to it entirely; for they are bought at the inestimable price of the Blood of the Lamb and of Divine Love. Do not allow Thyself to be hindered in this matter by Thy own lowliness and bashfulness; but overcome the fear which restrains Thee, for if Thou

22

Thyself art of small value and usefulness, the Most High is rich (I Pet. 1, 18), powerful, great, and by Himself performs all things (Rom. 10, 12). Thy promptness and affection will not go without its reward, although I wish Thee rather to be moved entirely by the pleasure of Thy Lord.

THE VISITATION

MOST HOLY MARY VISITS ELISABETH.

"And Mary rising up in those days," says the Sacred Text, "went into the hill country with haste, into a city of Jude" (Luke 1, 39). This rising up of Our Heavenly Queen signified not only Her exterior preparations and setting out from Nazareth on Her journey, but it referred to the movement of Her Spirit and to the Divine impulse and command which directed Her to arise interiorly from the humble retirement, which She had chosen in Her humility. She arose as it were from the feet of the Most High, Whose will and pleasure She eagerly sought to fulfill, like the lowliest handmaid, who according to the word of David (Ps. 122, 2) keeps Her eyes fixed upon the hands of Her Mistress, awaiting Her commands. Arising at the bidding of the Lord She lovingly hastened to accomplish His Most Holy Will, in procuring without delay the santification of the Precursor of the Incarnate Word, who was yet held prisoner in the womb of Elisabeth by the bonds of original sin. This was the purpose and object of this journey. Therefore the Princess of Heaven arose and proceeded in diligent haste, as mentioned by the Evangelist Saint Luke.

Leaving behind then the house of Her father and forgetting Her people (Ps. 44, 11), the most chaste spouses, Mary and Joseph, pursued Tehir way to the house of Zacharias in mountainous Judea. It was twenty-six leagues distant from Nazareth, and the greater part of the way was very rough and broken, unfit for such a delicate and tender Maiden. All the convenience at Their disposal for the arduous undertaking was an humble beast, on which She began and pursued Her journey. Although it was intended solely for Her comfort and service, yet Mary, the most humble and unpretentious of all creatures, many times dismounted and asked Her spouse

Saint Joseph to share with Her this commodity and to lighten the difficulties of the way by making use of the beast. Her discreet spouse never accepted this offer; and in order to yield somewhat to the solicitations of the Heavenly Lady, he permitted, Her now and then to walk with him part of the way, whenever it seemed to him that Her delicate strength could sustain the exertion without too great fatigue. But soon he would again ask Her, with great modesty and reverence, to accept of this slight alleviation and the Celestial Queen would they obey and again proceed on Her way seated in the saddle.

Thus alleviating their fatigue by humble and courteous contentions, the Most Holy Mary and Saint Joseph continued on Their journey, making good use of each single moment. They proceeded alone, without accompaniment of any human creatures; but all the thousand angels, which were set to guard the couch of Solomon, the Most Holy Mary, attended upon them (Cant. 3, 7). Although the angels accompanied them in corporeal form, serving their Great Queen and Her Most Holy Son in Her womb, they were visible only to Mary. In the company of the angels and of Saint Joseph, the Mother of Grace journeyed along, filling the fields and the mountains with the sweetest fragrance of Her presence and with the Divine Praises, in which She unceasingly occupied Herself. Sometimes She conversed with the angels and, alternately with them, sang divine canticles concerning the different mysteries of the Divinity and the works of Creation and of the Incarnation. Thus ever anew the Pure Heart of the Immaculate Lady was inflamed by the ardors of Divine Love. In all this Her spouse Saint Joseph contributed his share by maintaining a discreet silence, and by allowing his Beloved Spouse to pursue the flights of Her spirit; for, lost in highest contemplation, he was favored with some understanding of what was passing within Her Soul.

At other times the two would converse with each other and speak about the salvation of souls and the mercies of the Lord, of the coming of the Redeemer, of the prophecies given to the ancient Fathers concerning Him, and of other mysteries and sacraments of the Most High. Something happened on the way, which caused great wonder in Her holy spouse Joseph: he loved his Spouse most tenderly with a chaste and holy love, such as had been ordained in Him by the special grace and dispensation of the Divine Love Itself

(Cant. 2, 4); in addition to this privilege (which was certainly not a small one) the Saint was naturally of a most noble and courteous disposition, and his manners were most pleasing and charming; all this produced in him a most discreet and loving solicitude, which was yet increased by the great holiness, which he had seen from the beginning in his Spouse and which was ordained by heaven as the immediate object of all his privileges. Therefore the Saint anxiously attended upon Most Holy Mary and asked Her many times, whether She was tired or fatigued, and in what he could serve Her on the journey. But as the Queen of Heaven already carried within the virginal chamber the Divine Fire of the Incarnate Word, Holy Joseph, without fathoming the real cause, experienced in his soul new reactions, proceeding from the words and conversations of his Beloved Spouse. He felt himself so inflamed by Divine Love and imbued with such exalted knowledge of the mysteries touched upon in Their conversations, that he was entirely renewed and spiritualized by this burning interior light. The farther They proceeded and the more They conversed about these heavenly things, so much the stronger these affections grew, and he became aware, that it was the words of his Spouse, which thus filled his heart with love and inflamed his will with Divine Ardor.

Having pursued Their journey four days, the Most Holy Mary and Her spouse arrived at the town of Juda, where Zachary and Elisabeth then lived. This was the special and proper name of the place, where the parents of Saint John lived for a while, and therefore the Evangelist Saint Luke specifies it, calling it Juda, although the commentators have commonly believed that this was not the name of the town in which Elisabeth and Zacharias lived, but simply the name of the province, which was called Juda or Judea; just as for the same reason the mountains south of Jerusalem were called the mountains of Judea. But it was expressly revealed to me that the town was called Juda and that the Evangelist calls it by its proper name; although the learned expositors have understood by this name of Juda the province, in which that town was situated. This confusion arose from the fact that some years after the death of Christ the town Juda was destroyed, and, as the commentators found no trace of such a town, they inferred that Saint Luke meant the province and not a town; thus the great differences of opinion in regard to

26

the place, where Most Holy Mary visited Elisabeth, are easily explained.

It was at this city of Juda and at the house of Zacharias that Most Holy Mary and Joseph arrived. In order to announce Their visit, Saint Joseph hastened ahead of Mary and calling out saluted the inmates of the house, saying: "The Lord be with you and fill your souls with Divine Grace." Elisabeth was already forewarned, for the Lord Himself had informed her in a vision that Mary of Nazareth had departed to visit her. She had also in this vision been made aware that the Heavenly Lady was most pleasing in the eyes of the Most High; while the mystery of Her being the Mother of God was not revealed to her until the moment, when They both saluted each other in private. But Saint Elisabeth immediately issued forth with a few of her family, in order to welcome Most Holy Mary, who, as the more humble and younger in years, hastened to salute her cousin, saying: "The Lord be with you, my dearest cousin," and Elisabeth answered: "The same Lord reward you for having come in order to afford me this pleasure." With these words they entered the house of Zacharias and what happened I will relate in the following chapter.

When the most holy Mother Mary arrived at the house of Zacharias, the Precursor of Christ had completed the sixth month of his conception in the womb of Saint Elisabeth. The body of the child John had already attained a state of great natural perfection; much greater than that of other children, on account of the miracle of his conception by a sterile mother and on account of the intention of the Most High to make him the depository of greater sanctity than other men (Matth. 11, 11). Yet at that time his soul was yet filled with the darkness of sin, which he had contracted in the same way as the other children of Adam, the first and common father of the human race; and as, according to the universal and general law, mortals cannot receive the light of grace before they have issued forth to the light of the sun (Rom. 5, 7); so, after the first, the original sin contracted by our nature, the womb of the mother must serve as a dungeon or prison for all of us, who have laden upon ourselves this guilt of our father and head, Adam. Christ our Lord resolved to anticipate this great blessing in His Prophet and Precursor by conferring the light of His grace and justification upon him six months after his conception by Saint Elisabeth, in order that he might be distinguished as well in holiness, as he was in his office of Presursor and Baptist.

After the first salutation of Elisabeth by the Most Holy Mary, the two cousins retired, as I have said at the end of the preceding chapter. And immediately the Mother of Grace saluted anew her cousin saying: "May God save thee, my dearest cousin, and may His Divine Light communicate to thee Grace and Life" (Luke 1, 40). At the sound of Most Holy Mary's voice, Saint Elisabeth was filled by the Holy Ghost and so enlightened interiorly, that in one instant she perceived the most exalted mysteries and sacraments. These emotions, and those that at the same time were felt by the Child John in the womb of his mother, were caused by the presence of the Lord Made Flesh in the bridal chamber of Mary's womb, for, making use of the voice of Mary as His instrument, He, as Redeemer, began from that place to use the power given to Him by the eternal Father for the Salvation and Justification of the Souls. And since He now operated as man, though as yet of the diminutive size of one conceived eight days before, He assumed, in admirable humility, the form and posture of one praying and beseeching the Father. He asked in earnest prayer for the justification of His future Precursor and obtained it at the hands of the Blessed Trinity.

This happened before the Most Holy Mary had put Her salutation into words. At the pronunciation of the words mentioned above, God looked upon the child in the womb of Saint Elisabeth, and gave it perfect use of reason, enlightening it with His Divine Light, in order that He might prepare Himself by foreknowledge for the blessings which he was to receive. Together with this preparation he was sanctified from original sin, made an adopted son of God, and filled with the most abundant graces of the Holy Ghost and with the plenitude of all His gifts; his faculties were sanctified, subjected and subordinated to reason, thus verifying in himself what the Archangel Gabriel had said to Zacharias; that His son would be filled with the Holy Ghost from the womb of his mother (Luke 1, 17). At the same time the fortunate child, looking through the walls of the maternal womb as through clear glass upon the Incarnate Word, and assuming a kneeling posture, adored His Redeemer and Creator, whom he beheld in Most Holy Mary as if enclosed in a chamber made of the purest crystal. This was the movement of jubilation, which was felt by his mother Elisabeth as coming from the infant in her womb (Luke 1, 44). Many other acts of virtue the child John performed during this interview, exercising faith, hope, charity, worship, gratitude, humility, devotion and all the other virtues possible to him there. From that moment he began to merit and grow in sanctity, without ever losing it and without ever ceasing to exercise it with all the vigor of grace.

Saint Elisabeth was instructed at the same time in the mystery of the Incarnation, the sanctification of her own son and the sacramental purpose of this new wonder. She also became aware of the virginal purity and of the dignity of the Most Holy Mary. On this occasion, the Heavenly Queen, being absorbed in the vision of the Divinity and of the mysteries operated by it through Her Most Holy Son, became entirely Godlike, filled with the clear light of the divine gifts which She participated; and thus filled with majesty Saint Elisabeth saw Her. She saw the Word made man as through a most pure and clear glass in the Virginal Chamber, lying as it were on a couch of burning and enlivined crystal.

Filled with admiration at what She saw and heard in regard to these divine mysteries, Saint Elisabeth was wrapt in the joy of the Holy Ghost; and, looking upon the Queen of the world and what was contained in Her, she burst forth in loud voice of praise, pronouncing the words reported to us by saint Luke: "Blessed are Thou among women and blessed is the Fruit of Thy Womb, and whence is this to me, that the Mother of My Lord should come to me? For behold as soon as the voice of Thy salutation sounded in my ears, the infant in my womb leaped for joy, and blessed art Thou, that has believed, because those things shall be accomplished, that were spoken to Thee by the Lord." In these prophetic words Saint Elisabeth rehearsed the noble privileges of Most Holy Mary, perceiving by the Divine Light what the power of the Lord had done in Her, what He now performed and, what He was to accomplish through Her in time to come. All this also the child John perceived and understood, while listening to the words of his mother; for she was enlightened for the purpose of his sanctification, and since he could not from his place in the womb bless and thank her by word of mouth, she, both for herself and for her son, extolled the Most Holy Mary as being the instrument of their good fortune.

These words of praise, pronounced by Saint Elisabeth were

referred by the Mother of wisdom and humility to the Creator; and in the sweetest and softest voice She intoned the Magnificat as recorded by Saint Luke (Ch. 1, 46-55).

46. My soul doth magnify the Lord;

47. And my spirit hath rejoiced in God my Saviour.

48. Because He hath regarded the humility of His Handmaid; for behold from henceforth all generations shall call Me Blessed.

49. Because He that is mighty hath done great things to Me; and holy is His Name.

50. And His mercy is from generation unto generation to them that fear Him.

51. He hath showed might in His arm; He hath scattered the proud in the conceit of their heart.

52. He hath put down the mighty from their seat and hath exalted the humble.

53. He hath filled the hungry with good things; and the rich He hath sent empty away.

54. He hath received Israel, his servant, being mindful of His mercy;

55. As He spoke to our fathers, to Abraham and his seed forever."

Just as Saint Elisabeth was the first one who heard this sweet canticle from the mouth of Most Holy Mary, so she was also the first one who understood it and, by means of her infused knowledge, commented upon it. She penetrated some of the great mysteries, which its Authoress expressed therein in so few sentences. The Soul of Most Holy Mary magnified the Lord for the excellence of His Infinite Essence; to Him She referred and yielded all glory and praise (I Tim. 1, 17), both for the beginning and the accomplishment of Her works. She knew and confessed that in God alone every creature should glory and rejoice, since He alone is their entire happiness and salvation (II Cor. 10, 17). She confessed also the equity and magnificence of the Most High in attending to the humble and in conferring upon them His abundant Spirit of Divine Love (Ps. 137, 6). She saw how worthy of mortals it is to perceive, understand and ponder the gifts that were conferred on the humility of Her, whom all nations were to call Blessed, and how all the humble ones, each one according to his degree, could share the same good fortune. By one word also She expressed all the mercies, benefits and blessings, which the Almighty showered upon

30

Her in His Holy and Wonderful Name; for She calls them altogether "great things" since there was nothing small about anything that referred to This Great Queen and Lady.

And as the Mercies of the Most High overflowed from Mary's plenitude to the whole human race, and as She was the "Portal of Heaven," through which they issued and continue to issue, and through which we are to enter into the participation of the Divinity; therefore She confessed, that the Mercy of the Lord in regard to Her is spread out over all the generations, communicating itself to them that fear Him. And just as the infinite mercies raise up the humble and seek out those that fear God; so also the powerful arm of Divine Justice scatters and destroys those who are proud in the mind of their heart, and hurls them from their thrones in order to set in their place the poor and lowly. This justice of the Lord was exercised in wonderful splendor and glory upon the chief of all the proud, Lucifer and his followers, when the Almighty Arm of God scattered and hurled them (because they themselves precipitated themselves) from their exalted seats which befitted their angelic natures and their graces, and which they occupied according to the original (Isaias 14; Apoc. 12) decree of the Divine Love. For by it He intended that all should be blessed (I Tim. 2, 4) while they, in trying to ascend in their vain pride to positions, which they neither could attain nor should aspire to, on the contrary cast themselves from those which they occupied (Isaias 14, 13).

When it was time to come forth from their retirement, Saint Elisabeth offered herself and her whole family and all her house for the service of the Queen of Heaven. She asked Her to accept, as a quiet retreat, the room which she herself was accustomed to use for her prayers, and which was much retired and accommodated to that purpose. The Heavenly Princess accepted the chamber with humble thanks, and made use of it for recollecting Herself and sleeping therein, and no one ever entered it, except the two cousins. As for the rest She offered to serve and assist Elisabeth as a handmaid, for She said, that this was the purpose of visiting her and consoling her. O what friendship is so true, so sweet and inseparable, as that which is formed by the great bond of the Divine Love! How admirable is the Lord in manifesting this great sacrament of the Incarnation to three women before He would make it known to any one else in the human race! For the first was Saint Anne, as I have said in

31

its place; the second one was Her Daughter and the Mother of the Word, Most Holy Mary; the third one was Saint Elisabeth, and conjointly with Her, her son, for he being yet in the womb of his mother, cannot be considered as distinct from her. Thus "the foolishness of God is wiser than men," as Saint Paul says.

The Most Holy Mary and Elisabeth came forth from their retirement at nightfall, having passed a long time together; and the Queen saw Zacharias standing before Her in his muteness, and She asked him for his blessing as from a priest of the Lord, which the saint also gave to Her. Yet, although She tenderly pitied him for his affliction, She did not exert Her power to cure him, because She knew the mysterious occasion of his dumbness; yet She offered a prayer for him. Saint Elisabeth, who already knew the good fortune of the most chaste spouse Joseph, although he himself as yet was not aware of it, entertained and served him with great reverence and highest esteem. After staying three days in the house of Zacharias, however, he asked permission of his Heavenly Spouse Mary to return to Nazareth and leave Her in the company of Saint Elisabeth in order to assist her in her pregnancy. The holy husband left them with the understanding that he was to return in order to accompany the Queen home as soon as they should give him notice; Saint Elisabeth offered him some presents to take home with him; but he would take only a small part of them, yielding only to their earnest solicitations, for this man of God was not only a lover of poverty, but was possessed of a magnanimous and noble heart. Therewith he pursued his way back to Nazareth, taking along with him the little beast of burden, which they had brought with them. At home, in the absence of his Spouse, he was served by a neighboring woman and cousin of his, who, also when Most Holy Mary was at home, was wont to come and go on the necessary errands outside of the house.

When the Precursor John had been sanctified and Saint Elisabeth, his mother, had been endowed with such great gifts and blessings, and when thus the principal object of Mary's visit was fulfilled, the great Queen proceeded to arrange Her daily life in the house of Zacharias; for Her occupations could not be uniformly the same as those She was accustomed to in Her own house. In order to direct Her desire by the guidance of the Holy Ghost She retired and placed Herself in the presence of the Most High, asking Him as usual to guide Her and direct Her in that which She was to do during Her stay in the house of His servants Elisabeth and Zacharias; so that She might in all things be pleasing to Him and fulfill entirely His pleasure. The Lord heard Her petition and answered by saying: "My Spouse and my Dove, I will direct all Thy actions and I will direct thy footsteps in the fulfillment of My service and pleasure, and I will make known to Thee the day on which I wish Thee to return to Thy home. In the meanwhile remain in the house of My servant Elisabeth and converse with her. As for the rest, continue Thy exercises and prayers, especially for the salvation of men, and pray also, that I withhold My justice in dealing with their incessant offenses against My bounty. Conjointly with Thy prayers Thou shalt offer to Me The Lamb without spot (1 Pet. 1, 19) which thou bearest in Thy womb and which takes away the sins of the world (John 1, 291). Let these now be thy occupations."

In conformity with this instruction and new mandate of the Most High, the Princess of Heaven ordered all Her occupations in the house of Her cousin Elisabeth. She rose up at midnight in accordance with Her former custom, spending the hours in the continued contemplation of the Divine Mysteries and giving to waking and sleep the time, which most perfectly and exactly agreed with the natural state and conditions of Her body. In labor and repose She continued to receive new favors, illuminations, exaltation and caresses of the Lord. During these three months She had many visions of the Divinity, mostly abstractive in kind. More frequent still were the visions of the Most Holy Humanity of the Word in its hypostatic union; for Her virginal womb, in which She bore Him, served Her as Her continual altar and sanctuary. She beheld the daily growth of that Sacred Body. By this experience and by the sacraments, which every day were made manifest to Her in the boundless fields of the divine power and essence, the spirit of this exalted Lady expanded to vast proportions. Many times would She have been consumed and have died by the violence of Her affections, if She had not been strengthened by the power of the Lord. To these occupations, which were concealed from all, She added those, which the service and consolation of Her cousin Elisabeth demanded, although She did not apply one moment more to them, than charity required. These fulfilled, She turned immediately to Her solitude and recollection, where She could pour out the more freely Her Spirit before the Lord.

THE BIRTH OF OUR LORD
IN BETHLEHEM, JUDA

THE JOURNEY OF MOST HOLY MARY FROM NAZARETH
TO BETHLEHEM IN THE COMPANY OF THE HOLY
SPOUSE JOSEPH AND OF THE HOLY GUARDIAN ANGELS.

The Most Pure Mary and the Glorious Saint Joseph departed from Nazareth for Bethlehem alone, poor and humble in the eyes of the world. None of the mortals thought more of them than what was warranted by Their poverty and humility. But O the wonderful sacraments of the Most High, hidden to the proud, and unpenetrated by the wisdom of the flesh! They did not walk alone, poor or despised, but prosperous, rich and in magnificence. They were most worthy of the immense love of the Eternal Father and most estimable in His Eyes. They carried with them the Treasure of Heaven, the Deity Itself. The whole court of the celestial ministers venerated them. All the inanimate beings recognized the Living and True Ark of the Testament (Josue 3, 16) more readily than the waters of the Jordan recognized its type and shadow, when they courteously laid open and free the path for its passage and those that followed it. They were accompanied by the ten thousand angels which were appointed by God Himself as servants of Her Majesty during that whole journey.

Their journey lasted five days for on account of the pregnancy of his Spouse, Saint Joseph shortened each day's journey. The Sovereign Queen experienced no darkness of night on the way; for a few times when Their travel extended beyond nightfall the holy angels spread about such effulgence as not all the lights of heaven in their noontide splendor would have thrown forth in the clearest Heavens. During this whole journey the Queen was rejoiced by the sight of Her resplendent ministers and vassals and by the sweet conversation held with them.

With these wonderful favors and delights, however, The Lord joined some hardships and inconveniences which The Divine Mother encountered on the way. For the concourse of people in the taverns, occasioned by the imperial edict, was very annoying and disagreeable to the modest and retiring Virgin-Mother and spouse. On account of Their poverty and timid retirement They were treated with less hospitality and consideration than others, especially the well-to-do; for the world judges and usually confers its favors according to outward appearance and according to personal influence. Our Holy Pilgrims were obliged repeatedly to listen to sharp reprimands in the taverns, at which They arrived tired out by Their journey, and in some of them They were refused admittance as worthless and despicable people. Several times they assigned to the Mistress of Heaven and Earth some corner of the hallway; while at others She did not fare even so well, being obliged to retire with Her husband to places still more unbecoming in the estimation of the world. But in whatever places She tarried, how contemptable so ever it might be considered, the courtiers of heaven established their court around their Supreme King and Sovereign Queen. Immediately they surrounded and enclosed them like an impenetrable wall, securing the bridal chamber of Solomon against the terrors of the night. Her most faithful spouse Joseph, seeing the Mistress of Heaven so well guarded by the angelic hosts, betook himself to rest and sleep; for to this She urged him on account of the hardships of travel. She, however, continued her Celestial colloquies with the ten thousand angels of Her retinue.

Thus variously and wonderfully assisted, Our travelers arrived at the town of Bethlehem at four o'clock of the fifth day, a Saturday. As it was at the time of the winter solstice, the sun was already sinking and the night was falling. They entered the town, and wandered through many streets in search of a lodging-house or inn for staying over night. They knocked at the doors of their acquaintances and nearer family relations; but They were admitted nowhere and in many places they were met with harsh words and insults. The most modest Queen followed Her spouse through the crowds of people, while he went from house to house and from door

36

to door. Although She knew that the hearts and the houses of men were to be closed to Them, and although to expose Her state at Her age to the public gaze was more painful to Her modesty than their failure to procure a night-lodging, She nevertheless wished to obey Saint Joseph and suffer this indignity and unmerited shame. While wandering through the streets they passed the Office of the Public Registry and They inscribed their names and paid the fiscal tribute in order to comply with the edict and not be obliged to return. They continued their search, betaking themselves to other houses. But having already applied at more than fifty different places, They found themselves rejected and sent away from them all.

It was nine o'clock at night when the most faithful Joseph, full of bitter and heart rending sorrow, returned to his most Prudent Spouse and said: "My Sweetest Lady, my heart is broken with sorrow at the thought of not only being able to shelter Thee as Thou deservest and as I desire, but in not being able to offer Thee even any kind of protection from the weather, or a place of rest, a thing rarely or never denied to the most poor and despised in the world. No doubt Heaven, in thus allowing the hearts of men to be so unmoved as to refuse us a night-lodging, conceals some mystery. I now remember, Lady, that outside the city walls there is a cave, which serves as a shelter for the shepherds and their flocks. Let us seek it out; perhaps it is unoccupied, and we may there expect some assistance from Heaven, since we receive none from men on earth." The most prudent Virgin answered: "My spouse and My master, let not thy kindest heart be afflicted because the ardent wishes which the love of Thy Lord excites in thee cannot be fulfilled. Since I bear Him in My womb, let us, I beseech thee, give thanks for having disposed events in this way. The place of which thou speakest shall be most satisfactory to me. Let thy tears of sorrow be turned to tears of joy, and let us lovingly embrace poverty, which is the inestimable and precious treasure of My Most Holy Son. He came from Heaven in order to seek it, let us then afford Him an occasion to practice it in the joy of Our Souls; certainly I cannot be better delighted than to see thee procure it for me. Let us go gladly wherever the Lord shall guide us." The holy angels accompanied the heavenly pair, brilliantly lighting up the way, and when they arrived at the city gate they saw that the cave was forsaken and unoccupied.

The palace which the Supreme King of Kings and the

37

Lord of Lords had chosen for entertaining His Eternal and Incarnate Son in this World was a most poor and insignificant hut or cave, to which Most Holy Mary and Joseph betook themselves after they had been denied all hospitality and the most ordinary kindness by their fellow-men, as I have described in the foregoing chapter. This place was held in such contempt that though the town of Bethlehem was full of strangers in want of night-shelter, none would demean or degrade himself so far as to make use of it for a lodging; for there was none who deemed it suitable or desirable for such a purpose, except the Teachers of humility and poverty, Christ Our Savior and his Purest Mother. On this account the wisdom of the Eternal Father had reserved it for Them, consecrating it in all its bareness, loneliness and poverty as the "First Temple of Light" (Malachy 4, 2, Ps. 111, 4) and as the house of the True Sun of Justice, which was to arise for the upright of heart from the resplendent Aurora Mary, turning the night of sin into the daylight of grace.

Most Holy Mary and Saint Joseph entered the lodging thus provided for them and by the effulgence of the ten thousand angels of their guard they could easily ascertain its poverty and loneliness, which they esteemed as favors and welcomed with tears of consolation and joy. Without delay the two Holy Travelers fell on Their knees and praised the Lord, giving Him thanks for His benefit, which they knew had been provided by His wisdom for His own hidden designs. Of this mystery the Heavenly Princess Mary had a better insight; for as soon as She sanctified the interior of the cave by Her sacred footsteps She felt a fullness of joy which entirely elevated and vivified Her. She besought the Lord to bless with a liberal hand all the inhabitants of the neighboring city, because by rejecting Her they had given occasion to the vast favors, which She awaited in this neglected cavern. It was formed entirely of the bare and coarse rocks, without any natural beauty or artificial adornment; a place intended merely for the shelter of animals; yet the Eternal Father had selected it for the shelter and dwelling-place of His Own Son.

The angelic spirits, who like a celestial militia guarded their Queen and Mistress, formed themselves into cohorts in the manner of court guards in a royal palace. They showed themselves in their visible forms also to Saint Joseph; for on this occasion it was befitting that he should enjoy such a favor, on the one hand in order to assuage his sorrow by allowing him to behold this poor lodging thus beautified and adorned by their celestial presence, and on the other, in order to enliven and encourage him for the events which the Lord intended to bring about during that night, and in this forsaken place. The great Queen and Empress, who was already informed of the mystery to be transacted here, set about cleaning with Her Own hands the cave, which was so soon to serve as a royal throne and sacred mercy-seat; for neither did She want to miss this occasion for exercising Her humility, nor would She deprive Her Only-begotten Son of the worship and reverence implied by this preparation and cleansing of His temple.

Saint Joseph, mindful of the majesty of his Heavenly Spouse (which, it seemed to him, She was forgetting in Her ardent longing for humiliation), besought Her not to deprive Him of this work, which he considered as his alone; and he hastened to set about cleaning the floor and the corners of the cave, although the humble Queen continued to assist him therein. As the holy angels were then present in visible forms, they were (according to our mode of speaking) abashed at such eagerness for humiliation, and they speedily emulated with each other to join in this work; or rather, in order to say it more succinctly, in the shortest time possible they had cleansed and set in order that cave, filling it with holy fragrance. Saint Joseph started a fire with the material which he had brought for that purpose. As it was very cold, they sat at the fire in order to get warm. They partook of the food which they had brought, and they ate this, their frugal supper, with incomparable joy of their souls. The Queen of Heaven was so absorbed and taken up with the thought of the impending mystery of Her Divine delivery, that She would not have partaken of food if She had not been urged there to by obedience to Her spouse.

After their supper they gave thanks to the Lord as was their custom. Having spent a short time in this prayer and conferring about the mysteries of the Incarnate Word, the Most Prudent Virgin felt the approach of the Most Blessed Birth. She requested Her spouse Saint Joseph to betake himself to rest and sleep as the night was already far advanced. The man of God yielded to the request of his Spouse and urged Her to do the same; and for this purpose he arranged and prepared a sort of couch with the articles of wear in their possession, making use of a crib or manger, that had been left by the shepherds for their animals. Leaving Most Holy Mary in the portion of the cave thus furnished, Saint Joseph retired to a corner of the entrance, where he began to pray. He was immediately visited by the Divine Spirit and felt a most sweet and extraordinary influence, by which he was wrapt and elevated into an ecstasy. In it was shown him all that passed during that night in this blessed cave; for he did not return to consciousness until his Heavenly Spouse called him. Such was the sleep which Saint Joseph enjoyed in that night, more exalted and blessed than that of Adam in paradise (Gen. 21, 2).

The Queen of all creatures was called from Her resting place by a loud voice of the Most High, which strongly and sweetly raised Her above all created things and caused Her to feel new effects of divine power; for this was one of the most singular and admirable ecstasies of Her Most Holy Life. Immediately also She was filled with new enlightenment and divine influences, such as I have described in other places, until She reached the clear vision of the Divinity. The veil fell and She saw intuitively the Godhead Itself in such glory and plenitude of insight, as all the capacity of men and angels could not describe or fully understand. All the knowledge of the Divinity and humanity of Her Most Holy Son, which She had ever received in former visions was renewed and, moreover, other secrets of the inexhaustible archives of the bosom of God were revealed to Her. I have not ideas or words sufficient and adequate for expressing what I have been allowed to see of these Sacraments by the Divine Light; and their abundance and multiplicity convince me of the poverty and want of proper expression in created language.

The Most High announced to His Virgin Mother, that the time of His coming into the World had arrived and what would be the manner in which this was now to be fulfilled and executed. The Most Prudent Lady perceived in this vision the purpose and exalted scope of these wonderful Mysteries and Sacraments, as well in so far as related to the Lord Himself as also in so far as they concerned creatures, for whose benefit they had been primarily decreed. She prostrated Herself before the throne of His Divinity and gave Him glory, magnificence, thanks and praise for Herself and for all creatures, such as was befitting the ineffable mercy and condescension of His Divine Love. At the same time She asked of the Divine Majesty new light and grace in order to

40

be able worthily to undertake the service and worship and the rearing up of the Word made Flesh, whom She was to bear in Her arms and nourish with Her virginal milk. This petition the Heavenly Mother brought forward with the profoundest humility, as one who understood the greatness of this new sacrament. She held Herself unworthy of the office of rearing up and conversing as a Mother with a God Incarnate of which even the highest Seraphim are incapable. Prudently and humbly did the Mother of Wisdom ponder and weigh this matter. And because She humbled Herself to the dust and acknowledged Her nothingness in the presence of the Almighty, therefore His Majesty raised Her up and confirmed anew upon Her the title of *Mother of God*. He commanded Her to exercise this office and ministry of a legitimate and true Mother of Himself; that She should treat Him as the Son of the Eternal Father and at the same time the Son of Her womb. All this could be easily entrusted to such a Mother, in whom was contained an excellence that words cannot express.

The Most Holy Mary remained in this ecstasy and beatific vision for over an hour immediately preceding Her Divine delivery. At the moment when She issued from it and re-gained the use of Her senses She felt and saw that the Body of the Infant God began to move in Her virginal womb; how, releasing and freeing Himself from the place which in the course of nature He had occupied for nine months, He now prepared to issue forth from that sacred bridal chamber. This movement not only did not cause any pain or hardship, as happens with the other daughters of Adam and Eve in their childbirths; but filled Her with incomparable joy and delight, causing in Her Soul and in Her Virginal Body such exalted and Divine effects that they exceed all thoughts of men. Her body became so spiritualized with the beauty of heaven that She seemed no more a human and earthly creature. Her countenance emitted rays of light, like a sun incarnadined, and shone in indescribable earnestness and majesty, all inflamed with fervent love. She was kneeling in the manger, Her eyes raised to heaven, Her hands joined and folded at Her breast, Her soul wrapped in the Divinity and She Herself was entirely deified. In this position, and at the end of the heavenly rapture, the Most Exalted Lady gave to the World The Only-begotten of the Father and Her Own, Our Savior Jesus, True God and man, at the hour of mid-

41

night, on a Sunday, in the year of the creation of the world five thousand one hundred and ninety-nine (5199), which is the date given in the Roman Church, and which date has been manifested to me as the true and certain one.

At the end of the beatific rapture and vision of the Mother ever Virgin, which I have described above, was born the Sun of Justice, the Only-begotten of the Eternal Father and of Mary most pure, beautiful, refulgent and immaculate, leaving Her untouched in Her virginal integrity and purity and making Her more Godlike and forever sacred; for He did not divide, but penetrated the virginal chamber as the rays of the sun penetrate the crystal shrine, lighting it up in prismatic beauty.

The Infant God therefore was brought forth from the virginal chamber unencumbered by any corporeal or material substance foreign to Himself. But He came forth glorious and transfigured for the Divine and Infinite Wisdom decreed and ordained that the Glory of His Most Holy Soul should in His Birth overflow and communicate itself to His body, participating in the gifts of glory in the same way as happened afterwards in His Transfiguration on Mount Tabor in the presence of the Apostles (Matth. 17, 2). This miracle was not necessary in order to penetrate the virginal enclosure and to leave unimpaired the virginal integrity; for without this Transfiguration God could have brought this about by other miracles. Thus say the holy doctors, who see no other miracle in this Birth than that the Child was born without impairing the virginity of the Mother. It was the will of God that the Most Blessed Virgin should look upon the body of Her Son, the God-man, for this first time in a glorified state for two reasons. The one was in order that by this Divine Vision the Most Prudent Mother should conceive the highest reverence for the Majesty of Him whom She was to treat as Her Son, the True God-man. Although She was already informed of His two-fold nature, the Lord nevertheless ordained that by ocular demonstration She be filled with new graces, corresponding to the greatness of Her Most Holy Son, which was thus manifested to Her in a visible manner. The second reason was to reward by this wonder the fidelity and holiness of the Divine Mother; for Her most pure and chaste eyes, that had turned away from all earthly things for love of Her Most Holy Son, were to see Him at His very Birth in this

42

glory and thus be rejoiced and rewarded for Her loyalty and beautiful love.

The sacred evangelist Luke tells us that the Mother Virgin, having brought forth Her first begotten Son, wrapped Him in swathing clothes and placed Him in a manger. He does not say that She received Him in Her arms from Her virginal womb; for this did not pertain to the purpose of his narrative. But the two sovereign princes, Saint Michael and Saint Gabriel, were the assistants of the Virgin on this occasion. They stood by at proper distance in human corporeal forms at the moment when the Incarnate Word, penetrating the virginal chamber by Divine power, issued forth to the light, and they received Him in their hands with ineffable reverence. In the same manner as a priest exhibits the Sacred Host to the people for adoration, so these two celestial ministers presented to the Divine Mother Her Glorious and Refulgent Son. All this happened in a short space of time. In the same moment in which the Holy Angels thus presented the Divine Child to His Mother, both Son and Mother looked upon each other, and in this look, She wounded with love the Sweet Infant and was at the same time exalted and transformed in Him. From the arms of the Holy Princes the Prince of All the Heavens spoke to His Holy Mother: "Mother, become like unto Me, since on this day, for the human existence, which Thou hast today given Me, I will give Thee another more exalted existence in grace, assimilating Thy existence as a mere creature to the likeness of Me, who am God and Man." The Most Prudent Mother answered: "Trahe me post Te, curremus in odorem unguentorum tuorum" (Cant. 1, 3). Raise me, elevate Me, Lord, and I will run after Thee in the odor of Thy ointments. In the same way many of the hidden mysteries of the Canticles were fulfilled; and other sayings which passed between the Infant God and the Virgin Mother had been recorded in that book of songs, as for instance: "My Beloved to Me, and I to Him, and His desire is toward Me" (Cant. 2, 16). "Behold Thou art beautiful, my friend, and Thy eyes are dove's eyes. Behold, My beloved, for Thou art beautiful"; and many other sacramental words which to mention would unduly prolong this chapter.

The words, which Most Holy Mary heard from the mouth of Her Most Holy Son, served to make Her understand at the same time the interior acts of His Holiest Soul united with the Divinity; in order that by imitating them She might

43

become like unto Him. This was one of the greatest blessings, which the Most Faithful and Fortunate Mother received at the hands of her Son, the True God and man, not only because it was continued from that day on through all Her life, but because it furnished Her the means of copying His Own Divine life as faithfully as was possible to a mere creature. At the same time the Heavenly Lady perceived and felt the presence of the Most Holy Trinity, and She heard the voice of the Eternal Father saying: "This is My Beloved Son, in whom I am greatly pleased and delighted" (Matth. 17, 5). The Most Prudent Mother made entirely Godlike in the overflow of so many sacraments, answered: "Eternal Father and Exalted God, Lord and Creator of the Universe, give Me anew Thy permission and benediction to receive in My arms the Desired of Nations (Agg. 2, 8); and teach Me to fulfill as Thy unworthy Mother and lowly slave, Thy Holy Will." Immediately She heard a voice, which said: "Receive Thy Only be-gotten Son, imitate Him and rear Him; and remember, that Thou must sacrifice Him when I shall demand it of Thee." The divine Mother answered: "Behold the creature of Thy hands, adorn Me with Thy grace so that Thy Son and My God receive Me for His slave; and if Thou wilt come to My aid with Thy Omnipotence, I shall be faithful in His service; and do Thou count it no presumption in Thy insignificant creature, that She bear in Her arms and nourish at Her breast Her Own Lord and Creator."

After this interchange of Words, so full of mysteries, the Divine Child suspended the miracle of His Transfiguration, or rather He inaugurated the other miracle, that of suspending the effects of glory in His Most Holy Body, confining them solely to His Soul; and He now assumed the appearance of one capable of suffering. In this form the Most Pure Mother now saw Him and, still remaining in a kneeling position and adoring Him with profound humility and reverence, She received Him in Her arms from the hands of the Holy Angels. And when She saw Him in Her arms, She spoke to Him and said: "My sweetest Love and light of My eyes and being of My Soul, Thou hast arrived in good hour into this World as the Sun of Justice (Malach. 4, 2), in order to disperse the darkness of sin and death! True God of the True God, save Thy servants and let all flesh see Him, who shall draw upon it salvation (Is. 9, 2). Receive Me Thy servant as Thy slave and supply My deficiency, in order that I may properly serve Thee. Make Me, My Son, such as Thou desirest Me to be in Thy service." Then the Most Prudent Mother turned toward the Eternal Father to offer up to Him His Only be-gotten, saying: "Exalted Creator of all the Universe, here is the altar and the sacrifice acceptable in Thy eyes (Malachy 3, 4). From this hour on, O Lord, look upon the human race with mercy; and inasmuch as we have deserved Thy anger; it is now time that Thou be appeased in Thy Son and Mine. Let Thy justice now come to rest, and let Thy mercy be exalted; for on this account the Word has clothed Itself in the semblance of sinful flesh (Rom. 8, 3), and became a Brother of mortals and sinners (Philip 2, 7). In this title I recognize them as brothers and I intercede for them from my inmost soul. Thou, Lord, hast made me the Mother of Thy Only be-gotten without My merit, since this dignity is above all merit of a creature; but I partly owe to men the occasion of this incomparable good fortune; since it is on their account that I am the Mother of the Word made man and Redeemer of them all. I will not deny them My love, or remit My care and watchfulness for their salvation. Receive, Eternal God, My wishes and petitions for that which is according to Thy pleasure and good will."

The Mother of mercy turned also toward all mortals and addressed them, saying: "Be consoled ye afflicted and rejoice ye disconsolate, be raised up ye fallen, come to rest ye uneasy. Let the just be gladdened and the saints be rejoiced; let the heavenly spirits break out in new jubilee, let the Prophets and Patriarchs of limbo draw new hope, and let all the generations praise and magnify The Lord, who renews His wonders. Come, come ye poor; approach ye little ones, without fear, for in My arms I bear the Lion made a Lamb, the Almighty, become weak, the Invincible subdued. Come to draw life, hasten to obtain salvation, approach to gain eternal rest, since I have all this for all, and it will be given to you freely and communicated to you without envy. Do not be slow and heavy of heart, ye sons of men; and Thou, O Sweetest Joy of My Soul, give Me permission to receive from Thee that kiss desired by all creatures." Therewith the Most Blessed Mother applied Her most chaste and heavenly lips in order to receive the loving caresses of the Divine Child, Who on His part, as Her True Son, had desired them from Her.

Holding Him in Her arms She thus served as the altar and the sanctuary, where the ten thousand angels adored in visible human forms Their Creator Incarnate. And as the Most Blessed Trinity assisted in an especial manner at the Birth of the Word, Heaven was as it were emptied of its inhabitants, for the Whole Heavenly Court had betaken itself to that Blessed Cave of Bethlehem and was adoring the Creator in His garb and habit of a Pilgrim (Phil. 2, 7). And in their concert of praise the Holy Angels intoned the new canticle: "Gloria in excelsis Deo, et in terra pax hominibus bonae voluntatis" (Luke 2, 14). In sweetest and sonorous harmony they repeated it, transfixed in wonder at the new miracles then being fulfilled and at the unspeakable prudence, grace, humility and beauty of that tender Maiden of fifteen years, who had become the worthy Trustee and Minister of such vast and magnificent sacraments.

It was now time to call Saint Joseph, the faithful spouse of the most discreet and attentive Lady. As I have said above he was wrapped in ecstasy, in which he was informed by Divine Revelation of all the Mysteries of this Sacred Birth during this night. But it was becoming that he should see, and, before all other mortals, should in his corporeal faculties and senses be present and experience, adore and reverence the Word Made Flesh; for he of all others had been chosen to act as the faithful warden of this Great Sacrament. At the desire of his Heavenly Spouse he issued from his ecstasy and, on being restored to consciousness, the first sight of his eyes was the Divine Child in the arms of the Virgin Mother reclining against Her sacred countenance and breast. There he adored Him in profoundest humility and in tears of joy. He kissed his feet in great joy and admiration, which no doubt would have taken away and destroyed life in him, if divine power had not preserved it; and he certainly would have lost all the use of his senses, if the occasion had permitted. When Saint Joseph had begun to adore the Child, the Most Prudent Mother asked leave of Her Son to arise (for until then She had remained on Her knees) and, while Saint Joseph handed Her the wrappings and swaddling-clothes, which She had brought, She clothed Him with incomparable reverence, devotion and tenderness. Having thus swathed and clothed Him, His Mother, with Heavenly wisdom, laid Him in the crib, as related by Saint Luke (Luke 2, 7). For this purpose She had arranged some straw and hay upon a stone in order to prepare for the God-Man His first resting-place upon earth next to that which He had found in

Her arms. According to Divine ordainment an ox from the neighboring fields ran up in great haste and, entering the cave, joined the beast of burden brought by the Queen. The blessed Mother commanded them, with what show of reverence was possible to them to acknowledge and adore Their Creator. The humble animals obeyed their Mistress and prostrated themselves before the Child, warming Him with their breath and rendering Him the service refused by men. And thus the God made man was placed between two animals, wrapped in swaddling-clothes and wonderfully fulfilling the prophecy, that "the ox knoweth His owner, and the ass His master's crib; but Israel hath not known Me, and My people hath not understood." (Is. 13.)

WORDS OF THE QUEEN.

My daughter, if men would keep their heart disengaged and if they would rightly and worthily consider this great sacrament of the kindness of the Most High towards men, it would be a powerful means of conducting them in the pathway of life and subjecting them to the love of Their Creator and Redeemer. For as men are capable of reasoning, if they would only make use of their freedom to treat this SACRAMENT WITH THE REVERENCE DUE TO ITS GREATNESS, who would be so hardened as not to be moved to tenderness at the sight of Their God become man, humiliated in poverty, despised, unknown, entering the world in a cave, lying in a manger surrounded by brute animals, protected only by a poverty-stricken Mother, and cast off by the foolish arrogance of the world? Who will dare to love the vanity and pride, which was openly abhorred and condemned by the Creator of heaven and earth in His conduct? No one can despise the humility, poverty and indigence, which the Lord loved and chose for Himself as the very means of teaching the WAY of ETERNAL LIFE. Few there are, who stop to consider this Truth and Example: and on account of this vile ingratitude only the few will reap the fruit of THESE GREAT SACRAMENTS.

But if the condescension of My Most Holy Son was so great as to bestow so liberally upon Thee His light and knowledge concerning these vast blessings, ponder well how much Thou art bound to co-operate with this light. In order that thou mayest correspond to this obligation, I remind and exhort Thee to forget all that is of earth and lose it out of thy sight; that thou seek nothing, or engage thyself with nothing except what can help thee to withdraw and detach thee from the world and its inhabitants; so that, with a heart freed from all terrestrial affection, thou dispose thyself to celebrate in it the mysteries of the poverty, humility and Divine Love of the Incarnate God. Learn from My example the reverence, fear and respect, with which thou must treat Him, remembering how I acted, when I held Him in My arms; follow My example, whenever thou receivest Him in thy heart in the Venerable Sacrament of the Holy Eucharist, wherein is contained the same God-Man, who was born of My womb. In this Holy Sacrament thou receivest Him and possessest Him just as really, and He remains in thee just as actually, as I possessed Him and conversed with Him, although in another manner.

I desire that thou go even to extremes in this Holy Reverence and fear; and I wish that thou take notice and be convinced, that in entering into thy heart in the Holy Sacrament, Thy God exhorts thee in the same words, which thou hast recorded as spoken to Me: become like unto Me. His coming down from Heaven onto the earth, His being born in humility and poverty, His living and dying in it, giving such rare example of the contempt of the world and its deceits; the knowledge, which thou hast received concerning his conduct and which thou hast penetrated so deeply by Divine Intelligence: all these things should be for thee like living voices, which thou must heed and inscribe into the interior of thy heart. These privileges have all been granted to thee in order that thou discreetly use the common blessings to their fullest extent, and in order that thou mayest understand, how thankful thou must be to My Most Holy Son and Lord, and how thou shouldst strive to make as great a return for His Goodness, as if He had come from Heaven to redeem thee alone and as if He had Instituted all His Wonders and Doctrines in The Holy Church for none else than thee (Gal. 7, 12).

After the Courtiers of Heaven had thus celebrated the Birth of God made man near the portals of Bethlehem, some of them were immediately dispatched to different places, in order to announce the happy news to those, who according to the Divine Will were properly disposed to hear it. The Holy Prince Michael betook himself to the Holy Patriarchs in limbo and announced to them, how the Only be-gotten of the Eternal Father was already born into the world and was resting, humble and meek, as they had prophesied, in a manger between two beasts. He addressed also in a special manner Holy Joachim and Anne in the name of the Blessed Mother, who had enjoined this upon him; he congratulated them, that their Daughter now held in Her Arms the Desired of Nations and Him, Who had been foretold by all the Patriarchs and Prophets (Is. 7, 14; 9, 7, etc.). It was the most consoling and joyful day, which this great gathering of the just and the saints had yet had during their long banishment. All of them acknowledged this New Godman as the True Author of Eternal Salvation, and they composed and sang new Songs of Adoration and Worship in His praise.

Another of the Holy Angels that attended and guarded the Heavenly Mother was sent to Saint Elisabeth and her son John. On hearing this news of the Birth of the Redeemer, the prudent matron and her son, although he was yet of so tender an age, prostrated themselves upon the earth and adored Their God made man in spirit and in truth (John 4, 23). The child which had been consecrated as His Precursor, was renewed interiorly with a spirit more inflamed than that of Elias, causing new admiration and jubilation in the angels themselves.

Other angels were delegated to bring the news to Zachary, Simeon, and Anne, the prophetess, and to some other just and holy people, who were worthy to be trusted with this new mystery of our Redemption; for as the Lord found them prepared to receive this news with gratitude and with benefit to themselves, He considered it a just due to their virtue not to hide from them the blessing conferred upon the human race. Only among the just there were many, who by Divine impulse suspected or believed that God had come into the world; yet no one knew it with certainty, except those to whom it was revealed. Among these were the three Magi, to each of whom in their separate Oriental kingdoms angels of the Queen's guard were sent to inform them by interior and intellectual enlightenment that the Redeemer of the human race had been born in poverty and humility. At the same time they were inspired with the sudden desire of seeing and adoring Him and immediately they saw the star as a guide to Bethlehem.

Amongst all these, the shepherds of that region, who were

watching their flocks at the time of the Birth of Christ, were especially blessed (Luke 2, 8); not only because they accepted the labor and inconvenience of their calling with resignation from the hand of God; but also because, being poor and humble, and despised by the world, they belonged in sincerity and uprightness of heart to those Israelites, who fervently hoped and longed for the coming of the Messias, speaking and discoursing of Him among themselves many times. They resembled the Author of life, as they were removed from the riches, vanity and ostentation of the World and far from its diabolical cunning (John 10, 14). They exhibited in the circumstances of their calling the office, which the good Shepherd had come to fulfill in knowing His Sheep and being known to them. Hence they merited to be called and invited, as the first fruits of the saints by the Savior Himself, to be the very first ones, to whom the Eternal and Incarnate Word manifested Himself and by whom He wished to be praised, served and adored. Hence the Archangel Gabriel was sent to them as they watched on the field, appearing to them in human form and with great splendor.

The shepherds found themselves suddenly enveloped and bathed in the celestial radiance of the angel, and at his sight, being little versed in such visions, they were filled with great fear. The holy prince reassured them and said: "Ye upright men, be not afraid: for I announce to you tidings of great joy, which is, that for you is born today the Redeemer Christ, Our Lord, in the City of David. And as a sign of this truth, I announce to you, that you shall find the Infant wrapped in swaddling-clothes and placed in a manger" (Luke 2, 10, 12). At these words of the angel, suddenly appeared a great multitude of the celestial army, who in voices of sweet harmony sang to the Most High these words: "Glory to God in the highest and earth peace to men of good will." Rehearsing this Divine canticle, so new to the World, the Holy Angels disappeared. All this happened in the fourth watch of the night. By this angelic vision the humble and fortunate shepherds were filled with Divine enlightenment and were unanimously impelled by a fervent longing to make certain of this blessing and to witness with their own eyes the most high mystery of which they had been informed.

They departed without delay and entering the cave or portal, they found, as Saint Luke tells us, Mary and Joseph, and the Infant lying in a manger. Prostrating themselves on

50

the earth they adored the Word made Flesh. Not any more as ignorant rustics, but as wise and prudent men they adored Him, acknowledged and magnified Him as True God and Man, as Restorer and Redeemer of the human race.

Like other towns of Israel, the City of Bethlehem had its own synagogue, where the people came together to pray (wherefore it was also called the house of prayer), and to hear the law of Moses. This was read and explained by a Priest from the pulpit in a loud voice, in order that the people might understand its precepts. But in these synagogues no sacrifices were offered; this was reserved for the temple of Jerusalem, except when the Lord commanded otherwise. But the priest, who was the teacher or minister of the law in those places, was usually also charged with administering the circumcision; not that this was a binding law, for not only priests but any one could perform the circumcision; but because the pious mothers firmly believed that the infants would run less danger in being circumcised by the hands of a priest. Our Great Queen, not on account of any apprehension of danger, but because of the dignity of the Child, also wished a priest to administer this rite to Him; and therefore She sent Her most fortunate spouse to Bethlehem to call the priest of that town.

In order to show as much exterior reverence for the sacred rite of circumcision as was possible in that place, Saint Joseph lighted two wax candles. The priest requested the Virgin Mother to consign the Child to the arms of the two assistants and withdraw for a little while in order not to be obliged to witness the sacrifice. This command caused some hesitation in the Great Lady; for Her humility and spirit of obedience inclined Her to obey the priest, while on the other hand She was withheld by the love and reverence for Her Only Be-gotten. In order not to fail against either of these virtues, She humbly requested to be allowed to remain, saying that She desired to be present at the performance of this rite, since She held it in great esteem, and that She would have courage to hold Her Son in Her arms, as She wished not to leave Him alone on such an occasion. All that She would ask would be that the circumcision be performed with as much tenderness as possible on account of the delicacy of the Child. The priest promised to fulfill Her request, and permitted the Child to be held in the arms of His Mother for fulfilling the mystery.

51

In the meanwhile the priest asked the parents what name they wished to give to the Child in Circumcision; the Great Lady, always attentive to honor Her Spouse, asked Saint Joseph to mention the name. Saint Joseph turned toward Her in like reverence and gave Her to understand that He thought it proper this sweet name should first flow from Her mouth. Therefore, by divine interference, both Mary and Joseph said at the same time: "JESUS is His Name." The priest answered: "The parents are unanimously agreed, and great is the name which they give to the Child"; and thereupon he inscribed it in the tablet or register of the names of the rest of the children. While writing it the priest felt great interior movements, so that he shed copious tears; and wondering at what he felt yet not being able to account for, he said: "I am convinced that This Child is to be a Great Prophet of The Lord. Have great care in raising Him, and tell me in what I can relieve your needs." Most holy Mary and Joseph answered the priest with humble gratitude and dismissed him after offering him the gift of some candles and other articles.

The three Magi Kings, who came to find the Divine Infant after His Birth, were natives of Persia, Arabia, and Sabba (Ps. 71, 10), countries to the East of Palestine. These Three Kings were well versed in the natural sciences, and well read in the Scriptures of the people of God; and on account of their learning they were called Magi. By their knowledge of Scripture, and by conferring with some of the Jews, they were imbued with a belief in the coming of the Messias expected by the people. They were, moreover, upright men, truthful and very just in the government of their countries. In all things they communicated with each other as most faithful friends.

I have already mentioned that in the same night in which the Incarnate Word was born, they were informed of His Birth by the ministry of the Holy Angels. It happened in the following manner: one of the Guardian Angels of Our Queen of a higher order than that of the Guardian Angels of the Three Kings, was sent from the cave of the Nativity. By his superior faculties he enlightened the three guardian angels of the Kings informing them at the same time of the will and command of the Lord, that each of them should manifest to his charge the mystery of the Incarnation and of The Birth of Christ our Redeemer. Immediately and in the same hour each of the three angels spoke in dreams to the wise man under his care.

After receiving these heavenly revelations in their sleep, the Three Kings awoke at the same hour of the night, and prostrating themselves on the ground and humiliating themselves to the dust, they adored in spirit the immutable being of God. Then all three of them, governed by an impulse of the same Spirit, resolved to depart without delay for Judea in search of the Divine Child in order to adore Him. The Three Kings prepared gifts of gold, incense, and myrrh in equal quantities, being guided by the same mysterious impulse, and without having conferred with each other concerning their undertaking, the three of them arrived at the same plan of executing it.

At the same time the Holy Angel, who had brought the news from Bethlehem to the Kings, formed of the material air a most resplendent star, although not so large as those of the firmament; for it was not to ascend higher than was necessary for the purpose of its formation. It took its course through the atmospheric regions in order to guide and direct the Holy Kings to the cave, where the Child awaited them. Its splendor was of a different kind from that of the sun and the other stars; with its most beautiful light it illumined the night like a brilliant torch, and it mingled its own most active brilliancy with that of the sun by day. On coming out of their palaces each one of the kings saw this new star (Matth. 2, 2) although each from a different standpoint, because it was only one star and it was placed in such distance and height that it could be seen by each one at the same time. As the three of them followed the guidance of this miraculous star, they soon met.

The Magi pursued their journey under the guidance of the star without losing sight of it until they arrived at Jerusalem. As well on this account as also because this city was the capital and metropolis of the Jews, they suspected that this was the birthplace of Their Legitimate and True King. They entered into the city and openly inquired after Him, saying (Matth. 2, 8): "Where is the King of the Jews, who is born? For we have seen His star in the East, announcing to us His Birth and we have come to see Him and adore Him." Their inquiry came to the ears of Herod, who at that time unjustly reigned in Judea and lived in Jerusalem. The wicked king, panic-stricken at the thought that a more legitimate claimant to the throne, should have been born, felt much disturbed and outraged by this report. Immediately, as Saint Matthew relates, Herod called together a meeting of the principal priests and scribes in order to ask them where Christ was to be born according to the Prophecies and Holy Scriptures.

Thus informed of the birthplace of the New King of Israel, and insidiously plotting from that very moment to destroy Him, Herod dismissed the priests. Then he secretly called the Magi in order to learn of them at what time they had seen the star as harbinger of His Birth (Math. 2, 7). They ingenuously informed him, and he sent them away to Bethlehem, saying to them in covert malice: "Go and inquire after the Infant, and when you have found Him, announce it to me, in order that I, too, may go to recognize and adore Him."

On leaving Jerusalem the Magi again found the star, which at their entrance they had lost from view. By its light they were conducted to Bethlehem and to the cave of the Nativity. The Three Kings of the East entered and at the first sight of the Son and Mother they were for a considerable space of time overwhelmed with wonder. They prostrated themselves upon the earth, and in this position they worshiped and adored the Infant, Acknowledging Him as the True God and man, and as the Savior of the human race.

With the blessing of Jesus, Mary and Joseph, they departed, so moved by tenderest affection that it seemed to them they had left their hearts all melted into sighs and tears in that place. They chose another way for their return journey, in order not to meet Herod in Jerusalem; for thus they had been instructed by the angel on the preceding night. On their departure from Bethlehem the same or a similar star appeared in order to guide them home, conducting them on their new route to the place where they had first met, whence each one separated to reach his own country.

THE PRESENTATION

Already the forty days after the birth of a son, during which
a woman, according to the law, was considered unclean and
during which she was obliged to continue her purification for
her readmittance into the temple, were coming to a close
(Lev. 22, 4). In order to comply with this law and satisfy
another obligation contained in Exodus, chapter thirteenth,
which demanded the sanctification and presentation to the
Lord of all the first-born sons, the Mother of All Purity
prepared to go to Jerusalem, where She was to appear in the
temple with Her Son as the Only Be-gotten of the Eternal
Father and purify Herself according to the custom of other
women.

During the journey of Our Lady with the Infant God, it
happened in Jerusalem that Simeon, the high-priest was enlightened by the Holy Ghost concerning the coming of the
Incarnate Word and His presentation in the temple on the
arms of His Mother. The same revelation was given to the
holy widow Anne, and she was also informed of the poverty
and suffering of Saint Joseph and the Most Pure Lady on
Their way to Jerusalem. These two holy persons, immediately
conferring with each other about their revelations and enlightenments, called the chief procurator of the temporal
affairs of the temple, and, describing to him the signs,
whereby he should recognize the Holy Travelers, they ordered him to proceed to the gate leading out to Bethlehem
and receive Them into his house with all benevolence and
hospitality. This the procurator did and thus the Queen and
Her spouse were much relieved, since they had been anxious
about finding a proper lodging for the Divine Infant. Leaving

Them well provided in his house, the fortunate host returned in order to report to the high-priest.

The Sacred Humanity of Christ belonged to the Eternal Father not only because it was created like other beings, but it was His Special Property by virtue of the hypostatic union with the Person of the Word, for this Person of the Word, being His Only be-gotten Son, was engendered of His substance, True God of True God. Nevertheless the Eternal Father had decreed, that His Son should be presented to Him in the temple in mysterious compliance with the law, of which Christ Our Lord was the end (Rom. 10, 4). It was established for no other purpose than that the just men of the Old Testament should perpetually sanctify and offer to the Lord their first-born sons, in the hope that one thus presented might prove to be the Son of God and a Child of the Mother of the expected Messias (Exod. 13, 2). According to our way of thinking His Majesty acted like men, who are apt to repeat and enjoy over and over again a thing which has caused them enjoyment. For although the Father understood and knew all things in His Infinite Wisdom, He sought pleasure in the offering of the Incarnate Word, which by so many titles already belonged to Him.

This will of the Eternal Father, which was conformable to that of His Son in so far as He was God, was known to the Mother of Life and of the human nature of the Word; for She saw that all His interior actions were in unison with the Will of His Eternal Father. Full of this Holy Science the Great Princess passed the night before His presentation in the temple in divine colloquies. Speaking to the Father She said: "My Lord and God Most High, Father of My Lord, a festive day for Heaven and earth will be that, in which I shall bring and offer to Thee in Thy holy temple the Living Host, which is at the same time the Treasure of Thy Divinity. Rich, O My Lord and God, is this Oblation; and Thou canst well pour forth, in return for It, Thy mercies upon the human race: pardoning the sinners, that have turned from the straight path, consoling the afflicted, helping the needy, enriching the poor, succoring the weak, enlightening the blind, and meeting those who have strayed away. This is, My Lord, what I ask of Thee in offering to Thee Thy Only begotten, who, by Thy merciful condescension is also My Son. If Thou hast given Him to me as a God, I return Him to Thee as God and man; His value is Infinite, and what I ask of Thee is much less. In opulence do I

56

return to Thy Holy Temple, from which I departed poor; and My Soul shall magnify Thee forever, because Thy Divine right hand has shown itself toward Me so liberal and powerful."

On the next morning, the Sun of Heaven, being now ready to issue from its purest dawning, the Virgin Mary, on whose arms He reclined, and being about to rise up in full view of the World, the Heavenly Lady, having provided the turtle-dove and two candles, wrapped Him in swaddling-clothes and betook Herself with Saint Joseph from Their lodging to the Temple. The Holy Angels, Who had come with Them from Bethlehem, again formed in procession in corporeal and most beautiful forms, just as has been said concerning the journey of the preceding day. On this occasion however the Holy Spirits added many other hymns of the sweetest and most entrancing harmony in honor of the Infant God, which were heard only by the Most Pure Mary. Besides the ten thousand, who had formed the procession on the previous day, innumerable others descended from Heaven, who, accompanied by those that bore the shields of The Holy Name of Jesus, formed the guard of honor of the Incarnate Word on the occasion of His Presentation. These however were not in corporeal shapes and only the Heavenly Princess perceived Their presence. Having arrived at the temple-gate, the Most Blessed Mother was filled with new and exalted sentiments of devotion. Joining the other women, She bowed and knelt to adore the Lord in spirit and in truth in His Holy Temple and She presented Herself before the exalted Majesty of God with His Son upon Her arms (John 4, 23). Immediately She was immersed in an intellectual vision of the Most Holy Trinity and She heard a voice issuing from the Eternal Father, saying: "This is My beloved Son, in whom I am well pleased" (Matth. 27, 20). Saint Joseph, the most fortunate of men, felt at the same time a new sweetness of the Holy Ghost, which filled him with joy and divine light.

The holy high-priest Simeon, moved by the Holy Ghost as explained in the preceding chapter, also entered the temple at that time (Luke 2, 7). Approaching the place where the Queen stood with the Infant Jesus in Her arms, he saw both Mother and Child enveloped in splendor and glory. The prophetess Anne, who, as the Evangelist says, had come at the same hour, also saw Mary and Her Infant surrounded by this wonderful light. In the joy of Their spirit both of them approached the Queen of heaven, and the priest received the

57

Infant Jesus from Her arms upon his hands. Raising up his eyes to Heaven he offered Him up to the Eternal Father, pronouncing at the same time these words so full of mysteries: "Now dost thou dismiss Thy servant, O Lord, according to Thy Word in peace. Because my eyes have seen Thy Salvation, which Thou hast prepared before the face of all peoples: a light for the revelation of the gentiles, and the glory of Thy people Israel" (Luke 2, 29). It was as if He had said: "Now, Lord, thou wilt release me from the bondage of this mortal body and let me go free and in peace; for until now have I been detained in it by the hope of seeing Thy promises fulfilled and by the desire of seeing Thy Only Be-gotten made man. Now that my eyes have seen Thy Salvation, the Only Begotten made man, joined to our nature in order to give it Eternal Welfare according to the intention and Eternal decree of Thy Infinite Wisdom and Mercy, I shall enjoy true and secure peace. Now, O Lord, Thou hast prepared and placed before all mortals Thy Divine Light that it may shine upon the World and that all who wish may enjoy it throughout the universe and derive therefrom guidance and salvation. For this is the Light which is revealed to the gentiles for the glory of Thy chosen people of Israel" (John 1, 9, 32).

Most Holy Mary and Saint Joseph heard this canticle of Simeon, wondering at the exalted revelation it contained. The Evangelist calls them in this place the parents of the Divine Infant, for such they were in the estimation of the people who were present at this event. Simeon, addressing himself to the Most Holy Mother of the Infant Jesus, then added: "Behold this Child is set for the fall and for the resurrection of many in Israel, and for a sign which shall be contradicted. And Thy Own Soul a sword shall pierce, that out of many hearts thoughts may be revealed." Thus Saint Simeon; and being a priest he gave his blessing to the happy parents of the Child. Then also the prophetess Anne acknowledged the Incarnate Word, and full of the Holy Ghost, she spoke of the mysteries of the Messias to many, who were expecting the redemption of Israel. By these two holy old people public testimony of the coming of the Redeemer was given to the World.

At the moment when the priest Simeon mentioned the sword and the sign of contradiction, which were prophetical of the Passion and Death of The Lord, the Child bowed Its head. Thereby, and by many interior acts of obedience, Jesus ratified the prophecy of the priest and accepted it as the sentence of the Eternal Father pronounced by his minister. All this the Loving Mother noticed and understood; She presently began to feel the sorrow predicted by Simeon and thus in advance was She wounded by the sword, of which She had thus been warned. As in a mirror Her Spirit was made to see all the mysteries included in this prophecy; how Her Most Holy Son was to be the stone of stumbling, the perdition of the unbelievers, and the salvation of the faithful; the fall of the synagogue and the establishment of the Church among the heathens; She foresaw the triumph to be gained over the devils and over death, but also that a great price was to be paid for it, namely the frightful agony and death of the Cross (Colos. 2, 15). She foresaw the boundless opposition and contradiction, which The Lord Jesus was to sustain both personally and in His Church (John 15, 20). At the same time She also saw the glory and excellence of the predestined souls. Most Holy Mary knew it all and in the joy and sorrow of Her Most Pure Soul, excited by the prophecies of Simeon and these hidden mysteries, She performed heroic acts of virtue. All these sayings and happenings were indelibly impressed upon Her memory, and, of all that She understood and experienced, She forgot not the least iota. At all times She looked upon Her Most Holy Son with such a living sorrow, as we, mere human creatures with hearts so full of ingratitude, shall never be able to feel. The holy spouse Saint Joseph was by these prophecies also made to see many of the mysteries of the Redemption and of the labors and sufferings of Jesus. But the Lord did not reveal them to him so copiously and openly as they were perceived and understood by his Heavenly Spouse; for in him these revelations were to serve a different purpose, and besides, Saint Joseph was not to be an eye-witness of them during his mortal life.

The ceremony of the Presentation thus being over, the Great Lady kissed the hand of the priest and again asked his blessing. The same She did also to Anne, Her former teacher; for Her dignity as Mother of God, the highest possible to angels or men, did not prevent Her from these acts of deepest humility. Then, in the company of Saint Joseph, Her spouse, and of the fourteen thousand angels in procession, She returned with the Divine Infant to Her lodging. They remained, as I shall relate farther on, for some days in

Jerusalem, in order to satisfy Their devotion and during that time She spoke a few times with the priest about the mysteries of the Redemption and of the prophecies above mentioned.

When the Most Holy Mary and Glorious Saint Joseph returned from the Presentation of the Infant Jesus in the temple, They concluded to stay in Jerusalem for nine days in order to be able each day to visit the Temple and repeat the offering of the Sacred Victim, Their Divine Son, thus rendering fitting thanks for the immense blessing for which they had been singled out from among all men. The Heavenly Lady had a special veneration for this number in memory of the nine days, during which She had been prepared and adorned by God for the Incarnation of the Word, as I have related in the first ten chapters of this second part; also in memory of the nine months, during which She had borne Jesus in Her virginal womb. In honor of these events She wished to make this novena with Her Divine Child, presenting Him that many times to the Eternal Father as an acceptable offering for Her lofty purposes. They began the devotions of the novena every day before the third hour, praying in the Temple until nightfall. They chose the most obscure and retired place, meriting thereby the invitation of the master of the banquet in the Gospel: "Friend, go up higher."

As an answer to Her petitions He conceded to Her new and great privileges, among which was also this one, that, as long as the World should last, She should obtain all that She would ever ask for Her clients; that the greatest sinners, if they availed themselves of Her intercession, should find salvation; that in the New Church and Law of the Gospel She should be the Coöperatrix and Teacher of Salvation with Christ Her Most Holy Son. This was to be Her privilege especially after His Ascension into Heaven, when She should remain, as Queen of the Universe, as the Representative and Instrument of the Divine Power on Earth. This I will show more particularly in the third part of this history. Many other favors and mysteries the Most High confirmed upon the Heavenly Mother in answer to Her prayers. They, however, are beyond the reach of spoken language, and cannot be described by my short and limited terms.

In the course of these manifestations, on the fifth day of the novena after the Presentation and Purification, while the Heavenly Lady was in the Temple with the Infant on Her arms, the Deity revealed Itself to Her, although not intuitively, and She was wholly raised and filled by the Spirit. It is true, that this had been done to Her before; but as God's Power and Treasures are Infinite, He never gives so much as not to be able to give still more to the creatures. In this abstractive vision the Most High visited anew His Only Spouse, wishing to prepare Her for the labors, that were awaiting Her. Speaking to Her, He comforted Her saying: "My Spouse and my Dove, Thy wishes and intentions are pleasing in My eyes and I delight in them always. But Thou canst not finish the nine days' devotion, which Thou hast begun, for I have in store for Thee other exercises of Thy love. In order to save the Life of Thy Son and raise Him up, Thou must leave Thy Home and Thy Country, fly with Him and thy Spouse Joseph into Egypt, where Thou art to remain until I shall ordain otherwise: for Herod is seeking the Life of the Child. The journey is long, most laborious and most fatiguing; do Thou suffer it all for My sake; for I am, and always will be, with Thee."

Any other faith and virtue might have been disturbed (as the incredulous really have been) to see the powerful God flying from a miserable earthly being, and that He should do so in order to save His life, as if He, being both God and man, could be affected by the fear of death. But the Most Prudent and Obedient Mother advanced no objection or doubt: She was not in the least disturbed or moved by this unlooked for order. Answering, She said: "My Lord and Master, behold Thy servant with a heart prepared to die for Thy Love if necessary. Dispose of me according to Thy will. This only do I ask of thy immense goodness, that, overlooking My want of merit and gratitude, Thou permit not My Son and Lord to suffer, and that Thou turn all pains and labor upon Me, who am obliged to suffer them." The Lord referred Her to Saint Joseph, bidding Her to follow his directions in all things concerning the journey. Therewith She issued from Her vision, which She had enjoyed without losing the use of Her exterior senses and while holding in Her arms the Infant Jesus. She had been raised up in this vision only as to the superior part of Her Soul; but from it flowed other gifts, which spiritualized Her senses and testified to Her that Her Soul was living more in its love than in the earthly habitation of Her body.

On account of the incomparable love, which the Queen

bore toward Her Most Holy Son, Her Maternal and Compassionate Heart was somewhat harrowed at the thought of the labors which She foresaw in the vision impending upon the Infant God. Shedding many tears, She left the Temple to go to Her lodging-place, without manifesting to Her spouse the cause of Her sorrow. Saint Joseph therefore thought that She grieved on account of the prophecy of Simeon. As the most faithful Joseph loved Her so much, and as he was of a kind and solicitous disposition, he was troubled to see his Spouse so tearful and afflicted, and that She should not manifest to him the cause of this new affliction. This disturbance of his soul was one of the reasons why the Holy Angels spoke to him in sleep, as I have related above, when speaking of the pregnancy of the Queen. For in the same night, while Saint Joseph was asleep, the Angel of the Lord appeared to him, and spoke to him as recorded by Saint Matthew: "Arise, take the Child and Its Mother and fly into Egypt; there shalt thou remain until I shall return to give thee other advice; for Herod is seeking after the Child in order to take away His life." Immediately the holy spouse arose full of solicitude and sorrow, foreseeing also that of his Most Loving Spouse. Entering upon Her retirement, he said: "My Lady, God wills that we should be afflicted; for his Holy Angel has announced to me the pleasure and the decree of the Almighty, that we arise and fly with the Child into Egypt, because Herod is seeking to take away Its life. Encourage Thyself, my Lady, to bear the labors of this journey and tell me what I can do for Thy comfort, since I hold my life and being at the service of Thy Child and of Thee."

"My husband and My master," answered the Queen, "if we have received from the hands of the Most High such great blessings of grace, it is meet that we joyfully accept temporal afflictions (Job 2, 13). We bear with us the Creator of Heaven and Earth; if He has placed us so near to Him, what arms shall be able to harm us, even if it be the arm of Herod? Wherever we carry with us all our Good, the Highest Treasure of Heaven, Our Lord, Our Guide and True Light, there can be no desert; but He is Our Rest, Our Portion, and Our Country. All these goods we possess in having His company; let us proceed to fulfill His Will." Then Most Holy Mary and Joseph approached the crib where the Infant Jesus lay; and where He, not by chance, slept at that time. The Heavenly Mother uncovered Him without awakening Him;

then the Heavenly Mother, falling upon Her knees, awakened the Sweetest Infant, and took Him in Her arms. Jesus, in order to move Her to greater tenderness and in order to show Himself as true man, wept a little (O wonders of the Most High in things according to our judgments so small)! Yet He was soon again quieted; and when the Most Holy Mother and Saint Joseph asked His blessing He gave it them in visible manner. Gathering their poor clothing into the casket and loading it on the beast of burden which they had brought from Nazareth, they departed shortly after midnight, and hastened without delay on their journey to Egypt.

WORDS OF THE QUEEN.

My Daughter, what thou must especially learn from this chapter is, that thou accustom Thyself to humble thanksgiving for the benefits which Thou receivest, since Thou, among many generations, art so specially signalized by the riches of grace with which My Son and I visit Thee without any merit of thine. I was wont to repeat many times this verse of David: "What shall I render to the Lord for all the things that he hath rendered to me?" (Ps. 15, 12). In such sentiments I humiliated Myself to the dust, esteeming Myself altogether useless among creatures. Therefore, if thou knowest what I did as Mother of God, consider what then is thy obligation, since thou must with so much truth confess thyself unworthy and undeserving of all thou receivest, and so poorly furnished for giving thanks and for making payment. Thou must supply thy insufficiency and thy misery by offering up to the Eternal Father The Living Host of His Only Be-gotten Son, especially when thou receivest Him in the Holy Sacrament and possessest Him within thee: for in this thou shouldst also imitate David, who, after asking the Lord what return he should make for all his benefits, answers: "I will take the chalice of salvation; and I will call upon the name of the Lord" (Ps. 115, 13). Thou must accept the salvation offered to thee and bring forth its fruits by the perfection of thy works, calling upon the name of the Lord, offering up His Only Be-gotten. For He it is Who gave the virtue of salvation, Who merited it, Who alone can be an adequate return for the blessings conferred upon the human race and upon thee especially. I have given Him human form in order that He might converse with men and become the

63

property of each one. He conceals Himself under the appearances of bread and wine in order to accommodate Himself to the needs of each one, and that each one might consider Him as his personal property fit to offer to the Eternal Father. In this way He furnishes to each one an oblation which no one could otherwise offer, and the Most High rests satisfied with it, since there is not anything more acceptable nor anything more precious in the possession of creatures.

In addition to this offering is the resignation with which souls embrace and bear with equanimity and patience the labors and difficulties of mortal life. My Most Holy Son and I were eminent Masters in the practice of this doctrine. My Son began to teach it from the moment in which He was conceived in My womb. For already then He began to suffer, and as soon as He was born into the world He and I were banished by Herod into a desert, and His sufferings continued until He died on the Cross. I also labored to the end of My life, as thou wilt be informed more and more in the writing of this history. Since, therefore, We suffered so much for creatures and for their salvation, I desire thee to imitate Us in this Conformity to the Divine Will as being His Spouse and My Daughter. Suffer with a magnanimous heart, and labor to increase the possessions of Thy Lord and Master, namely, souls, which are so precious in His sight and which He has purchased with His Life-blood. Never shouldst thou fly from labors, difficulties, bitterness and sorrows, if by any of them thou canst gain a Soul for The Lord, or if thou canst thereby induce it to leave the path of sin and enter the path of life. Let not the thought that thou art so useless and poor, or that thy desires and labor avail but little, discourage Thee; since thou canst not know how the Lord will accept of them and in how far He shall consider Himself served thereby. At least thou shouldst wish to labor assiduously and eat no unearned bread in His House. (Prov. 31, 27).

Our Heavenly Pilgrims left Jerusalem and entered upon their banishment while yet the silence and obscurity of night held sway. They were full of solicitude for the Pledge of Heaven, which They carried with Them into a strange and unknown land. Although faith and hope strengthened them (for in no other beings could these virtues be more firmly and securely established than in Our Queen and Her most Faithful Spouse), nevertheless the Lord afforded them occasion for anxiety. Their love for the Infant Jesus would naturally excite in them anxiety and suffering on an occasion like this. They knew not what would happen during such a long journey, nor when it should end, nor how they would fare in Egypt, where they would be entire strangers, nor what comfort or convenience they would find there for raising the Child, nor even how they would be able to ward off great sufferings from Him on the way to Egypt. Therefore the hearts of These Holy Parents were filled with many misgivings and anxious thoughts when they parted with so much haste from their lodging-place; but their sorrow was much relieved when the ten thousand heavenly courtiers above mentioned again appeared to them in human forms and in their former splendor and beauty, and when they again changed the night into the brightest day for the Holy Pilgrims. As they set forth from the portals of the city the Holy Angels humiliated themselves and Adored the Incarnate Word in the arms of the Virgin Mother. They also encouraged Her by again offering their homage and service, stating that it was the will of The Lord that they guide and accompany Her on the journey.

THE FINDING OF THE CHRIST CHILD
IN THE TEMPLE

INTERIOR TRIALS OF MARY; JESUS IN THE TEMPLE.

Already Jesus, Mary and Joseph had settled in Nazareth and thus changed their poor and humble dwelling into a heaven. In order to describe the Mysteries and Sacraments which passed between the Divine Child and His Purest Mother before his twelfth year and later on, until His public preaching, many chapters and many books would be required; and in them all, I would be able to relate but the smallest part in view of the vastness of the subject and the insignificance of such an ignorant woman as I am. Even with the light given me by This Great Lady I can speak of only a few incidents and must leave the greater part unsaid. It is not possible or befitting to us mortals to comprehend all these mysteries in this life, since they are reserved for the future life.

Shortly after their return from Egypt to Nazareth the Lord resolved to try His Most holy Mother in the same manner as He had tried Her in Her childhood as the first-born Daughter of the new Law of grace, the most perfect copy of His ideals and the most pliant material, upon which, as on liquid wax, should be set the seal of His doctrine of holiness, so that the Son and the Mother might be the two true tablets of the New Law of the World (Exod. 31, 18). For this purpose of the Infinite Wisdom He manifested to Her all the mysteries of the evangelical law and of His doctrine; and this was the subject of His instructions from the time of their return from Egypt until His public preaching, as we shall see in the course of this history. In these hidden Sacraments the Incarnate Word and His Holy Mother occupied themselves during the twenty-three years of their stay in Nazareth. As all this concerned the Heavenly Mother alone (whose life the Holy Evangelists did not profess to narrate), the writers of the Gospel made no mention of it, excepting that which was related of the Child Jesus, when, in His twelfth year, He was lost in Jerusalem. During all those years Mary alone was the disciple of Christ.

In order to rear in the heart of the purest Virgin this edifice of holiness to a height beyond all that is not God, the Lord laid its foundations accordingly, trying the strength of Her love and of all Her other virtues. For this purpose the Lord withdrew Himself, causing Her to lose Him from Her sight, which until then had caused Her to revel in continual joy and delight. I do not wish to say, that the Lord left Her bodily; but, still remaining with Her and in Her by an ineffable presence and grace, He hid Himself from Her interior sight and suspended the tokens of His Most Sweet Affection. The Heavenly Lady in the meanwhile knew not the inward cause of this behavior, as the Lord gave Her no explanation. Moreover Her Divine Son, without any forewarning showed Himself very reserved and withdrew from Her society. Many times He retired and spoke but few words to Her, and even these with great earnestness and majesty.

This unannounced and unexpected change was the Crucible in which the Purest Gold of the Love of Our Queen was cleansed and assayed. Surprised at what was happening, She immediately took refuge in the humble opinion She had of Herself, deeming Herself unworthy of the vision of the Lord, who now had hidden Himself. She attributed it all to Her want of correspondence and to Her ingratitude for the blessings She had obtained from the Most Generous and Exalted Father of mercies. The Most Prudent Queen did not feel so much the privation of his delightful caresses, as the dread of having displeased Him and of having fallen short in His service. This was the arrow that pierced Her heart with grief. One filled with such true and noble love could not feel less; for all delight of love is founded in the pleasure and satisfaction given by the lover to the one beloved, and therefore He cannot rest, when he suspects that the beloved is not contented or pleased. The loving sighs of His Mother were highly pleasing to Her Most Holy Son. He was enamored with Her anew and the tender affection of His Only and Chosen One wounded His heart (Cant. 4, 9). But whenever the Sweet Mother sought him out in order to hold converse with Him He continued to show exterior reserve.

Just as the flame of a forge or a conflagration is intensified by the application of insufficient water, so the flame of love in the heart of the Sweetest Mother was fanned to an intenser blaze by this adversity.

The single-hearted Dove exercised Herself in heroic acts of all the virtues. She humbled Herself below the dust; She reverenced Her Son in deepest adoration; She blessed the Father, thanking Him for His admirable works and blessings and conforming Herself to His wishes and pleasure; She sought to know His will in order to fulfill it in all things; She unceasingly renewed Her acts of faith, hope and burning love; and in all Her actions and in all circumstances this most fragrant spikenard gave forth the odor of sweetness for Him, the King of Kings, who rested in Her heart as in His flowery and perfumed couch (Cant. 1, 11). She persevered in Her tearful prayers, with continual sighing and longing from Her inmost heart; She poured forth Her prayers in the presence of the Lord and recounted Her tribulation before the throne of the God (Ps. 141, 3).

Upon the request of the Loving Mother Saint Joseph had made a couch, which She covered with a single blanket and upon which the Child Jesus rested and took His sleep; for from the time in which He had left the cradle, when they were yet in Egypt, He would not accept of any other bed or of more covering. Although He did not stretch Himself out on this couch, nor even always made use of it, He sometimes reclined in a sitting posture upon it, resting upon a poor pillow made of wool by the same Lady. When She spoke of preparing for Him a better resting-place, Her Most Holy Son answered, that the only couch upon which He was to be stretched out, was that of His Cross, in order to teach men by His example (I Pet. 2, 21), that no one can enter eternal rest by things beloved of Babylon and that to suffer is our true relief in mortal life. Thenceforward the Heavenly Lady imitated Him in this manner of taking rest with new earnestness and attention.

Thirty days passed in this conflict; and they equalled many ages in the estimation of Her, who deemed it impossible to live even one moment without the love and without the Beloved of Her soul. After such delay (according to our way of speaking), the heart of the Child Jesus could no longer contain itself or resist further the immense force of His love for His Sweetest Mother; for also the Lord suffered a delightful and wonderful violence in thus holding Her in such a suspense and affliction. It happened that the humble and sovereign Queen one day approached Her Son Jesus, and, throwing Herself at His feet, with tears and sighs coming from Her inmost heart, spoke to Him as follows: "My Sweetest Love and Highest Good, of what account am I, the insignificant dust and ashes, before Thy vast power? What is the misery of a creature in comparison with Thy endless affluence? In all things Thou excellest our lowliness and Thy immense sea of mercy overwhelms our imperfections and defects. If I have not been zealous in serving Thee, as I am constrained to confess, do Thou chastise my negligence and pardon it. But let Me, My Son and Lord, see the gladness of Thy countenance, which is My Salvation and the wished-for Light of My Life and Being. Here at Thy feet I lay my poverty, mingling it with the dust, and I shall not rise from it until I can again look into the mirror, which reflects My Soul."

These and other pleadings, full of wisdom and most ardent love, the Great Queen poured humbly forth before Her Most Holy Son. And as His longings to restore Her to His delights were even greater than those of the Blessed Lady, He pronounced with great sweetness these few words: "My Mother, arise." As these words were pronounced by Him, who is Himself the Word of the Eternal Father, it had such an effect, that the Heavenly Mother was instantly transformed and elevated into a most exalted ecstasy, in which She saw the Divinity by an abstractive vision. In it the Lord received Her with sweetest welcome and embraces of a Father and Spouse, changing Her tears into rejoicing, Her sufferings into delight and Her bitterness into highest sweetness. The Lord manifested to Her great secrets of the scope of His New Evangelical Law. Wishing to write it entirely into Her Purest Heart, the Most Holy Trinity appointed and destined Her as His first-born Daughter and the First Disciple of the Incarnate Word and set Her up as the model and pattern for all the holy Apostles, Martyrs, Doctors, Confessors, Virgins and other just of the New Church and of the Law of Grace, which the Incarnate Word was to establish for the Redemption of man.

Some days after Our Queen and Lady with Her Most Holy Son and Saint Joseph had settled in Nazareth, the time of the year in which the Jews were obliged to present themselves before the Lord in the Temple of Jerusalem, was at hand. This commandment obliged the Jews to this duty three times each year, as can be seen in Exodus and Deuteronomy. But it obliged only the men, not the women (Exod. 23, 17); therefore the women could go or not, according to their devotion; for it was neither commanded nor prohibited to them. The heavenly Lady and Her spouse conferred with each other as to what they should do in this regard. The holy husband much desired the company of the Great Queen, his Wife, and of Her Most Holy Son; for he wished to offer Him anew to the Eternal Father in the Temple. The Most Pure Mother also was drawn by Her piety to worship the Lord in the temple; but as in things of that kind She did not permit Herself to decide without the counsel and direction of the Incarnate Word, Her Teacher, She asked His advice upon this matter. They finally arranged, that two times a year Saint Joseph was to go to Jerusalem by himself, while on the third occasion They would go together. The Israelites visited the temple on the feast of the Tabernacles (Deut. 16, 13), the feast of the Weeks, or Pentecost, and the feast of the Unleavened Breads or the Pasch of the preparation. To this latter the Sweetest Jesus, Most Pure Mary, and Joseph went up together. It lasted seven days and during that time happened what I shall relate in the next chapter. For the other solemnities Saint Joseph went alone, leaving the Child and the Mother at home.

As I have said, Mary and Joseph repeated their visit to the temple at the feast of the Unleavened Bread every year. Also when the divine Child was twelve years old and when it was time to allow the splendors of His inaccessible and Divine Light to shine forth, They went to the temple for this feast (Luke 2, 42). This festival of the unleavened Bread lasted seven days, according to the command of the Divine Law; and the more solemn days were the first and the last. On this account our Heavenly Pilgrims remained in Jerusalem during the whole week, spending their time in acts of worship and devotion as the rest of the Jews, although on account of the sacraments connected with each of Them their worship and devotion was entirely different and greatly exalted above that of the others. The Blessed Mother and Holy Joseph received during these days favors and blessings beyond the conception of the human mind.

Having thus spent all the seven days of the feast They

betook themselves on their way home to Nazareth. When His parents departed from Jerusalem and were pursuing their way homeward, the Child Jesus withdrew from them without their knowledge. For this purpose the Lord availed Himself of the separation of the men and women, which had become customary among the pilgrims for reasons of decency as well as for greater recollection during their return homeward. The children which accompanied their parents were taken in charge promiscuously either by the men or the women, since their company with either was a matter of indifference. Thus it happened that Saint Joseph could easily suppose that the Child Jesus had remained with His Most Holy Mother, with whom He generally remained. The thought that She would go without Him was far from his mind, since the heavenly Queen loved and delighted in Him more than any other creature human or angelic. The Great Lady did not have so many reasons for supposing that Her Most Holy Son was in the company of Saint Joseph: but the Lord Himself so diverted Her thoughts by holy and divine contemplations, that She did not notice His absence at first. When afterwards She because aware of Her not being accompanied by Her sweetest and beloved Son, She supposed that the Blessed Joseph had taken Him along and that the Lord accompanied His foster-father for His consolation.

Thus assured, Holy Mary and Joseph pursued their home journey for an entire day, as Saint Luke tells us. As the pilgrims proceeded onwards they gradually thinned out, each taking his own direction and joining again with his wife or family. The Most Holy Mary and Saint Joseph found themselves at length in the place where they had agreed to meet on the first evening after leaving Jerusalem. When the Great Lady saw that The Child was not with Saint Joseph and when the Holy Patriarch found that He was not with His Mother, the two were struck dumb with amazement and surprise for quite a while. Both, governed in their judgment by their most profound humility, felt overwhelmed with self-reproach at their remissness in watching over their Most Holy Son and thus blamed themselves for His absence; for neither of them had any suspicion of the mysterious manner in which He had been able to elude their vigilance. After a time they recovered somewhat from their astonishment and with deepest sorrow took counsel with each other as to what was to be done (Luke 2, 45). The loving Mother said to

71

Saint Joseph: "My Spouse and My Master, My Heart cannot rest, unless we return with all haste to Jerusalem in order to seek My Most Holy Son." This they proceeded to do, beginning their search among their relations and friends, of whom, however, none could give them any information or any comfort in their sorrow; on the contrary their answers only increased their anxiety, since none of them had so much as seen their Son since their departure from Jerusalem.

Thus this sincerest Dove persevered in Her tears and groans without cessation or rest, without sleeping or eating anything for three whole days. Although the ten thousand angels accompanied Her in corporeal forms and witnessed Her affliction and sorrow, yet they gave Her no clue to find Her lost Child. On the third day the Great Queen resolved to seek Him in the desert where Saint John was; for since She saw no indications that Archelaus had taken Him prisoner, She began to believe more firmly, that Her Most Holy Son was with Saint John. When She was about to execute Her resolve and was on the point of departing for the desert, the Holy Angels detained Her, urging Her not to undertake the journey, since the Divine Word was not there. She wanted also to go to Bethlehem, in the hope of finding Him in the cave of the Nativity; but this the Holy Angels likewise prevented, telling Her that He was not so far off. Although the Blessed Mother heard these answers and well perceived that the Holy Angels knew the whereabouts of the Child Jesus, She was so considerate and reserved in Her humility and prudence, that She gave no response, nor asked where She could find Him; for She understood that they withheld this information by command of the Lord. With such magnanimous reverence did the Queen of the Angels treat the Sacraments of the Most High and of His ministers and ambassadors (II Mach. 2, 9). This was one of the occasions in which the greatness of Her queenly and magnanimous heart was made manifest.

Not all the sorrows suffered by all the martyrs ever reached the height of the sorrows of Most Holy Mary in this trial; nor will the patience, resignation and tolerance of this Lady ever be equalled, nor can they; for the loss of Jesus was greater to Her than the loss of anything created, while Her love and appreciation of Him exceeded all that can be conceived by any other creature. Since She did not know the cause of the loss, Her anxiety was beyond all measure, as I

have already said. Moreover, during these three days the
Lord left Her to her natural resources of nature and of
grace, deprived of special privileges and favors; for, with the
exception of the company and intercourse with the angels,
He suspended all the other consolations and blessings so
constantly vouchsafed to Her Most Holy Soul. From all this
we can surmise what sorrow filled the loving heart of the
Heavenly Mother. But, O prodigy of holiness, prudence,
fortitude and perfection! in such unheard of affliction and
sorrow She was not disturbed, nor lost Her interior or exterior peace, nor did She entertain a thought of anger or
indignation, nor allowed Herself any improper movement or
expression, nor fell into any excess of grief or annoyance, as is
so common in great affliction with other children of Adam,
who allow all their passions and faculties to be disarranged,
yea even in small difficulties; The Mistress of all virtue held all
Her powers in heavenly order and harmony; though Her
sorrow was without comparison great and had pierced Her
inmost heart, She failed not in reverence and in the praise of
the Lord, nor ceased in Her prayers and petitions for the
human race, and for the finding of Her Most Holy Son.

With this heavenly wisdom and with greatest diligence She
sought Him for three successive days, roaming through the
streets of the city, asking different persons and describing to
the daughters of Jerusalem the marks of Her Beloved, searching the byways and the open squares of the city and
thereby fulfilling what was recorded in the Canticles of
Solomon (Cant. 5, 10). Some of the women asked Her what
were the distinctive marks of Her lost and only Son; and She
answered in the words of the Spouse: "My Beloved is white
and ruddy, chosen out of thousands." One of the women,
hearing Her thus describing Him, said: "This Child, with
those same marks, came yesterday to my door to ask for
alms, and I gave some to Him; and His Grace and Beauty
have ravished my heart. And when I gave Him alms, I felt
myself overcome by compassion to see a Child so gracious in
poverty and want." These were the first news the sorrowful
Mother heard of her Only-begotten in Jerusalem. A little
respited in Her sorrow, She pursued Her quest and met
other persons, who spoke of Him in like manner. Guided by
this information She directed Her steps to the hospital of the
city, thinking that among the afflicted She would find the
Spouse and the Originator of patient poverty among His own

legitimate brethren and friends (Matth. 5, 40). Inquiring at that place, She was informed that a Child of that description had paid His visits to the inmates, leaving some alms and speaking words of much consolation to the afflicted.

The report of these doings of Her Beloved caused sentiments of sweetest and most tender affection in the heart of the Heavenly Lady, which She sent forth from Her inmost heart as messengers to Her lost and absent Son. Then the thought struck Her, that, since He was not with the poor, He no doubt tarried in the Temple, as in the house of God and of prayer. The Holy Angels encouraged Her and said: "Our Queen and Lady, the hour of Thy consolation is at hand: soon wilt Thou see the Light of Thy eyes; hasten Thy footsteps and go to the Temple." The glorious patriarch Saint Joseph at this moment again met His Spouse, for, in order to increase their chance of finding the Divine Child, they had separated in different directions. By another angel he had now been likewise ordered to proceed to the temple. During all these three days he had suffered unspeakable sorrow and affliction, hastening from one place to another, sometimes without his Heavenly Spouse, sometimes with Her. He was in serious danger of losing his life during this time, if the hand of the Lord had not strengthened Him and if the Most Prudent Lady had not consoled him and forced him to take some food and rest. His sincere and exquisite love for the Divine Child made him so anxious and solicitous to find Him, that he would have allowed himself no time or care to take nourishment for the support of nature.

It was very near to the gate of the city, that the Divine Child turned and hastened back through the streets. Foreseeing in His Divine fore-knowledge all that was to happen, He offered it up to His Eternal Father for the benefit of souls. He asked for alms during these three days in order to ennoble from that time on humble mendicity as the first-born of holy poverty. He visited the hospitals of the poor, consoling them and giving them the alms which He had received; secretly He restored bodily health to some and spiritual health to many, by enlightening them interiorly and leading them back to the way of salvation. On some of the benefactors, who gave Him alms, He performed these wonders with a greater abundance of grace and light; thus fulfilling from that time on the promise, which He was afterwards to make to His Church; that he who gives to the just and to the prophet in the name of a prophet, shall receive the reward of the just (Matth. 10, 41).

Having thus busied Himself with these and other works of His Father, He betook Himself to the temple. On the day which the Evangelist mentions it happened that also the rabbis, who were the learned and the teachers of the Temple, met in a certain part of the buildings in order to confer among themselves concerning some doubtful points of Holy Scriptures. On this occasion the coming of the Messias was discussed; for on account of the report of the wonderful events, which had spread about since the birth of the Baptist and the visit of the Kings of the east, the rumor of the coming of the Redeemer and of His being already in the world, though yet unknown, had gained ground among the Jews. They were all seated in their places filled with the sense of authority customary to those who are teachers and considered as learned. The Child Jesus came to the meeting of these distinguished men; and He that was the King of Kings, and Lord of Lords (Apoc. 19, 16), the Infinite Wisdom Itself (I Cor. 1, 24), and who corrects the wise (Wis. 7, 15), presented Himself before the teachers of this world as an Humble Disciple, giving them to understand that He had come to hear their discussion and inform Himself on the question treated of, namely: whether the Messias was already come, or, if not, concerning the time in which He should come into the world. Therefore the Divine Child presented Himself to the disputants, manifesting the grace poured out over his lips (Ps. 44, 3). He stepped into their midst with exceeding majesty and grace, as one who would propose some doubt or solution. By His pleasing appearance He awakened in the hearts of these learned men a desire to hear Him attentively.

The scribes and learned men who heard Him were all dumbfounded. Convinced by His arguments they looked at each other and in great astonishment asked: "What miracle is this? and what prodigy of a boy! Whence has He come and who is the Child?" But though thus astonished, they did not recognize or suspect who it was, that thus taught and enlightened them concerning such an important truth. During this time and before Jesus had finished His argument, His Most Holy Mother and Saint Joseph Her most chaste spouse arrived, just in time to hear him advance his last arguments. When He had finished, all the teachers of the law arose with stupendous amazement. The Heavenly Lady, absorbed in joy, approached Her Most Loving Son and in the presence of the whole assembly, spoke to Him the words recorded by Saint Luke: "Son, why hast Thou done so to us? Behold Thy father and I have sought Thee sorrowing" (Luke 2, 48). This loving complaint the Heavenly Mother uttered with equal reverence and affection, adoring Him as God and manifesting Her maternal affliction. The Lord answered: "Why is it that You sought Me? Did you not know that I must be about My Father's business?"

The Evangelist says that They did not understand the mystery of these words (Luke 2, 50); for it was hidden at the time to Most Holy Mary and Saint Joseph. And for two reasons; on the one hand, the interior joy of now reaping what They had sown in so much sorrow, and the visible presence of Their Precious Treasure, entirely filled the faculties of their souls; and on the other hand, the time for the full comprehension of what had just been treated of in this discussion had not yet arrived for them. Moreover, for the most solicitous Queen there was another hindrance, just at that time, and it was, that the veil, concealing the interior of Her Most Holy Son had again intervened and was not removed until some time later. The learned men departed, commenting in their amazement upon the wonderful event, by which they had been privileged to hear the teaching of Eternal Wisdom, though they did not recognize it. Being thus left almost alone, the Blessed Mother, embracing Him with maternal affection, said to Him: "Permit my longing heart, My Son, to give expression to its sorrow and pain; so that it may not die of grief as long as it can be of use to Thee. Do not cast Me off from Thy sight; but accept Me as Thy Slave. If it was my negligence, which deprived Me of Thy presence, pardon Me and make Me worthy of Thy company, and do not punish Me with Thy absence." The Divine Child received Her with signs of pleasure and offered Himself as Her Teacher and Companion until the proper time should arrive. Thus was the dove-like and affectionate heart of the Great Lady appeased, and They departed for Nazareth.

They arrived at Nazareth, where They occupied themselves in what I shall record later on. The Evangelist Luke compendiously mentions all the mysteries in few words, saying the Child Jesus was subject to His parents, namely Most Holy Mary and Saint Joseph, and that His Heavenly Mother noted and preserved within Her Heart all these events; and that

Jesus advanced in wisdom, and age, and grace with God and men (Luke 2, 52), of which, as far as my understanding goes, I will speak later on. Just now I wish only to mention, that the humility and obedience of our God and Master toward His parents were the admiration of the angels. But so was also the dignity and excellence of His Most Blessed Mother, who thus merited that the Incarnate God should subject Himself and resign Himself to Her care; so much so, that She, with the assistance of Saint Joseph, governed Him and disposed of Him as Her own.

To the obedience and subjection of Her Most Holy Son the great Lady on Her part responded by heroic works. Among Her other excellences She conceived as it were an incomprehensible humility and a most heartfelt gratitude for having regained the companionship of Her Son. This blessing, of which the Heavenly Queen deemed Herself unworthy, vastly increased in Her most pure heart Her love and Her anxiety to serve Her divine Son. And She was so constant in showing Her gratitude, so punctual and solicitous to serve Him, kneeling before Him and lowering Herself to the dust, that it excited the admiration of the highest seraphim. Moreover, She sought with the closest attention to imitate Him in all His actions as they became known to Her and exerted Herself most anxiously to copy them and reproduce them in Her own life. The plenitude of Her perfection wounded the heart of our Christ and Lord, and, according to our way of speaking, held him bound to Her with chains of invincible love. (Osee 11, 4). His being thus bound as God and as Son to this Heavenly Princess, gave rise to such an interchange and divine reciprocity of intense love, as surpasses all created understanding. For into the ocean of Mary's soul entered all the vast floods of the graces and blessings of the Incarnate Word; and this ocean did not overflow (Eccles. 1, 7), because it contained the depth and expanse necessary to receive them.

WORDS OF THE QUEEN.

My daughter, all the works of My Most Holy Son and My own actions are full of mysterious instruction and doctrine for the mortals who contemplate them diligently and reverently. The Lord absented Himself from me in order that, seeking Him in sorrow and tears, I might find Him again in joy and with abundant fruits for my soul. I desire that thou imitate Me in this mystery and seek Him with such earnestness, as to be consumed with a continual longing without ever in thy whole life coming to any rest until thou holdst Him and canst lose Him no more (Can. 5, 4). In order that thou mayest understand better this sacrament of the Lord, remember, that the Infinite Wisdom made men capable of His Eternal Felicity and placed them on the way to this happiness, but left them in doubt of its attainment, as long as they have not yet acquired it and thus filled them with joyful hope and sorrowful fear of its final acquisition. This anxiety engenders in men a lifelong fear and abhorrence of sin, by which alone they can be deprived of beatitude and thus prevent them from being ensnared and misled by the corporeal and visible things of this earth. This anxiety the Creator assists by adding to the natural reasoning powers, faith and hope, which are the spurs of their love toward seeking and finding their last end. Besides these virtues and others infused at Baptism He sends His inspirations and helps to keep awake the soul in the absence of Its Lord and to prevent forgetfulness of Him and of itself while deprived of his amiable presence. Thus it pursues the right course until it finds the great goal, where all its inclinations and longing shall be satiated.

Hence thou canst estimate the listless ignorance of mortals and how few stop to consider the mysterious order of the creation and justification and all the works of the Almighty tending toward this exalted end. From this forgetfulness flow so many evils endured by men while they appropriate so many earthly goods and deceitful delights, as if they could ever find in them their ultimate end. The height of perversity opposed to the order of the Creator, is that mortals in this transitory and short life rejoice in visible things as if they were their last end, while they ought, on the contrary, to make use of creatures to gain, not to lose, the highest Good. Do thou, therefore, My Dearest, be mindful of this dangerous human folly. Consider all delights and joys of the world as insanity, its laughing as sorrow, sensible enjoyment as self deceit, as the source of foolishness, which intoxicates the heart and hinders and destroys all true wisdom. Live in constant and holy fear of losing Eternal Life and rejoice in nothing except in the Lord until thou obtainest full possession of Him.

I have already said in former chapters, that Our Great Lady was the first and specially privileged Disciple of Her Most Holy Son, chosen among all creatures as the model of the new evangelical law and its Author, according to which He was to mould all the saints of the new law and judge of all the results of the Redemption. In regard to Her the Incarnate Word proceeded like a most skillful artist, who understands the art of painting and all that pertains to it most thoroughly; who, throwing all His powers into one chosen work, seeks to gain from it alone renown and fame as from the full exposition of His art. It is certain that all the holiness and glory of the saints was the result of the love and merits of Christ: (Eph. 2, 3) but in comparison with the excellence of Mary, they seem insignificant and as it were only rough sketches; for in all the saints are found defects (I John 1, 8). But this Living Image of the Only be-gotten was free from all imperfections; and the first strokes of His pencil in Her were of greater beauty than the last touches in the highest angels and saints. She is the Model for all the perfection of holiness and virtues of all His elect, and the utmost limit to which the love of Christ can proceed in mere creatures. No one received any grace or glory that Most Holy Mary could not receive, and She received all that others were incapable of receiving; and Her Most Blessed Son gave to Her all that She could receive and that He could communicate.

The multitude and variety of the saints silently enhance the Artificer of their great sanctity, and the greatness of the highest is made more conspicuous by the beauty of the lowest: but all of them together are a glorification of Most Holy Mary. For by Her incomparable holiness they are all surpassed and they all partake of so much the greater felicity as they imitate Her, whose holiness redounds over all. If the most pure Mary has reached the highest pinnacle in the ranks of the just, She may also on this very account be considered as the instrument or the motive power through which the saints themselves have reached their station. As we must judge of Her excellence (even if only from afar), by the labor which Christ the Lord applied for Her formation, let us consider what labor He spent upon Her and how much upon the whole Church. To establish and to enrich His Church He deemed it sufficient to spend only three years in preaching, selecting the Apostles, teaching the people, and inculcating the evangelical law by His public life; and this was amply sufficient to accomplish the work enjoined upon Him by the Eternal Father and to justify and sanctify all the true believers. But in order to stamp upon His Most Holy Mother the image of His holiness, He consumed not three years, but ten times three years, engaging in this work with all the power of His Divine Love, without ever ceasing hour after hour to add grace to grace, gifts to gifts, blessings to blessings, and holiness to holiness. And at the end of all this He still left Her in a state, in which He could continue to add excellence after His Ascension to His Eternal Father as I will describe in the third part. Our reason is unbalanced, our words fail at the greatness of This Incomparable Lady; for She is Elect as the sun (Cant. 6, 9); and Her effulgence cannot be borne by terrestrial eyes, nor comprehended by any earthly creatures.

Christ our Redeemer began to manifest His designs in regard to His Heavenly Mother after they had come back from Egypt to Nazareth, as I have already mentioned; and from that time on He continued to follow up His purpose in His quality as Teacher and as the Divine Enlightener in all the mysteries of the Incarnation and Redemption. After They returned from Jerusalem in his twelfth year, the Great Queen had a vision of the Divinity, not an intuitive vision, but one consisting of intellectual images; one very exalted and full of the new influences of the Divinity and of the secrets of the Most High. She was especially enlightened in regard to the decrees of the Divine Will concerning the law of grace, which was now to be established by the Incarnate Word, and concerning the power, which was given to Him in the consistory of the Most Blessed Trinity. At the same time She saw how for this purpose the Eternal Father consigned to His Son the seven-sealed book, of which Saint John speaks (Apoc. 5, 1), and how none could be found either in heaven or on earth, who could unseal and open it, until the Lamb broke its seals by his Passion and Death and by His Doctrines and Merits. For in this figure God wished to intimate, that the secret of this book was nothing else than the new law of the Gospel and the Church founded upon it in this world.

Then the Heavenly Queen saw in spirit, that, by the decree of the Most Blessed Trinity, She was to be the first one to read and understand this book; that Her Only begotten was to open it for Her and manifest it all to Her, while She was to put it perfectly into practice; that She was the first one, who was to accompany The Word, and who was to occupy the first place next to Him on the Way To Heaven, which He had opened up for mortals and traced out in this book. In Her, as His True Mother, was to be deposited this New Testament. She saw how the Son of the Eternal Father and of Herself accepted this decree with great pleasure; and how His Sacred Humanity obeyed it with ineffable joy on Her account.

She issued from this ecstatic vision and betook Herself to Her Most Holy Son, prostrating Herself at His feet and saying: "My Lord, My Light and My Teacher, behold Thy Unworthy Mother prepared for the fulfillment of Thy wishes admit me anew as Thy disciple and servant and make use of Me as the instrument of Thy Wisdom and Power. Execute in Me Thy pleasure and that of Thy Eternal Father." Her Most Holy Son received Her with the majesty and authority of a Divine Teacher and instructed Her in most exalted mysteries. In most persuasive and powerful words He explained to Her the profoundest meanings of the works enjoined upon Him by the Eternal Father in regard to the Redemption of man, the founding of the Church and the establishment of the New Evangelical Law. He declared and reaffirmed, that in the execution of these high and hidden mysteries She was to be His Companion and Coadjutrix, receiving and enjoying the first-fruits of grace; and that therefore She, the Most Pure Lady, was to follow Him in His labors until His death on the Cross with a magnanimous and well prepared heart in invincible and unhesitating constancy. He added heavenly instruction such as enabled Her to prepare for the reception of the whole Evangelical Law, the understanding and practice of all its precepts and counsels in their highest perfection. Other sacramental secrets concerning His works in this world the Child Jesus manifested to His Most Blessed Mother on this occasion. And the Heavenly Lady met all His words and intentions with profound humility, obedience, reverence, thanksgiving and most ardent love.

WORDS OF THE QUEEN.

The Most High who in sheer goodness and bounty has given existence to all creatures and denies His providential care to none, faithfully supplies all souls with light, by which they can enter into the knowledge of Him and of Eternal Life provided they do not of their own free will prevent and obscure this light by sin or give up the quest of the kingdom of heaven. To the souls whom according to His secret judgments, He calls to His Church, He shows himself still more liberal. For with the grace of Baptism He infuses into them not only those virtues, which are called essentially infused and which the creature cannot merit by its own efforts; but also those, which are accidentally infused and which it can merit by its own labors and efforts. These the Lord gives freely before hand, in order that the soul may be more prepared and zealous in the observance of His Holy Law. In other souls, in addition to the common light of Faith, The Lord in His clemency grants supernatural gifts of knowledge and virtue for the better understanding of the evangelical mysteries and for the more zealous practice of good works. In this kind of gifts He has been more liberal with thee than with many generations; obliging thee thereby to distinguish thyself in loving correspondence due to Him and to humble thyself before Him to the very dust.

In order that thou mayest be well instructed and informed, I wish to warn thee as a solicitous and loving Mother of the cunning of satan for the destruction of these works of the Lord. From the very moment in which mortals begin to have the use of their reason, each one of them is followed by many watchful and relentless demons. For as soon as the souls are in a position to raise their thoughts to the knowledge of Their God and commence the practice of the virtues infused by Baptism, these demons, with incredible fury and astuteness, seek to root out the divine seed; and if they cannot succeed in this, they try to hinder its growth, and prevent it from bringing forth fruit by engaging men in vicious, useless, or trifling things. Thus they divert their thoughts from faith and hope and from the pursuit of other virtues, leading them to forget that they are Christians and diverting their attention from the knowledge of God and from the Mysteries of the Redemption and of Life Eternal. Moreover the same enemy instills into the parents a base neglectfulness and carnal love for their offspring; and he incites the teachers to carelessness, so that the children find no support against evil in their education, but become depraved and spoiled by many bad habits, losing sight of virtue and of their good inclinations and going the way of perdition.

But the Most Kind Lord does not forget them in this danger and He renews in them His Holy inspirations and special helps. He supplies them with the Holy Teachings of the Church by his preachers and ministers. He holds out to them the aid of the Sacraments and many other inducements to keep them on the path of life. That those who walk in the way of salvation are the smaller number, is due to the vice and depraved habits imbibed in youth and nourished in childhood. For that saying of Deuteronomy is very true: "As the days of thy youth, so also shall thy old age be" (Deut. 33, 25). Hence the demons gain courage and increase their tyrannical influence over souls in the early years of man's life, hoping that they will be able to induce men to commit so much the greater and the more frequent sins in later years, the more they have succeeded in drawing them into small and insignificant faults in their childhood. By these they draw them on to a state of blind presumption; for with each sin the soul loses more and more the power of resistance, subjects itself to the demon, and falls under the sway of its tyrannical enemies. The miserable yoke of wickedness is more and more and more firmly fastened upon it; the same is trodden underfoot by its own iniquity and urged onward under the sway of the devil from one precipice to another, from abyss to abyss (Ps. 41, 8): a chastisement merited by all those, that allow themselves to be overcome by evil-doing in the beginning. By these means Lucifer has hurled into hell so great a number of souls and continues so to hurl them every day, rising up in his pride against the Almighty. In this manner has he been able to introduce into the world his tyrannical power, spreading among men forgetfulness of death, judgement, heaven, and hell, and casting so many nations from abyss to abyss of darkness and bestial errors, such as are contained in the heresies and false sects of the infidels. Do thou therefore beware of this terrible danger, My Daughter, and let not the memory of the Law of Thy God, His precepts and Commands, and The Truths of the Catholic Church and the Doctrines of the Gospels ever fail in Thy mind. Let not a day pass in which thou dost not spend much time in meditating upon all these; and exhort Thy religious and all those who listen to Thee to do the same. For thy enemy and adversary is laboring with ceaseless vigilance to obscure Thy understanding in forgetfulness of the Divine

Law, seeking to withdraw Thy Will, which is a blind faculty, from the practice of justification. This, thou knowest, consists in acts of living faith, trustful hope, and ardent love, all coming from a contrite and humble heart (Ps. 50, 19).

THE FIVE SORROWFUL MYSTERIES

THE AGONY IN THE GARDEN

THE PRAYER IN GETHSEMANI AND HOW MARY JOINED THEREIN.

Christ had partaken of the prescribed supper with His Disciples reclining on the floor around a table, which was elevated from it a little more than the distance of six or seven fingers; for such was the custom of the Jews. But after the washing of the feet He ordered another, higher table to be prepared, such as we now use for our meals. By this arrangement He wished to put an end to the legal suppers and to the lower and figurative law and establish the New Supper of the Law of Grace. The table was covered with a very rich cloth and upon it was placed a plate or salver and a large cup in the shape of a chalice, capacious enough to hold the wine. All this was done in pursuance of the will of Christ Our Savior, who by His Divine Power and Wisdom directed all these particulars. The master of the house was inspired to offer these rich vessels, which were made of what seemed a precious stone like emerald. The Apostles often used it afterwards in consecrating, whenever the occasion permitted it. The Lord seated himself at this table with the Apostles and some of the other Disciples, and then ordered some unleavened bread to be placed on the table and some wine to be brought, of which He took sufficient to prepare the chalice.

Then the Master of Life spoke words of most endearing love to His Apostles, and, though His sayings were wont to penetrate to the inmost heart at all times, yet on this occasion they were like the flames of a great fire of charity, which consumed the souls of His hearers. He manifested to them anew the most Exalted Mysteries of His Divnity, humanity and of the works of the Redemption. He enjoined upon them peace and charity, of which He was now to leave a pledge in the Mysteries about to be celebrated. He reminded them, that in loving one another, they would be loved by the Eternal Father with the same love in which He was beloved. He gave them an understanding of the fulfillment of this promise in having chosen them to found the New Church and the Law of Grace. He renewed in them the light concerning the supreme dignity, excellence and prerogatives of His Most Pure Virgin Mother. The great Lady, from Her retreat, beheld in Divine Contemplation all these doings of Her Son in the Cenacle; and in Her profound intelligence She entered more deeply into their meaning than the Apostles and Angels, who also were present in bodily forms, adoring Their True Lord, Creator and King. By the hands of these Angels Enoch and Elias were brought to the Cenacle from their place of abode; for the Lord wished that these Fathers of the natural and of the written laws should be present at the establishment of the Law of the Gospel, and that they should participate in its Mysteries.

Thereupon Christ Our Lord took into His Venerable Hands the bread, which lay upon the plate, and interiorly asked the permission and co-operation of the Eternal Father, that now and ever afterwards in virtue of the words about to be uttered by Him, and later to be repeated in His Holy Church, He should really and truly become present in the Host, Himself to yield obedience to these Sacred Words. While making this petition He raised His Eyes toward Heaven with an expression of such sublime majesty, that He inspired the Apostles, the Angels and His Virgin Mother with new and deepest reverence. Then He pronounced the words of Consecration over the bread, changing its substance into the substance of His True Body and immediately thereupon He uttered the words of Consecration also over the wine, changing it into His True Blood. As an answer to these words of Consecration was heard the voice of the Eternal Father, saying: "This is my beloved Son in whom I delight, and shall take my delight to the end of the World; and He shall be with men during all the time of their banishment."

All the Apostles and Disciples, who, with the exception of the traitor, believed in This Holy Sacrament, adored it with great humility and reverence according to each ones disposition. The Great High Priest Christ raised up His Own Consecrated Body and Blood in order that all who were present at this first Mass might adore it in a special manner, as they also did.

Still greater was my admiration when Jesus Our God, having raised the Most Holy Sacrament, as I said before, for their adoration, divided it by His Own Sacred Hands, first partook of it Himself as being the First and Chief of all the priests. Recognizing Himself, as man, inferior to the Divinity, which He was now to receive in this His Own Consecrated Body and Blood. He humiliated and, as it were, with a trembling of the inferior part of his being, shrank within Himself before that Divinity, thereby not only teaching us the reverence with which holy Communion is to be received; but also showing us what was His sorrow at the temerity and presumption of many men during the reception and handling of this exalted and sublime Sacrament.

While receiving His Own Body and Blood Christ Our Lord composed a canticle of praise to the Eternal Father and offered Himself in the blessed Sacrament as a sacrifice for the salvation of man. He took another particle of the Consecrated Bread and handed it to the Archangel Gabriel who brought and communicated it to the Most Holy Mary. By having such a privilege conferred on one of their number, the Holy Angels considered themselves sufficiently recompensed for being excluded from the Sacerdotal Dignity and for yielding it to man. The privilege of merely having one of their number hold the Sacramental Body of Their Lord and True God filled them with new and immense joy. In abundant tears of consolation the Great Queen awaited Holy Communion. When Saint Gabriel with innumerable other Angels approached, She received it, the first after Her Son, imitating His Self-abasement, Reverence, and Holy Fear. The Most Blessed Sacrament was deposited in the breast and above the heart of the Most Holy Virgin Mother, as in the most legitimate shrine and tabernacle of the Most High.

After having thus favored the Heavenly Princess, Our Savior distributed The Sacramental Bread to the Apostles (Luke 22, 17), commanding them to divide it among themselves and partake of it. By this commandment He conferred upon them the Sacerdotal Dignity and they began to exercise it by giving Communion each to Himself. This they did with the greatest reverence, shedding copious tears and adoring the Body and Blood of Our Lord, whom They were receiving. They were established in the power of the Priesthood, as being founders of the Holy Church and enjoying the distinction of priority over all others (Ephes. 2, 20). Then Saint Peter, at the command of Christ The Lord, administered two of the particles of Holy Communion to the two Patriarchs. Enoch and Elias. This holy Communion so rejoiced these two holy men, that they were encouraged anew in their hope of the beatific vision, which for them was to be deferred for so many ages, and they were strengthened to live on in this hope until the end of the World. Having given most fervent and humble thanks to the Almighty for this blessing, they were brought back to their abiding-place by the hands of the Holy Angels.

Another very wonderful miracle happened at the Communion of the Apostles. The perfiduous and treacherous Judas, hearing the command of His Master to partake of Holy Communion, resolved in his unbelief not to comply, but if he could do so without being observed, determined to secrete the Sacred Body and bring it to the priests and pharisees in order to afford them a chance of incriminating Jesus by showing them what He had called His Own Body; or if he should not succeed therein, to consummate some other vile act of malice with the Divine Sacrament. The Mistress and Queen of Heaven, who by a clear vision was observing all that passed and knew the interior and exterior effects and affections in the Apostles at Holy Communion, saw also the accursed intentions of the obstinate Judas. All the zeal for the glory of Her Lord, existing in Her as His Mother, Spouse and Daughter, was aroused in Her Purest Heart. Knowing that it was The Divine Will, that She should make use of Her power as Mother and Queen, She commanded the Holy Angels to extract from the mouth of Judas the Consecrated Particles as well of the Bread as of the Wine and replace them from whence They had been taken. It well befitted Her on this occasion to defend the Honor of Her Divine Son and prevent Judas from heaping such an ignominious injury upon Christ the Lord. The Holy Angels obeyed Their Queen, and when it was the turn of Judas to communicate, they withdrew The Consecrated Species One after the Other, and, purifying them from their contact with Judas, the most wicked of living men, they restored Them to their place, altogether unobserved by the Apostles. Thus the Lord shielded the honor of His malicious and obstinate Apostle to the end. This was attended to by the Angels in the shortest

88

space of time and the others then received Holy Communion, for Judas was neither the first nor the last to communicate. Then our Savior offered thanks to the Eternal Father and therewith ended both the legal and the Sacramental Supper in order to begin the Mysteries of His Passion.

By the Wonderful Mysteries, which Our Savior Jesus had celebrated in the Cenacle, the reign which, according to His Inscrutable decree, His Eternal Father had consigned to Him, was well established; and the Thursday Night of His Last Supper having already advanced some hours. He chose to go forth to that dreadful battle of His Suffering and Death by which the Redemption was to be accomplished. The Lord then rose to depart from the hall of the Miraculous Feast and also Most Holy Mary left Her retreat in order to meet Him on the way. At this face to face meeting of the Prince of Eternity and of the Queen, a Sword of Sorrow pierced the heart of Son and Mother, inflicting a pang of grief beyond all human and angelic thought. The Sorrowful Mother threw Herself at the feet of Jesus, adoring Him as Her True God and Redeemer. The Lord, looking upon Her with a Majesty Divine and at the same time with the overflowing love of a Son, spoke to Her only these words: "My Mother, I shall be with Thee in tribulation; let Us accomplish the Will of the Eternal Father and the salvation of men." The Great Queen offered Herself as a sacrifice with Her whole heart and asked His blessing. Having received this She returned to Her retirement, where, by a special favor of the Lord, She was enabled to see all that passed in connection with Her Divine Son. Thus She was enabled to accompany Him and co-operate with Him in His activity as far as devolved upon Her. The owner of the house, who was present at this meeting, moved by a Divine Impulse, offered his house and all that it contained to the Mistress of Heaven, asking Her to make use of all that was his during Her stay in Jerusalem; and the Queen accepted his offer with humble thanks. The Thousand Angels of Her guard, in forms visible to Her, together with some of the pious women of Her company, remained with the Lady.

Our Redeemer and Master left the house of the Cenacle with all the men, who had been present at the celebration of the Mysterious Supper; and soon many of them dispersed in the different streets in order to attend to their own affairs. Followed by His Twelve Apostles, the Lord directed His steps toward Mount Olivet outside and close to the eastern walls of Jerusalem. Judas, alert in his treacherous solicitude for the betrayal of His Divine Master, conjectured that Jesus intended to pass the night in prayer as was His custom. This appeared to him a most opportune occasion for delivering his Master into the hands of his conferderates, the scribes and the pharisees. Having taken this dire resolve, he lagged behind and permitted the Master and His Apostles to proceed. Unnoticed by the latter he lost them from view and departed in all haste to his own ruin and destruction. Within him was the turmoil of sudden fear and anxiety, interior witnesses of the wicked deed he was about to commit. Driven on in the stormy hurricane of thoughts raised by his bad conscience, he arrived breathless at the house of the high priests. On the way it happened, that Lucifer, perceiving the haste of Judas in procuring the death of Jesus Christ, and (as I have related in chapter the tenth), fearing that after all Jesus might be the True Messias, came toward him in the shape of a very wicked man, a friend of Judas acquainted with the intended betrayal. In this shape Lucifer could speak to Judas without being recognized. He tried to persuade him that this project of selling his Master did at first seem advisable on account of the wicked deeds attributed to Jesus; but that, having more naturally considered the matter, he did not now deem it advisable to deliver Him over to the priests and pharisees; for Jesus was not so bad as Judas might imagine; nor did He deserve death; and besides He might free Himself by some miracles and involve his betrayer into great difficulties.

In the meanwhile Our Divine Lord with the Eleven Apostles was engaged in the work of Our Salvation and the Salvation of those who were scheming His death. Unheard of and wonderful contest between the deepest malice of man and the unmeasurable goodness and charity of God! If this stupendous struggle between good and evil began with the first man, it certainly reached its highest point in the death of the Repairer; for then good and evil stood face to face and exerted their highest powers: human malice in taking away the Life and Honor of The Creator and Redeemer, and His immense charity freely sacrificing both for men. According to our way of reasoning, it was as it were necessary that the Most Holy Soul of Christ, yea that even His Divinity, should revert to His Blessed Mother, in order that He might find some object in creation, in which His love should be recompensed and some excuse for disregarding the dictates of His justice. For in This Creature alone could He expect to see His Passion and Death bring forth full fruit; in Her immeasurable Holiness did His justice find some compensation for human malice; and in the humility and constant charity of This Great Lady could be deposited the Treasures of His merits, so that afterwards, as the new Phœnix from the rekindled ashes, His Church might arise from His Sacrifice. The consolation which the humanity of Christ drew from the certainty of His Blessed Mother's Holiness gave Him strength and, as it were, new courage to conquer the malice of mortals; and He counted Himself well recompensed for suffering such atrocious pains by the fact that to mankind belonged also His Most Beloved Mother.

Our Savior pursued His Way across the torrent of Cedron (John 18, 1) to Mount Olivet and entered the Garden of Gethsemani. Then He said to all the Apostles: "Wait for Me, and seat yourselves here while I go a short distance from here to pray (Matth. 26, 36); do you also pray, in order that you may not enter into temptation" (Luke 22, 40). The Divine Master gave them this advice, in order that they might be firm in the temptations, of which He had spoken to them at the Supper: that all of them should be scandalized on account of what they should see Him suffer that night, that Satan would assail them to sift and stir them up by his false suggestions; for the Pastor (as prophesied) was to be ill treated and wounded and the sheep were to be dispersed (Zach. 13, 7). Then the Master of Life, leaving the Band of Eight Apostles at that place and taking with Him Saint Peter, Saint John, and Saint James, retired to another place, where They could neither be seen nor heard by the rest (Mark 14, 33). Being with the three Apostles He raised His eyes up to the Eternal Father confessing and praising Him as was His custom; while interiorly He prayed in fulfillment of the prophecy of Zacharias, permitting death to approach the Most Innocent of Men and commanding the Sword of Divine Justice to be unsheathed over the Shepherd and descend upon the Godman with all its deathly force. In this prayer Christ Our Lord offered Himself anew to the Eternal Father in satisfaction of His Justice for the rescue of the human race; and He gave consent, that all the torments of His Passion and Death be let loose over that part of His Human Being, which was capable of suffering. From that moment He suspended and restrained whatever consolation or relief would otherwise overflow from the impassable to the passable part of His Being, so that in this dereliction His Passion and Sufferings might reach the highest degree possible. The Eternal Father granted these petitions and approved this total Sacrifice of the Sacred Humanity.

This prayer was as it were the floodgate through which the rivers of His Suffering were to find entrance like the resistless onslaught of the ocean, as was foretold by David (Ps. 68, 2). And immediately He began to be sorrowful and feel the anguish of His Soul and therefore said to the Apostles: "My Soul is Sorrowful unto Death" (Mark 14, 34).

He threw Himself with His Divine Face upon the ground and prayed to the Eternal Father: "Father, if it is possible, let this Chalice pass from Me" (Matth. 24, 38). This prayer Christ Our Lord uttered, though He had come down from Heaven with the express purpose of really suffering and dying for men; though He had counted as naught the shame of His Passion, had willingly embraced it and rejected all human consolation; though He was hastening with most ardent love into the jaws of death, to affronts, sorrows and afflictions; though He had set such a high price upon men, that He determined to redeem them at the shedding of His Life-blood. Since by virtue of His Divine and human wisdom and His inextinguishable love He had shown Himself so superior to the natural fear of death, that it seems this petition did not arise from any motive solely coming from Himself. That this was so in fact, was made known to me in the light which was vouchsafed me concerning the mysteries contained in this prayer of the Savior.

This agony of Christ Our Savior grew in proportion to the greatness of His charity and the certainty of His knowledge, that men would persist in neglecting to profit by His Passion and Death (Luke 22, 44). His Agony increased to such an extent, that great drops of bloody sweat were pressed from Him, which flowed to the very earth. Although this prayer was uttered subject to a condition and failed in regard to the reprobate who fell under this condition; yet He gained thereby a greater abundance and secured a greater frequency of favors for mortals. Through it the blessings were multiplied for those who placed no obstacles, the fruits of the Redemption were applied to the Saints and to the Just more abundantly, and many Gifts and Graces, of which the reprobates made themselves unworthy, were diverted to the Elect. The human will of Christ, conforming itself to that of the Divinity, then accepted suffering for each respectively: for the reprobate, as sufficient to procure them the necessary help, if they would make use of its merits, and for the predestined, as an efficacious means, of which they would avail themselves to secure their salvation by co-operating with grace. Thus was set in order, and as it were realized, the salvation of the Mystical Body of His Holy Church, of which Christ the Lord was the Creator and Head.

As a ratification of this Divine Decree, while yet Our Master was in His agony, the Eternal Father for the third time sent the Archangel Michael to the earth in order to comfort Him by a sensible message and confirmation of what He already knew by the infused science of His Most Holy Soul; for the Angel could not tell Our Lord anything He did not know, nor could he produce any additional effect on His Interior Consciousness for this purpose.

Let us now return to the Cenacle, where the Queen of Heaven had retired with the holy women of Her company. From Her retreat, by Divine enlightenment, She saw most clearly all the Mysteries and doings of Her Most Holy Son in the garden. At the moment when the Savior separated Himself with the Three Apostles Peter, John and James, the Heavenly Queen separated Herself from the other women and went into another room. Upon leaving them She exhorted them to pray and watch lest they enter into temptation, but She took with Her the Three Marys, treating Mary Magdalen as the superior of the rest. Secluding Herself with these three as Her more intimate companions, She begged the Eternal Father to suspend in Her all human alleviation and comfort, both in the sensitive and in the spiritual part of Her being, so that nothing might hinder Her from suffering to the highest degree in union with Her Divine Son. She prayed that She might be permitted to feel and participate in Her virginal body all the pains of the wounds and tortures about to be undergone by Jesus. This petition was granted by the Blessed Trinity and the Mother in consequence suffered all the torments of Her Most Holy Son in exact duplication, as I shall relate later. Although they were such, that, if the Right Hand of the Almighty had not preserved Her, they would have caused Her death many times over; yet, on the other hand, these sufferings, inflicted by God Himself, were like a pledge and a new lease of life. For in Her most ardent love She would have considered it incomparably more painful to see Her Divine Son suffer and die without being allowed to share in His torments.

The Three Marys were instructed by The Queen to accompany and assist Her in Her affliction, and for this purpose they were endowed with greater Light and Grace than the other women. In retiring with them the Most Pure Mother began to feel unwonted sorrow and anguish and She said to them: "My soul is sorrowful, because My Beloved Son is about to suffer and die, and it is not permitted me to suffer and die of His torments. Pray, My friends, in order that you may not be overcome by temptation." Having said this She went apart a short distance from them, and following the Lord in His supplications, She, as far as was possible to Her and as far as She knew it to be conformable to the human will of Her Son, continued Her prayers and petitions, feeling the same Agony as that of the Savior in the garden. She also returned at the same intervals to Her companions to exhort them, because She knew of the wrath of the demon against them. She wept at the perdition of the foreknown; for She was highly enlightened in the Mysteries of Eternal Predestination and Reprobation. In order to imitate and co-operate in all things with The Redeemer of the World, the Great Lady also suffered a bloody sweat, similar to that of Jesus in the garden, and by Divine intervention She was visited by the Archangel Saint Gabriel, as Christ Her Son was visited by the Archangel Michael. The Holy Prince expounded to Her the Will of the Most High in the same manner as Saint Michael had expounded it to Christ The Lord. In both of Them the prayer offered and the cause of sorrow was the same; and therefore They were also proportionally alike to One Another in Their actions and in Their knowledge.

While Our Savior occupied Himself in praying to His Father for the spiritual salvation of the human race, the perfidious disciple Judas sought to hasten the delivery of Christ into the hands of the priests and pharisees. At the same time Lucifer and his demons, not being able to divert the perverse will of Judas and of the other enemies of Christ from their designs on the life of Christ their Creator and Master, changed the tactics of their satanic malice and began to incite the Jews to greater cruelty and effrontery in their dealings with The Savior. As I have already said several times, the devil was filled with great suspicions lest this most extraordinary Man be the Messias and The True God.

Similar motives urged on the priests and pharisees. At the instigation of Judas they hastily gathered together a large band of people, composed of pagan soldiers, a tribune, and many Jews. Having consigned to them Judas as a hostage, they sent this band on its way to apprehend the Most Innocent Lamb, who was awaiting them and who was aware of all the thoughts and schemes of the sacrilegious priests, as foretold expressly by Jeremias (Jer. 11, 19). All these servants of malice, bearing arms and provided with ropes and chains, in the glaring torch and lantern light issued forth from the city in the direction of Mount Olivet.

While They were approaching, the Lord returned the third time to His Apostles and finding them asleep spoke to them: "Sleep ye now, and take your rest. It is enough: the hour is come; behold the Son of Man shall be betrayed into the hands of sinners. Rise up, let us go. Behold he that will betray Me is at hand" (Mark 14, 41). Such were the words of the Master of Holiness to the three most privileged Apostles; He was unwilling to reprehend them more severely than in this most meek and loving manner. Being oppressed, they did not know what to answer Their Lord, as Scripture says (Mark 14, 40). They arose and Jesus went with them to join the other eight Apostles. He found them likewise overcome and oppressed by their great sorrow and fallen asleep. The Master then gave orders, that all of them together, mystically forming one body with Him their Head, should advance toward the enemies, thereby teaching them the power of mutual and perfect unity for overcoming the demons and their followers and for avoiding defeat by them. For a triple cord is hard to tear, as says Ecclesiastes (4, 12), and he that is mighty against one, may be overcome by two, that being the effect of union. The Lord again exhorted all the Apostles and forewarned them of what was to happen. Already the confused noise of the advancing band of soldiers and their helpmates began to be heard. Our Savior then proceeded to meet them on the way, and, with incomparable love, magnanimous courage and tender piety prayed interiorly: "O sufferings longingly desired from My Inmost Soul, ye pains, wounds, affronts, labors, afflictions and ignominious death, come, come, come quickly, for the fire of love, which burns for the Salvation of men, is anxious to see you meet the Innocent One of all creatures. Well do I know your value, I have sought, desired, and solicited you and I meet you joyously of My Own Free Will; I have purchased you by My anxiety in searching for you and I esteem you for your merits. I desire to remedy and enhance your value and raise you to highest dignity. Let death come, in order that by My accepting it without having deserved it I may triumph over it and gain Life for those who have been punished by death for their sins (Osee 13, 14). I give permission to My friends to forsake Me; for I alone desire and am able to enter into this battle and gain for them triumph and victory" (Is. 53, 3).

During these words and prayers of the Author of Life Judas advanced in order to give the signal upon which he had agreed with his companions (Matth. 26, 48), namely the customary, but now feigned kiss of peace, by which they were to distinguish Jesus as the One whom they should single out from the rest and immediately seize. These precautions the unhappy Apostle had taken, not only out of avarice for the money and hatred against his Master, but also, on account of the fear with which he was filled. For he dreaded the inevitable necessity of meeting Him and encountering Him in the future, if Christ was not put to death on this occasion. Such a confusion he feared more than the death of his soul, or the death of his Divine Master, and, in order to forestall it, he hastened to complete his treachery and desired to see the Author of Life die at the hands of His enemies. The traitor then ran up to the Meekest Lord, and, as a consummate hypocrite, hiding his hatred, he imprinted on His countenance the kiss of peace, saying: "God save Thee, Master." By this so treacherous act the perdition of Judas was matured and God was justified in withholding His grace and help. On the part of the unfaithful Apostle, malice and temerity reached their highest degree; for, interiorly denying or disbelieving the uncreated and created wisdom by which Christ must know of his treason, and ignoring His power to destroy him, he sought to hide his malice under the cloak of the friendship of a true Apostle; and all this for the purpose of delivering over to such a frightful and cruel death his Creator and Master, to whom he was bound by so many obligations. In this one act of treason he committed so many and such formidable sins, that it is impossible to fathom their immensity; for he was treacherous, murderous, sacrilegious, ungrateful, inhuman, disobedient, false, lying, impious and unequalled in hypocrisy; and all this was included in one and the same crime perpetrated against the Person of God made Man.

The Most Pure Mother of Christ Our Lord was most attentive to all that passed in His capture, and by means of Her clear visions saw it more clearly than if She had been present in person; for by means of Her supernatural visions She penetrated into all the mysteries of His words and actions. When She beheld the band of soldiers and servants issuing from the house of the high priest, the prudent Lady foresaw the irreverence and insults with which they would treat Their Creator and Redeemer; and in order to do what was within Her power, She invited the Holy Angels and many others in union with Her to render adoration and praise to the Lord of Creation as an offset to the injuries and affronts He would sustain at the hands of those ministers of darkness. The same request She made to the holy women who were praying with Her. She told them, that Her Most Holy Son had now given permission to His enemies to take Him prisoner and illtreat Him, and that they were about to make use of this permission in a most impious and cruel manner. Assisted by the Holy Angels and the pious women the Faithful Queen engaged in interior and exterior acts of devoted faith and love, confessing, adoring, praising and magnifying the Infinite Deity and the Most Holy Humanity of Her Creator and Lord. The holy women imitated Her in the genuflections and prostrations, and the Angelic Princes responded to the canticles with which She magnified, celebrated and glorified the Divinity and Humanity of Christ. In the measure in which the children of malice increased their irreverence and injuries, She sought to compensate them by Her praise and veneration. Thus She continued to placate the Divine Justice, lest it should be roused against His persecutors and destroy them; for only Most Holy Mary was capable of staying the punishment of such great offenses.

And the Great Lady not only placated the Just Judge, but even obtained favors and blessings from the Divine Clemency for the very persons who irritated Him and thus secured a return of good for those who were heaping wrongs upon Christ the Lord for His Doctrine and benefits. This mercy attained its highest point in the disloyal and obstinate Judas; for the Tender Mother, seeing him deliver Jesus by the kiss of feigned friendship, and considering how shortly before his mouth had contained the Sacramental Body of the Lord, with whose Sacred Countenance so soon after those same foul lips were permitted to come in contact, was transfixed with sorrow and entranced by charity. She asked the Lord to grant new Graces, whereby this man, who had enjoyed the privilege of touching the Face whereon Angels desire to look, might, if he chose to use them, save himself from perdition. In response to this prayer of Most Holy Mary, Her Son and Lord granted Judas Powerful Graces in the very consummation of his treacherous delivery. If the unfortunate man had given heed and had commenced to respond to them, the Mother of Mercy would have obtained for him many others and at last also pardon for his sin. She has done so with many other great sinners, who were willing to give that glory to Her, and thus obtain Eternal Glory for themselves. But Judas failed to realize this and thus lost all chance of salvation, as I shall relate in the next chapter.

When the servants of the high priest laid hands on and bound The Savior, The Most Blessed Mother felt on Her own hands the pains caused by the ropes and chains, as if She Herself was being bound and fettered; in the same manner She felt in Her Body the blows and torments further inflicted upon the Lord, for, I have already said, this favor was granted to His Mother, as we shall see in the course of the Passion. This Her sensible participation in His sufferings was some kind of relief of the pain, which She would have suffered in Her Loving Soul at the thought of not being with Him in His torments.

WORDS OF THE QUEEN.

My Daughter, in all that thou art made to understand and write concerning these mysteries, thou drawest upon Thyself (and upon mortals) a severe judgment, if thou dost not overcome Thy pusillanimity, ingratitude and baseness by meditating day and night on the Passion and Death of Jesus crucified. This is the great science of the Saints, so little heeded by the worldly; it is the Bread of Life and the Spiritual Food of the little ones, which gives Wisdom to them and the want of which starves the lovers of this proud World (Wis. 15, 3). In this science I wish thee to be studious and wise, for with it thou canst buy thyself all good things (Wis.

7, 11). My Son and Lord taught us this Science when He said: "I am the Way, the Truth and the Life: no one cometh to My Father except through Me" (John 14, 6). Tell Me then, My Daughter: if My Lord and Master has made Himself the Life and the Way for men through His Passion and Death, is it not evident that in order to go that way and live up to this Truth, they must follow Christ crucified, afflicted, scourged and affronted? Consider the ignorance of men who wish to come to The Father without following Christ, since they expect to reign with God without suffering or imitating His Passion, yea without even a thought of accepting any part of His Suffering and Death, or of thanking Him for it. They want it to procure for them the pleasures of this life as well as of Eternal Life, while Christ their Creator has suffered the most bitter pains and torments in order to enter Heaven and to show them by His example how they are to find the Way of Light.

JESUS BROUGHT BEFORE ANNAS AND CAIPHAS.

Having been taken prisoner and firmly bound, the Most Meek Lamb Jesus was dragged from the garden to the house of the highpriests, first to the house of Annas (John 18, 13). The trubulent band of soldiers and servants, having been advised by the traitorous disciple that his Master was a sorcerer and could easily escape their hands, if they did not carefully bind and chain Him securely before starting on their way, took all precautions inspired by such a mistrust (Mark 14, 44). Lucifer and his compeers of darkness secretly irritated and provoked them to increase their impious and sacrilegious illtreatment of the Lord beyond all bounds of humanity and decency. As they were willing accomplices of Lucifer's malice, they omitted no outrage against the Person of their Creator within the limits set them by the Almighty. They bound Him with a heavy iron chain with such ingenuity, that it encircled as well the waist as the neck. The two ends of the chain, which remained free, were attached to large rings or handcuffs, with which they manacled the hands of the Lord, who created the Heavens, the Angels and the whole universe. The hands thus secured and bound, they fastened not in front, but behind. This chain they had brought from the house of Annas the highpriest, where it had served to raise the portcullis of a dungeon. They had wrenched it from its place and provided it with padlock handcuffs. But they were not satisfied with this unheard-of way of securing a prisoner; for in their distrust they added two pieces of strong rope: the one they wound around the throat of Jesus and, crossing it at the breast, bound it in heavy knots all about the body, leaving two long ends free in front, in order that the servants and soldiers might jerk Him in different directions along the way. The second rope served to tie His arms, being bound likewise around His waist. The two ends of this rope were left hanging free to be used by two other executioners for jerking Him from behind.

The Author of our Salvation, hiding His Power of annihilating His enemies in order that our Redemption might be the more abundant, submitted to all the consequences of the impious fury which Lucifer and his hellish squadron formented in the Jews. They dragged Him bound and chained under continued ill-treatment to the house of Annas, before whom they presented Him as a malefactor worthy of death. It was the custom of the Jews to present thus bound those criminals who merited capital punishment; and they now made use of this custom in regard to Jesus, in order to intimate His sentence even before the trial. The sacriligious priest Annas seated himself in proud and arrogant state on the platform or tribunal of a great hall. Immediately Lucifer placed himself at his side with a multitude of evil spirits.

Imperiously and haughtily the highpriest asked Him about His disciples (John 18, 191), and what doctrine He was preaching and teaching. This question was put merely for the purpose of misinterpreting His answer, if Jesus should utter any word that afforded such a chance. But the Master of Holiness, Who is the Guide and the Corrector of the most wise (Wis. 7, 15), offered to the Eternal Father the humiliation of being presented as a criminal before the highpriest and of being questioned by him as a prevaricator and author of a false doctrine. Our Redeemer with an humble and cheerful countenance answered the question as to His doctrines: "I have spoken openly to the world: I have always taught in the synagogue and in the temple, whither all the Jews resort: and in secret I have spoken nothing. Why askest thou Me, ask these, who have heard what I have spoken unto them, behold they know what I have said?" As the doctrine of Christ our Lord came from his Eternal Father,

He spoke for it and defended its honor. He referred them to his hearers, both because those by whom He was now surrounded, would not believe Him and wished to distort all He should say, and because the truth and force of His teachings recommended and forced themselves upon the minds of His greatest enemies by their own excellence.

Concerning the Apostles He said nothing, because it was not necessary on this occasion and because they were not reflecting much credit upon their Master by their present conduct. Though His answer was so full of wisdom and so well suited to the question, yet one of the servants of the highpriest rushed up with raised hand and audaciously struck the Venerable and Sacred Face of Jesus, saying: "Answerest Thou the high priest so?" The Lord accepted this boundless injury, praying for the one who had inflicted it; and holding Himself ready, if necessary, to turn and offer the other cheek for a second stroke, according to the doctrine He had Himself inculcated (Matth. 5, 39). But in order that the atrocious and daring offender might not shamelessly boast of His wickedness, the Lord replied with great tranquillity and meekness: "If I have spoken evil, give testimony of the evil; if well, why strikest thou Me?" O sight most astounding to the supernal spirits! Since this is He, at the mere sound of Whose voice the foundations of the heavens tremble and ought to tremble and the whole firmament is shaken! While this ill treatment of the Lord was going on, Saint Peter and the other disciple, who was none other than Saint John, arrived at the house of Annas. Saint John, as being well known there, readily obtained entrance, while Saint Peter remained outside. Afterwards the servant maid, who was an acquaintance of Saint John, allowed also Him to enter and see what would happen to the Lord (John 18, 16). The two Disciples remained in the portico adjoining the court-hall of the priest, and Saint Peter approached the fire, which the soldiers, on account of the coldness of the night, had built in the enclosure near the portico. The servant maid, on closer inspection, noticed the depressed bearing of Saint Peter. Coming up to Him she recognized Him as a Apostle of Jesus, and said: "Art Thou not perhaps one of the Apostles of this Man?" This question was asked by the maid with an air of contempt and reproach. Peter in His great weakness and hesitancy yielded to a sense of shame. Overcome also by His fear he answered: "I am not His Apostle." Having given this an-

101

swer, He slipped away to avoid further conversation, and left the premises. But he soon afterwards followed His Master to the house of Caiphas, where he denied Him again at two different times, as I shall relate farther on.

The denial of Peter caused greater pain to the Lord than the buffet which He had received; for this sin was directly opposed and abhorrent to His immense charity, while pains and sufferings were sweet and welcome to Him, since He could thereby atone for our sins. After this first denial of Peter, Christ prayed for Him to His Eternal Father and ordained that through the intercession of the Blessed Mary he should obtain pardon even after the third denial. The Great Lady witnessed all that passed from her oratory, as I have said. As She contained in Her own breast the propitiatory and sacrifice of Her Son and Lord in Sacramental Form, She directed Her petitions and loving aspirations to Him, eliciting most heroic acts of compassion, thanksgiving, adoration and worship. She bitterly wept over the denial of Saint Peter, and ceased not, until She perceived that the Lord would not refuse Him the necessary helps for effectualy rising from his fall.

After Jesus had thus been insulted and struck in the house of Annas, He was sent, bound and fettered as He was, to the priest Caiphas, the father-in-law of Annas, who in that year officiated as the prince and high priest; with him were gathered the scribes and distinguished men of the Jews in order to urge the condemnation of the Most Innocent Lamb (Matth. 26, 57).

The whole rabble of infernal spirits and merciless foes of Christ left the house of Annas and dragged our Lord Savior through the streets to the house of Caiphas, exercising upon Him all the cruelty of their ignominious fury. The highpriests and his attendants broke out in loud derision and laughter, when they saw Jesus brought amid tumultuous noise into their presence and beheld Him now subject to their power and jurisdiction without hope of escape. O Mystery of the Most Exalted Wisdom of Heaven! O foolishness and ignorance of hell, and blind stupidity of mortals! What a distance immeasurable do I see between the doings of the Most High and yours!

The highpriest Caiphas, filled with a deadly envy and hatred against the Master of Life, was seated in his chair of state or throne. With him were Lucifer and all his demons, who had come from the house of Annas. The scribes and pharisees, like bloodthirsty wolves, surrounded the Gentle Lamb; all of them were full of the exultation of the envious, who see the object of their envy confounded and brought down. By common consent they sought for witnesses, whom they could bribe to bring false testimonies against Jesus Our Savior (Matth. 26, 59). Those that had been procured, advanced to proffer their accusations and testimony; but their accusations neither agreed with each other, nor could any of their slander be made to apply to Him, who of His very Nature was Innocence and Holiness (Mark 25, 56; Heb. 7, 26).

Our Savior Jesus answered not a word to all the calumnies and lies brought forward against His Innocence. Caiphas, provoked by the patient silence of the Lord, rose up in his seat and said to Him: "Why dost Thou not answer to what so many witnesses testify against Thee?" But even to this the Lord made no response. For Caiphas and the rest were not only indisposed to believe Him; but they treacherously wished to make use of His answer in order to calumniate Him and satisfy the people in their proceedings against the Galileean, so that they might not be thought to have condemned Him to death without cause. This Humble Silence, which should have appeased the wicked priest, only infuriated him so much the more because it frustrated his evil purpose. Lucifer, who incited the high priest and all the rest, intently watched the conduct of the Savior. But the intention of the dragon was different from that of the high priest. He merely wanted to irritate the Lord, or to hear some word by which he could ascertain whether He was True God.

With this purpose satan stirred up Caiphas to the highest pitch of rage and to ask in great wrath and haughtiness: "I adjure Thee by the Living God, that Thou tell us, if Thou be the Christ, the Son of God." This question of the highpriest certainly convicted Him at once of the deepest folly and of dreaded blasphemy; for if it was sincere, he had permitted Christ to be brought before his tribunal in doubt whether He was the True God or not, which would make Him guilty of the most formidable and audacious crime. The doubt in such a matter should have been solved in quite another way, conformable to the demands of right reason and justice. Christ Our Savior, hearing Himself conjured by the Living God, inwardly adored and reverenced the Divinity, though appealed to by such sacriligious lips. Out of reverence for the name of God He therefore answered: "Thou hast said: I am He. Nevertheless I say to you, hereafter you shall see the Son of Man (Who I am) sitting on the Right Hand of the Power of God, and coming in the clouds of Heaven" (Matth. 26, 64).

But the highpriest, furious at the answer of the Lord, instead of looking upon it as a solution of his doubt, rose once more in his seat, and rending his garments as an outward manifestation of his zeal for the Honor of God, loudly cried out: "He hath blasphemed; what further need have we of witnesses? Behold, now you have heard the blasphemy, what think you?" (Matth. 26, 65.) The real blasphemy however consisted rather in these words of Caiphas, since he denied the certain fact that Christ was the Son of God by His very Nature, and since he attributed to the Divine Personality sinfulness, which was directly repugnant to His very Nature. Such was the folly of the wicked priest, who by his office should have recognized and proclaimed the Universal Truth. He made of himself an execrable blasphemer in maintaining that He, Who is Holiness itself, had blasphemed. Having previously, with satanical instinct, abused his high office in prophesying that the death of one man is better than the ruin of all the people, he now was hindered by his sins from understanding his own prophecy. As the example and the opinions of princes and prelates powerfully stirs up the flattery and subserviency of inferiors, that whole gathering of wickedness was incensed at the Savior Jesus, all exclaimed in a loud voice, "He is guilty of death (Matth. 26, 66), let Him die, let Him die!" Roused by satanic fury they all fell upon their Most Meek Master and discharged upon Him their wrath. Some of them struck Him in the Face, others kicked Him, others tore out His hair, others spat upon His Venerable Countenance, others slapped or struck Him in the neck, which was a treatment reserved among the Jews only for the most abject and vile of criminals. All these affronts, reproaches and insults were seen and felt by the Most Holy Mary, causing in Her the same pains and wounds in the same parts of Her Body and at the same time as inflicted upon the Lord. The only difference was, that in Our Lord the blows and torments were inflicted by the Jews themselves, while in His Most Pure Mother they were caused by the Almighty in a miraculous manner and upon request of the Lady. According to natural laws, the vehemence of Her interior sorrow and anxiety would have put an end to Her life; but She was strengthened by Divine Power, so as to be able to continue to suffer with Her Beloved Son and Lord.

The interior acts performed by the Savior under these barbarous and unheard of persecutions, cannot be fathomed by human reason or faculties. Mary alone understood them fully, so as to be able to imitate them with the highest perfection. But as the Divine Master now experienced in His own Person, how necessary His sympathy would be for those who were to follow Him and practice His Doctrine, He exerted Himself so much the more in procuring for them grace and blessings on this occasion, in which He was teaching them by His own example the narrow way of perfection. In the midst of these injuries and torments, and those which followed thereafter, the Lord established for His perfect and chosen souls the beatitudes, which He had promised and proposed to them some time before. He looked upon the poor in spirit, who were to imitate Him in this virtue and said: "Blessed are you in being stripped of the earthly goods, for by My Passion and Death I am to entail upon you the heavenly kingdom as a secure and certain possession of voluntary poverty. Blessed are those who meekly suffer and bear adversities and tribulations, for besides the joy of having imitated Me, they shall possess the land of the hearts and the good will of men through the peacefulness of their intercourse and the sweetness of their virtues. Blessed are they that weep while they sow in tears, for in them, they shall receive the bread of understanding and life, and they shall afterwards harvest the fruits of Everlasting Joy and Bliss."

"Blessed are also those who hunger and thirst for justice and truth, for I shall earn for them satiation far beyond all their desires, as well in the reign of grace as in the reign of glory. Blessed are they, who, imitating Me in My offers of pardon and friendship, mercifully pity those that offend and persecute them, for I promise them the fulness of mercy from My Father. Blessed be the pure of heart, who imitate Me in crucifying their flesh in order to preserve the purity of their souls. I promise them the vision of peace and of My Divinity, by becoming like unto Me and by partaking of Me. Blessed are the peaceful, who, yielding their rights, do not resist the evil-minded and deal with them with a sincere and tranquil heart without vengeance; they shall be called My children, because they imitate My Eternal Father and I shall write them in My memory and in My mind as My adopted sons. Those that suffer persecution for justice's sake, shall be the blessed heirs of My Celestial Kingdom, since they suffer with Me; and where I am, there also they shall be in Eternity. Rejoice, ye poor, be consoled all ye that are and shall be afflicted, glory in your lot ye little ones and despised ones of this world, you who suffer in humility and longanimity, suffer with an interior rejoicing, since all of you are following Me in the path of truth. Renounce vanity, despise the pomp and haughtiness of the false and deceitful Babylon, pass ye through the fires and the waters of tribulation until you reach Me, Who am the Light, the Truth and Your Guide to the Eternal Rest and Refreshment."

Saint Peter had followed the Lord Jesus from the house of Annas to that of Caiphas, although he took care to walk at some distance behind the crowd of enemies for fear that the Jews might seize him. He partly repressed this fear on account of the love of His Master and by the natural courage of his heart. Among the great multitude which crowded in and out of the house of Caiphas and in the darkness, it was not difficult for the Apostle to find entrance into the house of Caiphas. In the gates of the courtyard a servant-maid, who was a portress as in the house of Annas, likewise noticed Saint Peter; she immediately went up to the soldiers, who stood at the fire with him and said: "This man is one of those who were wont to accompany Jesus of Nazareth." One of the bystanders said: "Thou art surely a Galileean and one of them." Saint Peter denied it and added an oath, that he was not a Apostle of Jesus, immediately leaving the company at the fire. Yet, in his eagerness to see the end, although he left the courtyard, he did not leave the neighborhood. His natural love and compassion for The Lord still caused him to linger in the place, where he saw Him suffer so much. So the Apostle moved about, sometimes nearer, sometimes farther from the hall of justice for nearly an hour. Then a relative of that Malchus, whose ear he had severed, recognized him and said: "Thou art a Galileean and a Apostle of Jesus; I saw thee with Him in the garden." Then Peter deeming himself discovered, was seized with still greater fear, and he began to assert with oaths and imprecations, that he knew not The

106

Man (Matth. 26, 72). Immediately thereupon the cock crowed the second time, and the prediction of His Divine Master, that he should deny Him thrice before the cock crowed twice, was fulfilled to the letter.

The Holy Evangelists pass over in silence what and where the Savior suffered after the ill-treatment in the house of Caiphas and the denial of Saint Peter. But they all take up again the thread of events, when they speak of the council held by them in the morning in order to deliver Him over to Pilate. I had some doubts as to the propriety of speaking of this intervening time of manifesting that which was made known to me concerning it.

By the ill-treatment, which the Lord received in the presence of Caiphas, the wrath of this highpriest and of all his supporters and ministers was much gratified, though not at all satiated. But as it was already past midnight, the whole council of these wicked men resolved to take good care, that the Savior be securely watched and confined until the morning, lest He should escape while they were asleep. For this purpose they ordered Him to be locked, bound as He was, in one of the subterranean dungeons, a prison cell set apart for the most audacious robbers and criminals of the state. Scarcely any light penetrated into this prison to dispel its darkness. It was filled with such uncleanness and stench, that it would have infected the whole house, if it had not been so remote and so well enclosed; for it had not been cleaned for many years, both because it was so deep down and because of the degradation of the criminals that were confined in it; for none thought it worth while making it more habitable than for mere wild beasts, unworthy of all human kindness.

WORDS OF THE QUEEN.

My daughter, to great deeds art thou called and invited on account of the Divine Enlightenment thou receivest concerning the mysteries of the Sufferings of My Most Holy Son and of Myself for the human race, and on account of the knowledge which thou hast obtained concerning the small return made by heartless and ungrateful men for all Our pains. Thou livest yet in mortal flesh and art thyself subject to this ignorance and weakness; but by the force of truth thou art now roused to great wonder, sorrow and compassion at the want of attention displayed by mortals toward these

107

Great Sacraments and at the losses sustained by them through their lukewarmness and negligence. What then are the thoughts of the Angels and Saints, and what are My thoughts in beholding this world and all the faithful in such a dangerous and dreadful state of carelessness, when they have the Passion and Death of My Divine Son before their eyes, and when they have Me, for their Mother and Intercessor and His Most Pure Life and Mine for an example? I tell thee truly, My dearest, only My Intercession and the Merits of His Son, which I offer to the Eternal Father, can delay the punishment and placate His wrath, can retard the destruction of the world and the severe chastisement of the children of the Church, who know His Will and fail to fulfill it (John 15, 15). But I am much incensed to find so few who condole with Me and try to console My Son in His sorrows, as David says (Ps. 68, 21). This hardness of heart will cause great confusion to them on the day of judgment; since they will then see with irreparable sorrow, not only that they were ungrateful, but inhuman and cruel toward My Divine Son, toward Me and toward themselves.

Consider then thy duty, My dearest, and raise thyself above all earthly things and above thyself; for I am calling thee and choose thee to imitate and follow Me into the solitude, in which I am left by creatures, whom My Son and I have pursued with so many blessings and favors. Weigh in thy heart, how much it cost My Lord to reconcile mankind to the Eternal Father (Colos. 1, 22) and regain for them His friendship. Weep and afflict thyself that so many should live in such forgetfulness and that so many should labor with all their might at destroying and losing what was bought by the Blood of God Itself and all that I from the first moment of My Conception have sought to procure and am procuring for their salvation. Awaken in thy heart the deepest grief, that in His Holy Church there should be many followers of the hypocritical and sacriligious priests who, under cover of a false piety, still condemn Christ; that pride and sumptuousness with other grave vices should be raised to authority and exalted, while humility, truth, justice and all virtues be so oppressed and debased and avarice and vanity should prevail. Few know the Poverty of Christ, and fewer embrace it. Holy Faith is hindered and is not spread among the nations on account of the boundless ambition of the mighty of this earth; in many Catholics it is inactive and dead, and whatever

108

should be living, is near to death and to Eternal Perdition. The Counsels of the Gospel are forgotten, its precepts trodden under foot, charity almost extinct. My Son and True God offers His Cheeks in patience and meekness to be buffeted and wounded (Thren. 3, 30). Who pardons an insult for the sake of imitating Him? Just the contrary is set up as law in this world, not only by the infidels, but by the very children of the Faith and of Light.

In recognizing these sins I desire that thou imitate Me in what I did during the Passion and during My whole life, namely practice the virtues opposed to these vices. As a recompense for their blasphemies, I blessed God; for their oaths, I praised Him; for their unbelief, I excited acts of Faith, and so for all the rest of the sins committed. This is what I desire thee to do while living in this world. Fly also the dangerous intercourse with creatures, taught by the example of Peter, for thou art not stronger than he, the Apostle of Christ; and if thou fall in thy weakness, weep over thy fault and immediately seek My Intercession. Make up for thy ordinary faults and weaknesses by thy patience in adversities, accept them with a joyous mien and without disturbance, no matter what they may be, whether they be sickness or the molestations coming from creatures, or whether they arise from the opposition of the flesh to the spirit, or from the conflicts with visible or invisible enemies. In all these things canst thou suffer and must thou bear up in faith, hope and magnanimous sentiment. I remind thee, that there is no exercise more profitable and useful for the soul than to suffer: for suffering gives Light, undeceives, detaches the heart from visible things and raises it up to the Lord. He will come to meet those in suffering, because He is with the afflicted and sends to them His Protection and Help (Ps. 40, 15).

THE SECOND AND THIRD
SORROWFUL MYSTERIES

JESUS BROUGHT BEFORE PILATE. THE SCOURGING AND
CROWNING WITH THORNS.

At the dawn of Friday morning, say the Evangelists
(Matth. 27, 1; Mark 15, 1; Luke 22, 66; John 11, 47), the
ancients, the chief priests and scribes, who according to the
law were looked upon with greatest respect by the people,
gathered together in order to come to a common decision
concerning the Death of Christ. This they all desired; however they were anxious to preserve the semblance of justice
before the people. This council was held in the house of Caiphas, where the Lord was imprisoned. Once more they
commanded Him to be brought from the dungeon to the hall
of the council in order to be examined. The satellites of
justice rushed below to drag Him forth bound and fettered as
He was.

They again asked Him to tell them, whether He was the
Christ (Luke 22, 1), that is, the Anointed. Just as all their
previous questions, so this was put with the malicious deter-
mination not to listen or to admit the Truth, but to calumniate
and fabricate a charge against Him. But the Lord, being
perfectly willing to die for the Truth, denied it not; at the
same time He did not wish to confess it in such a manner
that they could despise it, or borrow out of it some color for
their calumny; for this was not becoming His Innocence and
Wisdom. Therefore He veiled His answer in such a way, that
if the pharisees chose to yield to even the least kindly feeling,
they would be able to trace up the mystery hidden in His
words; but if they had no such feeling, then should it become
clear through their answer, that the evil which they imputed
to Him was the result of their wicked intentions and lay not
in His answer. He therefore said to them: "If I tell you that

I am He of Whom you ask, you will not believe what I say; and if I shall ask you, you will not answer, nor release Me. But I tell you, that the Son of Man, after this, shall seat Himself at the Right Hand of the Power of God" (Luke 22, 67). The priests answered: "Then thou art the Son of God?" and the Lord replied: "You say that I am." This was as if He had said: You have made a very correct inference, that I am the Son of God; for My works, My doctrines, and your own Scripture, as well as what you are now doing with Me, testify to the fact, that I am the Christ, the One promised in the Law.

But this council of the wicked was not disposed to assent to Divine Truth, although they themselves inferred it very correctly from the antecedents and could easily have believed it. They would neither give assent nor belief, but preferred to call it a blasphemy deserving death. Since the Lord had now reaffirmed what He had said before, they all cried out: "What need have we of further witnesses, since He Himself asserts it by His Own lips?" And they immediately came to the unanimous conclusion that He should, as one worthy of death, be brought before Pontius Pilate, who governed Judea in the name of the Roman emperor and was the temporal Lord of Palestine.

The executioners therefore brought Our Savior Jesus Christ to the house of Pilate, in order to present Him, still bound with the same chains and ropes in which they had taken Him from the garden, before his Tribunal. The city of Jerusalem was full of strangers, who had come from all Palestine to celebrate the great Pasch of the Lamb and of the unleavened bread. As the rumor of this arrest was already spread among the people, and as the Master of Life was known to all of them, a countless multitude gathered in the streets to see Him brought in chains through the streets. They were divided in their opinion concerning the Messiah; some of them shouted out: "Let Him die, let Him die, this wicked imposter, who deceives the whole world." Others answered: "His Doctrines do not appear to be so bad, nor His works; for He has done good to many." Still others, who had believed in Him, were much afflicted and wept; while the whole city was in confusion and uproar concerning the Nazarene.

The sun had already arisen while these things happened and the Most Holy Mother, who saw it all from afar, now resolved to leave Her retreat and follow Her Divine Son to the house of Pilate and to His Death on the Cross. When the Great Queen and Lady was about to set forth from the Cenacle, Saint John arrived, in order to give an account of all that was happening; for the Beloved Disciple at that time did not know of the visions, by which all the doings and sufferings of Her Most Holy Son were manifest to the Blessed Mother. After the denial of Saint Peter, Saint John had retired and had observed, more from afar what was going on. Recognizing also the wickedness of his flight in the Garden, he confessed it to the Mother of God and asked Her pardon as soon as he came into Her presence; and then he gave an account of all that passed in his heart and of what he had done and what he had seen in following his Master. Saint John thought it well to prepare the afflicted Mother for Her meeting with Her Most Holy Son, in order that She might not be overcome by the fearful spectacle of His present condition. Therefore He sought to impress Her beforehand with some image of His sufferings by saying: "O my Lady, in what a state of suffering is Our Divine Master! The sight of Him cannot but break one's heart; for by the buffets and the blows and by the spittle, His Most Beautiful Countenance is so disfigured and defiled, that Thou wilt scarcely recognize Him with Thy Own eyes." The Most Prudent Lady listened to his description, as if She knew nothing of the events; but She broke out in bitterest tears of heart-rending sorrow. The Holy Women, who had came forth with the Lady, also listened to Saint John, and all of them were filled with grief and terror at his words. The Queen of Heaven asked the Apostle to accompany Her and the devout women, and, exhorting them all, She said: "Let us hasten our steps, in order that My eyes may see the Son of the Eternal Father, Who took Human Form in My womb; and you shall see, My dearest friends, to what the Love of mankind has driven Him, My Lord and God, and what it costs Him to redeem men from sin and death, and to open for them the Gates of Heaven."

The Queen of Heaven set forth through the streets of Jerusalem accompanied by Saint John and by some Holy Women. Of these not all, but only the three Marys and other very pious women, followed Her to the end. With Her were also the Angels of Her guard, whom She asked to open a way for Her to Her Divine Son. The Holy Angels obeyed and acted as Her guard. On the streets She heard the people expressing their various opinions and sentiments concerning the sorrowful events now transpiring in reference to Jesus of Nazareth. The more kindly hearted lamented over his fate, and they were fewest in number. Others spoke about the intention of His enemies to crucify Him; others related where He now was and how He was conducted through the streets, bound as a criminal; others spoke of the illtreatment He was undergoing; others asked, what evil He had done, that He should be so misused; others again in their astonishment and in their doubts, exclaimed: To this then have His miracles brought Him! Without a doubt they were all impostures, since He cannot defend or free Himself!

Through the swarming and confused crowds the Angels conducted the Empress of Heaven to a sharp turn of the street, where She met Her Most Holy Son. With the profoundest reverence She prostrated Herself before His Sovereign Person and adored it more fervently and with a reverence more deep and more ardent than ever was given or ever shall be given to it by all the creatures. She arose and then the Mother and Son looked upon Each Other with ineffable tenderness, interiorly conversing with Each Other in transports of an unspeakable sorrow. The Most Prudent Lady stepped aside and then followed Christ Our Lord, continuing at a distance Her interior communication with Him and with the Eternal Father. The words of Her Soul are not for the mortal and corruptible tongue.

The image of Her Divine Son, thus wounded, defiled and bound, remained so firmly fixed and imprinted in the Soul of Our Queen, that during Her life it was never effaced, and remained in Her mind as distinctly, as if She were continually beholding Him with Her Own eyes. Christ Our God arrived at the house of Pilate, followed by many of the council and a countless multitude of the people. The Jews, wishing to preserve themselves as clean before the law as possible for the celebration of the Pasch and the unleavened bread, excused themselves before Pilate for their refusing to enter the pretorium or court of Pilate in presenting Jesus. As most absurd hypocrites they paid no attention to the sacrilegious uncleanness, with which their souls were affected in becoming the murderers of the innocent Godman. Pilate, although a heathen, yielded to their ceremonious scruples, and seeing that they hesitated to enter his pretorium, he went out to meet them. According to the formality customary among the

Romans, he asked them (John 18, 28): "What accusation have you against this Man?" They answered: "If He were not a criminal, we would not have brought Him to thee thus bound and fettered." This was as much as to say: We have convinced ourselves of the misdeeds and we are so attached to justice and to our obligations, that we would not have begun any proceedings against Him, if He were not a great malefactor. But Pilate pressed his inquiry and said: "What then are the misdeeds, of which He has made Himself guilty?" They answered: "He is convicted of disturbing the commonwealth, He wishes to make Himself our king and forbids paying tribute to Cæsar (Luke 23, 2); He claims to be the Son of God, and has preached a New Doctrine, commencing in Galilee, through all Judea and Jerusalem." "Take Him then yourselves," said Pilate, "and judge Him according to your laws; I do not find a just cause for proceeding against Him." But the Jews replied: "It is not permitted us to sentence any one to death, nor to execute such a sentence."

The Most Holy Mary, with Saint John and the women who followed Her, was present at this interview; for the Holy Angels made room for them where they could hear and see all that was passing. Shielded by Her mantle She wept Tears of Blood, pressed forth by the sorrow which pierced Her Virginal Heart. In Her interior acts of virtue She faithfully reproduced those practiced by Her Most Holy Son, while in Her pains and endurance She copied those of His Body. She asked the Eternal Father to grant Her the favor of not losing sight of Her Divine Son, as far as was naturally possible, until His Death; and this was conceded to Her, excepting during the time in which He was in prison.

One of the accusations of the Jews and the priests before Pilate was, that Jesus Our Savior had begun to stir up the people by His preaching in the province of Galilee (Luke 23, 6). This caused Pilate to inquire, whether He was a Galileean; and as they told him, that Jesus was born and raised in that country, he thought this circumstance useful for the solution of his difficulties in regard to Jesus and for escaping the molestations of the Jews, who so urgently demanded His death. Herod was at that time in Jerusalem, celebrating the Pasch of the Jews. He was the son of the first Herod, who had murdered the Innocents to procure the death of Jesus soon after His birth (Matth 2, 16). This murderer had become a proselyte of the Jews at the time of his marriage with a Jewish woman. On this account his son Herod likewise observed the law of Moses, and he had come to Jerusalem from Galilee, of which he was governor. Pilate was at enmity with Herod, for the two governed the two principal provinces of Palestine, namely, Judea and Galilee, and a short time before it had happened that Pilate, in his zeal for the supremacy of the Roman empire, had murdered some Galileeans during a public function in the temple, mixing the blood of the insurgents with that of the holy sacrifices. Herod was highly incensed at this sacrilege, and Pilate, in order to afford him some satisfaction without much trouble to himself, resolved to send to him Christ the Lord to be examined and judged as one of the subjects of Herod's sway. Pilate also expected that Herod would set Jesus free as being innocent and a Victim of the malice and envy of the priests and scribes.

When Herod was informed that Pilate would send Jesus of Nazareth to him, he was highly pleased. He knew that Jesus was a great friend of John the Baptist, whom he had ordered to be put to death (Mark 6, 27), and had heard many reports of his preaching. In vain and foolish curiosity he harbored the desire of seeing Jesus do something new and extraordinary for his entertainment and wonder (Luke 23, 8). The Author of Life therefore came into the presence of the murderer Herod, against whom the blood of the Baptist was calling more loudly to this same Lord for vengeance, than in its time the blood of Abel (Gen. 4, 10). But the unhappy adulterer, ignorant of the terrible judgment of the Almighty, received Him with loud laughter as an enchanter and conjurer. In this dreadful misconception he commenced to examine and question Him, persuaded that he could thereby induce Him to work some miracle to satisfy his curiosity. But the Master of Wisdom and Prudence, standing with an humble reserve before His most unworthy judge, answered him not a word. For on account of his evil-doing he well merited the punishment of not hearing the words of life, which he would certainly have heard if he had been disposed to listen to them with reverence.

The princes and priests of the Jews stood around, continually rehearsing the same accusations and charges which they had advanced in the presence of Pilate. But the Lord maintained silence also in regard to these calumnies, much to the disappointment of Herod. In his presence the Lord would not open His lips, neither in order to answer his questions, nor in order to refute the accusations. Herod was altogether unworthy of hearing the truth, this being his greatest punishment and the punishment most to be dreaded by all the princes and the powerful of this earth. Herod was much put out by the silence and meekness of Our Savior and was much disappointed in his vain curiosity. But the unjust judge tried to hide his confusion by mocking and ridiculing the innocent Master with his whole cohort of soldiers and ordering Him to be sent back to Pilate.

Pilate was again confronted with Jesus in his palace and was bestormed anew by the Jews to condemn Him to death of the cross. Convinced of the innocence of Christ and of the mortal envy of the Jews, he was much put out at Herod's again referring the disagreeable decision to his own tribunal. Feeling himself obliged in his quality of judge to give this decision, he sought to placate the Jews in different ways. One of these was a private interview with some of the servants and friends of the highpriests and priests. He urged them to prevail upon their masters and friends, not any more to ask for the release of the malefactor Barabbas, but instead demand the release of Our Redeemer; and to be satisfied with some punishment he was willing to administer before setting Him free. This measure Pilate had taken before they arrived a second time to press their demand for a sentence upon Jesus. The proposal to choose between freeing either Barabbas or Jesus was made to the Jews, not only once, but two or three times. The first time before sending Him to Herod and the second time after His return; this is related by the Evangelists with some variation, though not essentially contradicting Truth (Matth. 27, 17). Pilate spoke to the Jews and said: "You have brought this Man before me, accusing Him of perverting the people by His doctrines; and having examined Him in your presence, I was not convinced of the truth of your accusations. And Herod, to whom I have sent Him and before whom you repeated your accusations, refused to condemn Him to death. It will be sufficient to correct and chastise Him for the present, in order that He may amend. As I am to release some malefactor for the feast of the Pasch, I will release Christ, if you will have Him freed, and punish Barabbas." But the multitude of the Jews, thus informed how much Pilate desired to set Jesus free, shouted with one voice: "Enough, enough, not Christ, but Barabbas deliver unto us."

While Pilate was thus disputing with the Jews in the pretorium, his wife, Procula, happened to hear of his doings and she sent him a message telling him: "What hast thou to do with this Man? Let him go free; for I warn thee that I have had this very day some visions in regard to Him!" This warning of Procula originated through the activity of Lucifer and his demons. For they, observing all that was happening in regard to the Person of Christ and the unchangeable patience with which He bore all injuries, were more and more confused and staggered in their rabid fury. Despairing of success the demons betook themselves to the wife of Pilate and spoke to her in dreams, representing to her that this Man was just and without guilt, that if her husband should sentence Him he would be deprived of his rank and she herself would meet with great adversity. They urged her to advise Pilate to release Jesus and punish Barabbas, if she did not wish to draw misfortune upon their house and their persons.

Procula was filled with great fear and terror at these visions, and as soon as she heard what was passing between the Jews and her husband, she sent him the message mentioned by Saint Matthew, not to meddle with this Man nor condemn One to death, whom she held to be just. The demon also injected similar misgivings into the mind of Pilate and these warnings of his wife only increased them. Yet, as all his considerations rested upon worldly policy, and as he had not co-operated with the true helps given him by the Savior, all these fears retarded his unjust proceedings only so long as no other more powerful consideration arose, as will be seen in effect. But just now he began for the third time to argue (as Saint Luke tells us), insisting upon the innocence of Christ Our Lord and that he found no crime in Him nor any guilt worthy of death, and therefore he would punish and then dismiss Him (Luke 23, 22). As we shall see in the next chapter, he did really punish Christ in order to see whether the Jews would be satisfied. But the Jews, on the contrary, demanded that Christ be crucified. Thereupon Pilate asked for water and released Barabbas. Then he washed his hands in the presence of all the people, saying: "I have no share in the death of this Just Man, whom you condemn. Look to yourselves in what you are doing, for I wash my hands in order that you may understand they are not sullied in the

117

blood of the Innocent." Pilate thought that by this ceremony he could excuse himself entirely and that he thereby could put its blame upon the princes of the Jews and upon the people who demanded it. The wrath of the Jews was so blind and foolish that for the satisfaction of seeing Jesus crucified, they entered upon this agreement with Pilate and took upon themselves and upon their children the responsibility for this crime. Loudly proclaiming this terrible sentence and curse, they exclaimed: "His blood come upon us and upon our children" (Matth. 27, 25).

In the house of Pilate, through the ministry of the Holy Angels, Our Queen was placed in such a position that She could hear the disputes of the iniquitous judge with the scribes and priests concerning the innocence of Christ Our Savior, and concerning the release of Barabbas in preference to Him. All the clamors of these human tigers She heard in silence and admirable meekness, as the living counterpart of Her Most Holy Son. Although She preserved the unchanging propriety and modesty of Her exterior, all the malicious words of the Jews pierced Her Sorrowful Heart like a two-edged sword. But the voices of Her unspoken sorrows resounded in the ears of the Eternal Father more pleasantly and sweetly than the lamentation of the beautiful Rachel who, as Jeremias says, was beweeping her children because they cannot be restored (Jer. 31, 15). Our Most Beautiful Rachel, the Purest Mary, sought not revenge, but pardon for her enemies, who were depriving Her of the Only-begotten of the Father and Her Only Son. She imitated all the actions of the Most Holy Soul of Christ and accompanied Him in the works of Most Exalted Holiness and Perfection; for neither could Her torments hinder Her charity, nor Her affliction diminish Her fervor, nor could the tumult distract Her attention, nor the outrageous injuries of the multitudes prevent Her interior recollection: under all circumstances She practiced the most exalted virtues in the most eminent degree.

Pilate, aware of the obstinate hostility of the Jews against Jesus of Nazareth, and unwilling to condemn Him to death, of which he knew Him to be innocent, thought that a severe scourging of Jesus might placate the fury of the ungrateful people, and soothe the envy of the priests and the scribes. But these perfidious Jews were clothed in the guise of demons, or rather transformed into demons, who exert the more furious rage against those who are rendered more helpless and wretched; who, when they see any one most helpless, say: let us pursue him now, since He has none to defend nor free him from our hands.

Such was the implacable fury of the priests and of their confederates, the pharisees, against the Author of Life. For Lucifer, despairing of being able to hinder his murder by the Jews, inspired them with his own dreadful malice and outrageous cruelty. Pilate, placed between the known truth and his human and terrestrial considerations, chose to follow the erroneous leading of the latter, and order Jesus to be severely scourged, though he had himself declared Him free from guilt (John 19, 1). Thereupon those ministers of satan, with many others, brought Jesus Our Savior to the place of punishment, which was a courtyard or enclosure attached to the house and set apart for the torture of criminals in order to force them to confess their crimes. It was surrounded by a low, open building, surrounded by columns, some of which supported the roof, while others were lower and stood free. To one of these columns, which was of marble, they bound Jesus very securely; for they still thought Him a magician and feared His escape.

They first took off the white garment with not less ignominy than when they clothed Him therein in the house of the adulterous homicide Herod. In loosening the ropes and chains, which He had borne since His capture in the garden, they cruelly widened the wounds which His bonds had made in His arms and wrists. Having freed His hands, they commanded Him with infamous blasphemies to despoil Himself of the seamless tunic which He wore. This was the identical garment with which His Most Blessed Mother had clothed Him in Egypt when He first began to walk.

Thus the Lord stood uncovered in the presence of a great multitude and the six torturers bound Him brutally to one of the columns in order to chastise Him so much the more at their ease. Then, two and two at a time, they began to scourge Him with such inhuman cruelty, as was possible only in men possessed by Lucifer, as were these executioners. The first two scourged the Innocent Savior with hard and thick cords, full of rough knots, and in their sacrilegious fury strained all the powers of their body to inflict the blows. This first scourging raised in the Deified Body of the Lord great welts and livid tumors, so that the Sacred Blood gathered beneath the skin and disfigured His entire body. Already it began to ooze through the Wounds. The first two having at length desisted, the second pair continued the scourging in still greater emulation; with hardened leather thongs they leveled their strokes upon the places already sore and caused the discolored tumors to break open and shed forth the Sacred Blood until it bespattered and drenched the garments of the sacriligious torturers, running down also in streams to the pavement. Those two gave way to the third pair of scourgers, who commenced to beat the Lord with extremely tough rawhides, dried hard like osier twigs. They scourged Him still more cruelly, because they were wounding, not so much His Virginal Body, as cutting into the wounds already produced by the previous scourging. Besides they had been secretly incited to greater fury by the demons, who were filled with new rage at the Patience of Christ.

As the veins of the Sacred Body had now been opened and His whole Person seemed but one continued Wound, the third pair found no more room for new wounds. Their ceaseless blows inhumanly tore the Immaculate and Virginal Flesh of Christ Our Redeemer and scattered many pieces of it about the pavement; so much so that a large portion of the shoulder-bones were exposed and showed red through the flowing Blood; in other places also the bones were laid bare larger than the palm of the hand. In order to wipe out entirely that Beauty, which exceeded that of all other men (Ps. 44, 3), they beat Him in the face and in the feet and hands, thus leaving unwounded not a single spot in which they could exert their fury and wrath against the Most Innocent Lamb. The Divine blood flowed to the ground, gathering here and there in great abundance. The scourging in the face, and in the hands and feet, was unspeakably painful, because these parts are so full of sensitive and delicate nerves. His Venerable Countenance became so swollen and wounded that the Blood and the swellings blinded Him. In addition to their blows the executioners spirted upon His Person their disgusting spittle and loaded Him with insulting epithets (Thren. 3, 30). The exact number of blows dealt out to the Savior from head to foot was 5,115. The Great Lord and Author of all creation who, by His Divine Nature was incapable of suffering, was, in His Human Flesh and for our sake, reduced to a Man of Sorrows as prophesied, and was made to experience our infirmities, becoming the Last of Men (Is. 53, 3), a Man of Sorrows and the outcast of the people.

The multitudes who had followed the Lord, filled up the courtyard of Pilate's house and the surrounding streets; for all of them waited for the issue of this event, discussing and arguing about it according to each one's views. Amid all this confusion the Virgin Mother endured unheard of insults, and She was deeply afflicted by the injuries and blasphemies heaped upon Her Divine Son by the Jews and gentiles. When they brought Jesus to the scourging place She retired in the company of the Marys and Saint John to a corner of the courtyard. Assisted by Her Divine Visions, She there witnessed all the scourging and the torments of Our Savior. Although She did not see it with the eyes of Her Body nothing was hidden to Her, no more than if She had been standing quite near. Human thoughts cannot comprehend how great and how diverse were the afflictions and sorrows of the Great Queen and Mistress of the Angels: together with many other Mysteries of the Divinity they shall become manifest in the next life, for the Glory of the Son and Mother. I have already mentioned in other places of this history, and especially in that of the Passion, that the Blessed Mother felt in Her Own Body all the torments of Her Son. This was true also of the scourging, which She felt in all the parts of Her Virginal Body, in the same intensity as they were felt by Christ in His Body. Although She shed no blood except what flowed from Her eyes with Her tears, nor was lacerated in Her flesh; yet the bodily pains so changed and disfigured Her, that Saint John and the Holy Women failed to find in Her any resemblance of Herself. Besides the tortures of the body She suffered ineffable sorrows of the soul; there sorrow was augmented in proportion to the immensity of Her insight (Eccles. 1, 18). For Her sorrows flowed not only from the natural love of a mother and a supreme love of Christ as Her God, but it was proportioned to Her power of judging more accurately than all creatures of the innocence of Christ, the dignity of His Divine Person, the atrocity of the insults coming from the perfidious Jews and the children of Adam, whom He was freeing from Eternal death.

THE THIRD SORROWFUL MYSTERY,

THE CROWNING WITH THORNS

Thereupon they took Jesus to the pretorium, where, with the same cruelty and contempt, they again despoiled Him of His garments and in order to deride Him before all the people as a counterfeit king, clothed Him in a much torn and soiled mantle of purple color. They placed also upon His Sacred Head a cap made of woven thorns, to serve Him as a crown (John 19, 2). This cap was woven of thorn branches and in such a manner that many of the hard and sharp thorns would penetrate into the skull, some of them to the ears and others to the eyes. Hence one of the greatest tortures suffered by the Lord was that of the Crown of Thorns. Instead of a sceptre they placed into His hands a contemptible reed. They also threw over His shoulders a violet colored mantle, something of the style of capes worn in churches; for such a garment belonged to the vestiture of a king. In this array of a mock-king the perfidious Jews decked out Him, who by His nature and by every right was the King of Kings and the Lord of Lords (Apoc. 19, 16). Then all the soldiers, in the presence of the priests and pharisees, gathered around Him and heaped upon Him their blasphemous mockery and derision. Some of them bent their knees and mockingly said to Him, God save Thee, King of the Jews. Others buffeted Him; others snatched the cane from His hands and struck Him on His crowned head; other ejected their disgusting spittle upon Him; all of them, instigated by furious demons, insulted and affronted Him in different manners.

It seemed to Pilate that the spectacle of a man so illtreated as Jesus of Nazareth would move and fill with shame the hearts of that ungrateful people. He therefore commanded Jesus to be brought from the pretorium to an open window, where all could see Him crowned with thorns, disfigured by the scourging and the ignominious vestiture of a mock-king. Pilate himself spoke to the people, calling out to them: "Ecce Homo," "Behold, what a man!" (John 19, 5). See this Man, whom you hold as your enemy! What more can I do with Him than to have punished Him in this severe manner? You certainly have nothing more to fear from Him. I do not find any cause of death in Him." As the priests and pharisees, in their eager and insatiable hostility, were irrevocably bent upon taking away the Life of Christ Our Savior, nothing but His Death would content or satisfy them; therefore they answered Pilate: "Crucify Him, Crucify Him!" (John 19, 6).

When the Blessed Among Women, Most Holy Mary, saw her Divine Son as Pilate showed Him to the people and heard him say: "Ecce homo!" She fell upon Her knees and openly adored Him as the True Godman. The same was also done by Saint John and the Holy Women, together with all the Holy Angels of the Queen and Lady; for they saw that not only Mary, as the Mother of the Savior, but that God Himself desired them thus to act.

WORDS OF THE QUEEN.

Think well, then, My Dearest, which of these lots thou wishest to choose in the sight of My Son and Me. If thou seest Thy Redeemer, Thy Spouse and Thy Chief tormented, afflicted, crowned with thorns, and saturated with reproaches and at the same time desirest to have a part in Him and be a member of His Mystical Body, it is not becoming, or even possible, that thou live steeped in the pleasures of the flesh. Thou must be the persecuted and not a persecutor, the oppressed and not the oppressor; the one that bears the cross, that encounters the scandal, and not that gives it; the one that suffers, and at the same time makes none of the neighbors suffer. On the contrary, thou must exert thyself for their conversion and salvation in as far as is compatible with the perfection of thy state and vocation. This is the portion of the friends of God and the inheritance of His children in mortal life; in this consists the participation in grace and glory, which by His torments and reproaches and by His Death of the Cross My Son and Lord has purchased for them. I too have co-operated in this work and have paid the sorrows and afflictions, which thou hast understood and which I wish thou shalt never allow to be blotted out from My inmost memory. The Almighty would indeed have been powerful enough to exalt His predestined in this world, to give them riches and favors beyond those of others, to make them strong as lions for reducing the rest of mankind to their invincible power. But it was inopportune to exalt them in this manner, in order that men might not be led into the error of thinking that greatness consists in what is visible and happiness in earthly goods; lest, being induced to forsake virtues and obscure the Glory of the Lord, they fail to experience the efficacy of Divine Grace and cease to aspire toward spiritual and Eternal things. This is the Science which I wish thee to study continually and in which thou must advance day by day, putting into practice all that thou learnest to understand and know.

JESUS CARRIES THE HEAVY CROSS

THE WAY OF THE CROSS.

To the great satisfaction and joy of the priests and pharisees Pilate then decreed the sentence of death on the Cross against Life itself, Jesus Our Savior. Having announced it to the One they had thus condemned in spite of His innocence, they brought Him to another part of the house of Pilate, where they stripped Him of the purple mantle, in which they had derided Him as mock-king. All happened by the mysterious dispensation of God; though on their part it was due to the concerted malice of the Jews; for they wished to see Him undergo the punishment of the Cross in His Own clothes so that in them He might be recognized by all. Only by His garments could He now be recognized by the people, since His Face had been disfigured beyond recognition by the scourging, the impure spittle, and the crown of thorns. They again clothed Him with the seamless tunic, which at the command of the Queen was brought to Him by the Angels; for the executioners had thrown it into a corner of another room in the house, where they left it to place upon Him the mocking and scandalous purple cloak.

The sentence of Pilate against Our Savior having been published in a loud voice before all the people, the executioners loaded the heavy Cross, on which He was to be crucified, upon His tender and wounded shoulders. In order that He might carry it they loosened the bonds holding His hands, but not the others, since they wished to drag Him along by the loose ends of the ropes that bound His body. In order to torment Him the more they drew two loops around His throat. The Cross was fifteen feet long, of thick and heavy timbers. The herald began to proclaim the sentence and the whole confused and turbulent multitude of the people, the executioners and soldiers, with great noise, uproar and disor-

125

der began to move from the house of Pilate to Mount Calvary through the streets of Jerusalem. The Master and Redeemer of the World, Jesus, before receiving the Cross, looked upon it with a countenance full of extreme joy and exultation such as would be shown by a bridegroom looking at the rich adornments of his bride, and on receiving it, He addressed it as follows:

"O Cross, beloved of My soul, now prepared and ready to still My longings, come to Me, that I may be received in thy arms, and that, attached to them as on an altar, I may be accepted by the Eternal Father as the Sacrifice of His everlasting reconciliation with the human race. In order to die upon thee, I have descended from Heaven and assumed mortal and passible flesh; for thou art to be the sceptre with which I shall triumph over all My enemies, the key with which I shall open the gates of Heaven for all the predestined (Is. 22, 22), the sanctuary in which the guilty sons of Adam shall find mercy, and the treasurehouse for the enrichment of their poverty. Upon thee I desire to exalt and recommend dishonor and reproach among men, in order that My friends may embrace them with joy, seek them with anxious longings, and follow Me on the path which I through thee shall open up before them. My Father and Eternal God, I confess Thee as the Lord of Heaven and Earth (Matth. 11, 25), subjecting Myself to Thy power and to Thy Divine wishes, I take upon My shoulders the wood for the sacrifice of My innocent and passible humanity and I accept it willingly for the salvation of men. Receive Thou, Eternal Father, this Sacrifice as acceptable to Thy justice, in order that from today on they may not any more be servants, but sons and heirs of Thy Kingdom together with Me" (Rom. 8, 17).

None of these Sacred mysteries and happenings were hidden from the Great Lady of the World, Mary; for She had a most intimate knowledge and understanding of them, far beyond that of all the Angels. The events, which She could not see with the eyes of Her body, She perceived by Her intelligence and Revealed Science, which manifested to Her the interior operation of Her Most Holy Son. By this Divine Light She recognized the Infinite Value of the Wood of the Cross after once it had come in contact with the Deified humanity of Jesus Our Redeemer. Immediately She venerated and adored it in a manner befitting it. The same was also done by the Heavenly Spirits attending upon the Queen. She imitated Her Divine Son in the tokens of affections, with which He received the Cross, addressing it in the words suited to Her office as Coadjutrix of the Redeemer. By Her prayers to the Eternal Father She followed Him in His exalted sentiments as the living original and exemplar, without failing in the least point. When She heard the voice of the herald publishing and rehearsing the sentence through the streets, the Heavenly Mother, in protest against the accusations contained in the sentence and in the form of comments on the Glory and Honor of the Lord, composed a canticle of praise and worship of the innocence and sinlessness of Her All-Holy Son and God. The Most Loving Mother was so admirably faithful in Her sufferings and in imitating the example of Christ Our God, that She never permitted Herself any easement either of Her bodily pains, such as rest, or nourishment, or sleep; nor any relaxation of the spirit, such as any consoling thoughts or considerations, except when She was visited from on high by Divine influence. Then only would She humbly and thankfully accept relief, in order that She might recover strength to attend still more fervently to the object of Her sorrows and to the cause of His sufferings. The same wise consideration She applied to the malicious behavior of the Jews and their servants, to the needs of the human race, to their threatening ruin, and to the ingratitude of men, for whom He suffered. Thus She perfectly and intimately knew of all these things and felt it more deeply than all the creatures.

Another hidden and astonishing miracle was wrought by the right hand of God through the instrumentality of the Blessed Mary against Lucifer and his infernal spirits. It took place in the following manner: The dragon and his associates, though they could not understand the humiliation of the Lord, were most attentive to all that happened in the Passion of the Lord. Now, when He took upon Himself the Cross, all these enemies felt a new and mysterious tremor and weakness, which caused in them great consternation and confused distress. Conscious of these unwonted and invincible feelings the prince of darkness feared, that in the Passion and Death of Christ our Lord some dire and irreparable destruction of his reign was imminent. In order not to be overtaken by it in the presence of Christ Our God, the dragon resolved to retire and fly with all his followers to the caverns of hell. But when he sought to execute this resolve, he was prevented by the

Great Queen and Mistress of all creation; for the Most High, enlightening Her and intimating to Her what She was to do, at the same time invested Her with His power. The Heavenly Mother, turning toward Lucifer and his squadrons, by Her imperial command hindered them from flying; ordering them to await and witness the Passion to the end on Mount Calvary. The demons could not resist the command of the Mighty Queen; for they recognized and felt the Divine Power operating in Her. Subject to Her sway they followed Christ as so many prisoners dragged along in chains to Calvary, where the Eternal Wisdom had decreed to triumph over them from the Throne of the Cross, as we shall see later on. There is nothing which can exemplify the discouragement and dismay, which from that moment began to oppress Lucifer and his demons. According to our way of speaking, they walked along to Calvary like criminals condemned to a terrible death, and seized by the dismay and consternation of an inevitable punishment.

The executioners, bare of all human compassion and kindness, dragged Our Savior Jesus along with incredible cruelty and insults. Some of them jerked Him forward by the ropes in order to accelerate His passage, while others pulled from behind in order to retard it. On account of this jerking and the weight of the Cross they caused Him to sway to and fro and often to fall to the ground. By the hard knocks He thus received on the rough stones great wounds were opened, especially on the two knees and they were widened at each repeated fall. The heavy Cross also inflicted a wound on the shoulder on which it was carried. The unsteadiness caused the Cross sometimes to knock against His Sacred Head, and sometimes the head against the Cross; thus the thorns of His crown penetrated deeper and wounded the parts, which they had not yet reached. To these torments of the body the ministers of evil added many insulting words and execrable affronts, ejecting their impure spittle and throwing the dirt of the pavement into His face so mercilessly, that they blinded the eyes that looked upon them with such Divine Mercy. Thus they of their own account condemned themselves to the loss of the graces, with which His very looks were fraught. By the haste with which they dragged Him along in their eagerness to see Him die, they did not allow Him to catch His breath; for His most innocent body, having been in so few hours overwhelmed with such a storm of torments, was so weakened and bruised, that to all appearances He was ready to yield up life under His pains and sorrows.

From the house of Pilate the Sorrowful and Stricken Mother followed with the multitudes on the way of Her Divine Son, accompanied by Saint John and the pious women. As the surging crowds hindered Her from getting very near to the Lord, She asked the Eternal Father to be permitted to stand at the Foot of the Cross of Her Blessed Son and see Him die with Her own eyes. With the Divine consent She ordered Her Holy Angels to manage things in such a way as to make it possible for Her to execute Her wishes. The Holy Angels obeyed Her with great reverence; and they speedily led the Queen through some bystreet, in order that She might meet Her Son. Thus it came that both of Them met face to face in sweetest recognition of each Other and in mutual renewal of each Other's interior sorrows. Yet They did not speak to one another, nor would the fierce cruelty of the executioners have permitted such an intercourse. But the most prudent Mother adored Her Divine Son and True God, laden with the Cross; and interiorly besought Him, that, since She could not relieve Him of the weight of the Cross and since She was not permitted to command Her Holy Angels to lighten it, He would inspire these ministers of cruelty to procure some one for His assistance. This prayer was heard by the Lord Christ; and so it happened, that Simon of Cyrene was afterwards impressed to carry the Cross with the Lord (Matth. 27, 32). The pharisees and the executioners were moved to this measure, some of them out of natural compassion, others for fear lest Christ, the Author of life, should lose His life by exhaustion before it could be taken from Him on the Cross.

PRAYER OF OUR HOLY MOTHER

Beyond all human thought and estimation was the sorrow of the most sincere Dove and Virgin Mother while She thus witnessed with Her own eyes Her Son carrying the Cross to Mount Calvary; for She alone could fittingly know and love Him according to His true worth. It would have been impossible for Her to live through this ordeal, if the Divine Power had not strengthened Her and preserved Her life. With bitterest sorrow She addressed the Lord and spoke to Him in

Her heart: "My Son and Eternal God, Light of My eyes and Life of My soul, receive, O Lord, the sacrifice of My not being able to relieve Thee of the burden of the Cross and carry it Myself, who am a Daughter of Adam; for it is I who should die upon it in love of Thee, as Thou now wishest to die in most ardent love of the human race. O most loving Mediator between guilt and justice! How dost Thou cherish mercy in the midst of so great injuries and such heinous offenses! O charity without measure or bounds, which permits such torments and affronts in order to afford it a wider scope for its ardor and efficacy! O infinite and sweetest love, would that the hearts and the wills of men were all Mine, so that they could give no such thankless return for all that Thou endurest! O who will speak to the hearts of the mortals to teach them what they owe to Thee, since Thou hast paid so dearly for their salvation from ruin!"

WORDS OF THE QUEEN.

I desire that the fruit of the obedience with which thou writest the history of My life shall be, that thou become a true disciple of My Most Holy Son and of Myself. The main purpose of the exalted and venerable mysteries, which are made known to thee, and of the teachings, which I so often repeat to thee, is that thou deny and strip thyself, estranging thy heart from all affection to creatures, neither wishing to possess them nor accept them for other uses. By this precaution thou wilt overcome the impediments, which the devils seek to place in the way of the dangerous softness of thy nature. I who know thee, thus advise and lead thee by the way of instruction and correction as Thy Mother and Instructress. By the Divine teaching thou knowest the Mysteries of the Passion and Death of Christ and the one true way of life, which is the Cross; and thou knowest that not all who are called, are chosen. Many there are who wish to follow Christ and very few who truly dispose themselves to imitate Him; for as soon as they feel the sufferings of the Cross they cast it aside. Laborious exertions are very painful and averse to human nature according to the flesh; and the Fruits of the Spirit are more hidden and few guide themselves by the Light. On this account there are so many among mortals, who, forgetful of the Eternal Truths, seek the flesh and the continual indulgence of its pleasures. They ardently seek honors and fly from injuries: they strive after riches, and contemn poverty; they long after pleasure and dread mortification. All these are enemies of the Cross of Christ (Phil. 3, 18), and with dreadful aversion they fly from it, deeming it sheer ignomiy, just like those who crucified Christ, The Lord.

Another deceit has spread through the world: many imagine that they are following Christ their Master, though they neither suffer affliction nor engage in any exertion or labor. They are content with avoiding boldness in committing sins, and place all their perfection in a certain prudence or hollow self-love, which prevents them from denying anything to their will and from practicing any virtues at the cost of their flesh. They would easily escape this deception, if they would consider that My Son was not only the Redeemer, but their Teacher; and that He left in this world the treasures of His Redemption not only as a remedy against its Eternal ruin, but as a necessary medicine for the sickness of sin in human nature. No one knew so much as My Son and Lord; no one could better understand the quality of love than the Divine Lord, who was and is wisdom and charity itself; and no one was more able to fulfill all His wishes (I John 4, 16). Nevertheless, although He well could do it, He chose not a life of softness and ease for the flesh, but one full of labors and pains; for He judged His instructions to be incomplete and insufficient to redeem man, if He failed to teach them how to overcome the demon, the flesh and their own self. He wished to inculcate, that this magnificent victory is gained by the Cross, by labors, penances, mortifications and the acceptance of contempt: all of which are the trade-marks and evidences of true love and the special watchwords of the predestined.

THE CRUCIFIXION AND DEATH
OF OUR LORD ON THE CROSS

Our Savior then, the new and true Isaac, the Son of the Eternal Father, reached the mountain of sacrifice, which is the same one to which his prototype and figure, Isaac, was brought by the patriarch Abraham (Gen. 22, 9). Upon the most innocent Lamb of God was to be executed the rigor of the sentence, which had been suspended in favor of the son of the Patriarch. Mount Calvary was held to be a place of defilement and ignominy, as being reserved for the chastisement of condemned criminals, whose cadavers spread around it their stench and attached to it a still more evil fame. Our Most Loving Jesus arrived at its summit so worn out, wounded, torn and disfigured, that He seemed altogether transformed into an object of pain and sorrows. The Sorrowful and Afflicted Mother, in the bitterness of Her soul, also arrived at the summit of the Mount and remained very close to Her Divine Son, but in the sorrows of Her Soul She was as it were beside Herself, being entirely transformed by Her love and by the pains which She saw Jesus suffer. Near Her were Saint John and the three Marys; for they alone, through Her intercession and the favor of the Eternal Father, had obtained the privilege of remaining so constantly near to The Savior and to His Cross.

When the most prudent Mother perceived that now the Mysteries of the Redemption were to be fulfilled and that the executioners were about to strip Jesus of His clothes for crucifixion, She turned in spirit to the Eternal Father and prayed as follows: "My Lord and Eternal God, Thou art the Father of Thy only begotten Son. By Eternal generation He is engendered, God of the True God, namely Thyself, and as man He was born of My womb and received from Me this human nature, in which He now suffers. I have nursed and sustained Him at My own breast; and as the best of sons that ever can be born of any creature, I love Him with maternal love. As His Mother I have a natural right in the Person of His Most Holy Humanity and Thy Providence will never infringe upon any rights held by Thy creatures. This right of a Mother then, I now yield to Thee and once more place in Thy hands Thy and My Son as a Sacrifice for the Redemption of man. Accept, My Lord, this pleasing offering, since this is more than I can ever offer by submitting My own self as a victim or to suffering. This sacrifice is greater, not only because My Son is the True God and of Thy own substance, but because this sacrifice costs me a much greater sorrow and pain. For if the lots were changed and I should be permitted to die in order to preserve His Most Holy Life, I would consider it a great relief and the fulfillment of My dearest wishes." The Eternal Father received this prayer of the Exalted Queen with ineffable pleasure and complacency. The patriarch Abraham was permitted to go no further than to prefigure and attempt the sacrifice of a son, because the real execution of such a sacrifice God reserved to Himself and to His Only begotten. Nor was Sara, the mother of Isaac, informed of the mystical ceremony, this being prevented not only by the promptness of Abraham's obedience, but also because he mistrusted, lest the maternal love of Sara, though she was a just and holy woman, should impel her to prevent the execution of the Divine command. But not so was it with Most Holy Mary, to whom the Eternal Father could fearlessly manifest His unchangeable Will in order that She might, as far as Her powers were concerned, unite with Him in the Sacrifice of His Only be-gotten.

It was already the sixth hour, which corresponds to our noontime, and the executioners, intending to crucify the Savior naked, despoiled Him of the seamless tunic and of His garments. As the tunic was large and without opening in front, they pulled it over the head of Jesus without taking off the Crown of Thorns; but on account of the rudeness with which they proceeded, they inhumanly tore off the Crown with the tunic. Thus they opened anew all the wounds of His head, and in some of them remained the thorns, which, in spite of their being so hard and sharp, were wrenched off by the violence with which the executioners despoiled Him of his tunic and, with it, of the Crown. With heartless cruelty they again forced it down upon His Sacred Head, opening up wounds upon wounds. By the rude tearing off of the tunic

133

were renewed also the wounds of His whole body, since the tunic had dried into the open places and its removal was, as David says, adding new pains to his wounds (Ps. 68, 27). Four times during the Passion did they despoil Jesus of His garments and again vest Him. The first time in order to scourge Him at the pillar; the second time in order to clothe Him in the mock purple; the third, when they took this off in order to clothe Him in His tunic; the fourth, when they finally took away His clothes. This last was the most painful, because His wounds were more numerous, His Holy Humanity was much weakened, and there was less shelter against the sharp wind on Mount Calvary; for also this element was permitted to increase the sufferings of His death-struggle by sending its cold blasts across the mount.

To all these sufferings was added the confusion of being bereft of His garments in the presence of His Most Blessed Mother, of Her pious companions, and in full sight of the multitudes gathered around. By His Divine Power He, however, reserved for Himself the nether garment which His Mother had wound around his loins in Egypt; for neither at the scourging, nor at the crucifixion could the executioners remove it, and He was laid in the sepulchre still covered with this cloth.

The Holy Cross was lying on the ground and the executioners were busy making the necessary preparations for crucifying Him and the two thieves. In the meanwhile Our Redeemer and Master prayed to the Father in the following terms:

"Eternal Father and My Lord God, to the incomprehensible Majesty of Thy infinite goodness and justice I offer My entire humanity and all that according to Thy will it has accomplished in descending from Thy bosom to assume passible and mortal flesh for the Redemption of men, My brethren. I offer Thee, Lord, with Myself, also My Most Loving Mother, Her love, Her most perfect works, Her sorrows, Her sufferings, Her anxious and prudent solicitude in serving Me, imitating Me and accompanying Me unto death. I offer Thee the little flock of My Apostles, the Holy Church and congregation of the faithful, such as it is now and as it shall be to the end of the world; and with it I offer to Thee all the mortal children of Adam. All this I place in Thy hands as the True and Almighty Lord and God. As far as My wishes are concerned, I suffer and die for all, and I desire that all shall be saved, under the condition that all follow Me and profit of My Redemption. Thus may they pass from the slavery of the devil to be Thy children, My brethren and co-heirs of the grace merited by Me. Especially, O My Lord, do I offer to Thee the poor, the despised and afflicted, who are My friends and who follow Me on the Way to the Cross. I desire that the just and the predestined be written in Thy Eternal memory. I beseech Thee, My Father, to withhold Thy chastisement and not to raise the scourge of Thy justice over men; let them not be punished as they merit for their sins. Be Thou from now on their Father as Thou art Mine. I beseech Thee also, that they may be helped to ponder upon My Death in pious affection and be enlightened from above; and I pray for those who are persecuting Me, in order that they may be converted to the truth. Above all do I ask Thee for the exaltation of Thy Ineffable and Most Holy Name."

This prayer and supplication of Our Savior Jesus were known to the Most Blessed Mother, and She imitated Him and made the same petitions to the Eternal Father in as far as She was concerned. The Most Prudent Virgin never forgot or disregarded the first word which She had heard from the mouth of Her Divine Son as an infant: "Become like unto Me, My Beloved." His promise, that in return for the new human existence which She had given Him in Her virginal womb, He would, by His almighty power, give Her a new existence of Divine and eminent grace above all other creatures, was continually fulfilled.

In order to find the places for the auger-holes on the Cross, the executioners haughtily commanded the Creator of the universe (O dreadful temerity!), to stretch Himself out upon it. The Teacher of humility obeyed without hesitation. But they, following their inhuman instinct of cruelty, marked the places for the holes, not according to the size of His body, but larger, having in mind a new torture for their Victim. This inhuman intent was known to the Mother of Light, and the knowledge of it was one of the greatest afflictions of Her chastest heart during the whole Passion. She saw through the intentions of these ministers of sin and She anticipated the torments to be endured by Her Beloved Son when His limbs should be wrenched from their sockets in being nailed to the Cross. But She could not do anything to prevent it, as it was the Will of the Lord to suffer these pains for men. When He rose from the Cross, and they set about boring the holes, the Great Lady approached and took hold of one of His hands, adoring Him and kissing it with greatest reverence. The executioners allowed this because they thought that the sight of His Mother would cause so much the greater affliction to the Lord; for they wished to spare Him no sorrow they could cause Him. But they were ignorant of the hidden mysteries; for the Lord during His Passion had no greater source of consolation and interior joy than to see in the soul of His Most Blessed Mother, the beautiful likeness of Himself and the full fruits of His Passion and Death. This joy, to a certain extent, comforted Christ Our Lord also in that hour.

Presently one of the executioners seized the hand of Jesus Our Savior and placed it upon the auger-hole, while another hammered a large and rough nail through the palm. The veins and sinews were torn, and the bones of the Sacred Hand, which made the heavens and all that exists, were forced apart. When they stretched out the other hand, they found that it did not reach up to the auger-hole; for the sinews of the other arm had been shortened and the executioners had maliciously set the holes too far apart, as I have mentioned above. In order to overcome the difficulty, they took the chain, with which the Savior had been bound in the garden, and looping one end through a ring around His wrist, they, with unheard of cruelty, pulled the hand over the hole and fastened it with another nail. Thereupon they seized His feet, and placing them one above the other, they tied the same chain around both and stretched them with barbarous ferocity down to the third hole. Then they drove through both feet a large nail into the Cross. Thus the Sacred Body, in which dwelled the Divinity, was nailed motionless to the Holy Cross, and the handiwork of His deified members, formed by the Holy Ghost, was so stretched and torn asunder, that the bones of His body, dislocated and forced from their natural position, could all be counted. The bones of His breast, of His shoulders and arms, and of His whole body yielded to the cruel violence and were torn from their sinews.

After the Savior was nailed to the Cross, the executioners judged it necessary to bend the points of the nails which projected through the back of the wood, in order that they might not be loosened and drawn out by the weight of the body. For this purpose they raised up the Cross in order to turn it over, so that The Body of The Lord would rest face downward upon the ground with the weight of the Cross upon Him. This new cruelty appalled all the bystanders and a shout of pity arose in the crowd. But the sorrowful and compassionate Mother intervened by Her prayers, and asked the Eternal Father not to permit this boundless outrage to happen in the way the executioners had intended. She commanded Her Holy Angels to come to the assistance of Their Creator. When, therefore, the executioners raised up the Cross to let it fall, with the Crucified Lord face downward upon the ground, the Holy Angels supported Him and the Cross above the stony and fetid ground, so that His Divine Countenance did not come in contact with the rocks and pebbles. Thus altogether ignorant of the miracle the executioners bent over the points of the nails; for the Sacred Body was so near to the ground and the Cross was so firmly held by the Angels, that the Jews thought it rested upon the hard rock.

Then they dragged the lower end of the Cross with the crucified God near to the hole, wherein it was to be planted. Some of them getting under the upper part of the Cross with their shoulders, others pushing upward with their halberds and lances, they raised the Savior on His Cross and fastened its foot in the hole they had drilled into the ground. Thus Our True Life and Salvation now hung in the air upon the Sacred wood in full view of the innumerable multitudes of different nations and countries. I must not omit mentioning another barbarity inflicted upon the Lord as they raised Him: for some of them placed the sharp points of their lances and halberds to His body and fearfully lacerating Him under the armpits in helping to push the Cross into position. At this spectacle new cries of protest arose with still more vehemence and confusion from the multitude of people. The Jews blasphemed, the kind-hearted lamented, the strangers were astounded, some of them called the attention of the bystanders to the proceedings, others turned away their heads in horror and pity; others took to themselves a warning from this spectacle of suffering, and still others proclaimed Him a just Man. All these different sentiments were like arrows piercing the heart of the afflicted Mother. The Sacred Body now shed much blood from the nail wounds, which, by its weight and the shock of the Cross falling into the hole, had widened. They were the fountains, now opened up, to which Isaias invites us to hasten with joy to quench our thirst and wash off the stains of our sins (Is. 12, 3). No one shall be excused who does not quickly approach to drink of them.

Then they crucified also the two thieves and planted their crosses to the right and the left of the Savior; for thereby they wished to indicate that He deserved the most conspicuous place as being the greatest malefactor. The pharisees and priests, forgetting the two thieves, turned all the venom of their fury against the sinless and Holy One by nature. Wagging their heads in scorn and mockery (Matth. 27, 39) they threw stones and dirt at the Cross of the Lord and His Royal Person, saying: "Ah Thou, who destroyest the temple and in three days rebuildest it, save now Thyself; others He has made whole, Himself He cannot save; if this be the Son of God let Him descend from the Cross, and we will believe in Him" (Matth. 27, 42). The two thieves in the beginning also mocked the Lord and said: "If Thou art the Son of God, save Thyself and us." These blasphemies of the two thieves caused special sorrow to Our Lord, since they were so near to death and were losing the fruit of their death-pains, by which they could have satisfied in part for their justly punished crimes. Soon after, however, one of them availed himself of the greatest opportunity that a sinner ever had in this world, and was converted from his sins.

All the inanimate creatures, by Divine Will, obeyed the command of the Most Holy Mary. From the noon hour until three o'clock in the afternoon, which was called the ninth hour, when the Lord expired, they exhibited great disturbances and changes mentioned in the Gospels. The sun hid its light, the planets showed great alterations, the earth quaked, many mountains were rent; the rocks shook one against the other, the graves opened and sent forth some of the dead alive. The changes in the elements and in the whole universe were so notable and extraordinary that they were evident on the whole earth. All the Jews of Jerusalem were dismayed and astonished; although their outrageous perfidy and malice made them unworthy of the truth and hindered them from accepting what all the insensible creatures preached to them.

The soldiers who had crucified Jesus Our Savior, according to a custom permitting the executioners to take possession of the property of those whom they executed, now proceeded to divide the garments of the innocent Lamb. The cloak or outside mantle, which by Divine Disposition they had brought to Mount Calvary and which was the one Christ had laid aside at the washing of the feet, they divided among themselves, cutting it into four parts (John 19, 23). But the seamless tunic, by a Mysterious Decree of Providence they did not divide, but they drew lots and assigned it entirely to the one who drew the lot for it; thus fulfilling the prophecy in the twenty-first Psalm.

As the Wood of the Cross was the Throne of His Majesty and the Chair of the Doctrine of Life, and as He was now raised upon it, confirming His Doctrine by His example, Christ now uttered those words of highest charity and perfection: "Father, forgive them, for they know not what they do!" (Luke 23, 34.) This principle of charity and fraternal love the Divine Teacher had appropriated to Himself and proclaimed by His own lips (John 15, 12; Matth. 15, 44). He now confirmed and executed it upon the Cross, not only pardoning and loving His enemies, but excusing those under the plea of ignorance whose malice had reached the highest point possible to men in persecuting, blaspheming and crucifying their God and Redeemer. Such was the difference between the behavior of ungrateful men favored with so great enlightenment, instruction and blessing; and the behavior of Jesus in His most burning charity while suffering the Crown of Thorns, the Nails, and the Cross and unheard of blasphemy at the hands of men. O incomprehensible love! O ineffable sweetness! O patience inconceivable to man, admirable to the Angels and fearful to the devils! One of the two thieves, called Dismas, became aware of some of the mysteries. Being assisted at the same time by the prayers and intercession of Most Holy Mary, he was interiorly enlightened concerning his Rescuer and Master by the First Word on the Cross. Moved by true sorrow and contrition for his sins, he turned to his companion and said: "Neither dost thou fear God, seeing that thou art under the same condemnation? And we indeed justly, for we receive the due reward of our deeds; but this Man hath done no evil." And thereupon speaking to Jesus, he said: "Lord, remember me when Thou shalt come into Thy kingdom!" (Luke 23, 40.)

In this happiest of thieves, in the centurion, and in the others who confessed Jesus Christ on the Cross, began to appear the results of the Redemption. But the one most favored was this Dismas, who merited to hear the Second Word of the Savior on the Cross: "Amen, I say to thee, this day shalt thou be with Me in Paradise."

Having thus justified the good thief, Jesus turned His loving gaze upon His afflicted Mother, who with Saint John was standing at the Foot of the Cross. Speaking to both, he first addressed His Mother, saying: "Woman, behold thy son!" and then to the Apostle: "Behold thy Mother!" (John 19, 26.) The Lord called Her Woman and not Mother, because this name of Mother had in it something of sweetness and consolation, the very pronouncing of which would have been a sensible relief. During His Passion He would admit of no exterior consolation, having renounced for that time all exterior alleviation and easement, as I have mentioned above. By this word "woman" he tacitly and by implication wished to say: Woman blessed among all women, the most prudent among all the daughters of Adam, Woman, strong and constant, unconquered by any fault of Thy own, unfailing in My service and most faithful in Thy love toward Me, which even the mighty waters of My Passion could not extinguish or resist (Cant. 8, 7), I am going to My Father and cannot accompany Thee further; My Beloved Apostle will attend upon Thee and serve Thee as his Mother, and he will be Thy son. All this the Heavenly Queen understood. The Holy Apostle on his part received Her as his own from that hour on; for he was enlightened anew in order to understand and appreciate the greatest treasure of the Divinity in the whole creation next to the humanity of Christ Our Savior. In this light He reverenced and served Her for the rest of Her life, as I will relate farther on. Our Lady also accepted him as Her son in humble subjection and obedience.

Already the ninth hour of the day was approaching, although the darkness and confusion of nature made it appear to be rather a chaotic night. Our Savior spoke the Fourth Word from the Cross in a loud and strong voice, so that all the bystanders could hear it: "My God, My God, why hast Thou forsaken Me?" (Matth. 27, 46.) Although the Lord had uttered these words in His own Hebrew language, they were not understood by all. Since they began with: "Eli, eli," some of them thought He was calling upon Elias, and a number of them mocked Him saying: "Let us see whether Elias shall come to free Him from our hands?" He grieved that his copious and superabundant Redemption, offered for the whole human race, should not be efficacious in the reprobate and that He should find Himself deprived of them in the Eternal happiness, for which He had created and redeemed them. As this was to happen in consequence of the decree of His Father's Eternal Will, He lovingly and sorrowfully complained of it in the words: "My God, My God, why hast Thou forsaken Me?" that is, in so far as God deprived Him of the salvation of the reprobate.

In confirmation of this sorrow the Lord added: "I thirst!" The sufferings of the Lord and His anguish could easily cause a natural thirst. But for Him this was not a time to complain of this thirst or to quench it; and therefore Jesus would not have spoken of it so near to its expiration, unless in order to give expression to a most exalted mystery. He was thirsting to see the captive children of Adam make use of the liberty, which He merited for them and offered to them, and which so many were abusing. He was athirst with the anxious desire that all should correspond with Him in the faith and love due to Him, that they profit by His merits and sufferings, accept His friendship and grace now acquired for them, and that they should not lose the Eternal happiness which He was to leave as an inheritance to those that wished to merit and accept it. This was the thirst of our Savior and Master; and the Most Blessed Mary alone understood it perfectly and began, with ardent affection and charity, to invite and interiorly to call upon all the poor, the afflicted, the humble, the despised and downtrodden to approach their Savior and thus quench, at least in part, His thirst which they could not quench entirely. But the perfidious Jews and the executioners, evidencing their unhappy hard-heartedness, fastened a sponge soaked in gall and vinegar to a reed and mockingly raised it to His mouth, in order that He might drink of it. Thus was fulfilled the prophecy of David: "In My thirst they gave me vinegar to drink" (John 16, 28; Ps. 68, 22).

In connection with this same mystery the Savior then pronounced the Sixth Word: "Consummatum est," "It is consummated" (John 19, 29). Now is consummated this work of My coming from Heaven and I have obeyed the command of My Eternal Father, who sent Me to suffer and die for the salvation of mankind. Now are fulfilled the Holy Scriptures, the prophecies and figures of the Old Testament, and the course of My earthly and mortal life assumed in the womb of My Mother. Now are established on earth My example, My doctrines, My Sacraments and My remedies for the sickness of sin. Now is appeased the justice of My Eternal Father in regard to the debt of the children of

141

Adam. Now is My Holy Church enriched with the remedies for the sins committed by men; the whole work of My coming into the world is perfected in so far as concerns Me, its Restorer; the secure foundation of the triumphant Church is now laid in the Church militant, so that nothing can overthrow or change it. These are the mysteries contained in the few words: "Consummatum est."

Having finished and established the work of Redemption in all its perfection, it was becoming that the Incarnate Word, just as He came forth from the Father to enter mortal life (John 16, 8), should enter into immortal life of the Father through death. Therefore Christ Our Savior added the last words uttered by Him: "Father, into Thy hands I commend My spirit." The Lord spoke these words in a loud and strong voice, so that the bystanders heard them. In pronouncing them He raised His eyes to Heaven, as one speaking with the Eternal Father, and with the last accent He gave up His spirit and inclined His head. By the Divine force of these words Lucifer with all his demons were hurled into the deepest caverns of hell, there they lay motionless, as I shall relate in the next chapter. The invincible Queen and Mistress of all virtues understood these mysteries beyond the understanding of all creatures, as She was the Mother of the Savior and the Coadjutrix of His Passion. In order that She might participate in it to the end, just as She had felt in Her own body the other torments of Her Son, She now, though remaining alive, felt and suffered the pangs and agony of His death. She did not die in reality; but this was because God miraculously preserved Her life, when according to the natural course death should have followed. This miraculous aid was more wonderful than all the other favors She received during the Passion. For this last pain was more intense and penetrating; and all that the martyrs and the men sentenced to death have suffered from the beginning of the world cannot equal what the Blessed Mary suffered during the Passion. The Great Lady remained at the Foot of the Cross until evening, when the Sacred Body (as I shall relate) was interred. But in return for this last anguish of death, all that was still of this mortal life in the virginal body of the purest Mother, was more than ever exalted and spiritualized.

My Daughter, seek with all the powers of thy mind during thy whole life to remember the mysteries manifested to thee in this chapter. I, as thy Mother and thy Instructress, shall ask the Lord by His Divine Power to impress in thy heart the knowledge, which I have vouchsafed thee, in order that it may remain fixed and ever present to thee as long as thou livest. In virtue of this blessing keep in thy memory Christ crucified, who is My Divine Son and thy Spouse, and never forget the sufferings of the Cross and the doctrine taught by Him upon it. This is the mirror by which thou must arrange all thy adornments and the source from which thou art to draw thy interior beauty, like a true daughter of the Prince (Ps. 44, 14), in order that thou mayest be prepared, proceed and reign as the spouse of the Supreme King. As this honorable title obliges thee to seek with all thy power to imitate Him as far as is becoming thy station and possible to thee by His grace, and as this is to be the true fruit of My doctrine, I wish that from today on thou live crucified with Christ, entirely assimilated to thy exemplar and model and dead to this earthly life (II Cor. 5, 15).

MARY THE HEIRESS OF THE MERITS OF CHRIST.

Of many of the Sacraments and mysteries connected with the doings of Christ Our Savior on the Cross the Evangelists make no mention; and we as Catholics can only form prudent conjectures founded upon the infallible certainty of our faith. But among those which have been manifested to me in this history, and concerning this part of the Passion, is a prayer, which Christ addressed to His Eternal Father before speaking the seven words on the Cross recorded by the Evangelists. I call it a prayer because it was addressed to the Father; but in reality it was a last bequest or testament, which He made as a true and most wise Father in order to consign His possessions to His family, that is, to the whole human race. Even natural reason teaches us, that he who is the head of a family or the lord over many or few possessions, would not be a prudent dispenser of his goods, and inattentive to his office or dignity, if at the hour of his death he would not make known his will in regard to the disposition of his goods and his estate, in order that each one of his family may know what belongs to him and may possess it justly and peacefully without recourse to lawsuits. Although earthly things could not disturb Our Savior, since He neither possessed them, nor, if He had possessed any, could He be embarrassed by them in His infinite power; yet it was fitting, that He should in that hour dispose of the spiritual riches and treasures which He had amassed for mankind in the course of His pilgrimage.

Of these Eternal goods the Saviour made His last disposition on the Cross, distributing them and pointing out those who should be legitimate heirs and those who should be disinherited, and mentioning the reasons for the one as well as the other. All this He did in conference with His Eternal Father, as the Supreme Lord and Most Just Judge of all creatures; for in this testament are rehearsed the mysteries of the predestination of the Saints and of the reprobation of the wicked. It was a testament hidden and sealed for mankind; only the Blessed Mary understood it, because, in addition to Her being informed of the operations of the Divine Soul of Christ, She was also to be the Universal Heiress of all creation. As She was the Coadjutrix of Salvation, She was also to be the testamentary Executrix. For the Son placed all things in Her hands, just as the Father had assigned the whole creation to Him. She was to execute His will and She was to distribute all the treasures acquired and due to Her Son as God on account of His infinite merits. This understanding has been given me as part of this history for the exaltation of Our Queen and in order that sinners might approach Her as the Custodian of all the treasures gained by Her Son and Our Redeemer in the sight of His Eternal Father. All help and assistance is in the hands of Most Holy Mary and She is to distribute it according to Her most sweet kindness and liberality.

When the Holy Wood of the Cross had been raised on Mount Calvary, bearing aloft with it the Incarnate Word crucified before speaking any of the seven words, Christ prayed interiorly to His Heavenly Father and said: "My Father and Eternal God, I confess and magnify Thee from this tree of the Cross, and I offer Thee a sacrifice of praise in My Passion and Death; for, by the hypostatic union with the Divine Nature, Thou hast raised My humanity to the highest dignity, that of Christ, the Godman, anointed with Thy own Divinity. I confess Thee on account of the plenitude of the

144

highest possible graces and glory, which from the first instant of My Incarnation Thou hast communicated to My humanity, and because from all eternity up to this present hour Thou hast consigned to Me full dominion of the universe both in the order of grace and of nature. Thou hast made Me the Lord of the heavens and of the elements (Matth. 28, 18), of the sun, the moon and the stars; of fire and air, of the earth and the sea, of all the animate and inanimate creatures therein; Thou hast made Me the Disposer of the seasons, of the days and nights, with full lordship and possession according to My free will, and Thou hast set Me as the Head, the King and Lord of all Angels and men (Ephes. 1, 21), to govern and command them, to punish the wicked and to reward the good (John 5, 22); Thou hast given Me the dominion and power of disposing all things from highest heavens to deepest abysses of hell (Apoc. 20, 1). Thou hast placed in My hands the Eternal justification of men, the empires, kingdoms and principalities, the great and the little, the rich and the poor; and of all that are capable of Thy grace and glory, Thou hast made Me the Justifier, the Redeemer and Glorifier, the Universal Lord of all the human race, of life and death, of the Holy Church, its treasures, laws and blessings of grace: all hast Thou, My Father, consigned to My hands, subjected to My will and My decrees, and for this I confess, exalt and magnify Thy holy name."

"Now, at this moment, My Lord and Eternal Father, when I am returning from this world to Thy right hand through this death on the Cross, by which I completed the task of the Redemption of men assigned to Me, I desire that this same Cross shall be the tribunal of Our justice and mercy. Nailed to it, I desire to judge those for whom I give My life. Having justified My cause, I wish to dispense the treasures of my coming into the world and of My Passion and Death to the just and the reprobate according as each one merits by his works of love or hatred. I have sought to gain all mortals and invited them to partake of My friendship and grace; from the first moment of My Incarnation I have ceaselessly labored for them; I have borne inconveniences, fatigues, insults, ignominies, reproaches, scourges, a crown of thorns, and now suffer the bitter death of the Cross; I have implored Thy vast kindness upon all of them; I have watched in prayer, fasted and wandered about teaching them the way of Eternal Life.

145

As far as in Me lay I have sought to secure Eternal happiness for all men, just as I merited it for all, without excluding any one. I have established and built up the law of grace and have firmly and forever established the Church in which all human beings can be saved."

"But in our knowledge and foresight We are aware, My God and Father, that on account of their malice and rebellious obstinacy not all men desire to accept Our Eternal Salvation, nor avail themselves of Our mercy and of the way I have opened to them by My labors, life and death; but that many will prefer to follow their sinful ways unto perdition. Thou art just, My Lord and Father, and most equitable are Thy judgments (Ps. 68, 137); and therefore it is right, since Thou hast made Me the Judge of the living and the dead, of the good and the bad (Act 10, 3), that I give to the good the reward of having served and followed Me, and to sinners the chastisement of their perverse obstinacy; that the just should share in My goods, and the wicked be deprived of the inheritance, which they refuse to accept. Now then, My Eternal Father, in My and Thy name and for Thy glorification, I make My last bequest according to My human will, which is conformable to Thy Eternal and Divine Will. First shall be mentioned My Most Pure Mother, who gave Me human existence; Her I constitute My sole and universal Heiress of all the gifts of Nature, of Grace and of Glory that are Mine. She shall be Mistress and Possessor of them all. The gifts of Grace, of which as a mere creature She is capable, She shall actually receive now, while those of Glory I promise to confer upon Her in their time. I desire that She shall be Mistress of Angels and men, claim over them full possession and dominion and command the service and obedience of all. The demons shall fear Her and be subject to Her. All the irrational creatures, the heavens, the stars, the planets, the elements with all the living beings, the birds, the fishes and the animals contained in them, shall likewise be subject to Her and acknowledge Her as Mistress, exalting and glorifying Her with Me. I wish also that She be the Treasurer and Dispenser of all the goods in Heaven and on earth. Whatever She ordains and disposes in My Church for My children, the sons of men, shall be confirmed by the Three Divine Persons; and whatever She shall ask for mortals now, afterwards and forever, We shall concede according to Her will and wishes."

"To the Holy Angels, who have obeyed Thy Holy and Just

146

Will, I assign as habitation the highest heavens as their proper and Eternal abode, and with it the joys of Eternal Vision and fruition of our Divinity. I desire that they enjoy its everlasting possession together with Our company and friendship. I decree, that they recognize My Mother as their legitimate Queen and Lady, that they serve Her, accompany and attend upon Her, bear Her up in their hands in all places and times, obeying Her in all that She wishes to ordain and command. The demons, rebellious to Our perfect and Holy Will, I cast out and deprive of Our vision and company; again do I condemn them to Our abhorrence, to Eternal loss of Our friendship and glory, to privation of the vision of My Mother, of the Saints and of My friends, the just. I appoint and assign to them as their Eternal dwelling the place most remote from Our royal throne, namely the infernal caverns, the centre of the earth, deprived of light and full of the horrors of sensible darkness (Jude 6). I decree this to be their portion and inheritance, as chosen by them in their pride and obstinacy against the Divine Being and decrees. In those Eternal dungeons of darkness they shall be tormented by everlasting and inextinguishable fire."

"From the multitudes of men, in the fulness of My good will, I call, select and separate all the just and the predestined, who through My grace save themselves by imitating Me, doing My will and obeying My Holy Law. These, next to My Most Pure Mother, I appoint as the inheritors of all My mysteries, My blessings, My sacramental treasures, of the mysteries concealed in the Holy Scriptures; of My humility, meekness of heart; of the virtues of faith, hope, and charity; of prudence, justice, fortitude and temperance; of My Divine gifts and favors; of My Cross, labors, contempt, poverty and nakedness. This shall be their portion and inheritance in this present and mortal life. Since they must choose these in order to labor profitably, I assign to them the trials I have chosen for Myself in this life, as a pledge of My friendship, in order that they may undergo them with joy. I offer them My protection and defense, My holy inspirations, My favors and powerful assistance, My blessings and My justification, according to each one's disposition and degree of love. I promise to be to them a Father, a Brother and a Friend, and they shall be My chosen and beloved children, and as such I appoint them as the inheritors of all My merits and treasures without limitation. I desire that all who dispose themselves,

147

shall partake of the goods of My Holy Church and of the Sacraments; that, if they should lose My friendship, they shall be able to restore themselves and recover My graces and blessings through My cleansing blood. For all of them shall be open the intercession of My Mother and of the Saints, and She shall recognize them as Her children, shielding them and holding them as Her own. My Angels shall defend them, guide them, protect them and bear them up in their hands lest they stumble, and if they fall, they shall help them to rise" (Ps. 90, 11, 12).

"Likewise it is My will that My just and chosen ones shall stand high above the reprobate and the demons, that they shall be feared and obeyed by My enemies; that all the rational and irrational creatures shall serve them; that all the influences of the heavens, the planets and the stars shall favor them and give them life; that the earth, its elements and animals, shall sustain them; all the creatures, that are mine and serve Me, shall be theirs, and shall serve also them as My children and friends (I Cor. 3, 22; Wis. 16, 24), and their blessing shall be in the dew of heaven and in the fruits of the earth (Genes. 27, 28). I wish to hold with them My delights (Pros. 8, 31), communicate to them My secrets, converse with them intimately and live with them in the militant Church in the species of bread and wine, as an earnest and an infallible pledge of the Eternal happiness and glory promised to them; of it, I make them partakers and heirs, in order that they may enjoy it with Me in heaven by perpetual right and in unfailing beatitude."

"I consent that the foreknown and reprobate (though they were created for another and much higher end), shall be permitted to possess as their portion and inheritance the concupiscence of the flesh and the eyes (John 1, 2-16), pride in all its effects; that they eat and be satisfied with the dust of the earth, namely, with riches; with the fumes and the corruption of the flesh and its delights, and with the vanity and presumption of the world. For such possessions have they labored, and applied all the diligence of their mind and body; in such occupations have they consumed their powers, their gifts and blessings bestowed upon them by Us, and they have of their own free will chosen deceit, despising the truth I have taught them in the Holy law (Rom. 2, 8). They have rejected the law which I have written in their hearts and the one inspired by My grace; they have despised My teachings and My blessings, and listened to My and their own enemies; they have accepted their deceits, have loved vanity (Ps. 4, 3), wrought injustice, followed their ambitions, sought their delight in vengeance, persecuted the poor, humiliated the just, mocked the simple and the innocent, strove to exalt themselves and desired to be raised above all the cedars of Lebanon in following the laws of injustice" (Ps. 36, 35).

"Since they have done all this in opposition to Our Divine goodness and remained obstinate in their malice, and since they have renounced the rights of sonship merited for them by Me, I disinherit them of My friendship and glory. Just as Abraham separated the children of the slave, setting aside some possessions for them and reserving the principal heritage for Isaac, the son of the freedwoman Sarah (Gen. 25, 5), thus I set aside their claims on My inheritance by giving them the transitory goods, which they themselves have chosen. Separating them from Our company and from that of My Mother, of the Angels and Saints, I condemn them to the Eternal dungeons and the fire of hell in the company of Lucifer and his demons, whom they have freely served, I deprive them forever of all hope of relief. This is, O My Father, the sentence which I pronounce as the Head and the Judge of men and angels (Eph. 4, 15; Col. 2, 10), and this is the testament made at my Death, this is the effect of My Redemption, whereby each one is rewarded with that which he has justly merited according to his works and according to Thy incomprehensible wisdom in the equity of Thy strictest justice" (II Tim. 4, 8). Such was the prayer of Christ Our Savior on the Cross to His Eternal Father. It was sealed and deposited in the heart of the Most Holy Mary as the mysterious and sacramental testament, in order that through Her intercession and solicitous care it might at its time, and even from that moment, be executed in the Church, just as it had before this time been prepared and perfected by the wise providence of God, in whom all the past and the future is always one with the present.

THE VICTORY OF CHRIST OVER HELL.

The hidden and venerable mysteries of this chapter correspond to many others scattered through the whole extent of this history. One of them is, that Lucifer and his demons in the course of the life and miracles of Our Savior, never could

149

ascertain fully whether the Lord was True God and Redeemer of the world, and consequently what was the dignity of the Most Holy Mary. This was so disposed by Divine Providence, in order that the whole mystery of the Incarnation and the Redemption of the human race might be more fittingly accomplished. Lucifer, although knowing that God was to assume human flesh, nevertheless knew nothing of the manner and the circumstances of the Incarnation. As he was permitted to form an opinion of this mystery in accordance with his pride, he was full of hallucinations, sometimes believing Christ to be God on account of His miracles, sometimes rejecting such an opinion on account of seeing Him poor, humiliated, afflicted and fatigued. Harassed by these contradicting evidences, he remained in doubt and continued his inquiries until the predestined hour of Christ's Death on the Cross, where, in virtue of the Passion and Death of the Sacred humanity, which he had himself brought about, he was to be both undeceived and vanquished by the full solution of these mysteries.

Lucifer and his demons, as soon as they saw the Lord taking the Cross upon His Sacred shoulders, wished to fly and cast themselves into hell; for at that moment they began to feel with greater force the operations of His Divine Power. By Divine intervention this new torment made them aware that the Death of this innocent Man, whose destruction they had plotted and who could not be a mere man, threatened great ruin to themselves. They therefore desired to withdraw and they ceased to incite the Jews and the executioners, as they had done hitherto. But the command of the Most Blessed Mary, enforced by the Divine Power, detained them and, enchained like fiercest dragons, compelled them to accompany Christ to Calvary. The ends of the mysterious chain that bound them were placed into the hands of Mary, the great Queen, who, by the power of Her Divine Son, held them all in subjection and bondage. Although they many times sought to break away and raged in helpless fury, they could not overcome the power of the Heavenly Lady. She forced them to come to Calvary and stand around the Cross, where She commanded them to remain motionless and witness the end of the great mysteries there enacted for the salvation of men and the ruin of themselves.

Lucifer and his infernal hosts were so overwhelmed with pains and torments by the presence of the Lord and His

Blessed Mother, and with the fear of their impending ruin, that they would have felt greatly relieved to be allowed to cast themselves into the darkness of hell. As this was not permitted them, they fell upon one another and furiously fought with each other like hornets disturbed in their nest, or like a brood of vermin confusedly seeking some dark shelter. But their rabid fury was not that of animals, but that of demons more cruel than dragons.

The time had now come for this ancient dragon to be vanquished by the Master of life. As this was to be the hour of his disillusionment, and as this poisonous asp was not to escape it by stopping his ears to the voice of the Enchanter (Ps. 57, 5), the Lord began to speak the seven words from His Cross, at the same time providing that Lucifer and his demons should understand the mysteries therein contained. For it was by this disclosure that the Lord wished to triumph over them, over sin and death, and despoil them of their tyrannous power over the human race. The Savior then pronounced the first word: "Father, forgive them, for they know not what they do!" (Luke 23, 34). By these words the princes of darkness came to the full conviction, that Christ Our Lord was speaking to the Eternal Father, that He was His natural Son and the true God with Him and the Holy Ghost, that He had permitted death in His Most Sacred and perfect humanity, united to the Divinity for the salvation of the whole human race; that now He offered His infinitely precious merits for the pardon of the sins of all those children of Adam, who should avail themselves thereof for their rescue, not excepting even the wretches that crucified Him. At this discovery Lucifer and his demons were thrown into such fury and despair that they instantly wished to hurl themselves impetuously to the depths of hell and strained all their powers to accomplish it in spite of the powerful Queen.

In the second word spoken by the Lord to the fortunate thief: "Amen I say to thee, today thou shalt be with Me in paradise," the demons understood that the fruits of the Redemption in the justification of sinners ended in the glorification of the just. They were made aware that from this hour the merits of Christ would commence to act with a new force and strength, that through them should be opened the gates of Paradise, which had been closed by the first sin, and that from now on men would enter upon Eternal happiness and occupy their destined heavenly seats, which until now had been impossible for them. They perceived the power of Christ to call sinners, justify and beautify them, and they felt the triumphs gained over themselves by the exalted virtues, the humility, patience, meekness and all the virtues of His life. The confusion and torment of Lucifer at seeing this cannot be explained by human tongue; but it was so great, that he humiliated himself so far as to beg the Most Blessed Virgin to permit them to descend into hell and be cast out from Her presence; but the Great Queen would not consent, as the time had not yet arrived.

At the third word spoken by the Lord to His Mother: "Woman, behold Thy son!" the demons discovered that this Heavenly Lady was the True Mother of the Godman, the same Woman whose likeness and prophetic sign had been shown to them in the heavens at their creation, and who was to crush their head as announced by the Lord in the terrestrial paradise. They were informed of the dignity and excellence of this Great Lady over all creatures, and of Her power which they were even now experiencing. As they had from the beginning of the world and from the creation of the first woman, used all their astuteness to find out who this great woman that was announced in the heavens could be, and as they now discovered Her in Mary, whom they had until now overlooked, these dragons were seized with inexpressible fury; their having been thus mistaken crushed their arrogance beyond all their other torments, and in their fury they raged against their own selves like bloodthirsty lions, while their helpless wrath against the Heavenly Lady was increased a thousandfold. Moreover, they discerned that Saint John was appointed by Christ Our Lord as the Angel Guardian of His Mother, endowed with the powers of the priesthood. This they understood to be in the nature of a threat against their own wrath, which was well known to Saint John. Lucifer saw not only the power of the Evangelist, but that given to all the priests in virtue of their participation in the dignity and power of Our Redeemer; and that the rest of the just, even though no priests, were placed under the special protection of the Lord and made powerful against Hell. All this paralyzed the strength of Lucifer and his demons.

The fourth word of Christ was addressed to the Eternal Father: "God, My God, why hast Thou forsaken Me?" The evil spirits discovered in these words that the charity of God toward men was boundless and everlasting; that, in order to satisfy it, He had mysteriously suspended the influence of the Divinity over His Most Sacred Humanity, thus permitting His sufferings to reach the highest degree and to draw from them the most abundant fruits; that He was aware and lovingly complained of His being deprived of the salvation of a part of the human race; how ready He was to suffer more, if such would be ordained by the Eternal Father. Man's good fortune in being so beloved by God increased the envy of Lucifer and his demons, and they foresaw the Divine Omnipotence following out this immense love without limitation. This knowledge crushed the haughty malice of the enemies and they were made well aware of their own weakness and helplessness in opposing this love, if men themselves should not choose to neglect its influence.

The fifth word of Christ, "I thirst," confirmed Christ's triumph over the devil and his followers; they were filled with wrath and fury because the Lord clearly let them see their total overthrow. By these words they understood Him to say to them: If what I suffer for men and My love for them seem great to you, be assured that My love for them is still unsatiated, that it continues to long for their Eternal salvation, and that the mighty waters of torments and sufferings have not extinguished it (Cant. 8, 7). Much more would I suffer for them, if it were necessary, in order to deliver them from your tyranny and make them powerful and strong against your malice and pride.

In the sixth word of the Lord: "It is consummated!" Lucifer and his hordes were informed that the Mystery of the Incarnation and Redemption was now accomplished and entirely perfected according to the decree of Divine wisdom. For they were made to feel that Christ Our Redeemer had obediently fulfilled the Will of the Eternal Father; that He had accomplished all the promises and prophecies made to the world by the ancient Fathers; that His humility and obedience had compensated for their own pride and disobedience in Heaven in not having subjected themselves and acknowledged Him as their Superior in human flesh; and that they were now through the wisdom of God justly humbled and vanquished by the very Lord whom they despised. The great dignity and the infinite merits of Christ demanded that in this very hour He should exercise His office and power of Judge over Angels and men, such as had been conceded to

Him by the Eternal Father. He now applied this power by hurling this sentence at Lucifer and all his followers, that, being condemned to Eternal fire, they instantly depart into the deepest dungeons of hell. This very sentence was included in the pronouncing of the seventh word: "Father, into Thy hands I commend My spirt!" (Luke 23, 46.) The Mighty Queen and Mother concurred with the will of Her Son Jesus and united with His Her command that Lucifer and all demons depart to the infernal depths. In virtue of these decrees of the Supreme King and of the Queen, the evil spirits were routed from Calvary and precipitated to deepest hell more violently and suddenly than a flash of light through the riven clouds.

The rout of Lucifer and his angels from Calvary to the abyss of hell was more violent and disastrous than their first expulsion from heaven. Though, as holy Job says (Job 10, 21), that place is a land of darkness, covered with the shades of death, full of gloomy disorder, misery, torments and confusion; yet on this occasion the chaos and disorder was a thousandfold increased; because the damned were made to feel new horror and additional punishments at the sudden meeting of the ferocious demons in their rabid fury. It is certain that the devils have not the power of assigning the damned to a place of greater or lesser torment; for all their torments are decreed by Divine justice according to the measure of the demerits of each of the condemned.

As soon as Lucifer was permitted to proceed in these matters and arise from the consternation in which he remained for some time, he set about proposing to his fellow-demons new plans of his pride. For this purpose he called them all together and placing himself in an elevated position, he spoke to them: "To you, who have for so many ages followed and still follow my standards for the vengeance of my wrongs, is known the injury which I have now sustained at the hands of this Mangod, and how for thirty-three years He has led me about in deceit, hiding His Divinity and concealing the operations of His soul, and how He has now triumphed over us by the very Death which we have brought upon Him. Before He assumed flesh I hated Him and refused to acknowledge Him as being more worthy than I to be adored by the rest of creation. Although on account of this resistance I was cast out from Heaven with you and was degraded to this abominable condition so unworthy of my

154

greatness and former beauty, I am even more tormented to see myself thus vanquished and oppressed by this Man and by His Mother. From the day on which the first man was created I have sleeplessly sought to find Them and destroy Them; or if I should not be able to destroy Them, I at least wished to bring destruction upon all his creatures and induce them not to acknowledge Him as their God, and that none of them should ever draw any benefit from His works. This has been my intent, to this all my solicitude and efforts were directed. But in vain, since He has overcome me by his humility and poverty, crushed me by his patience, and at last has despoiled me of the sovereignty of the world by His Passion and frightful Death. This causes me such an excruciating pain, that, even if I succeeded in hurling Him from the right hand of His Father, where He sits triumphant, and if I should draw all the souls redeemed down into this hell, my wrath would not be satiated or my fury placated."

"Is it possible that the human nature, so inferior to my own, shall be exalted above all the creatures! That it should be so loved and favored, as to be united to the Creator in the person of the Eternal World! That He should first make war upon me before executing this work, and afterwards overwhelm me with such confusion! From the beginning I have held this humanity as my greatest enemy; it has always filled me with intolerable abhorrence. O men, so favored and gifted by your God, whom I abhor, and so ardently loved by Him! How shall I hinder your good fortune? How shall I bring upon you my unhappiness, since I cannot destroy the existence you have received? What shall we now begin, O my followers? How shall we restore our reign? How shall we recover our power over men? How shall we overcome them? For if men from now on shall not be most senseless and ungrateful, if they are not worse disposed than we ourselves toward this Godman, who has redeemed them with so much love, it is clear that all of them will eagerly follow Him; none will take notice of our deceits; they will abhor the honors which we insidiously offer them, and will love contempt; they will seek the mortification of the flesh and will discover the danger of carnal pleasure and ease; they will despise riches and treasures, and love the poverty so much honored by their Master; and all that we can offer to their appetites they will abhor in imitation of their True Redeemer. Thus will our reign be destroyed, since no one will be added to our number in this

155

place of confusion and torments; all will reach the happiness which we have lost, all will humiliate themselves to the dust and suffer with patience; and my wrath and haughtiness will avail me nothing."

"Ah, woe is me, what torment does this mistake cause me! When I tempted Him in the desert, the only result was to afford Him a chance to leave the example of this victory, by following which men can overcome me so much the more easily. My persecutions only brought out more clearly His doctrine of humility and patience. In persuading Judas to betray Him, and the Jews to subject Him to the deadly torture of the Cross, I merely hastened my ruin and the salvation of men, while the doctrine I sought to blot out was only the more firmly implanted. How could One who is God humiliate Himself to such an extent? How could He bear so much from men who are evil? How could I myself have been led to assist so much in making this salvation so copious and wonderful? O how Godlike is the power of that Man which could torment and weaken me so? And how can this Woman, His Mother and my Enemy, be so mighty and invincible in Her opposition to me? New is such power in a mere creature, and no doubt She derived it from the Divine Word, whom She clothed in human flesh. Through this Woman the Almighty has ceaselessly waged war against me, though I have hated Her in my pride from the moment I recognized Her in Her image or heavenly sign. But if my proud indignation is not to be assuaged, I benefit nothing by my perpetual war against this Redeemer, against His Mother and against men. Now then, ye demons who follow me, now is the time to give way to our wrath against God. Come all of ye to take counsel what we are to do; for I desire to hear your opinions."

Some of the principal demons gave their answers to this dreadful proposal, encouraging Lucifer by suggesting diverse schemes for hindering the fruit of the Redemption among men. They all agreed that it was not possible to injure the person of Christ, to diminish the immense value of His merits, to destroy the efficacy of the Sacraments, to falsify or abolish the doctrine which Christ had preached; yet they resolved that, in accordance with the new order of assistance and favor established by God for the salvation of men, they should now seek new ways of hindering and preventing the work of God by so much the greater deceits and temptations.

In reference to these plans some of the astute and malicious demons said: "It is true, that men now have at their disposal a new and very powerful doctrine and law, new and efficacious Sacraments, a new Model and Instructor of virtues, a powerful Intercessor and Advocate in this Woman; yet the natural inclinations and passions of the flesh remain just the same, and the sensible and delectable creatures have not changed their nature. Let us then, making use of this situation with increased astuteness, foil as far as in us lies the effects of what this Godman has wrought for men. Let us begin strenuous warfare against mankind by suggesting new attractions, exciting them to follow their passions in forgetfulness of all else. Thus men, being taken up with these dangerous things, cannot attend to the contrary."

Acting upon this counsel they redistributed the spheres of work among themselves, in order that each squadron of demons might, with a specialized astuteness, tempt men to different vices. They resolved to continue to propagate idolatry in the world, so that men might not come to the knowledge of the True God and the Redemption. Wherever idolatry would fail, they concluded to establish sects and heresies, for which they would select the most perverse and depraved of the human race as leaders and teachers of error. Then and there was concocted among these malignant spirits the sect of Mahomet, the heresies of Arius, Pelagius, Nestorius, and whatever other heresies have been started in the world from the first ages of the Church until now, together with those which they have in readiness, but which it is neither necessary nor proper to mention here. Lucifer showed himself content with these infernal counsels as being opposed to Divine truth and destructive of the very foundation of man's rescue, namely Divine faith. He lavished flattering praise and high offices upon those demons, who showed themselves willing and who undertook to find the impious orginators of these errors.

Some of the devils charged themselves with perverting the inclinations of children at their conception and birth; others to induce parents to be negligent in the education and instruction of their children, either through an inordinate love or aversion, and to cause a hatred of parents among the children. Some offered to create hatred between husbands and wives, to place them in the way of adultery, or to think little of the fidelity promised to their conjugal partners. All agreed to sow among men the seeds of discord, hatred and vengeance, proud and sensual thoughts, desire of riches or honors, and by suggesting sophistical reasons against all the virtues Christ has taught; above all they intended to weaken the remembrance of His Passion and Death, of the means of salvation, and of the Eternal pains of hell. By these means the demons hoped to burden all the powers and the faculties of men with solicitude for earthly affairs and sensual pleasures, leaving them little time for spiritual thoughts and their own salvation.

Lucifer heard these different suggestions of the demons, and answering them, he said: "I am much beholden to you for your opinions: I approve of them and adopt them all; it will be easy to put them into practice with those, who do not profess the law given by this Redeemer to men, though with those who accept and embrace these laws, it will be a difficult enterprise. But against this law and against those that follow it, I intend to direct all my wrath and fury and I shall most bitterly persecute those who hear the doctrine of this Redeemer and become His Disciples; against these must our most relentless battle be waged to the end of the world. In this new Church I must strive to sow my cockle (Matth. 14, 25), the ambitions, the avarice, the sensuality, and the deadly hatreds, with all the other vices, of which I am the head. For if once these sins multiply and increase among the faithful, they will, with their concomitant malice and ingratitude, irritate God and justly deprive men of the helps of grace left to them by the merits of the Redeemer. If once they have thus despoiled themselves of these means of salvation, we shall have assured victory over them. We must also exert ourselves to weaken piety and all that is Spiritual and Divine; so that they do not realize the power of the Sacraments and receive them in mortal sin, or at least without fervor and devotion. For since these Sacraments are spiritual, it is necessary to receive them with well-disposed will, in order to reap their fruits. If once they despise the medicine, they shall languish in their sickness and be less able to withstand our temptations; they will not see through our deceits, they will let the memory of their Redeemer and of the intercession of His Mother slip from their minds. Thus will their foul ingratitude make them unworthy of grace and so irritate their God and Savior, as to deprive them of His helps. In all this I wish, that all of you assist me strenuously, losing neither time nor occasion for executing my commands."

It is not possible to rehearse all the schemes of this dragon and his allies concocted at that time against the Holy Church and her children, in order that these waters of Jordan might be swallowed up in his throat (Job 40, 18). It is enough to state that they spent nearly a full year after the Death of Christ in conferring and considering among themselves the state of the world up to that time and the changes wrought by Christ our God and Master through His Death and after having manifested the light of His faith by so many miracles, blessings and examples of holy men. If all these labors have not sufficed to draw all men to the way of salvation, it can be easily understood, that Lucifer should have prevailed and that his wrath should be so great, as to cause us justly to say with Saint John: "Woe to the earth, for satan is come down to you full of wrath and fury!" But alas! that truths so infallible and so much to be dreaded and avoided by men, should in our days be blotted from the minds of mortals to the irreparable danger of the whole world! Our enemy is astute, cruel and watchful: we sleepy, lukewarm and careless! What wonder that Lucifer has intrenched himself so firmly in the world, when so many listen to him, accept and follow his deceits, so few resist him, and entirely forget the Eternal death, which he so furiously and maliciously seeks to draw upon them? I beseech those, who read this, not to forget this dreadful danger. If they are not convinced of this danger through the evil condition of the world and through the evils each one experiences himself, let them at least learn of this danger by the vast and powerful remedies and helps, which the Savior thought it necessary to leave behind in His Church. For He would not have provided such antidotes if our ailment and danger of Eternal death were not so great and formidable.

WORDS OF THE QUEEN.

This close imitation and living reproduction of Christ, confronting the demons in the first children of the Church, they feared so much, that they dared not approach and they precipitously fled from the Apostles and the just ones imbued with the doctrines of My Divine Son. In them were offered up to the Almighty the first fruits of grace, and of Redemption. What is seen in the Saints and in perfect Christians in

159

those times, would happen in the present times with all the Catholics if they would accept grace and work with it instead of permitting it to go to waste, and if they would seek the Way of the Cross; for Lucifer fears it just as much now as in the times thou hast been writing of. But soon the charity, zeal and devotion in many of the faithful began to grow cold and they forgot the blessings of the Redemption; they yielded to their carnal inclinations and desires, they loved vanity and avarice, and permitted themselves to be fascinated and deceived by the false pretenses of Lucifer, obscuring the glory of their Savior and inveigling them into the meshes of their mortal enemies. This foul ingratitude has thrown the world into the present state and has encouraged the demons to rise up in their pride against God, audaciously presuming to possess themselves of all the children of Adam on account of this forgetfulness and carelessness of Catholics. They presume to plot the destruction of the whole Church by the perversion of so many who have fallen away from it; and by inducing those who are in it, to think little of it, or by hindering them from producing the fruits of the blood and death of their Redeemer. The greatest misfortune is, that many Catholics fail to recognize this great damage and do not seriously think of a remedy, although they can presume that the times, of which Jesus forewarned the women of Jerusalem, have arrived; namely, those in which the sterile should be happy, and in which many would call upon the mountains and the hills to cover and fall upon them, in order not to see the devastation of wickedness cutting down the sons of perdition, the dried trees, barren of all the fruits of virtue.

THE SIDE OF CHRIST IS OPENED WITH A LANCE AS HIS BODY HANGS ON THE CROSS; HE IS TAKEN DOWN AND BURIED

The Evangelist Saint John tells us that near the Cross stood Mary, the Most Holy Mother of Jesus, with Mary Cleophas and Mary Magdalen. Although this is said of the time before Jesus expired, it must be understood, that the Unconquerable Queen remained also afterwards, always standing beneath the Cross and adoring Her Dead Jesus and His Divinity inseparably united to his Sacred Body. But now She was especially solicitous for the burial of the Sacred

Body of Her Divine Son and how to procure some one to take It down from the Cross.

She soon saw an armed band approaching Calvary; and in Her dread of some new outrage against the Deceased Savior, She spoke to Saint John and the pious women: "Alas, now shall My affliction reach its utmost and transfix My heart! Is it not possible, that the executioners and the Jews are not yet satisfied with having put to death My Son and Lord? Shall they now heap more injury upon His Dead body?" It was the evening of the great Sabbath of the Jews, and in order to celebrate it with unburdened minds, they had asked Pilate for permission to shatter the limbs of the three men sentenced, so that, their death being hastened, they might be taken from the crosses and not be left on them for the following day. With this intent the company of soldiers, which Mary now saw, had come to Mount Calvary. As they perceived the two thieves still alive, they broke their limbs and so hastened their end (John 19, 31). But when they examined Jesus they found Him already dead, and therefore did not break His bones, thus fulfilling the mysterious prophecy in Exodus (Ex. 12, 46), commanding that no bones be broken in the Figurative Lamb to be eaten for the Pasch. But a soldier, by the name of Longinus, approaching the Cross of Christ, thrust his lance through the side of the Savior. Immediately water and blood flowed from the wound, as Saint John, who saw it and who gives testimony of the truth, assures us (John 19, 34). The Most Prudent Queen then perceived the Mystery of this lance-thrust, namely that in this last pouring forth of the Blood and Water issued forth the New Church, cleansed and washed by the Passion and Death of Jesus, and that from His Sacred side, as from the roots, should now spread out through the whole World the fruits of Life Eternal.

The evening of that day of the parasceve was already approaching, and The Loving Mother had as yet no solution of the difficulty of the burial of Her Dead Son, which She desired so much; but the Lord ordained, that the tribulations should be relieved by Joseph of Arimathea and Nikodemus, whom He had inspired with the thought of caring for the burial of Their Master. They were both just men and disciples of The Lord, although not of the seventy-two; for they had not as yet openly confessed themselves as disciples for fear of the Jews, who suspected and hated as enemies all those that followed Christ and acknowledged Him as

Teacher. The dispositions of Divine Providence concerning the burial of Her Son had not been made known to the Most Prudent Virgin and thus Her painful anxiety increased to such an extent, that She saw no way out of the difficulty. In Her affliction She raised Her Eyes to Heaven and said: "Eternal Father and My Lord, by the condescension of Thy Goodness and Infinite wisdom I was raised to the exalted dignity of being The Mother of Thy Son; and by that same bounty of An Immense God Thou hast permitted Me to nurse Him at My breast, nourish Him, and accompany Him to His death. Now it behooves Me as His Mother to give honorable burial to His Sacred Body, though I can go no farther than to desire it and deeply grieve because I am unable to fulfill My wishes. I beseech Thy Divine Majesty to provide some way for accomplishing My desires."

This prayer The Loving Mother offered up after The Sacred Body of the Lord was perforated by the lance. Soon after She saw another group of men coming toward Calvary with ladders and other apparatus seemingly for the purpose of taking from the Cross Her priceless Treasure; but as She did not know their intentions, She was tortured by new fears of the cruelty of the Jews, and turning to Saint John, She said: "My Son, what may be the object of these people in coming with all these instruments?" The Apostle answered: "Do not fear them that are coming, My Lady; for they are Joseph and Nikodemus with some of their servants, all of them friends and servants of Thy Divine Son and My Lord." Although Joseph had been a secret Disciple of The Lord, yet at His Death, in consequence of the efficacious influence of the Redemption, he openly confessed his adherence. Setting aside all fear of the envy of the Jews and caring nothing for the power of the Romans, he went boldly to Pilate and asked for the Body of Jesus (Mark 15, 43), in order to take Him down from the Cross and give Him honorable burial. Pilate dared not refuse the request of Joseph, but gave him full permission to dispose of the Dead Body of Jesus as he thought fit.

They approached Most Holy Mary, who, in the company of Saint John and the holy women, stood in inconceivable sorrow at the foot of the Cross. Instead of a salute, their sorrow at the sight of so painful a spectacle as that of The Divine Crucified, was roused to such vehemence and bitterness, that Joseph and Nikodemus remained for a time pros-

162

trate at the feet of the Queen and all of them at the foot of the Cross without speaking a word.

It seemed to Joseph, that the sorrow of the Heavenly Lady would be renewed, when the Sacred Body should be lowered and She should touch it, and therefore he advised the Apostle to take Her aside in order to draw away Her attention. But Saint John, who knew better the Invincible Heart of The Queen, answered that from the beginning She had stood by to witness the torments of The Lord and that She would not leave Him whom She venerated as Her God and loved as The Son of Her Womb.

Thereupon they began to arrange for the taking down of the Body. Then The Great Lady placed Herself on Her knees and held the unfolded cloth in Her outstretched arms ready to receive The Dead Body of her Son. In order to assist Joseph and Nikodemus, Saint John supported the Head, and Mary Magdalen the feet, of Christ and thus they tearfully and reverently placed Him into the arms of His Sweetest Mother. This was to Her an event of mixed sorrow and consolation; for in seeing Him thus wounded and all His beauty disfigured beyond all children of men (Ps. 44, 3), the sorrows of Her Most Chaste Heart were again renewed; and in holding Him in Her arms and at Her breast, Her incomparable sorrow was rejoiced and Her love satiated by the possession of her Treasure. She looked upon Him with supreme worship and reverence, shedding tears of blood. In union with Her, as He rested in Her arms, all the multitude of Her attendant Angels worshipped Him, although unseen by all others except Mary. Then Saint John first, and after him all those present in their turn Adored the Sacred Body. The Most Prudent Mother, seated on the ground, in the meanwhile held Him in Her arms in order that they might satisfy their devotion.

Some time passed during which The Sorrowful Mother held at Her Breast The Dead Jesus, and as evening was far advancing, Saint John and Joseph besought Her to allow the burial of Her Son and God to proceed. The most Prudent Mother yielded; and they now embalmed the Sacred body, using all the hundred pounds of the spices and the aromatic ointments brought by Nikodemus. Thus anointed the Deified Body was placed on a bier, in order to be carried to the sepulchre. The Heavenly Queen, most attentive in Her Zealous Love, called from Heaven many choirs of Angels, who

163

together with those of Her guard, should accompany the burial of Their Creator. Immediately they descended from on high in shapes visible to their Queen and Lady, though not to the rest. A procession of Heavenly Spirits was formed and another of men, and the Sacred Body was borne along by Saint John, Joseph, Nikodemus and the centurion, who had confessed the Lord and now assisted at His burial. They were followed by the Blessed Mother, by Mary Magdalen and the rest of the women Disciples. Besides these a large number of the faithful assisted, for many had been moved by the Divine Light and had come to Calvary after the lance-thrust. All of them, in silence and in tears, joined the procession. They proceeded toward a nearby garden, where Joseph had hewn into the rock a new grave, in which nobody had as yet been buried or deposited (John 19, 41). In this Most Blessed Sepulchre they placed the Sacred Body of Jesus. Before they closed it up with the heavy stone, the Devout and Prudent Mother adored Christ anew, causing the admiration of men and Angels. They imitated Her, all of them adoring the crucified Savior now resting in His Grave; thereupon they closed the sepulchre with the stone, which, according to the Evangelist, was very heavy (Matth. 27, 60).

The Jews, confused and disturbed by the events, went to Pilate on the morning of the Sabbath and asked him for soldiers to guard the Sepulchre; for Christ, this seducer, they said, had openly announced, that after three days He would arise; hence His Disciples might steal the body and then say that He had arisen. Pilate yielded to this malicious measure and gave them the guard they desired, which they stationed at the Sepulchre (Matth. 28, 12).

THE FIVE GLORIOUS MYSTERIES

THE RESURRECTION OF OUR LORD FROM THE DEAD

The fullness of wisdom in the Soul of Our Great Queen and Lady amid all Her sorrows permitted no defect or remissness in noticing and attending to all the duties of each occasion and at all times. By this heavenly foresight She met Her obligations and practiced the highest and most eminent of all the virtues. As I have said, the Queen retired, after the burial of Christ, to the house of the Cenacle. Remaining in the hall of the Last Supper in the company of Saint John, the Marys, and the Other Women who had followed Christ from Galilee, She spoke to them and the Apostle, thanking them in profound humility and abundant tears for persevering with Her up to this time throughout the Passion of Her Beloved Son and promising them in His name the reward of having followed Him with so much constancy and devotion. At the same time She offered Herself as a servant and as a friend to Those Holy Women. All of them with Saint John acknowledged this great favor, kissed Her hands and asked for Her blessing. They also begged Her to take some rest and some bodily refreshment. But the Queen answered: "My rest and My consolation shall be to see My Son and Lord arisen from the dead. Do you, My dearest friends, satisfy your wants according to your necessities, while I retire alone with My Son." In Her retirement during this evening the Great Lady contemplated the doings of the Most Holy Soul of her Son after It left the Sacred Body. For from the first the Blessed Mother knew that the Soul of Christ, united to the Divinity, descended to Limbo in order to release the Holy Fathers from the subterranean prison, where They had been detained since the death of the first just man that had died in expectance of the Advent of the Redeemer of the whole human race. By the presence of the Most Holy Soul this obscure cavern was converted into a heaven and was filled with a wonderful splendor; and to the Souls therein contained was imparted the clear vision of the Divinity. In one instant they passed from the state of long-deferred Hope to the possession of Glory, and from darkness to the Inaccessible Light, which they now began to enjoy. All of them recognized their True God and Redeemer, and gave Him thanks and glory, breaking forth in canticles of praise saying: "The Lamb that was slain is worthy to receive power and Divinity, and wisdom, and strength, and honor, and glory and benediction. Thou hast redeemed us, Lord, in Thy Blood, out of every tribe, and tongue, and people, and nation; and hast made us to Our God a Kingdom and Priests, and we shall reign on the earth (Apoc. 59, 12). Thine is, O Lord, the power," Thine the reign, and Thine is the glory of Thy works." Then the Lord commanded the Angels to bring all the Souls in Purgatory, and this was immediately done. As if in earnest of the human Redemption they were absolved then and there by the Redeemer from the punishments still due to them, and they were glorified with the other souls of the just by the Beatific Vision. Thus on that day of the presence of the King were depopulated the prisonhouses of both Limbo and Purgatory.

The Divine Soul of Christ Our Redeemer remained in Limbo from half past three of Friday afternoon, until after three of the Sunday morning following. During this hour He returned to the Sepulchre as the victorious Prince of the Angels and of the Saints, whom He had delivered from those nether prisons as spoils of His Victory and as an earnest of His glorious triumph over the chastised and prostrate rebels of hell. In the sepulchre were many Angels as its guard, venerating the Sacred Body united to the Divinity. Some of them, obeying the command of Their Queen and Mistress, had gathered the relics of the Sacred Blood shed by Her Divine Son, the particles of flesh scattered about, the hair torn from His Divine face and head, and all else that belonged to the perfection and integrity of His Most Sacred humanity. On these the Mother of prudence lavished Her solicitous care. The Angels took charge of these relics, each one filled with joy at being privileged to hold the particles, which he was able to secure. Before any change was made, the Body of the Redeemer was shown to the Holy Fathers, in the same wounded, lacerated and disfigured state in which it was left by the cruelty of the Jews. Beholding Him thus disfigured in death, the Patriarchs and Prophets and other Saints adored Him and again confessed Him as the Incarnate Word, Who had truly taken upon Himself our infirmities and sorrows (Is. 53, 4) and paid abundantly our debts, satisfying in His innocence and guiltlessness for what we ourselves owed to the justice of the Eternal Father. There did Our First Parents Adam and Eve see the havoc wrought by their disobedience, the priceless remedy it necessitated, the immense goodness and mercy of the Redeemer. As they felt the effects of His Copious Redemption in the glory of their souls, they praised anew the Omnipotent and Saint of Saints, who had with such marvelous wisdom wrought such a salvation.

Then, in the presence of all those Saints, through the ministry of those Angels, were united to the Sacred Body all the Relics, which they had gathered, restoring it to its natural perfection and integrity. In the same moment the Most Holy Soul reunited with the Body, giving It Immortal Life and Glory. Instead of the winding-sheets and the ointments, in which it had been buried, it was clothed with the Four Gifts of Glory, namely: with Clearness, Impassibility, Agility and Subtility (John 19, 40). These gifts overflowed from the immense glory of the Soul of Christ into the Sacred Body. Although these gifts were due to it as a natural inheritance and participation from the instant of its conception, because from that very moment His Soul was glorified and His whole humanity was united to the Divinity; yet they had been suspended in their effects upon the Purest Body, in order to permit It to remain passable and capable of meriting for us our own glory. In the Resurrection these gifts were justly called into activity in the proper degree corresponding to the Glory of His Soul and to His union with the Divinity. As the glory of the Most Holy Soul of Christ Our Savior is incomprehensible and ineffable to man, it is also impossible entirely to describe in our words or by our examples the glorious gifts of his Deified Body; for in comparison to Its Purity, crystal would be obscure. The light inherent and shining forth from His body so far exceeds that of the others, as the day does the night, or as many suns the light of one star; and all the beauty of creatures, if it were joined, would appear ugliness in comparison with His, nothing else being comparable to it in all creation.

167

The excellence of these gifts in the Resurrection were far beyond the Glory of His Transfiguration or that manifested on other occasions of the kind mentioned in this history. For on these occasions He received it transitorily and for special purposes, while now He received it in plenitude and forever. Through "Impassibility" His body became invincible to all created power, since no power can ever move or change Him. By "Subtility" the gross and earthly matter was so purified, that it could now penetrate other matter like a pure spirit. Accordingly He penetrated through the rocks of the sepulchre without removing or displacing them, just as He had issued forth from the womb of His Most Blessed Mother. "Agility" so freed Him from the weight and slowness of matter, that it exceeded the agility of the immaterial angels, while He himself could move about more quickly than they, as shown in His Apparitions to the Apostles and on other occasions. The Sacred Wounds, which had disfigured his body, now shone forth from His hands and feet and side so refulgent and brilliant, that they added a most entrancing beauty and charm. In all this Glory and Heavenly Adornment The Savior now arose from the grave; and in the presence of the Saints and Patriarchs He promised universal resurrection in their own flesh and body to all men, and that they moreover, as an effect of His Own Resurrection, should be similarly glorified. As an earnest and as a pledge of the universal resurrection, The Lord commanded the Souls of many Saints there present to reunite with Their Bodies and rise up to Immortal life. Immediately This Divine Command was executed, and their bodies arose, as is mentioned by Saint Matthew, in anticipation of this mystery (Matthew 27, 52). Among them was Saint Anne, Saint Joseph and Saint Joachim, and others of the ancient Fathers and Patriarchs, who had distinguished themselves in the Faith and Hope of the Incarnation, and had desired and prayed for it with greater earnestness to The Lord. As a reward for their zeal, the Resurrection and Glory of Their Bodies was now anticipated.

Of all these Mysteries the Great Queen of heaven was aware and She participated in them from Her retreat in the Cenacle. In the same instant in which the Most Holy Soul of Christ entered and gave life to His body the joy of Her Immaculate Soul, which I mentioned in the foregoing chapter as being restrained and, as it were, withheld, overflowed into

Her Immaculate Body. And this overflow was so exquisite in its effects, that She was transformed from sorrow to joy, from pain to delight, from grief to ineffable jubilation and rest. It happened that just at this time the Evangelist John, as he had done on the previous morning, stepped in to visit Her and console Her in Her bitter solitude, and thus unexpectedly, in the midst of splendor and glory, met Her, whom he had before scarcely recognized on account of Her overwhelming sorrow. The Apostle now beheld Her with wonder and deepest reverence and concluded that the Lord had risen, since His Blessed Mother was thus transfigured with joy.

In this new joy and under The Divine influences of Her Supernatural Vision the Great Lady began to prepare Herself for the visit of The Lord, which was near at hand. While eliciting acts of praise, and in Her canticles and prayers, She immediately felt within Her a new kind of jubilation and celestial delight, reaching far beyond the first joy, and corresponding in a wonderful manner to the sorrows and tribulations She had undergone in the Passion; and this new favor was different and much more exalted than the joys overflowing naturally from Her Soul into Her Body. Moreover She perceived within Herself another third and still more different effect, implying new divine favors.

The Blessed Mary being thus prepared, Christ Our Savior, arisen and glorious, in the company of all the Saints and Patriarchs, made His appearance. The ever humble Queen prostrated Herself upon the ground and adored Her Divine Son; and the Lord raised Her up and drew Her to Himself. In this contact, which was more intimate than the contact with the humanity and the wounds of the Savior sought by Magdalen, the Virgin Mother participated in an extraordinary favor, which She alone, as exempt from sin, could merit. Although it was not the greatest of the favors She attained on this occasion, yet She could not have received it without failing of Her faculties, if She had not been previously strengthened by the Angels and by the Lord Himself. This favor was, that the Glorious Body of the Son so closely united itself to that of His Purest Mother, that He penetrated into it or She into His, as when, for instance, a crystal globe takes up within itself the light of the sun and is saturated with the splendor and beauty of its light. In the same way the Body of the Most Holy Mary entered into that of Her divine Son by this heavenly embrace; it was, as it were, the portal of Her intimate knowledge concerning the Glory of the Most Holy Soul and Body of her Lord. As a consequence of these favors, constituting higher and higher degrees of ineffable gifts, the spirit of the Virgin Mother rose to the knowledge of the most hidden sacraments. In the midst of them She heard a voice saying to Her: "My beloved, ascend higher!" (Luke 18, 10). By the power of these words She was entirely transformed and saw the Divinity clearly and intuitively, wherein She found complete, though only temporary, rest and reward for all Her sorrows and labors. Silence alone here is proper, since reason and language are entirely inadequate to comprehend or express what passed in the Blessed Mary during this beatific vision, the highest She had until then enjoyed. Let us celebrate this day in wonder and praise, with congratulations and loving and humble thanks for what She then merited for us, and for Her exaltation and joy.

For some hours the Heavenly Princess continued to enjoy the essence of God with Her Divine Son, participating now in His triumph as She had in His torments. Then by similar degrees She again descended from this vision and found Herself in the end reclining on the right arm of the most sacred humanity and regaled in other ways by the right hand of His Divinity (Cant. 2, 6). She held sweetest converse with Her Son concerning the mysteries of His Passion and of His Glory. In these conferences She was again inebriated with the wine of love and charity, which now She drank unmeasured from the original fount. All that a mere creature can receive was conferred upon the Blessed Mary on this occasion; for, according to our way of conceiving such things, The Divine equity wished to compensate the injury (thus I must call it, because I cannot find a more proper word), which a Creature so pure and immaculate had undergone in suffering the sorrows and torments of the Passion. For, as I have mentioned many times before, She suffered the same pains as Her Son, and now in this mystery She was inundated with a proportionate joy and delight.

WORDS OF THE QUEEN.

Thou already knowest that the gifts of the soul are Vision, Comprehension, and Fruition, while thou hast already mentioned those of the body as being: Clearness, Impassibility, Subtility and Agility.

Each of these gifts are correspondingly augmented in him who in the state of grace performs the least meritorious work, even if it be no more than removing a straw or giving a cup of water for the love of God (Matth. 10, 42). For each of the most insignificant works the creature gains an increase of these gifts; an increase of clearness exceeding many times the sunlight and added to its state of Blessedness; an increase of Impassibility, by which man recedes from human and earthly corruption farther than what all created efforts and strength could ever effect in resisting or separating itself from such infirmity or changefulness; an increase of Subtility, by which he advances beyond all that could offer it resistance and gains new power of penetration; an increase of Agility, surpassing all the activity of birds, of winds, and all other active creatures, such as fire and the elements tending to their centre. From this increase of the gifts of the body merited by good works, thou wilt understand the augmentation of the gifts of the soul; for those of the body are derived from those of the soul and correspond with them. In the beatific vision each merit secures greater clearness and insight into the divine attributes and perfections than that acquired by all the doctors and enlightened members of the Church. Likewise the gift of Apprehension, or Possession of the Divine Object, is augmented; for the security of the possession of the highest and Infinite Good makes the tranquillity and rest of its enjoyment more estimable than if the soul possessed all that is precious and rich, desirable and worthy of attainment in all creation, even if possessed all at one time. Fruition, the third gift of the soul, on account of the love with which man performs the smallest acts, so exalts the degrees of functional love, that the greatest love of men here on earth can never be compared thereto; nor can the delight resulting therefrom ever be compared with all the delights of this mortal life.

After Jesus Our Savior, arisen and glorified, had visited and filled with glory His Most Blessed Mother, He resolved, as the loving Father and Pastor, to gather the sheep of His Flock, which the scandal of His sufferings had disturbed and scattered. For the purpose of making His Ressurection known to His Apostles, He began by showing Himself to the women, not on account of their weakness, but because they were stronger in their belief of the Ressurection; for this is the reason why they merited the privilege of being the first to see Him arisen.

171

The Evangelist Mark (Mark 15, 47) mentions the special notice, which Mary Magdalen and Mary Joseph took of the place where they had seen the Body of Jesus deposited. Accordingly they, with other Holy Women, went forth on the evening of the Sabbath from the Cenacle to the city and bought additional ointments and spices in order to return, early the following morning, to the sepulchre, and show their veneration by visiting and anointing the Holy Body once more. On the Sunday, entirely ignorant of the grave's having been sealed and placed under guard by order of Pilate (Matth. 27, 65), they arose before dawn in order to execute their pious design. On their way they thought only of the difficulty of removing the large stone, which they now remembered had been rolled before the opening of the sepulchre; but their love made light of this hindrance, though they did not know how to remove it. When they came forth from the house of the Cenacle, it was yet dark, but before they arrived at the sepulchre the sun had already dawned and risen; for on that day the three hours of darkness which had intervened at the Death of the Savior, were compensated by an earlier sun-rise.

A little before the Marys thought and spoke of the difficulty of removing the stone, a violent and wonderful quaking or trembling of the earth took place; at the same time an Angel of The Lord opened the sepulchre and cast aside the stone that covered and obstructed the entrance (Matth. 28, 2). At this noise and the earthquake the guards of the sepulchre fell prostrate to the earth, struck motionless with fear and consternation, although they did not see the Lord. For the body of the Lord was no more in the grave; He had already arisen and issued from the monument before the Angel cast aside the stone. The Marys, though in some fear, took heart and were encouraged by God to approach and enter the vault. Near the entrance they saw the Angel who had thrown aside the stone, seated upon it, refulgent in countenance and in snow-white garments (Mark 16, 5). He spoke to them saying: "Be not afrightened; you seek Jesus of Nazareth, Who was crucified: He is risen, He is not here; behold the place where they laid Him." The Holy Women entered, and seeing the sepulchre vacant they were filled with grief; for as yet they were more deeply affected at seeing The Lord absent, than by the words of the Angel. Then they saw two other Angels seated at each end of the slab, who said to them: "Why seek you the Living with the dead? Remember how He spoke unto you, when He was yet in Galilee (Luke 26, 4-5), that He was to rise on the third day. But go, tell His Apostles and Peter, that He goeth before you into Galilee, there shall you see Him (Mark 16, 7)."

Being thus reminded by the Angels the Marys remembered what Their Divine Master had said. Assured of His Resurrection they hastened away from the sepulchre and gave account to the eleven Apostles and other followers of the Lord. But many of these were so shaken in their faith and so forgetful of the words of Their Master and Redeemer, that they thought this story of the Holy Women a mere hallucination (Luke 24, 11).

Although the Disciples and Apostles considered the tale of the Marys mere preposterous talk, Saint Peter and Saint John, desirous of convincing themselves with their own eyes, departed in all haste to the sepulchre, closely followed by the Holy Women (John 20, 3). Saint John arrived first, and without entering saw the winding-sheets laid to one side. He waited for the arrival of Saint Peter, who, passing the other Apostle, entered first. Both of them saw that the Sacred Body was not in the tomb. Saint John then was assured of what he had begun to believe, when he had seen the great change in the Queen of Heaven, as I have related in the foregoing chapter, and he then professed his belief. The two Apostles returned to give an account of the wonder they had seen in the sepulchre. The Marys remained in a place apart from the sepulchre and wonderingly commented on the events. Mary Magdalen, in great excitement and tears, re-entered the sepulchre to reconnoitre. Although the Apostles had not seen the Angels, she saw them and they asked her: "Woman, why dost thou weep?" (John 20, 5). She answered: "Because they have taken away My Lord; and I know not where they have laid Him." With this answer she left the garden where the sepulchre was, and met The Lord. She did not know Him, but thought it was the gardener. And the Lord also asked her: "Woman, why weepest thou, whom dost thou seek?" (John 15). Magdalen, ignorant of His being the Lord, answered Him as if He were the gardener and, without further reflection said: "Sir, if thou hast taken Him hence, tell me where thou hast laid Him, and I will take Him away." Then the loving Master said: "Mary," and in pronouncing her name He permitted Himself to be recognized by the tone of His voice.

173

Then Magdalen left, filled with consolation and jubilee. Shortly she met the other Marys. Scarcely had they heard what had happened to her and how she had seen Jesus arisen from the grave, and while they were yet standing together conferring with each other in wonder and tears of joy, He appeared to them and said: "God save you." They all recognized Him and, as Saint Matthew tells us, they worshipped at His Sacred Feet. The Lord again commanded them to go to the Apostles and tell them, that they had seen Him and that they should go to Galilee, where they should see Him arisen (Matth. 22, 9). Jesus then disappeared and the Holy Women hastened to the Cenacle to tell the Apostles all that had happened to them, but the Apostles continued to hesitate in their belief (Luke 24, 11).

The Evangelists do not state when The Lord appeared to Saint Peter, although Saint Luke supposes it; but it was after He had appeared to the women. He appeared to him in private as the head of the Church and before He appeared to all of the Apostles together or to any one of them. This happened on that same day, after the Holy Women had informed him of His apparition to them. Soon after also happened the apparition of the Lord to the two Disciples going that afternoon to Emmaus. The one of them was called Cleophas and the other was Saint Luke himself. It took place in the following manner: The two Disciples left Jerusalem, after they had heard the reports of the women. On the way they continued to converse about the events of the Passion, the Holiness of Their Master and the cruelty of the Jews.

In the midst of this and similar conversation Jesus appeared to them in the habit of a pilgrim and as one who happened to meet them on the way. He saluted them and said: "Of what do you speak, for it seems to Me you are sad?" Cleophas answered: "Art Thou the only stranger in Jerusalem, that Thou dost not know what has happened during these days in the city?" The Lord said: "What has happened, then?" to which the Disciple replied: "Dost thou not know what the princes and priests have done to Jesus of Nazareth, a Man holy and powerful in words and deeds; how they condemned and crucified Him? We had hopes that He would redeem Israel by rising from the dead; now the third day has already come, and we do not know what has happened. And some of the women of our party have terrified us since they went early this morning to the sepulchre and did not find the body. They maintain that they saw some Angels who told them that He had risen. Then some of our associates went to the grave and found true, what the women had said. We are going to Emmaus in order to await the drift of these events." Then The Lord answered: "O foolish and slow of heart to believe, since you do not understand, that it might be so, that Christ suffer all these pains and so frightful a death in order to enter into His Glory." And when they were already near to the castle of Emmaus, the Divine Master gave them to understand, that He was to pass on in His journey; but they eagerly begged Him to stay with them, as it was getting late in the evening. The Lord yielded and, invited by the disciples, sat down to supper with them according to the manner of the Jews. The Lord took the bread, blessing it and breaking it as usual, He imparted to them, with it, the certainty that He was their Redeemer and Master.

They knew Him, because He opened the eyes of their souls. In the same instant He disappeared from their bodily eyes and they saw Him no more. But they were left in a state of wonder and full of joy, conferring with each other about the ardors of charity they had felt on the way, when He had conversed with them and explained to them the Scriptures. Without delay they returned to Jerusalem (Luke 24, 33), although night had already set in. They went to the house, where the rest of the Apostles had secreted themselves for fear of the Jews and they found them discussing the news of the Risen Savior and how He had already appeared to Peter. To this the two Disciples added all that had happened to them on the way to Emmaus. At this meeting was present also Saint Thomas, who, although hearing the arguments of the Apostles and the testimony of Saint Peter asserting that he had seen the Master risen, refused credit to the three Disciples and the Women, persevering in doubt and unbelief. In a somewhat hasty manner, caused by his incredulity, he left their company. Shortly after, when Thomas had left and the doors had been locked, the Lord entered and appeared to the others. In their midst He saluted them, saying: "Peace be with you. It is I; do not fear."

Having thus instructed them, He said again: "Peace be with you. As the Father has sent Me, so I send you, in order that you may teach the World the knowledge of the Truth, of God and of Eternal Life, preaching repentance for sins and forgiveness of them in My Name." Breathing upon them, He added and said: "Receive ye the Holy Ghost in order that the sins which you forgive may be forgiven, and those which you do not forgive may not be forgiven. Preach ye to all nations, beginning in Jerusalem." Then the Savior, having thus consoled and confirmed them in faith, and having given them and all priests the power to forgive sins, disappeared from their midst.

All this took place in the absence of Thomas; but soon after, the Lord so disposing, he returned to the assembly, and the Apostles told Him what had happened during His absence. Yet, though he found them so changed in joyful exultation, he remained incredulous and obstinate, maintaining, that he would not believe what all of them affirmed, unless he himself should see with his own eyes and touch with his own hands and fingers the Wounds of the Savior's side and those of the nails (John 20, 25). In this obstinacy the incredulous Thomas persevered for eight days, when the Savior again returned through locked doors and appeared in the midst of the Apostles including Thomas. He saluted them as usual, saying: "Peace be with you," and then calling Thomas, He sweetly reprimanded him. "Come, Thomas, and with your hands touch the openings of My hands and of My side, and be not so incredulous, but convinced and believing." Thomas touched the Divine Wounds and was interiorly enlightened to believe and to acknowledge his ignorance. Prostrating himself to the ground he said: "My Lord and My God!" to which the Lord replied: "Because thou hast seen Me, thou hast believed; but blessed are those who do not see Me and believe Me." The Lord then disappeared, leaving the Apostles and Thomas filled with light and joy. They immediately sought Most Holy Mary in order to relate to Her what had happened, just as they had done after the first apparition of the Lord.

THE ASCENSION
OF OUR LORD INTO HEAVEN

A few days before the Ascension of The Lord, while the Blessed Mary was engaged in the one of the above-mentioned exercises, the Eternal Father and the Holy Ghost appeared in the Cenacle upon a throne of ineffable splendor surrounded by the choirs of angels and saints there present and other heavenly spirits, which had now come with the Divine Persons. Then the Incarnate Word ascended the throne and seated Himself with the other Two. The ever humble Mother of the Most High, prostrate in a corner of a room, in deepest reverence adored the Most Blessed Trinity, and in it Her Own Incarnate Son. The Eternal Father commanded two of the highest angels to call Mary, which they did by approaching Her, and in sweetest voices intimating to Her the Divine Will. She arose from the dust with the most profound humility, modesty and reverence. Accompanied by the Angels She approached the foot of the Throne, humbling Herself anew. The Eternal Father said to Her: "Beloved, ascend higher!" (Luke 14, 10). As these words at the same time effected what they signified, She was raised up and placed on the throne of Royal Majesty with the three Divine Persons. New admiration was caused in the Saints to see a mere Creature exalted to such dignity. Being made to understand the sanctity and equity of the works of the Most High, they gave new glory and praise proclaiming Him immense, Just, Holy and Admirable in all His counsels.

The Father then spoke to the Blessed Mary saying: "My Daughter, to Thee do I entrust the Church founded by My Only Begotten, the new law of grace He established in the World, and the people, which He redeemed; to Thee do I consign them all." There upon also the Holy Ghost spoke to Her: "My Spouse, chosen from all creatures, I communicate to Thee My Wisdom and Grace together with which shall be deposited in Thy heart the Mysteries, the works and teachings and all that the Incarnate Word has accomplished in the world." And the Son also said: "My Most Beloved Mother, I go to My Father and in My stead I shall leave Thee and I charge Thee with the care of My Church; to Thee do I commend its children and my brethren, as the Father has consigned them to Me." Then the three Divine Persons, addressing the choir of holy angels and the other saints, said: "This is the Queen of all created things in heaven and earth; She is the Protectress of the Church, the Mistress of creatures, the Mother of piety, the Intercessor of the faithful, the Advocate of sinners, the Mother of beautiful love and holy hope (Eccli. 24, 24); She is mighty in drawing our will to mercy and clemency. In Her shall be deposited the treasures of Our Grace and Her Most Faithful Heart shall be the tablet whereon shall be written and engraved Our Holy Law. In Her are contained the mysteries of Our Omnipotence for the salvation of mankind. She is the perfect work of our hands, through whom the plentiude of our desires shall be communicated and satisfied without hindrance in the currents of Our Divine Perfections. Whoever shall call upon Her from his heart shall not perish; whoever shall obtain Her intercession shall secure for himself eternal life. What She asks of Us, shall be granted, and We shall always hear Her requests and prayers and fulfill Her will; for She has consecrated Herself perfectly to what pleases Us." The Most Blessed Mary, hearing Herself thus exalted, humiliated Herself so much the deeper the more highly She was raised by the right hand of the Most High above all the human and angelic creatures. As if She were the least of all, She adored the Lord and offered Herself, in the most prudent terms and in the most ardent love, to work as a faithful servant in the Church and to obey promptly all the biddings of the Divine Will. From that day on She took upon Herself anew the care of the Evangelical Church, as a Loving Mother of all its children; She renewed all the petitions She had until then made, so that during the whole further course of Her life they were most fervent and incessant, as we shall see in the third part, where will appear more clearly what the Church owes to This Great Queen and Lady, and what blessings She gained and merited for it.

On that same day, by divine dispensation, while the Lord was at table with the eleven Apostles, other disciples and pious women gathered at the Cenacle to the number of one hundred and twenty; for the Divine Master wished them to be present at His Ascension. Moreover, just as He had instructed the Apostles, so He now wanted to instruct these faithful respectively in what each was to know before His leaving them and ascending into heaven. All of them being thus gathered and united in peace and charity within those walls in the Hall of the Last Supper, the Author of life manifested Himself to them as a kind of loving Father and said to them:

"My sweetest children, I am about to ascend to My Father, from whose bosom I descended in order to rescue and save men. I leave with you in my stead My Own Mother as your Protectress, Consoler and Advocate, and as your Mother, whom you are to hear and obey in all things. Just as I have told you, that he who sees Me sees my Father, and he who knows Me, knows also Him; so I now tell you, that He who knows my Mother, knows Me; he who hears Her, hears Me; and who honors Her, honors Me. All of you shall have Her as your Mother, as your Superior and Head, and so shall also your successors. She shall answer your doubts, solve your difficulties; in Her, those who seek Me shall always find Me; for I shall remain in Her until the end of the World, and I am in Her now, although you do not understand how." This the Lord said, because He was sacramentally present in the bosom of His Mother; for the Sacred Species, which She had received at the Last Supper, were preserved in Her until Consecration of the First Mass, as I shall relate further on. The Lord thus fulfilled that which He promised in saint Matthew: "I am with you to the consummation of the World" (Matth. 28, 20). The Lord added and said: "You will have Peter as the Supreme Head of the Church, for I leave him as My Vicar; and you shall obey him as the chief highpriest. Saint John you shall hold as the son of My Mother; for I have chosen and appointed him for This Office on the Cross." The Lord then looked upon his Most Beloved Mother, who was there present, and intimated His desire of expressly commanding that whole congregation to worship and reverence Her in a manner suited to the dignity of Mother of God, and of leaving this command under form of a precept for the whole Church. But the most humble Lady besought her Only Begotten to be pleased not to secure Her more honor than was absolutely necessary for executing all that He had charged Her with; and that the new children of

179

the Church should not be induced to show Her greater honor than they had shown until then. On the contrary, She desired to divert all the sacred worship of the Church immediately upon the Lord Himself and to make the propagation of the Gospel redound entirely to the exaltation of His Holy Name. Christ Our Savior yielded to this most prudent petition of His Mother, reserving to Himself the duty of spreading the knowledge of Her at a more convenient and opportune time; yet in secret He conferred upon Her new extraordinary favors, as shall appear in the rest of this history.

In considering the loving exhortations of Their Divine Master, the mysteries which He had revealed to them, and the prospect of His leaving them, that whole congregation was moved to their inmost hearts; for He had enkindled in them the Divine Love by the vivid faith of his Divinity and humanity. Reviving within them the memory of His words and His teachings of Eternal Life, the delights of His most loving intercourse and company, and sorrowfully realizing, that they were now all at once to be deprived of these blessings, they wept most tenderly and sighed from their inmost souls. They longed to detain Him, although they could not, because they saw it was not befitting; words of parting rose to their lips, but they could not bring themselves to utter them; each one felt sentiments of sorrow arising amid feelings both of joy and yet also of pious regret. How shall we live without such a Master they thought? Who can ever speak to us such words of life and consolation as He? Who will receive us so lovingly and kindly? Who shall be our Father and protector? We shall be helpless children and orphans in this world. Some of them broke their silence and exclaimed: "O Most Loving Lord and Father! O joy and life of our souls! Now that we know Thee as Our Redeemer, Thou departest and leavest us! Take us along with Thee, O Lord; banish us not from Thy sight. Our Blessed Hope, what shall we do without Thy presence? Whither shall we turn, if Thou goest away? Whither shall we direct our steps, if we cannot follow Thee, Our Father, Our Chief, and Our Teacher?" To these and other pleadings the Lord answered by bidding them not to leave Jerusalem and to persevere in prayer until He should send the Holy Spirit, the Consoler, as promised by the Father and as already foretold to the Apostles at the Last Supper. Thereupon happened, what I shall relate in the next chapter.

The most auspicious hour, in which the Only Begotten of the Eternal Father, after descending from heaven in order to assume human flesh, was to ascend by His own power and in a most wonderful manner to the right hand of God, the Inheritor of His Eternities, one and equal with Him in nature and infinite glory. He was to ascend, also, because He had previously descended to the lowest regions of the earth, as the Apostle says (Ephes. 4, 9), having fulfilled all that had been written and prophesied concerning His coming into the world, His Life, Death and the Redemption of man, and having penetrated, as the Lord of all, to the very centre of the earth. By this Ascension He sealed all the mysteries and hastened the fulfillment of His promise, according to which He was, with the Father, to send the Paraclete upon His Church after He himself should have ascended into heaven (John 16, 7). In order to celebrate this festive and mysterious day, Christ Our Lord selected as witnesses the hundred and twenty persons, to whom, as related in the foregoing chapter, He had spoken in the Cenacle. They were the Most Holy Mary, the eleven Apostles, the seventy-two Disciples, Mary Magdalen, Lazarus their brother, the other Marys and the faithful men and women making up the above-mentioned number of one hundred and twenty.

With this little flock Our Divine Shepherd Jesus left the Cenacle, and, with His Most Blessed Mother at His side, He conducted them all through the streets of Jerusalem. The Apostles and all the rest in their order, proceeded in the direction of Bethany, which was less than half a league over the brow of Mount Olivet. The company of angels and saints from limbo and purgatory followed the Victor with new songs of praise, although Mary alone was privileged to see them. The Resurrection of Jesus of Nazareth was already divulged throughout Jerusalem and Palestine. Although the perfidious and malicious princes and priests had spread about the false testimony of His being stolen by the disciples, yet many would not accept their testimony, nor give it any credit. It was divinely provided, that none of the inhabitants of the city, and none of the unbelievers or doubters, should pay any attention to this holy procession, or hinder it on its way from the Cenacle. All, except the one hundred and twenty just, who were chosen by The Lord to witness His Ascension into heaven, were justly punished by being prevented from noticing this wonderful mystery, and the Chieftain and Head of this procession remained invisible to them.

The Lord having thus secured them this privacy, they all ascended Mount Olivet to its highest point. There they formed three choirs, one of the Angels, another of the Saints, and a third of the Apostles and faithful, which again divided into two bands, while Christ the Savior presided. Then the Most Prudent Mother prostrated Herself at the feet of Her Son and, worshipping Him with admirable humility, She adored Him as the True God and as the Redeemer of the World, asking His last blessing. All the faithful there present imitated Her and did the same. Weeping and sighing, they asked the Lord, whether He was now to restore the Kingdom of Israel (Acts 1, 6). The Lord answered, that this was a secret of the Eternal Father and not to be made known to them; but, for the present, it was necessary and befitting, that they receive the Holy Ghost and preach, in Jerusalem, in Samaria and in all the world, the Mysteries of the Redemption of the World.

Jesus, having taken leave of this holy and fortunate gathering of the faithful, His countenance beaming forth peace and majesty, joined His hands and, by His own power, began to raise Himself from the earth, leaving thereon the impression of His sacred feet. In gentlest motion He was wafted toward the aerial regions, drawing after Him the eyes and the hearts of those first-born children, who amid sighs and tears vented their affection. And as, at the moving of the First Cause of all motion, it is proper that also the nether spheres should be set in motion, so the Savior Jesus drew after Him also the Celestial Choirs of the Angels, the holy Patriarchs and the rest of the Glorified Saints, some of them with body and soul, others only as to their soul. All of them in heavenly order were raised up together from the earth, accompanying and following Their King, Their Chief and Head. The new and mysterious sacrament, which the right hand of the Most High wrought on this occasion for His Most Holy Mother, was that He raised Her up with Him in order to put Her in possession of the glory, which He had assigned to Her as His True Mother and which She had by Her merits prepared and earned for Herself. Of this favor the Great Queen was capable even before it happened; for Her Divine Son had offered it to Her during the forty days which He spent in Her company after His Resurrection. In order that this sacrament might be kept secret from all other living creatures at that time, and in order that the Heavenly Mistress might be present in the gathering of the Apostles and the faithful in their prayerful waiting upon the coming of the Holy Ghost (Acts 1, 14), the divine power enabled the Blessed Mother miraculously to be in two places at once; remaining with the children of the Church for their comfort during their stay in the Cenacle and at the same time ascending with the Redeemer of the World to His heavenly throne, where She remained for three days. There She enjoyed the perfect use of all Her powers and faculties, whereas She was more restricted in the use of them during that time in the Cenacle.

Amidst this jubilee and other rejoicings exceeding all our conceptions that new divinely arranged procession approached the Empyrean Heavens. Between the two choirs of angels and saints, Christ and His Most Blessed Mother made Their entry. All in their order gave supreme honor to Each respectively and to Both together, breaking forth in hymns of praise in honor of the Authors of grace and of life. Then the Eternal Father placed upon the Throne of His Divinity at His right hand, The Incarnate Word, and in such glory and majesty, that He filled with new admiration and reverential fear all the inhabitants of heaven. In clear and intuitive vision they recognized the Infinite Glory and perfection of the Divinity inseparably and substantially united in one personality to the most holy humanity, beautified and exalted by the pre-eminence and glory due to this union, such as eyes have not seen, nor ears heard, nor ever has entered into the thoughts of creatures (Is. 54, 4).

On this occasion the humility and wisdom of our Most Prudent Queen reached their highest point; for, overwhelmed by such divine and admirable favors, She hovered at the footstool of the royal throne, annihilated in the consciousness of being a mere earthly creature. Prostrate She adored the Father and broke out in new canticles of praise for the glory communicated to His Son and for elevating in Him the deified humanity to such greatness and splendor. Again the Angels and Saints were filled with admiration and joy to see the most prudent humility of Their Queen, whose living example of virtue, as exhibited on that occasion, they emulated among themselves in copying. Then the voice of The Eternal Father was heard saying: "My Daughter, ascend higher!" Her Divine Son also called Her, saying: "My Mother, rise up and

183

take possession of the place, which I owe Thee for having followed and imitated Me." The Holy Ghost said: "My Spouse and Beloved, come to My Eternal embraces!" Immediately was proclaimed to all the decree of the Most Holy Trinity, by which the Most Blessed Mother, for having furnished Her own life-blood toward the Incarnation and for having nourished, served, imitated and followed Him with all the perfection possible to a creature, was exalted and placed at the right hand of Her Son for all eternity. None other of the human creatures should ever hold that place or position, nor rival Her in the unfailing glory connected with it; but it was to be reserved to the Queen and to be Her possession by right after Her earthly life, as of one who pre-eminently excelled all the rest of the saints.

In fulfillment of this decree, the Most Blessed Mary was raised to the throne of the Holy Trinity at the right hand of Her Son. At the same time She, with all the Saints, was informed, that She was given possession of this throne not only for all the ages of eternity, but that it was left to Her choice to remain there even now and without returning to the earth. For it was the conditional will of the Divine Persons, that as far as they were concerned, She should now remain in that state. In order that She might make Her own choice, She was shown anew the state of the Church upon earth, the orphaned and necessitous condition of the faithful, whom She was left free to assist. This admirable proceeding of the Divine Providence was to afford the Mother of Mercy an occasion of going beyond, so to say, even Her own Self in doing good and in obliging the human race with an act of tenderest love similar to that of Her Son in assuming a passible state and in suspending the glory due to His Body during and for our Redemption. The Most Blessed Mother imitated Him also in this respect, so that She might be in all things like the Incarnate Word. The Great Lady therefore, having clearly before Her eyes all the sacrifices included in this proposition, left the throne and, prostrating Herself at the feet of the Three Persons, said: "Eternal and Almighty God, My Lord, to accept at once this reward, which Thy condescending kindness offers me, would be to secure my rest; but to return to the world and continue to labor in mortal life for the good of the children of Adam and the faithful of Thy Holy Church, would be to the glory and according to the pleasure of Thy Majesty and would benefit

184

my sojourning and banished children on earth. I accept this labor and renounce for the present the peace and joy of Thy presence. Well do I know, what I possess and receive, but I will sacrifice it to further the love Thou hast for men. Accept, Lord and Master of all My Being, this sacrifice and let Thy Divine strength govern Me in the undertaking confided to Me. Let faith in Thee be spread, let Thy Holy Name be exalted, let Thy Holy Church be enlarged, for Thou hast acquired it by the Blood of Thy Only Begotten and Mine; I offer Myself anew to labor for Thy Glory, and for the conquest of the souls, as far as I am able."

Such was the sacrifice made by the Most Loving Mother and Queen, one greater than ever was conceived by creature, and it was so pleasing to The Lord, that He immediately rewarded it by operating in Her those purifications and enlightenments, which I have at other times mentioned as necessary to the intuitive vision of the Divinity; for so far She had on this occasion seen It only by abstractive vision. Thus elevated She partook of the Beatific Vision and was filled with splendor and celestial gifts, altogether beyond the power of man to describe or conceive in mortal life.

In order to finish this chapter, and with it this second part, I return to the congregation of the faithful, whom we left so sorrowful on Mount Olivet. The Most Holy Mary did not forget them in the midst of Her Glory; as they stood weeping and lost in grief and, as it were, absorbed in looking into the aerial regions, into which Their Redeemer and Master had disappeared, She turned Her eyes upon them from the cloud on which She had ascended, in order to send them Her assistance. Moved by their sorrow, She besought Jesus lovingly to console these little children, whom He had left as orphans upon the earth. Moved by the prayers of His Mother, The Redeemer of the human race sent down two angels in white and resplendent garments, who appeared to all the disciples and the faithful and spoke to them: "Ye men of Galilee, do not look up to heaven in so great astonishment, for This Lord Jesus, who departed from you and has ascended into heaven, shall again return with the same Glory and Majesty in which you have just seen Him" (Acts 1, 11). By such words and others which they added they consoled the Apostles and Disciples and all the rest, so that they might not grow faint, but in their retirement hope for the coming

185

and the consolation of the Holy Ghost promised by Their Divine Master.

My Daughter, thou wilt appropriately close this second part of My life by remembering the lesson concerning the most efficacious sweetness of the Divine Love and the immense liberality of God with those souls, that do not hinder its flowing. It is in conformity with the inclinations of His Holy and Perfect Will to regale rather than afflict creatures, to console them rather than cause them sorrow, to reward them rather than to chastise them, to rejoice rather than grieve them. But mortals ignore this Divine Science, because they desire from the hands of the Most High such consolations, delights and rewards, as are earthly and dangerous, and they prefer them to the true and more secure blessings. The Divine Love then corrects this fault by the lessons conveyed in tribulations and punishments. Human nature is slow, coarse and uneducated; and if it is not cultivated and softened, it gives no fruit in season, and on account of its evil inclinations, will never of itself become fit for the most loving and sweet intercourse with The Highest Good. Therefore it must be shaped and reduced by the hammer of adversities, refined in the crucible of tribulation, in order that it may become fit and capable of The Divine gifts and favors and may learn to despise terrestrial and fallacious goods, wherein death is concealed.

I counted for little all that I endured, when I saw the reward which The Divine Goodness had prepared for Me; and therefore He ordained, in His admirable Providence, that I should return to the Militant Church of My own free will and choice. This I knew would redound to My greater glory and to the exaltation of His Holy Name, while it would provide assistance to His Church and to His children in an admirable and holy manner (I Tim. 1, 17). It seemed to me a sacred duty, that I deprive myself of the Eternal Felicity of which I was in possession and, returning from heaven to earth, gain new fruits of labor and love for the Almighty; all this I owed to the Divine Goodness, which had raised Me up from the dust. Learn therefore, My Beloved, from My example, and excite Thyself to imitate Me most eagerly during these times, in which The Holy Church is so disconsolate and overwhelmed by tribulations and in which there are none of her children to console her. In this cause I desire that Thou labor strenuously, ready to suffer in prayer and supplication, and crying from the bottom of Thy heart to the Omnipotent. And if it were necessary Thou shouldst be willing to give Thy life. I assure thee, My Daughter, Thy solicitude shall be very pleasing in the eyes of My Divine Son and in Mine.

Let it all be for the Glory and Honor of the Most High, the King of the ages, the Immortal and Invisible (I Tim. 1, 17), and for that of His Mother, the Most Blessed Mary, through all the Eternities!

THE DESCENT OF THE HOLY GHOST
UPON THE APOSTLES AND
THE BLESSED MOTHER

DESCENT OF THE HOLY GHOST, MARY'S INTUITIVE VISION
OF HIM.

In the company of the Great Queen of Heaven, and encouraged by Her, the twelve Apostles and the rest of the Disciples and Faithful joyfully waited for the fulfillment of the promise of The Savior, that He would send them the Holy Ghost, the Consoler, who should instruct them and administer unto them all that they had heard in the teaching of Their Lord (John 14, 26). They were so unanimous and united in charity, that during all these days none of them had any thought, affection or inclination contrary to those of the rest. They were of one heart and soul in thought and action. Although the election of Saint Mathias had occurred, not the least movement or sign of discord arose among all those first-born children of the Church; yet this was a transaction, which is otherwise apt to arouse differences of opinion in the most excellently disposed; since each one is apt to follow his own insight and does not easily yield to the opinion of others. But into this Holy Congregation no discord found entrance, because they were united in prayer, in fasting and in the expectation of the Holy Ghost, who does not seek repose in discordant and unyielding hearts. In order that it may be inferred, how powerful was this union in charity, not only for disposing them toward the reception of the Holy Ghost, but for overcoming and dispersing the evil spirits, I will say; that the demons, who since the death of the Savior had lain prostrate in hell, felt in themselves a new kind of oppression and terror, resulting from the virtues of those assembled in the Cenacle. Although they could not explain it to themselves, they perceived a new terrifying force, emanating from that place, and when they perceived the effects of the doctrine and example of Christ in the behavior of the Disciples, they feared the ruin of their dominion.

The Queen of the Angels, Most Holy Mary, in the plenitude of Her wisdom and grace, knew the time and predestined hour for the sending of the Holy Ghost upon the Apostolic College. When the days of Pentecost were about to be fulfilled (Act 2, 1), (which happened fifty days after the Resurrection of the Lord our Redeemer), the Most Blessed Mother saw, how in heaven the Humanity (John 14, 26) of the Word conferred with The Eternal Father concerning the promised sending of The Divine Paraclete to the Apostles, and that the time predetermined by His Infinite Wisdom for planting the faith and all His gifts in His Holy Church, was at hand. The Lord also referred to the merits acquired by Him in the flesh through His Most Holy Life, Passion and Death, to the Mysteries wrought by Him for the salvation of the human race and to the fact, that He was the Mediator, Advocate and Intercessor between the Eternal Father and men, and that among them lived His Sweetest Mother, in whom the Divine Persons were so well pleased. He besought His Father also, that, besides bringing Grace and the Invisible Gifts the Holy Ghost appear in the world in visible form, that so the Evangelical Law might be honored before all the World; that the Apostles and faithful, who were to spread the Divine Truth, might be encouraged, and that the enemies of the Lord, who had in this life persecuted and despised Him unto the death of the Cross, might be filled with terror.

This petition of our Redeemer in Heaven was supported on earth by Most Holy Mary in a manner befitting the Merciful Mother of the Faithful. Prostrated upon the earth in the form of a cross and in profoundest humility, She saw, how in that consistory of the Blessed Trinity, the request of the Savior was favorably accepted, and how, to fulfill and execute it, the persons of the Father and the Son, as the Principle from which the Holy Ghost proceeded, decreed the active mission of the Holy Spirit; for to These Two is attributed the sending of the Third Person, because He proceeds from Both; and the Third Person passively took upon Himself this mission and consented to come into the World.

On Pentecost morning the Blessed Virgin Mary exhorted the Apostles, the disciples and the pious women, numbering about one hundred and twenty, to pray more fervently and renew their hopes, since the hour was at hand in which they were to be visited by the Divine Spirit from on high. At the third hour (nine o'clock), when all of them were gathered around Their Heavenly Mistress and engaged in fervent prayer, the air resounded with a tremendous thunder and the blowing of a violent wind mixed with the brightness of fire or lightning, all centering upon the house of the Cenacle. The house was enveloped in light and the Divine Fire was poured out over all of that holy gathering (Acts 2, 2). Over the head of each of the hundred and twenty persons appeared a tongue of that same fire, in which the Holy Ghost had come, filling each one with Divine Influences and Heavenly Gifts and causing at one and the same time the most diverse and contrary effects in the Cenacle and in the whole of Jerusalem, according to the diversity of the persons affected.

In the Most Holy Mary these effects were altogether Divine, and most wonderful in the sight of all the heavenly courtiers; for as regard us men, we are incapable of understanding and explaining them. The Purest Lady was transformed and exalted in God; for She saw intuitively and clearly the Holy Ghost, and for a short time enjoyed the Beatific Vision of the Divinity. Of His gifts and Divine influences She by Herself received more than all the rest of the Saints. Her glory for that space of time, exceeded that of the Angels and of the Blessed. She alone gave to the Lord more glory, praise and thanksgiving than all the universe for the benefit of the descent of His Holy Spirit upon His Church and for His having pledged Himself so many times to send Him and through Him to govern it to the end of the World. The Blessed Trinity was so pleased with the conduct of Mary on this occasion, that It considered Itself fully repaid and compensated for having created the World; and not only compensated, but God acted as if He were under a certain obligation for possessing such a peerless Creature, whom the Father could look upon as His Daughter, the Son as His Mother, and the Holy Ghost as His Spouse; and whom (according to our way of thinking) He was now obliged to visit and enrich after having conferred upon Her such high dignity. In this Exalted and Blessed Spouse were renewed all the Gifts and Graces of the Holy Spirit, creating new effects and operations altogether beyond our capacity to understand.

The Apostles, as Saint Luke says (Acts 2, 11), were also

replenished and filled with the Holy Ghost; for they received a wonderful increase of justifying grace of a most exalted degree. The twelve Apostles were confirmed in this Sanctifying Grace and were never to lose it. In all of them, according to each one's condition, were infused the habits of the seven gifts: Wisdom, Understanding, Science, Piety, Counsel, Fortitude and Fear. In this magnificent blessing, as new as it was admirable in the World, the twelve Apostles were created fit ministers of the New Testament and founders of the Evangelical Church for the whole World: for this new grace and blessing communicated to them a Divine strength most efficacious and sweet, which inclined them to practice the most heroic virtue and the highest sanctity. Thus strengthened they prayed, they labored willingly and accomplished the most difficult and arduous tasks, engaging in their labors not with sorrow or from necessity, but with the greatest joy and alacrity.

In all the rest of the disciples and the faithful, who received the Holy Ghost in the Cenacle, the Most High wrought proportionally and respectively the same effects, except that they were not confirmed in Grace like the Apostles. According to the disposition of each the Gifts of Grace were communicated in greater or less abundance in view of the ministry they were to hold in the Holy Church. The same proportion was maintained in regard to the Apostles; yet Saint Peter and Saint John were more singularly favored on account of the high offices assigned to them: the one to govern the Church as its head, and the other to attend upon and serve the Queen and Mistress of Heaven and of Earth, Most Holy Mary. The sacred text of Saint Luke says, that the Holy Ghost filled the whole house in which this Happy Congregation was gathered (Acts 2, 7), not only because all of them were filled with the Holy Ghost and His admirable gifts, but because the house itself was filled with wonderful light and splendor. This plenitude of wonders and prodigies overflowed and communicated itself also to others outside of the Cenacle; for it caused diverse and various effects of the Holy Spirit among the inhabitants of Jerusalem and its vicinity. All those, who with some piety had compassioned Our Savior Jesus in His Passion and Death, deprecating His most bitter torments and reverencing His Sacred Person, were interiorly visited with new light and grace, which disposed them afterwards to accept the doctrine of the

191

Apostles. Those that were converted by the first sermon of Saint Peter, were to a great extent of the number of those who, by their compassion and sorrow at the death of The Lord, had merited for themselves such a great blessing. Others of the just who were in Jerusalem outside of the Cenacle, also felt great interior consolations, by which they were moved and predisposed by new effects of Grace wrought in each one proportionately by the Holy Ghost.

Not less wonderful, although more hidden, were some contrary effects produced on that day by the Holy Ghost in Jerusalem. By the dreadful thunders and violent commotion of the atmosphere and the lightnings accompanying His Advent, He disturbed and terrified the enemies of The Lord in that city, each one according to his own malice and perfidy. This chastisement was particularly evident in those who had actively concurred in procuring the death of Christ, and who had signalized themselves in their rabid fury against Him. All these fell to the ground on their faces and remained thus for three hours. Those that had scourged the Lord were suddenly choked in their own blood, which shot forth from their veins in punishment for shedding that of The Master. The audacious servant, who had buffeted The Lord, not only suddenly died, but was hurled into hell body and soul. Others of the Jews, although they did not die, were chastised with intense pains and abominable sicknesses. These disorders, consequent upon shedding The Blood of Christ, descended to their posterity and even to this day continue to afflict their children with most horrible impurities. This chastisement became notorious in Jerusalem, although the priests and pharisees diligently sought to cover it up, just as they had tried to conceal the Resurrection of The Savior. As these events, however, were not so important, neither the Apostles nor the Evangelists wrote about them, and in the confusion of the city the multitude soon forgot them.

WORDS OF THE QUEEN.

My Daughter, in small esteem and thankfulness do the children of the Church hold this blessing of the Most High, by which, in addition to sending of His Son as Their Master and Redeemer, He sent also the Holy Ghost into His Church. So great was the love, by which He sought to draw them to Himself, that, in order to make them sharers of His Divine perfections, He sent them first The Son, who is wisdom (John 3, 16) and afterwards the Holy Ghost, who is love, so that all might be enriched in the manner in which they were capable. The Divine Spirit, in coming for the first time upon the Apostles and the others gathered with them, intended it as a pledge and testimony, that He would confer the same favor on the rest of the children of the Church, of light and of the Gospel, and that He was ready to communicate His Gifts to all, if all will dispose themselves toward receiving them. In witness to this truth The Holy Ghost came upon many of the faithful in visible form and with visible effects (Acts 8, 17; 10, 44; 11, 15), because they were truly faithful servants, humble and sincere, pure and ready of heart to receive Him. Also in our times He comes to many just souls, although not with such open manifestations, because it is neither necessary nor proper. The interior effects and gifts are all of the same nature, acting according to the disposition and state of the one who receives them.

Blessed is the soul which sighs and aspires after this Blessing and seeks to participate in this Divine Fire, which enkindles, enlightens and consumes all that is terrestrial and carnal, which purifies and raises it up to a new existence, union and participation with God Himself.

SERMON OF THE APOSTLES. MARY'S CARE FOR THE CONVERTS.

On account of the visible and open signs, by which the Holy Ghost descended upon the Apostles, the whole city of Jerusalem with its inhabitants was stirred to wonder. When the news of the astounding events at the house of the Cenacle spread about, the multitude of the people gathered in crowds to know more of the happenings (Acts 2, 6). On that day was being celebrated one of the Paschs or Feasts of the Jews; and as well on this account, as on account of the special dispensation of heaven, the city was crowded with foreigners and strangers from all parts of the World. For to them the Most High wished to manifest the wonders of the first preaching and spreading of the New Law of Grace, which The Incarnate Word, Our Redeemer and Master, had ordained for the Salvation of men.

The Sacred Apostles, who were filled with charity by the plenitude of the Gifts of the Holy Ghost and who knew that all Jerusalem was gathering at the doors of the Cenacle, asked permission of Their Mistress and Queen to go forth and preach to them; in order that such great graces might not even for a moment fail to redound to the benefit of souls and to new Glory of Their Author. They all left the house of the Cenacle and, placing themselves before the multitudes, began to preach the Mysteries of the Faith and of Eternal Life. Though until then they had been so shy and seclusive, they now stepped forth with unhesitating boldness and poured forth burning words, that like a flashing fire penetrated to the souls of their hearers.

This miracle, that all the men of so many different tongues then assembled in Jerusalem should hear the Apostles in their own language, joined to the doctrine which they preached, caused great astonishment. Yet I wish to remark, that though all the Apostles, on account of the plenitude of science and of gifts gratuitously received, were able to speak in the languages of all nations, because that was necessary for the preaching of the Gospel, yet on that occasion they all spoke the language of Palestine. Using only this idiom they were understood by all the different nationalities there present, as if they had spoken in the several idioms. This miracle the Lord wrought at the time in order that they might be understood and believed by those different nations, and in order that Saint Peter might not be obliged to repeat in the different languages of those present, what he preached to them concerning the Mysteries of Faith. He preached only once and all heard and understood him, each in his own language, and so it happened also with the other Apostles. For if each one had spoken in the language of those who heard them, and which they knew as their mother tongue, it would have been necessary for them to repeat what they said at least seven or eight times according to the different nationalities mentioned by Saint Luke (Acts 2, 9). This would have consumed a longer time than is intimated by the Sacred Text, and it would have caused great confusion and trouble to repeat the same doctrines over and over again or to speak so many languages on one occasion; nor would the miracle be so intelligible to us as the one mentioned.

The people who heard the Apostles did not understand the miracle, although they wondered at hearing each their own idiom. What Saint Luke says about their speaking different languages, must be understood as meaning, that the Apostles

194

were then and there able to understand them, as I shall mention later on (Acts 2, 4), and because on that day, those that came to the Cenacle understood them all speaking in their own language. But this miracle and wonderment caused in their hearers different effects and opinions, according to the dispositions of each one. Those that listened piously received a deep understanding of the Divinity and of the Redemption of man, now so eloquently and fervently propounded to them. They were moved eagerly to desire the knowledge of the Truth; by the Divine Light they were filled with compunction and sorrow for their sins and with desire of Divine Mercy and forgiveness. With tears in their eyes they cried out to the Apostles and asked what they must do to gain Eternal Life. Others, who hardened their hearts, altogether untouched by the Divine Truths preached by them, became indignant at the Apostles, and instead of yielding to them, called them innovators and adventurers. Many of the Jews, more impious in their perfidy and envy, inveighed against the Apostles, saying they were drunk and insane (Acts 2, 13). Among these were some of those who had again come to their senses after having fallen to the ground at the thunder caused by the coming of the Holy Ghost; for they had risen still more obstinate and rebellious against God.

The three thousand, who were converted by the first sermon of Saint Peter, were from all the nations then gathered in Jerusalem, so that forthwith all nations, without excluding any, might partake of the fruits of the Redemption, all might be gathered to the Church, and all might experience the Grace of the Holy Spirit; for the Holy Church was to be composed of all nations and tribes. Many were Jews, who had followed Christ Our Savior with kindly feelings and witnessed His sufferings and Death with compassion, as I said above. Some also of those, who had concurred in His Passion, were converted, though these were few, because many would not alter their disposition; for, if they had done so, all of them would have been admitted to mercy and received pardon for their error. After their preaching the Apostles retired that evening within the Cenacle, in order to give an account to the Mother of Mercy, the Purest Mary. With them also entered a great number of the new children of the Church, in order that they might come to know and venerate The Mother of Mercy.

But the Great Queen of the Angels was ignorant of

nothing that had happened; for from Her retreat She had heard the preaching of the Apostles and She knew the secret hearts and thoughts of all the hearers. The tenderest Mother remained prostrate with Her face upon the ground during the whole time, tearfully praying for the conversion of all that subjected themselves to the Faith of the Savior, and for all the rest, if they should consent to co-operate with the Helps and the Graces of the Lord. In order to help the Apostles in their great work of beginning to preach, and the bystanders in properly listening to them, the Most Holy Mary sent many of Her accompanying Angels with holy inspirations, encouraging the Sacred Apostles and giving them strength to inquire and to manifest more explicitly the hidden Mysteries of the humanity and Divinity of Christ our Redeemer. The Angels fulfilled all the commands of Their Queen, while She Herself exercised Her Own power and gifts according to the circumstances of the occasion. When the Apostles came to Her with those copious first fruits of their preaching and of the Holy Ghost, She received them with incredible joy and sweetness and with the most loving kindness of a True Mother.

The Apostle Saint Peter spoke to the recently converted and said to them: "My brethren, and servants of the Most High, this is the Mother of Our Redeemer and Master, Jesus Christ, whose faith you have received in acknowledging Him as True God and man. She has given Him the human form, conceiving Him in Her womb, and She bore Him, remaining a Virgin before, during and after His birth. Receive Her as your Mother, as your Refuge and Intercessor, for through Her you and we shall receive light, direction, and release from our sins and miseries." At these words of the Apostle and at the sight of Most Holy Mary these new adherents of the faith were filled with admirable light and consolation; for this privilege of conferring great interior blessings and of giving light to those who looked upon Her with pious veneration, was renewed and extended in Her at the time when She was at the right hand of Her Divine Son in Heaven. As all of those faithful partook of these blessings in the presence of Their Queen, they prostrated themselves at Her feet and with tears besought Her assistance and blessing. But the humble and prudent Queen evaded this latter, because of the presence of the Apostles, who were Priests, and of Saint Peter, the Vicar of Christ. Then this Apostle said to Her: "Lady, do not refuse to these faithful what they piously ask for the consolation of their souls." The Blessed Mary obeyed the head of the Church and in humble serenity of a Queen She gave Her blessing to the newly converted.

The love which filled their hearts made them desire to hear from Their Heavenly Mother some words of consolation; yet their humility and reverence prevented them from asking for this favor. As they perceived how obediently She had yielded to Saint Peter, they turned to him and begged him to ask Her not to send them away without some word of encouragement. Saint Peter, though he considered this favor very proper for these souls who had been born again to Christ by His preaching and that of the other Apostles, nevertheless, aware that the Mother of Wisdom knew well what was to be done, presumed to say no more than these words; "Lady, listen to the petitions of Thy servants and children." Then the Great Lady obeyed and said to the converts: "My dearest brethren in the Lord, give thanks and praise with your whole hearts to the Almighty God, because from among all men He has called and drawn you to the sure path of eternal life in the knowledge of the Holy Faith you have received. Be firm in your confession of it from all your hearts and in hearing and believing all that the Law of Grace contains as preached and ordained by its True Teacher Jesus, My Son and Your Redeemer. Be eager to hear and obey His Apostles, who teach and instruct you, so that you may be signed and marked by Baptism in the character of children of the Most High. I offer Myself as your Handmaid to assist you in all that serves toward your consolation, and I shall ask Him to look upon you as a kind Father and to manifest to you the true joy of His countenance, communicating to you also His Grace."

By this sweetest of exhortations those new children of the Church were filled with consolation, light, veneration and admiration of what they saw of the Mistress of the World; asking again for Her blessing, they for that day left Her presence, renewed and replete with the wonderful gifts of the Most High. The Apostles and Disciples from that day on continued without intermission their preaching and their miracles, and through the entire octave they instructed not only the three thousand, who had been converted on Pentecost Day, but multitudes of others, who day by day accepted the faith. Since they came from all parts of the world, they conversed and spoke with each one in His own language; for as I have said above, they spoke in various languages from that time on. This grace was given not only to the Apostles, although it was more complete and noticeable in them; also the Disciples and all the one hundred and twenty, who were in the Cenacle at the time, and also the Holy Women, who received the Holy Ghost, were thus favored. This was really necessary at the time on account of the great multitudes, who came to the Faith. Although all the men and many of the women came to the Apostles, yet many, after having heard them, went to Magdalen and her companions, who catechized, instructed and converted them and others that came at the report of the miracles they performed. For this gift was also conferred on the women, who, by the imposition of hands, cured all the sicknesses, gave sight to the blind, tongue to the mute, motion to the lame, and life to many of the dead. These and other wonders were principally wrought by the Apostles, nevertheless both their miracles and those of the women excited the wonder and astonishment of all Jerusalem; so that nothing else was talked about except the prodigies and the preaching of the Apostles of Jesus, of His Disciples, and followers of His doctrine.

This was the happy beginning and the Golden Age of the Evangelical Church, where the rushing of the stream rejoiced the City of God (Ps. 45, 5) and the current of Grace and the Gifts of the Holy Ghost fertilized this new paradise recently planted by the hands of the Savior Jesus, while in its midst stood the tree of life, Most Holy Mary. Then was faith alive, hope firm, charity ardent, sincerity pure, humility true, justice most equitable, when the faithful neither knew avarice nor followed vanity, when they trod under foot vain pomp, were free from covetousness, pride, ambition, which later prevailed among the professors of the faith, who while confessing themselves followers of Christ, denied Him in their works.

It will be possible in this third part to describe only a minute portion of the wonderful and great works accomplished by the Mighty Queen in the primitive Church; but from those which I will describe, and from Her life in this World after the Ascension, much can be inferred. For She did not rest or lose one moment or occasion of conferring some singular favor either upon the Whole Church or some of its members. For She consumed Herself either in praying and beseeching Her Divine Son, without ever experiencing a refusal; or in exhorting, instructing, counseling, and, as Treasurer and Dispenser of the Divine Favors, distributing Graces in diverse manners among the children of the Gospel. Among the hidden mysteries, which were made known to me concerning this power of the Blessed Mary, was also this, that in those first ages, during which She lived in the Holy Church, the number of the damned was proportionately very small; and that, comparatively, in those few years a greater number were saved than in many succeeding ages.

I acknowledge, that, if the lapse of time had decreased the power, the charity and clemency of that Highest Sovereign, the good fortune of those living in that happy time might cause a holy envy in those living by the light of faith in our more protracted and less favored times. It is true we have not the happiness of seeing Her, conversing with Her and listening to Her with our bodily senses; and in this respect those first children of the Church were more fortunate. But let us all remember, that in the heavenly knowledge and charity of this Most Loving Mother we were all present to Her, also during those times (Vol. III., 78); for She saw and knew us all in the order and succession in which we were to be born in the Church; and She prayed and interceded for us no less than for those who lived in Her times. Nor is She at present less powerful in Heaven, than She was then upon earth; nor less Our Mother, than of those first children; and She held us as Her own, just as well as them. But alas! that our faith and our fervor and devotion should be so very different! Not She has changed, nor is Her love less ardent, nor would we experience less of Her intercession and protection, if in these troubled times we would hasten to Her with the same sentiments of humility and fervor, asking for Her prayers and trustfully relying upon Her for help, as was the case with those devoted Christians in the first beginning. Without a doubt the whole Catholic Church would then immediately experience the same assistance of the Queen throughout the whole world.

Many of those new faithful, highly impressed with Her greatness by their conversation with the Heavenly Mistress, returned to present to Her jewels and the richest gifts; especially the women despoiled themselves of fineries to lay them at Her feet. But she would receive or permit none of these gifts. When it seemed to Her appropriate not to refuse entirely, She secretly inspired the minds of the givers to bring them to the Apostles, in order that they might be equitably and justly distributed in charity among the most poor and needy of the faithful. But the Humble Mother gratefully acknowledged them as if they had been given to Her. The poor and the sick She received with ineffable kindness, and many of them She cured of inveterate and long-standing infirmities. Through the hands of Saint John She supplied many secret wants, never omitting the least point of virtue. As the Apostles and Disciples were engaged all day in preaching the faith and in converting those that came, the Great Queen busied Herself in perparing their food and attending to their comfort; and at stated times She served the Priests on Her knees and with incredible humility and reverence asked to kiss their hands. This She observed especially with the Apostles, knowing and beholding their souls confirmed in grace, endowed with all that the Holy Ghost had wrought in them and exalted by their dignity of being the Highpriests and the founders of the Church (Eph. 2, 20). Sometimes She saw them clothed in great splendor, which elicited from Her increased reverence and veneration.

WORDS OF THE QUEEN.

My Daughter, in what thou hast come to know of the events related in this chapter, thou wilt find a great deal that points to the mystery of the predestination of souls. Be convinced that, since the Redemption was so overflowing and copious, it was sufficient for the salvation of all men (Rom. 5, 20). The Divine Truth was made known to all, whoever heard its preaching or who saw the effects of the coming of the Godman into the World. Besides the outward preaching and knowledge of the remedy, all received interior inspirations and helps in order to seek and accept the means. You are surprised that, in spite of all this, only three thousand were converted by the first sermon of the Apostle among all that great multitude then in Jerusalem. It should cause a greater surprise that in our times so few are converted to the way of Eternal Life, as the Gospel is more widespread, its preaching is frequent, its ministers numerous, the light of the Church clearer and the knowledge of the Divine Mysteries more definite. With all this men are blinder, the hearts more hardened, pride more inflated, avarice more bold, and all the vices are practiced without fear of God and without consideration.

In this most perverse and unhappy state mortals cannot complain of the most high and equitable providence of the Lord, who offers to all and every one His Fatherly Mercy, and points out to them both the way of life and the way of death; so that if any man hardens his heart, God can permit it in strictest justice. The reprobate will have none but themselves to blame, if afterwards, when there is no more time, they shall be uselessly dismayed with what in opportune time they could and should have known. If in the short and transient life, which is given to them in order to merit the Eternal, they close their eyes and ears to the Truth and to the Light, and if they listen to the demon, giving themselves up to all the promptings of his malice; if they thus abuse the goodness and clemency of the Lord, what can they then allege as their excuse? If they do not know how to pardon an injury and for the slightest offense meditate the direst vengeance; if, for the sake of increasing their property, they prevent the entire order of reason and of natural brotherhood; if for a passing delight they forget the Eternal pains, and if, in addition to all this, they despise the warnings, helps and admonitions sent to them by God to inspire them with the fear of perdition and induce them to avoid it, how shall they afterwards find fault with the Divine Clemency? Let then mortals, who have sinned against God, undeceive themselves: without penance there shall be no grace, without reform no pardon, without pardon no glory. But just as these are not conceded to those that are unworthy, so they are also never denied to those that are worthy; nor is ever the Mercy of God withheld from any one who seeks to obtain it.

BAPTISM OF THE CONVERTS. THE FIRST MASS. PERPETUAL PRESENCE OF THE HOLY SPECIES IN MARY.

As the Apostles continued their preaching and wonders in Jerusalem the number of the faithful increased and, as Saint Luke says in the fourth chapter of the Acts, after seven days reached five thousand. All of them were busy catechising the newcomers in preparation for Baptism, though that work was done principally by the Disciples; for the Apostles were preaching and were conducting some controversies with the pharisees and sadducees. The Queen, with the assistance of

Her Angels and of the other Marys, proceeded to prepare and adorn the hall, in which Her divine Son had celebrated the Last Supper; and with Her own hands She cleansed it and scrubbed it for His return in the Consecration to be performed on the next day. She asked the owner to furnish it in the same way as I have described for the Thursday of the Last Supper and the devout host deferred to Her wishes with deepest reverence. She also prepared the unleavened bread and the wine necessary for the Consecration, together with the same paten and chalice in which the Savior had consecrated. For the Baptism She provided pure water and the basins for administering it with ease and reverence. Then the loving Mother retired and passed the night in most fervent aspirations, prostrations, thanksgiving and other exercises of exalted prayer; offering to the Eternal Father all that She, in Her Heavenly Wisdom, knew would help worthily to prepare Herself and all the rest for the worthy administration of Baptism.

Early the next day, which was the octave of the coming of the Holy Ghost, all the faithful and catechumens gathered with the Apostles and Disciples in the house of the Cenacle. Saint Peter preached to this gathering instructing them in the nature and excellence of Baptism, the need in which they stood of it and its Divine Effects, how they would, through it, be made members of the Mystical Body of the Church, receive an interior character; be regenerated to a new existence as children of God and inheritors of His glory through the remission of sins and sanctifying grace. He exhorted them to the observance of the Divine Law, to which they subjected themselves by their own free will, and to humble thanksgiving for this benefit and for all the others, which they received from the hands of the Most High. He explained to them also the Mysterious and Sacred Truth of the Holy Eucharist, which was to be celebrated in the Consecration of the True Body and Blood of Jesus Christ, and he admonished all those especially, who were to receive Holy Communion after their Baptism.

Through this sermon all the converts were inspired with additional fervor; for their dispositions were altogether sincere, the words of the Apostles full of life and penetration, and the interior grace very abundant. Then the Apostles themselves began to baptize amid the most devout and orderly attention of the others. The catechumens entered one door of the Cenacle and after being baptized, they passed out through another, while the Disciples and other of the faithful acted as ushers. The Most Holy Mary was present at the entire ceremony, although keeping to one side of the hall. She prayed for all of them and broke forth in canticles of praise. She recognized the effects of Baptism in each one, according to the greater or less degree of virtues infused in their souls. She beheld them renewed and washed in the Blood of the Lamb, and their souls restored to a Divine Purity and spotlessness. In witness of these effects, a most clear light, visible to all that were present, descended upon each one that was baptized. By this miracle God wished to authenticate the first beginnings of This Sacrament in His Holy Church, and to console both those first children and us, who are made partakers of this blessing without much adverting to it or giving thanks for it.

This administration of Baptism was continued on that day until all were baptized, although there were about five thousand to receive it. While the baptized were making their thanksgiving for this admirable blessing, the Apostles with all the Disciples and the faithful spent some time in prayer. All of them prostrated themselves on the ground adoring the Infinite and Immutable God, and confessing their own unworthiness of receiving Him in the Most August Sacrament of the Altar. In this profound humility and adoration they prepared themselves more immediately for Communion. And then they recited the same psalms and prayers which Christ had recited before consecrating, imitating faithfully that Sacred Function just as they had seen it performed by Their Divine Master. Saint Peter took in his hands the unleavened bread, and, after raising up his eyes to heaven with admirable devotion, he pronounced over the bread the Words of Consecration of the Most Holy Body of Christ, as had been done before the Lord Jesus (II Cor. 9, 24). Immediately the Cenacle was filled with the visible splendor of innumerable angels; and this light converged in a most singular manner on the Queen of Heaven and Earth and was seen by all those present. Then Saint Peter consecrated the Chalice and performed all the ceremonies, which Christ had observed with the Consecrated Body and Blood, raising them up for the adoration of all the faithful. The Apostle partook himself of the Sacrament and communicated it to the eleven Apostles as Most Holy Mary had instructed him. Thereupon, at the hands of Saint Peter, the Heavenly Mother partook of it, while the Celestial Spirits there present attended with ineffable reverence. In approaching the altar the Great Lady made three profound prostrations, touching the ground with her face.

She returned to Her place, and it is impossible to describe in words the effects of this participation of The Holy Eucharist in this most exalted of creatures. She was entirely transformed and elevated, completely absorbed in this Divine Conflagration of the love of Her Most Holy Son, whom She had now received bodily. She remained in a trance, elevated from the floor; but the holy angels shielded Her somewhat from view according to Her own wish, in order that the attention of those present might not be unduly attracted by the Divine effects apparent in Her. The disciples continued to distribute Holy Communion, first to the Disciples and then to the others who had been believers before the Ascension. But of the five thousand newly baptized only one thousand received Communion on that day; because not all were entirely prepared or furnished with the insight and attention required for receiving the Lord in This Great Sacrament and Mystery of the Altar.

To explain the rare and prodigious favor, that the Sacramental Body of Christ in the Sacred Species should be preserved continually in the bosom of Mary, it is not necessary to seek for another cause than that underlying all the other favors with which God distinguished this great Lady, namely: that it was His Holy Will and according to His Infinite Wisdom, by which He performs according to measure and weight all that is befitting (Wis. 11, 21). Christian prudence and piety will be content to know as a reason, that God had singled this mere Creature out to be His natural Mother, and that therefore She alone, of all creatures, deserved this distinction. As this miracle of Her Mothership was unique and without parallel, it would be shameful ignorance to seek proofs of what The Lord did in Her by comparing it with what He did or ever will do in other souls; since Mary alone rises supereminently above the common order of all. Yet, though all this is true, the Lord nevertheless wishes that by the light of Faith and by other enlightenment, we seek the reasons of the propriety and equity, according to which the powerful arm of the Almighty wrought these wonders in His Most Worthy Mother, so that in them we may know and bless Him in Her and through Her; and so that we may understand, how secure our salvation, all our hope, and our lot are in the hands of that Powerful Queen, toward whom Her Son has directed all the excess of His Love. In accordance with these truths I will explain what has been made known to me of This Mystery.

The Heavenly Mother lived thirty-three years in the company of Her Son and True God; and from the time when He was born of Her virginal womb She never left Him to the time of His death on the Cross. She nursed Him, served Him, followed Him and imitated Him, conducting Herself always as a Mother, Daughter and Spouse, as a most faithful Servant and Friend; She enjoyed the sight of Him, His conversation, His Doctrine and the favors, which, by all these meritorious services, She attained in this mortal life. Christ ascended into Heaven, and the force of love and right reason demanded, that He should take to Heaven with Him His Most Loving Mother, in order that He should not be deprived of Her there, nor She in this world of His presence and company. But the most ardent love which both of Them had for men, dissolved in a manner these bonds of union, inducing Our Kindest Mother to return to the World in order to establish the Church; and moving the Son to give His consent to Her absence from Him during that time. But as the Son of God was powerful enough to recompense Her for this privation to a certain extent, it became for Him an obligation of His Love to make such a recompense. And the fulfillment of this obligation would not have been so publicly acknowledged or made so manifest, if He denied His Blessed Mother the favor of accompanying Her upon earth, while He remained seated at the Glory of the right hand of His Father. Besides, the most ardent love of the Blessed Mother, having been accustomed and nourished in the presence of the Lord Her Son, would have inflicted upon Her insufferable violence, if for so many years She was to be deprived of that kind of presence of Him, which was possible during Her stay in the Church.

From the understanding which has been given me of the mystery of the Love of Christ the Lord for His Most Holy Mother and of the force with which He was drawn toward Her, I would go so far as to say, that if He had not found this way of remaining with Her in the Sacramental Species, He would have come down from the right hand of the

Father to the World in order to render companionship to His Mother while She sojourned with His Church. And if it had been necessary that the heavenly mansions and the Celestial Courtiers should be deprived of the presence of the most sacred humanity from that time, He would have considered that of less importance than to be deprived of the company of His Mother. It is no exaggeration to say this, when we all must confess, that in the purest Mary the Lord found a correspondence and a degree of love more conformable to His Will than in all the blessed combined; and consequently, His Own Love for Her exceeded His Love for all others. If the Shepherd of the Gospel leaves the ninety-nine sheep in order to go in search of only one that is lost, and if we nevertheless dare not say of Him that He leaves the greater for the less; it should not cause wonder in us that This Divine Shepherd should leave all the rest of the saints in order to be in the company of His Most Sincere Sheep, who clothed Him with Her own nature and raised and nourished Him as a Mother. Without a doubt the eyes of His Beloved Spouse and Mother would attract Him in swiftest flight from those heights (Cant. 6, 4) to that earth, where He had lived, whither He had before this come for the salvation of the children of Adam, toward whom He was less attracted, yea rather repelled by their sins and by the necessity of suffering for them. If now He descended to live with His Beloved Mother, it would not be to suffer and die; but to enjoy the delights of Her company. Fortunately it was not necessary to rob Heaven of His presence; since by descending in Sacramental Form He could satisfy both His Own Love and that of His Most Blessed Mother, in whose heart, as in his couch, this true Solomon could take up His rest without leaving the right hand of His Eternal Father (Cant. 3, 7).

WORDS OF THE QUEEN.

Consider attentively the common deception of mortals and the woeful damage they suffer. For in the decisions of their will they ordinarily are moved solely by what they perceive through the senses, and they immediately proceed to act upon their choice without further consideration or counsel. Since the sensible impressions immediately move the animal passions and inclinations, it is evident that men do not act according to right reason, but according to the impulse of passion, excited by the senses and their objects. Hence, he that considers only the injury and pain caused, is straightway moved to vengeance; he that follows only his hankering after strange property, as soon as he lays his eyes upon it, is impelled to injustice. In the same manner act so many unfortunates, who follow the concupiscence of the eyes, the movements of the flesh, and the pride of life, because these are the only things offered by the world and the devil. In their blind deception they follow darkness as their light, taste the bitter as sweet, take deadly poison for remedy of their souls, and hold that for wisdom which is nothing but diabolical and earthly ignorance. Do thou guard thyself against these pernicious errors, and never resolve on anything, or govern thyself by anything that is merely sensible or arising from sensible impressions, nor pursue the advantages held out through them. In thy actions take counsel first of all from the interior knowledge and light communicated to thee by God, in order that thou mayest not go blindly forward; and He shall always grant thee sufficient guidance. Immediately seek the advice of thy superiors and teachers, if thou canst do so before making thy choice. And if thy superior or teacher is not at hand, seek counsel of others, even inferiors; for this is more secure than to follow thy own will, which may be disturbed and blinded by passion. This is the rule to be followed especially in the exterior works, pursuing them with recollection, with secrecy, and according to the demands of circumstances and fraternal charity as they occur. In all of them it is necessary not to lose out of sight the north-star of interior light, while moving in the profound gulf of the intercourse with creatures, where there is continual danger of perishing.

SOLICITUDE OF MARY FOR THE APOSTLES AND THE FAITHFUL.

As the New Law of Grace continued to spread in Jerusalem so the number of the faithful increased and the New Evangelical Church was augmented day by day (Acts 5, 14). In like manner did the solicitude and attention of Its Great Queen and Teacher, Mary, expand toward the new children engendered by the Apostles through their preaching. As they were the foundation-stones of the Church, on which the security of that building was to depend, the Most Prudent

Lady lavished especial care upon the Apostolic College. Her heavenly solicitude augmented in proportion to the wrath of Lucifer against the followers of Christ and especially against the Apostles, as the Ministers of Eternal Salvation to the other faithful. It will never be possible to describe or to estimate in this life the blessings and favors conferred by Her upon the Church and upon each of Its Mystical members. This happened especially in regard to the Apostles and Disciples; for as has been revealed to me not a day or hour passed, in which She did not work for them many wonders. I will relate in this chapter some of the events, which are very instructive on account of the secrets of Divine Providence therein contained. From them we can form an estimate of the most vigilant charity and zeal of the Blessed Mary for souls.

All the Apostles She loved and served with incredible affection and reverence, both on account of their great holiness and on account of their dignity as Priests, as Ministers, Preachers and founders of the Gospel. During all their stay in Jerusalem She attended upon them, counseled and directed them in the manner noted above. With the increase of the Church they were obliged to go outside of Jerusalem in order to baptize and admit to the Faith many of the inhabitants of the neighboring places; but they always returned to the city, because they had purposely delayed separating from each other, or leaving Jerusalem, until they should receive orders to do so. From the Acts we learn that Saint Peter went to Lydda and Jaffa, where he raised Tabitha from the dead and performed other miracles, returning again to Jerusalem. Although Saint Luke relates these excursions after speaking of the death of Saint Stephen (of which I shall treat in the following chapter), yet during these events, many were converted throughout Palestine, and it was necessary, that the Apostles go forth to preach to them and to confirm them in the Faith, always returning in order to give an account of their doings to Their Heavenly Mistress.

During all their journeys and preachings the common enemy of all sought to hinder the spread of the Divine Word, or its fruit, by rousing the unbelievers to many contradictions and altercations with the Apostles and their listeners or converts; for it seemed to the infernal dragon more easy to assault them, when he saw them removed and far from the protection of Their Mistress. So formidable the Great Queen of the Angels appeared to the hellish hosts, that in spite of the eminent holiness of the Apostles, Lucifer imagined them disarmed and at his mercy, easily approachable to his temptations, as soon as they left the presence of Mary. The furious pride of this dragon, as is written in Job (Job 41, 18), esteems the toughest steel as weak straw, and the hardest bronze as a stick of rotten wood. He fears not the dart nor the sling; but he dreaded the protection of the Most Blessed Mary, and in tempting the Apostles, he waited until they should have left Her presence.

But Her protection failed them not on that account; for the Great Lady, from the watch-tower of Her exalted knowledge, reached out in every direction. Like a most vigilant sentinel She discovered the assaults of Lucifer and hastened to the relief of Her sons and Ministers of Her Lord. When in Her absence She could not speak to the Apostles in any of their afflictions, She immediately sent Her Holy Angels to their assistance in order to encourage, forewarn and console them; and sometimes also to drive away the assaulting demons. All this the Celestial Spirits executed promptly in compliance with the orders of Their Queen. At times they would do it secretly by inspirations and interior consolations; at others, and more frequently, they manifested themselves visibly, assuming most beautiful and refulgent bodies and informing the Apostles of what was proper for the occasion, or what had been ordered by Their Mistress. This happened very often on account of their purity and holiness and on account of the necessity of favoring them with such abundance of consolation and encouragement. In all their difficulties and labors the Most Loving Mother thus assisted them, besides offering up for them Her continual prayers and thanksgiving. She was the strong Woman, whose domestics were sheltered by double garments; the Mother of the family, who supplied all with nourishment and who by the labors of Her hands planted the vineyard of the Lord.

With all the other faithful She proportionately exhibited the same care; and although there were many converts in Jerusalem and in Palestine, She remembered them all in their necessities and tribulations. And She thought not only of the needs of their souls, but of those of the body, and many She cured of most grave sicknesses. Others, whom She knew were not to be cured miraculously, She visited and assisted in person. Of the poor She took a still greater care, with Her own hand administering to them food on their beds of sickness, and seeing to their being kept clean, as if She were the servant of all, infirm with the infirm. So great was the humility, the charity and solicitude of the Great Queen of the World, that She refused no service or lowliest ministry to the faithful, no matter how humble and insignificant the condition of those applying for Her assistance. She filled each one with joy and consolation and lightened all their labors. Those upon whom on account of their absence She could not personally attend, She assisted secretly through Her Holy Angels or by Her prayers and petitions.

In an especial manner Her Maternal Kindness exhibited itself to those who were in the agony of death; for she attended many of the dying and would not leave them, until they had secured their eternal salvation. For those who went to purgatory She offered up most fervent prayers and performed some works of penance, such as prostrations in the form of a cross, genuflections and other exercises, by which She satisfied for their faults. Then She sent one of Her Angels in order to draw them from purgatory and present them to Her Son in Heaven as His own and as the fruits of His Blood and Redemption. This happiness the Queen of heaven procured to many souls during Her stay upon earth. And, as far as was made known to me, this favor is not denied in our days to those, who during their earthly life dispose themselves properly for meriting her presence.

SAINT GABRIEL BRINGS NOTICE OF DEATH.

In writing of what still remains of the history of Our Lady, of Our Only and Heavenly Phœnix, the Most Blessed Mary, it is no more than right that our hearts be filled with tenderness and our eyes with tears at the sweet and touching marvels of the last years of Her life. I should wish to exhort the devout faithful not to read of them nor consider them as past and absent, since the powerful virtue of faith can make these truths present to the mind; and if we look upon them with the proper piety and Christian devotion, without a doubt we shall gather the sweetest fruit, and our hearts shall feel the effects and rejoice in the good, which our eyes cannot see.

The Most Holy Mary had arrived at the age of sixty-seven years without having tarried in Her career, ceased in Her flight, mitigated the flame of Her Love, or lessened the increase of Her merits from the first instant of Her Conception. As all this had continued to grow in each moment of Her life, the ineffable gifts, benefits and favors of the Lord had made Her entirely Godlike and spiritual; the affectionate ardors and desires of Her most chaste heart did not allow Her any rest outside the centre of Her Love; the bounds of the flesh were most violently irksome; the overwhelming attraction of the Divinity to unite Itself with Her with Eternal and most close bonds, (according to our mode of speaking) had attained the summit of power in Her; and the earth itself, made unworthy by the sins of mortals to contain the Treasure of Heaven, could no longer bear the strain of withholding Her from Her True Lord. The eternal Father desired His Only and True Daughter; the Son His beloved and Most Loving Mother; and the Holy Ghost the embraces of His Most Beautiful Spouse. The angels longed for Their Queen, the Saints for Their Great Lady; and all the heavens mutely awaited the presence of Their Empress Who should fill Them with glory, with Her beauty and delight. All that could be alleged in favor of Her still remaining in the world and in the Church, was the need of such a Mother and Mistress, and the love, which God Himself had for the miserable children of Adam.

But as some term and end was to be placed to the earthly career of our Queen, the Divine Consistory (according to our mode of understanding), conferred upon the manner of glorifying the Most Blessed Mother and established the kind of loving reward due to Her for having so copiously fulfilled all the designs of the Divine Mercy among the children of Adam during the many years in which She had been the Foundress and Teacher of his Holy Church. The Almighty therefore resolved to delight and console Her by giving Her definite notice of the term still remaining of Her life and revealing to Her the day and hour of the longed for end of Her earthly banishment. For this purpose the Most Blessed Trinity dispatched the Archangel Gabriel with many others of the Celestial Heirarchies, who should announce to the Queen when and how Her mortal life should come to an end and pass over into the eternal.

The Holy Prince descended with the rest to the Cenacle in Jerusalem and entered the oratory of The Great Lady, where they found Her prostrate on the ground in the form of a

211

cross, asking mercy for sinners. But hearing the sound of their music and perceiving them present, She rose to Her knees in order to hear the message and show respect to the Ambassador of Heaven and His companions, Who in white and refulgent garments surrounded Her with wonderful delight and reverence. All of them had come with crowns and palms in their hands, each one with a different one; but all of them represented the diverse premiums and rewards of inestimable beauty and value to be conferred upon Their Great Queen and Lady. Gabriel saluted Her with the Ave Maria, and added thereto: "Our Empress and Lady, the Omnipotent and the Holy of the Holy sends us from His Heavenly Court to announce to Thee in His name the most happy end of Thy pilgrimage and banishment upon earth in mortal life. Soon, O Lady, is that day and hour approaching, in which, according to Thy longing desires, Thou shalt pass through natural death to the possession of the Eternal and Immortal Life, which awaits Thee in the glory and at the right hand of Thy Divine Son, our God. Exactly three years from today Thou shalt be taken up and received into the everlasting joy of the Lord, where all its inhabitants await Thee, longing for Thy presence."

The Most Holy Mary heard this message with ineffable jubilee of Her purest and most loving spirit, and, prostrating Herself again upon the earth, She answered in the same words as at the Incarnation of the Word: "Ecce ancilla Domini, fiat mihi secundum verbum tuum." "Behold the handmaid of the Lord, be it done according to Thy word" (Luke 1, 38). Then She asked the Holy Angels and Ministers of the Most High to help Her give thanks for this welcome and joyful news. The Blessed Mother alternately with the Seraphim and other Angels, sang the responses of a canticle that lasted for two hours. Although by Their nature and supernatural gifts the Angelic Spirits are so subtle, wise and excellent, They were nevertheless excelled in all this by Their Queen and Lady, as vassals are by their sovereign; for in Her, grace and wisdom abounded as in a Teacher, in them, only as in disciples. Having finished this canticle and humiliating Herself anew, She charged the supernal Spirits to beseech the Lord to prepare Her for Her passage from mortal to Eternal Life, and to ask all the other Angels and Saints in Heaven to pray for the same favor. They offered to obey Her in all things, and therewith Saint Gabriel took leave and returned with all His Company to the Empyrean Heaven.

The Great Queen and Lady of all the universe remained alone in Her oratory, and amid tears of humble joy prostrated Herself upon the earth, embraced it as the Common Mother of us all, saying: "Earth, I give thee thanks as I ought, because without My merit thou hast sustained Me sixty-seven years. Thou art a creature of the Most High and by His Will thou hast sustained Me until now. I ask thee now to help Me during the rest of My dwelling upon thee, so that, just as I have been created of thee and upon thee, I may through thee and from thee be raised to the Blessed Vision of My Maker." She addressed also other creatures, saying: "Ye heavens, planets, stars and elements, created by the Powerful Hands of My Beloved, faithful witnesses and proclaimers of His Greatness and Beauty, you also I thank for the preservation of My life; help Me then from today on, that, with the Divine Favor, I may begin anew to perfect My life during the time left of My career, in order that I may show Myself thankful to My and your Creator."

The Devout Queen resolved to take leave of the holy places before Her departure into heaven, and having obtained the consent of Saint John She left the house with him and with the thousand Angels of Her guard. Although these Sovereign Princes had always served and accompanied Her in all Her errands, occupations and journeys, without having absented themselves for one moment since the instant of Her birth; yet on this occasion they manifested themselves to Her with greater beauty and refulgence, as if they felt special joy in seeing themselves already at the beginning of Her last journey into heaven. The Heavenly Princess, setting aside human occupations in order to enter upon Her journey to the real and true fatherland, visited all the memorable places of our Redemption, marking each with the sweet abundance of Her tears, recalling the sorrowful memories of what Her Son there suffered, and fervently renewing its effects by most fervent acts of love, clamors and petitions for all the faithful, who should devoutly and reverently visit these holy places during the future ages of the Church. On Calvary She remained a longer time, asking of Her Divine Son the full effects of His redeeming Death for all the multitudes of souls there snatched from destruction. The ardor of Her ineffable charity during this prayer rose to such a pitch, that it would

213

have destroyed Her life, if it had not been sustained by Divine Power.

The Queen asked also the Angels of the Sanctuaries and the Evangelist to give Her their blessing in this last leave-taking; and therewith She returned to Her oratory shedding tears of tenderest affection for what She loved so much upon earth. There She prostrated Herself with Her face upon the earth and poured forth another long and most fervent prayer for the Church; and She persevered in it, until in an abstractive vision of the Divinity, the Lord had given Her assurance that He had heard and conceded Her petitions at the Throne of His mercy. In order to give the last touch of Holiness to Her works, She asked permission of the Lord to take leave of the Holy Church, saying: "Exalted and Most High God, Redeemer of the world, Head of the Saints and the Predestined, Justifier and Glorifier of souls, I am a Child of the Holy Church, planted and acquired by Thy Blood. Give Me, O Lord, permission to take leave of such a Loving Mother, and of all My brethren, Thy children, belonging to it." She was made aware of the consent of the Lord and therefore turned to the Mystical Body of the Church, addressing it in sweet tears as follows:

"Holy Catholic Church, which in the coming ages shall be called the Roman, My Mother and Mistress, true treasure of My soul, Thou hast been the only Consolation of My banishment; the refuge and ease of My labors; My recreation, My joy and My hope; Thou hast sustained Me in My course; in Thee have I lived as a pilgrim to the Fatherland; and Thou hast nourished Me after I had received in Thee My existence in grace through Thy Head, Christ Jesus, My Son and My Lord. In Thee are the treasures and the riches of His infinite merits; Thou shalt be for His faithful children the secure way to the promised land, and Thou shalt safeguard them on their dangerous and difficult pilgrimage. Thou shalt be the Mistress of the nations to whom all owe reverence; in Thee are the rich and inestimable jewels of the anxieties, labors, affronts, hardships, torments, of the Cross and of death, which all are consecrated by those of My Lord, Thy Progenitor, Thy Master, Thy Chief, and are reserved for His more distinguished servants and His dearest friends. Thou hast adorned and enriched Me with Thy jewels in order that I might enter in the nuptials of the Spouse; Thou hast made Me wealthy, prosperous and happy, and Thou containest within Thee Thy Author in the Most Holy Sacrament. My happy Mother, Church Militant, rich art Thou and abundant in treasures! For Thee have I always reserved My heart and My solicitude; but now is the time come to part from Thee and leave Thy sweet companionship, in order to reach the end of My course. Make Me partaker of Thy great goods; bathe Me copiously in the sacred liquor of the Blood of the Lamb, preserved in Thee as a powerful means of sanctifying many worlds. At the cost of My life a thousand times would I bring to Thee all the nations and tribes of mortals, that they might enjoy Thy treasures. My Beloved Church, My honor and My glory, I am about to leave Thee in mortal life; but in the eternal life I will find Thee joyful in an existence which includes all good. From that place I shall look upon Thee with love, and pray always for Thy increase, Thy prosperity and Thy progress."

This was the parting of the Most Blessed Mary from the Mystical Body of the Holy Roman Catholic Church, the Mother of the Faithful, in order that all who should hear of Her, might know by Her sweet tears and endearments, in what veneration, love and esteem She held that Holy Church. After thus taking leave, the Great Mistress, as the Mother of Wisdom, prepared to make Her testament and Last Will. When She manifested this most prudent wish to the Lord, He deigned to approve of it by His own royal presence. For this purpose, with myriads of attending Angels, the Three Persons of the Most Blessed Trinity descended to the oratory of Their Daughter and Spouse, and when the Queen had adored the Infinite Being of God, She heard a voice speaking to Her: "Our Chosen Spouse, make Thy last will as thou desirest, for We shall confirm it and execute it entirely by Our Infinite Power." The Most Prudent Mother remained for some time lost in the profoundness of Her humility, seeking to know first the Will of the Most High before She should manifest Her own. The Lord responded to Her modest desires and the Person of the Father said to Her: "My Daughter, Thy will shall be pleasing and acceptable to Me; for Thou art not wanting in the merits of good works in parting from this mortal life, that I should not satisfy Thy desires." The same encouragement was given to Her by the Son and the Holy Ghost. Therewith the Most Blessed Mary made Her will in this form:

"Highest Lord and Eternal God, I, a vile wormlet of the earth, confess and adore Thee with all the reverence of My inmost soul as the Father, the Son and the Holy Ghost, Three Persons distinct in One Undivided and Eternal Essence, One Substance, One in Infinite Majesty of attributes and perfection. I confess Thee as the One True Creator and Preserver of all that has being. In Thy kingly presence I declare and say, that My last will is this: Of the goods of mortal life and of the world in which I live, I possess none that I can leave; for never have I possessed or loved anything beside Thee, Who art My good and all My possession. To the heavens, the stars and planets, to the elements and all creatures in them I give thanks, because according to Thy will they have sustained Me without My merit, and lovingly I desire and ask them to serve and praise Thee in the offices and ministries assigned to them, and that they continue to sustain and benefit My brethren and fellowmen. In order that they may do it so much the better, I renounce and assign to mankind the possession, and as far as possible, the dominion of them, which Thy Majesty has given Me over these irrational creatures, so that they may now serve and sustain My fellowmen. Two tunics and a cloak, which served to cover Me, I leave to John for His disposal, since I hold Him as a son. My Body I ask the earth to receive again for Thy service, since it is the common mother and serves Thee as Thy creature; My soul, despoiled of its body and of all visible things, O my God, I resign into Thy hands, in order that it may love and magnify Thee through all Thy eternities. My merits and all the treasures, which with Thy Grace through My works and exertions I have acquired, I leave to the Holy Church, My Mother and My Mistress, as My Residuary Heiress and with Thy permission I there deposit them, wishing them to be much greater. And I desire that before all else they redound to the exaltation of Thy Holy Name and procure the fulfillment of Thy Will on earth as it is done in heaven, and that all the nations come to the knowledge, love and veneration of Thee, the True God."

"In the second place I offer these merits for My Masters the Apostles and Priests, of the present and of the future ages, so that in view of Them Thy Ineffable Clemency may make them apt ministers, worthy of their office and state, filed with wisdom, virtue and holiness, by which they may edify and sanctify the souls redeemed by Thy Blood. In the

216

third place I offer them for the spiritual good of My devoted servants, who invoke and call upon Me, in order that they may receive Thy Protection and Grace, and afterwards Eternal Life. In the fourth place I desire that My services and labors may move Thee to mercy toward all the sinning children of Adam, in order that they may withdraw from their sinful state. From this hour on I propose and desire to continue My prayers for them in Thy Divine Presence, as long as the world shall last. This, Lord and My God, is My last Will, always subject to Thy Own." At the conclusion of this testament of the Queen, the Most Blessed Trinity approved and confirmed it; and Christ the Redeemer, as if authorizing it all, witnessed it by writing in the Heart of His Mother these words: "Let it be done as Thou wishest and ordainest."

If all we children of Adam, and especially we who are born in the law of grace, had no other obligation toward the Most Blessed Mary than this of having been constituted heirs of Her immense merits and of all that is mentioned in this short and mysterious testament, we could never repay our debt, even if in return we should offer our lives and endure all the sufferings of the most courageous martyrs and saints.

WORDS OF THE QUEEN.

Among the absurd fallacies introduced by the demon into the world none is greater or more pernicious than the forgetfulness of the hour of death and of what is to happen at the court of the rigorous Judge. Consider, My daughter, that through this portal sin entered into the world; for the serpent sought to convince the first woman principally, that she would not die and need not think of that matter (Gen. 11, 4). Thus continually deceived, there are uncountable fools who live without thought of death and who die forgetful of the unhappy lot that awaits them. In order that thou mayest not be seized by this human perversity, begin to convince thyself now that thou must die irrevocably; that thou hast received much and paid little; that the account shall be so much the more rigorous, as the Judge has been more liberal in the gifts and talents lavished upon thee in thy sphere. I do not ask of thee more, and also not less, that what thou owest to thy Spouse and to thy Lord, which is always to operate the best in all places, times and occasions, without permitting any forgetfulness, intermission or carelessness.

THE GLORIOUS TRANSITION OF THE VIRGIN MARY.

And now, according to the decree of the Divine Will, the day was approaching in which the True and Living Ark of the Covenant was to be placed in the temple of the celestial Jerusalem, with a greater glory and higher jubilee than its prophetic figure was installed by Solomon in the sanctuary beneath the wings of the Cherubim (III King 8, 8). Three days before the most happy Transition of the Great Lady the Apostles and Disciples were gathered in Jerusalem and in the Cenacle. The first one to arrive was Saint Peter, Who was transported from Rome by the hands of an Angel. At that place the Angel appeared to Him and told Him that the passing away of the Most Blessed Mary was imminent and that the Lord commanded Him to go to Jerusalem in order to be present at that event. Thereupon the Angel took Him up and brought Him from Italy to the Cenacle. Thither the Queen of the World had retired, somewhat weakened in body by the force of Her Divine Love; for since She was so near to Her end, She was subjected more completely to love's effects.

The Great Lady came to the entrance of Her oratory in order to receive the Vicar of Christ our Savior. Kneeling at His feet She asked His blessing and said: "I give thanks and praise to the Almighty, that He has brought to Me the Holy Father for assisting Me in the hour of My death." Then came Saint Paul, to whom the Queen showed the same reverence with similar tokens of Her pleasure at seeing Him. The Apostles saluted Her as the Mother of God, as their Queen and as Mistress of all creation; but with a sorrow equal to their reverence, because they knew that they had come to witness Her passing away. After these Apostles came the others and the Disciples still living. Three days after, they were all assembled in the Cenacle. The Heavenly Mother received them all with profound humility, reverence and love, asking each one to bless Her. All of them complied, and saluted Her with admirable reverence. By orders of the Lady given to Saint John, and with the assistance of Saint James the less, they were all hospitably entertained and accommodated.

Some of the Apostles who had been transported by the Angels and informed by them of the purpose of their coming, were seized with tenderest grief and shed abundant tears at the thought of losing their only Protection and Consolation. Others were as yet ignorant of their approaching loss, especially the Disciples, who had not been positively informed by the Angels, but were moved by interior inspirations and a sweet and forcible intimation of God's Will to come to Jerusalem. They immediately conferred with Saint Peter, desirous of knowing the occasion of their meeting; for all of them were convinced, that if there had been no special occasion, the Lord would not have urged them so strongly to come. The apostle Saint Peter, as the Head of the Church, called them all together in order to tell them of the cause of their coming, and spoke to the assembly: "My dearest children and brethren, the Lord has called and brought us to Jerusalem from remote regions not without a cause most urgent and sorrowful to us. The Most High wishes now to raise up to the Throne of Eternal Glory His Most Blessed Mother, our Mistress, our Consolation and Protection. His Divine Decree is that we all be present at Her most happy and glorious Transition. When our Master and Redeemer ascended to the right hand of His Father, although He left us orphaned of His most delightful presence, we still retained His Most Blessed Mother and our light now leaves us, what shall we do? What help or hope have we to encourage us on our pilgrimage? I find none except the hope that we all shall follow Her in due time."

Saint Peter could speak no farther, because uncontrollable tears and sighs interrupted Him. Neither could the rest of the Apostles answer for a long time, during which, amid copious and tenderest tears, they gave vent to the groans of their inmost heart. After some time the Vicar of Christ recovered Himself and added: "My children, let us seek the presence of our Mother and Lady. Let us spend the time left of Her life in Her company and ask Her to bless us." They all betook themselves to the oratory of the Great Queen and found Her kneeling upon a couch, on which She was wont to recline for a short rest. They saw Her full of beauty and celestial light, surrounded by the thousand Angels of Her guard.

The natural condition and appearance of Her Sacred and Virginal Body were the same as at Her thirty-third year; for, as I have already stated, from that age onward it experienced no change. It was not affected by the passing years, showing no signs of age, no wrinkles in Her face or body, nor giving signs of weakening or fading, as in other children of Adam, who gradually fall away and drop from the natural perfection of early man or womanhood. This unchangeableness was the privilege of the Most Blessed Mary alone, as well because it consorted with the stability of Her Purest Soul, as because it was the natural consequence of Her immunity from the sin of Adam, the effects of which in this regard touched neither Her Sacred Body nor her Purest Soul. The Apostles and Disciples, and some of the other faithful, occupied Her chamber, all of them preserving the utmost order in Her presence. Saint Peter and Saint John placed themselves at the head of the couch. The Great Lady looked upon them all with Her accustomed modesty and reverence and spoke to them as follows: "My dearest children, give permission to your Servant to speak in your presence and to disclose My humble desires." Saint Peter answered that all listened with attention and would obey Her in all things; and He begged Her to seat Herself upon the couch, while speaking to them. It seemed to Saint Peter that She was exhausted from kneeling so long and that She had taken that position in order to pray to the Lord, and that in speaking to them, it was proper She should be seated as their Queen.

But She, who was the Teacher of humility and obedience unto death, practiced both these virtues in that hour. She answered that She would obey in asking of them their blessing, and besought them to afford Her this consolation. With the permission of Saint Peter She left the couch and, kneeling before the Apostle, said to Him: "My lord, I beseech thee, as the Universal Pastor and Head of the Holy Church, to give Me Thy blessing in Thy own and in Its name. Pardon Me Thy Handmaid for the smallness of the service I have rendered in My life. Grant that John dispose of My vestments, the two tunics, giving them to the two poor maidens, who have always obliged Me by their charity." She then prostrated Herself and kisssd the feet of Saint Peter as the Vicar of Christ, by Her abundant tears eliciting not less the admiration than the tears of the Apostle and of all the bystanders. From Saint Peter She went to Saint John, and kneeling likewise at His feet, said: "Pardon, My Son and My Master, My not having fulfilled toward Thee the duties of a Mother as I ought and as the Lord had commanded Me, when from the Cross He appointed Thee as My son and Me as Thy mother (John 19, 27). I humbly and from My heart thank Thee for the kindness which Thou hast shown Me as a son. Give Me Thy benediction for entering into the vision and company of Him who created me."

The Sweetest Mother proceeded in Her leave-taking, speaking to each of the Apostles in particular and to some of the Disciples; and then to all the assembly together; for there were a great number. She rose to Her feet and addressed them all, saying: "Dearest children and My Masters, always have I kept you in My Soul and written in My Heart. I have loved you with that tender love and charity, which was given to Me by My Divine Son, whom I have seen in you, His chosen friends. In obedience to His Holy and Eternal Will, I now go to the Eternal Mansions, where I promise you as a Mother I will look upon you by the clearest light of the Divinity, the vision of which My Soul hopes and desires in security. I commend unto you My Mother, the Church, the Exaltation of the Name of the Most High, the spread of the Evangelical Law, the honor and veneration for the Words of My Divine Son, the memory of His Passion and Death, the practice of His Doctrine. My children, love the Church, and love one another with that bond of charity, which your Master has always inculcated upon you (John 13, 34). To Thee, Peter, Holy Pontiff, I commend My Son John and all the rest."

The words of the Most Blessed Mary, like arrows of a divine fire, penetrated the hearts of all the Apostles and hearers, and as She ceased speaking, all of them were dissolved in streams of tears and, seized with irreparable sorrow, cast themselves upon the ground with sighs and groans sufficient to move to compassion the very earth. All of them wept, and with them wept also the Sweetest Mary, who could not resist this bitter and well-founded sorrow of Her Children. After some time She spoke to them again, and asked them to pray with Her and for Her in silence, which they did. During this quietness the Incarnate Word descended from Heaven on a throne of Ineffable Glory, accompanied by all the Saints and innumerable Angels, and the house of the Cenacle was filled with Glory. The Most Blessed Mary adored the Lord and kissed His feet. Prostrate before Him She made the last and most profound act of faith and humility in Her mortal life. On this occasion the Most Pure Creature, the Queen of the Heavens, shrank within Herself and lowered Herself to the earth more profoundly than all men together ever have or ever will humiliate themselves for all their sins. Her Divine Son gave Her His blessing and in the presence of the courtiers of heaven spoke to Her these words: "My Dearest Mother, Whom I have chosen for My Dwelling-place, the hour is come in which thou art to pass from the life of this death and of the world into the glory of My Father and Mine, where Thou shalt possess the Throne prepared for Thee at My Right Hand and enjoy it through all eternity. And since, by My Power and as My Mother, I have caused Thee to enter the world free and exempt from sin, therefore also death shall have no right or permission to touch Thee at Thy exit from this world. If Thou wishest not to pass through it, come with Me now to partake of My glory, which Thou hast merited."

The Most Prudent Mother prostrated Herself at the feet of Her Son and with a joyous countenance answered: "My Son and My Lord, I beseech Thee let Thy Mother and Thy Servant enter into Eternal Life by the Common Portal of natural death, like the other children of Adam. Thou, Who art My True God, hast suffered death without being obliged to do so; it is proper that, as I have followed Thee in Life, so I follow Thee also in Death." Christ the Savior approved of the Decision and the Sacrifice of His Most Blessed Mother, and consented to its fulfillment. Then all the Angels began to sing in celestial harmony some of the verses of the Canticles of Solomon and other new ones. Although only Saint John and some of the Apostles were enlightened as to the presence of Christ the Savior, yet the others felt in their interior His Divine and Powerful Effects; but the music was heard as well by the Apostles and Disciples, as by many others of the faithful there present. A Divine Fragrance also spread about, which penetrated even to the street. The house of the Cenacle was filled with a wonderful effulgence, visible to all, and the Lord ordained that multitudes of the people of Jerusalem gathered in the streets as witnesses to this new miracle.

When the Angels began their music, the Most Blessed Mary reclined back upon Her couch or bed. Her tunic was folded about Her Sacred Body, Her hands were joined and Her eyes fixed upon Her Divine Son, and She was entirely inflamed with the Fire of Divine Love. And as the Angels intoned those verses of the second chapter of the Canticles:

"Surge, propera, amica mea," that is to say: "Arise, haste, My Beloved, My Dove, My Beautiful One, and come, the winter has passed," etc., She pronounced those Words of Her Son on the Cross: "Into Thy Hands, O Lord, I commend My Spirit." Then She closed Her virginal Eyes and expired. The sickness which took away Her life was love, without any other weakness or accidental intervention of whatever kind. She died at the moment when the Divine Power suspended the Assistance, which until then had counteracted the sensible ardors of Her burning Love of God. As soon as this Miraculous Assistance was withdrawn, the fire of Her Love consumed the life-humors of Her Heart and thus caused the cessation of Her earthly existence.

Then this Most Pure Soul passed from Her Virginal Body to be placed in boundless glory, on the Throne at the Right Hand of Her Divine Son. Immediately the music of the Angels seemed to withdraw to the upper air; for that whole procession of Angels and Saints accompanied the King and Queen to the Empyrean Heavens. The Sacred Body of the Most Blessed Mary, which had been the Temple and Sanctuary of God in life, continued to shine with an Effulgent Light and breathed forth such a wonderful and unheard of fragrance, that all the bystanders were filled with interior and exterior sweetness. The Thousand Angels of Her guard remained to watch over the inestimable treasure of Her Virginal Body. The Apostles and Disciples, amid the tears and the joy of the wonders they had seen, were absorbed in admiration for some time, and then sang many hymns and psalms in honor of the Most Blessed Mary now departed. This Glorious Transition of the Great Queen took place in the hour in which Her Divine Son had died, at three o'clock on a Friday, the Thirteenth day of August, She being Seventy years of age, less the Twenty-six days intervening between the Thirteenth of August, on which She died, and the Eighth of September, the day of Her birth. The Heavenly Mother had survived the death of Christ the Savior Twenty-one years, Four months and Nineteen days; and His Virginal Birth, Fifty-five years. This reckoning can be easily made in the following manner: when Christ our Savior was born, His Virginal Mother was Fifteen years, Three months and Seventeen days of age. The Lord lived Thirty-three years and Three months; so that at the time of His Sacred Passion the Most Blessed Lady was Forty-eight years, Six months and

Seventeen days old; adding to these another Twenty-one years, Four months and Nineteen days, we ascertain Her age as Seventy years, less Twenty-five or Twenty-six days.*

*In figures as follows:

Birth of Christ,	15 years,	3 months,	17 days.
Death of Christ,	33 years,	3 months,	.. days.
	48 years,	6 months,	17 days.
Death of Mary,	21 years,	4 months,	19 days.
Age at death,	69 years,	11 months,	5 or 6 days.

Great Wonders and Prodigies happened at the Precious Death of the Queen; for the sun was eclipsed (as I have mentioned above) and its light was hidden in sorrow for some hours. Many birds of different kinds gathered around the Cenacle, and by their sorrowful clamors and groans for a while caused the bystanders themselves to weep. All Jerusalem was in commotion, and many of the inhabitants collected in astonished crowds, confessing loudly the Power of God and the Greatness of His Works. Others were astounded and as if beside themselves. The Apostles and Disciples with others of the faithful broke forth in tears and sighs. Many sick persons came who all were cured. The souls in purgatory were released. But the Greatest Miracle was that three persons, a man in Jerusalem and two women living in the immediate neighborhood of the Cenacle, died in sin and impenitent in that same hour, subject to eternal damnation; but when their cause came before the Tribunal of Christ, His Sweetest Mother interceded for them and they were restored to life. They so mended their conduct, that afterwards they died in grace and were saved. This privilege was not extended to others that died on that day in the world, but was restricted to those three who happened to die in that hour in Jerusalem. What festivities were celebrated on that occasion in Heaven I will describe in another chapter, lest Heavenly Things be mixed up with the Sacred Things of earth.

WORDS OF THE QUEEN.

My daughter, besides what thou hast understood and written of My glorious Transition, I wish to inform thee of another privilege, which was conceded to Me by My Divine Son in that hour. Thou hast already recorded, that the Lord offered Me the choice of entering into Beatific Vision either with or without passing through the portals of death. If I had preferred not to die, the Most High would have conceded this favor, because sin had no part in Me, and hence also not its punishment, which is death. Thus it would also have been with My Divine Son, and with a greater right, if He had not taken upon Himself the satisfaction of the Divine Justice for men through His Passion and Death. Hence I chose death freely in order to imitate and follow Him, as also I did during His grievous Passion. Since I had seen My Son and True God die, I would not have satisfied the love I owe Him, if I had refused death, and I would have left a great gap in My conformity to and My imitation of My Lord the Godman, whereas He wished Me to bear a great likeness to Him in His Most Sacred Humanity. As I would thereafter never be able to make up for such a defect, My Soul would not enjoy the plenitude of the delight of having died as did My Lord and God.

Hence My choosing to die was so pleasing to Him, and My Prudent Love therein obliged Him to such an extent, that in return He immediately conceded to Me a singular favor for the benefit of the children of the Church and conformable to My wishes. It was this, that all those devoted to Me, who should call upon Me at the hour of death, constituting Me as their Advocate in memory of My Happy Transition and of My desiring to imitate Him in death, shall be under My special protection in that hour, shall have Me as a defense against the demons, as a help and protection, and shall be presented by Me before the Tribunal of His mercy and there experience My intercession. In consequence the Lord gave Me a new power and commission and He promised to confer great helps of His grace for a good death and for a purer life on all those who in veneration of this mystery of My precious death, should invoke My aid. Hence I desire thee, My beloved daughter, from this day on to keep in thy inmost heart a devout and loving memory of this mystery, and to bless, praise, and magnify the Omnipotent, because He wrought such sacred miracles for Me and for the mortals. By this solicitude thou wilt oblige the Lord and Me to come to thy aid in that last hour.

And since death follows upon life and ordinarily corresponds with it, therefore the surest pledge of a good death is a good life; a life in which the heart is freed and detached from earthly love. For this it is, which in that last hour afflicts and oppresses the soul and which is like a heavy chain restraining its liberty and preventing it from rising above the things loved in this world. O My daughter! How greatly do mortals misunderstand this truth, and how far they err from it in their actions! The Lord gives them life in order that they may free themselves from the effects of original sin, so as to be unhampered by them at the hour of their death; and the ignorant and miserable children of Adam spend all their life in loading upon themselves new burdens and fetters, so that they die captives of their passions and in the tyranny of their hellish foes. I had no share in original sin and none of its effects had any power over My faculties; nevertheless I lived in the greatest constraint, in poverty and detached from earthly things, Most Perfect and Holy; and this holy freedom I did indeed experience at the hour of My death. Consider then, My daughter, and be mindful of this living example; free thy heart more and more each day, so that with advancing years thou mayest find thyself more free, more detached and averted from visible things, and so that when the Spouse shall call thee to His nuptials, thou wilt not need to seek in vain the required freedom and prudence.

THE ASSUMPTION OF THE BLESSED
VIRGIN MARY INTO HEAVEN

BURIAL AND ASSUMPTION OF THE VIRGIN.

In order that the Apostles, the Disciples, and many others of the faithful might not be too deeply oppressed by sorrow, and in order that some of them might not die of grief caused by the passing away of the Most Blessed Mary, it was necessary that the Divine Power, by an especial providence, furnish them with consolation and dilate their heart for new influences in their incomparable affliction. For the feeling, that their loss was irretrievable in the present life, could not be repressed; the privation of such a Treasure could never find a recompense; and as most sweet, loving and amiable intercourse and conversation of their Great Queen had ravished the heart of each one, the ceasing of Her protection and company left them as it were without the breath of life. But the Lord, who well knew how to estimate the just cause of their sorrow, secretly upheld them by His encouragements and so they set about the fitting burial of the Sacred Body and whatever the occasion demanded.

Accordingly the Holy Apostles, on whom this duty specially devolved, held a conference concerning the burial of the Most Sacred Body of their Queen and Lady. They selected for that purpose a new sepulchre, which had been prepared mysteriously by the providence of Her Divine Son. As they remembered, that, according to the custom of the Jews at burial, the Deified Body of Their Master had been anointed with precious ointments and spices and wrapped in the sacred burial cloths; they thought not of doing otherwise with the Virginal Body of His Most Holy Mother. Accordingly they called the two maidens, who had assisted the Queen during Her life and who had been designated as the heiresses of Her tunics, and instructed them to anoint the

Body of the Mother of God with highest reverence and modesty and wrap it in the winding-sheets before it should be placed in the casket. With great reverence and fear the two maidens entered the room, where the Body of the Blessed Lady lay upon its couch; but the refulgence issuing from it barred and blinded them in such a manner that they could neither see nor touch the Body, nor even ascertain in what particular place it rested.

In fear and reverence still greater than on their entrance, the maidens left the room; and in great excitement and wonder they told the Apostles what had happened. They, not without Divine Inspiration, came to the conclusion, that this Sacred Ark of the Covenant was not to be touched or handled in the common way. Then Saint Peter and Saint John entered the oratory and perceived the effulgence, and at the same time they heard the celestial music of the Angels, who were singing: "Hail Mary, full of grace, the Lord is with Thee." Others responded: "A Virgin before childbirth, in childbirth and after childbirth." From that time on many of the faithful expressed their devotion toward the Most Blessed Mary in these words of praise; and from them they were handed down to be repeated by us with the approbation of the Holy Church. The two Holy Apostles, Saint Peter and Saint John, were for a time lost in admiration at what they saw and heard of their Queen; and in order to decide what to do, they sank on their knees, beseeching the Lord to make it known. Then they heard a voice saying: "Let not the Sacred Body be either uncovered or touched."

Having thus been informed of the Will of God, they brought a bier, and, the effulgence having diminished somewhat, they approached the couch and with their own hands reverently took hold of the tunic at the two ends. Thus, without changing its posture, they raised the Sacred and Virginal Treasure and placed it on the bier in the same position as it had occupied on the couch. They could easily do this, because they felt no more weight than that of the tunic. On this bier the former effulgence of the Body moderated still more, and all of them, by disposition of the Lord and for the consolation of all those present, could now perceive and study the beauty of that Virginal Countenance and of Her hands. As for the rest, the Omnipotence of God protected this His Heavenly Dwelling, so that neither in life nor in death any one should behold any other part except what is common in ordinary conversation, namely, Her most inspiring countenance, by which She had been known, and Her hands, by which She had labored.

So great was the care and solicitude for His Most Blessed Mother, that in this particular He used not so much precaution in regard to His own Body, as that of the Most Pure Virgin. In Her Immaculate Conception He made Her like to Himself; likewise at Her birth, in as far as it did not take place in the common and natural manner of other men. He preserved Her also from impure temptations and thoughts. But, as He was man and the Redeemer of the world through His Passion and Death, He permitted with His own Body, what He would not allow with Hers, as that of a woman, and therefore He kept her Virginal Body entirely concealed; in fact the Most Pure Lady during Her life had Herself asked that no one should be permitted to look upon it in death; which petition He fulfilled. Then the Apostles consulted further about Her burial. Their decision becoming known among the multitudes of the faithful in Jerusalem, they brought many candles to be lighted at the bier, and it happened that all the lights burned through that day and the two following days without any of the candles being consumed or wasted in any shape or manner.

In order that this and many other miracles wrought by the Power of God on this occasion might become better known to the world, the Lord Himself inspired all the inhabitants of Jerusalem to be present at the burial of His Most Blessed Mother, so that there was scarcely any person in Jerusalem, even of the Jews or the gentiles, who were not attracted by the novelty of this spectacle. The Apostles took upon their shoulders the Sacred Body and the Tabernacle of God and, as Priests of the Evangelical Law, bore the Propitiatory of the Divine Oracles and Blessings in orderly procession from the Cenacle in the city to the valley of Josaphat. This was the visible accompaniment of the dwellers of Jerusalem.

In the midst of this celestial and earthly accompaniment, visible and invisible, the Apostles bore along the Sacred Body, and on the way happened great miracles, which would take much time to relate. In particular all the sick, of which there were many of the different kinds, were entirely cured. Many of the possessed were freed from the demons; for the evil spirits did not dare to wait until the Sacred Body came near the persons thus afflicted. Greater still were the miracles

229

of conversions wrought among many Jews and gentiles, for on this occasion were opened up the Treasures of Divine Mercy, so that many souls came to the knowledge of Christ Our Savior and loudly confessed Him as the True God and Redeemer, demanding Baptism. Many days thereafter the Apostles and Disciples labored hard in catechizing and baptising those, who on that day had been converted to the Holy Faith. The Apostles in carrying the Sacred Body felt wonderful effects of Divine Light and Consolation, in which the Disciples shared according to their measure. All the multitudes of the people were seized with astonishment at the fragrance diffused about, the sweet music and the other prodigies. They proclaimed God great and powerful in this Creature and in testimony of their acknowledgment, they struck their breasts in sorrow and compunction.

When the procession came to the Holy Sepulchre in the valley of Josaphat, the same two Apostles, Saint Peter and Saint John, who had laid the Celestial Treasure from the couch onto the bier, with joyful reverence placed it in the Sepulchre and covered it with a linen cloth, the hands of the Angels performing more of these last rites than the hands of the Apostles. They closed up the Sepulchre with a large stone, according to custom at other burials. The Celestial Courtiers returned to heaven, while the Thousand Angels of the Queen continued their watch, guarding the Sacred Body and keeping up the music as at Her burial. The concourse of the people lessened and the Holy Apostles and Disciples, dissolved in tender tears, returned to the Cenacle. During a whole year the exquisite fragrance exhaled by the Body of the Queen was noticeable throughout the Cenacle, and in Her oratory, for many years. This sanctuary remained a place of refuge for all those that were burdened with labor and difficulties; all found miraculous assistance, as well in sickness as in hardships and necessities of other kind. After these miracles had continued for some years in Jerusalem, the sins of Jerusalem and of its inhabitants drew upon this city, among other punishments, that of being deprived of this inestimable blessing.

Having again gathered in the Cenacle, the Apostles came to the conclusion that some of them and of the Disciples should watch at the Sepulchre of their Queen as long as they should hear the celestial music, for all of them were wondering when the end of that miracle should be. Accordingly

230

some of them attended to the affairs of the Church in catechizing and baptizing the new converts; and others immediately returned to the Sepulchre, while all of them paid frequent visits to it during the next three days. Saint Peter and Saint John, however, were more zealous in their attendance, coming only a few times to the Cenacle and immediately returning to where was laid the Treasure of their heart.

Of the glory and felicity of the saints in the beatific vision Saint Paul says with Isaias (1 Cor. 2, 9; Is. 64, 4), that neither have mortal eyes seen, nor ears heard, nor can it enter into the heart of man what God has prepared for those who love Him and who hope in Him. In accordance with this Catholic Truth, we should not wonder at what is related of Saint Augustine, the Great Light of the Church, that, in setting out to write a book on the Glory of the Blessed, he was visited by his friend, Saint Jerome, who had just died and entered into the Glory of the Lord, and was admonished by his visitor, that he would not be able to compass His design; since no tongue or pen of man could describe the least part of the blessings enjoyed by the saints in the beatific vision.

If on this account the glory even of the least of the Saints is eneffable, what shall we say of the Glory of the Most Blessed Mary, since among the Saints She is the Most Holy and She by Herself is more like to Her Son than all the Saints together, and since Her grace and glory exceed those of all the rest, as those of an empress or sovereign over Her vassals? This truth can and should be believed; but in mortal life it cannot be understood, or the least part of it be explained; for the inadequacy and deficiency of our words and expressions rather tend to obscure than to set forth its greatness. Let us in this life apply our labor, not in seeking to comprehend it, but in seeking to merit its manifestation in glory, where we shall experience more or less of this happiness according to our works.

Our Redeemer Jesus entered heaven conducting the Purest Soul of His Mother at His right hand. She alone of all the mortals deserved exemption from particular judgment; hence for Her there was none; no account was asked or demanded of Her for what She had received; for such was the promise that had been given to Her, when She was exempted from the common guilt and chosen as the Queen privileged above the laws of the children of Adam. For the same reason, instead of being judged with the rest, She shall be seated at the right hand of the Judge to judge with Him all the creatures. If in the first instant of Her Conception She was the brightest Aurora, effulgent with the rays of the sun of the Divinity beyond all the brightness of the Most Exalted Seraphim, and if afterwards She was still further illumined by the contact of the Hypostatic Word, who derived His Humanity from Her Purest Substance, it necessarily follows that She should be His Companion for all eternity, possessing such a likeness to Him, that none greater can be possible between a Godman and a creature. In this light the Redeemer Himself presented Her before the Throne of the Divinity; and speaking to the Eternal Father in the presence of all the Blessed, who were ravished at this wonder, the most Sacred Humanity uttered these words: "Eternal Father, My Most Beloved Mother, Thy Beloved Daughter and the Cherished Spouse of the Holy Ghost, now comes to take possession of the Crown and Glory, which We have prepared as a reward for Her merit. She is the One Who was born as the Rose among thorns, untouched, pure and beautiful, worthy of being embraced by Us and of being placed upon a Throne to which none of our creatures can ever attain, and to which those conceived in sin cannot aspire. This is Our chosen and Our only One, distinguished above all else, to Whom We communicated Our Grace and Our Perfections beyond the measure accorded to other creatures; in Whom We have deposited the Treasure of our Incomprehensible Divinity and Its gifts; Who most faithfully preserved and made fruitful the talents, which We gave Her; who never swerved from Our Will, and who found grace and pleasure in Our eyes. My Father, Most Equitous is the Tribunal of Our Justice and Mercy, and in it the services of Our friends are repaid in the most superabundant manner. It is right that to My Mother be given the reward of a Mother; and if during Her whole life and in all Her work She was as like to Me as is possible for a creature to be, let Her also be as like to Me in glory and on the Throne of Our Majesty, so that where Holiness is in essence, there it may also be found in its highest participation."

This Decree of the Incarnate Word was approved by the Father and the Holy Ghost. The Most Holy Soul of Mary was immediately raised to the Right Hand of Her Son and True God, and placed on the Royal Throne of the Most Holy

Trinity, which neither men, nor Angels nor the Seraphim themselves attain, and will not attain for all eternity. This is the most exalted and supereminent privilege of our Queen and Lady, that She is seated on the Throne with the Three Divine Persons and holds Her place as Empress, while all the rest are set as servants and ministers to the Highest King. To the eminence and majesty of that position, inaccessible to all other creatures, correspond Her gifts of glory, comprehension, vision and fruition; because She enjoys, above all and more than all, that Infinite Object, which the other Blessed enjoy in an endless variety of degrees. She knows, penetrates and understands much deeper the Eternal Being and its infinite attributes; She lovingly delights in its mysteries and most hidden secrets, more than all the rest of the Blessed.

Just as little can be explained the extra joy, which the Blessed experienced on that day in singing the new songs of praise to the Omnipotent and in celebrating the glory of His Daughter, Mother and Spouse; for in Her He had exalted all the works of His Right Hand. Although to the Lord Himself could come no new or essential Glory, because He possessed and possesses it immutably infinite through all eternity; yet the exterior manifestations of His pleasure and satisfaction at the fulfillment of His eternal decrees were greater on that day.

On the third day after the most pure soul of Mary had taken possession of this Glory never to leave it, the Lord manifested to the Saints His Divine Will, that She should return to the World, resuscitate Her Sacred Body and unite Herself with it, so that She might in body and soul be again raised to the right hand of Her Divine Son without waiting for the general resurrection of the dead. The appropriateness of this favor, its accordance with the others received by the Most Blessed Queen and with Her supereminent dignity, the Saints could not but see; since even to mortals it is so credible, that even if the Church had not certified it, we would judge those impious and foolish, who would dare deny it. But the blessed saw it with greater clearness, together with the determined time and hour as manifested to them in God himself. When the time for this wonder had arrived, Christ Our Savior Himself descended from heaven bringing with Him at His right hand the soul of His Most Blessed Mother and accompanied by many legions of the Angels, the Patri-

233

archs and ancient Prophets. They came to the sepulchre in the valley of Josaphat, and all being gathered in sight of the virginal temple, The Lord spoke the following words to the Saints.

"My Mother was conceived without stain of sin, in order that from Her virginal substance I might stainlessly clothe Myself in the humanity in which I came to the world and redeemed it from sin. My flesh is Her flesh; She co-operated with Me in the works of the Redemption; hence I must raise Her, just as I rose from the dead, and this shall be at the same time and hour. For I wish to make Her like Me in all things." All the ancient Saints of the human race then gave thanks for this new favor in songs of praise and glory to the Lord. Those that especially distinguished themselves in their thanksgiving were our first parents Adam and Eve, Saint Anne, Saint Joachim and Saint Joseph, as being the more close partakers in this miracle of His Omnipotence. Then the Purest Soul of the Queen, at the command of the Lord, entered the Virginal Body, reanimated it and raised it up, giving it a new life of immortality and glory and communicating to it the four gifts of Clearness, Impassibility, Agility and Subtlety, corresponding to those of the soul and overflowing from it into the body.

Endowed with these gifts the Most Blessed Mary issued from the tomb in body and soul, without raising the stone cover and without disturbing the position of the tunic and the mantle that had enveloped Her Sacred Body. Since it is impossible to describe Her beauty and refulgent glory, I will not make the attempt. It is sufficient to say, that just as the Heavenly Mother had given to Her Divine Son in Her womb the form of man, pure, unstained and sinless, for the Redemption of the World, so in return The Lord, in this Resurrection and new regeneration, gave to Her a glory and beauty similar to His Own. In this mysterious and Divine interchange each One did what was possible: Most Holy Mary engendered Christ, assimilating Him as much as possible to Herself, and Christ resuscitated Her, communicating to Her of His Glory as far as She was capable as a creature.

Then from the sepulchre was started a most solemn procession, moving with celestial music through the regions of the air and toward the Empyrean Heaven. This happened in the hour immediately after midnight, in which also the

Lord had risen from the grave; and therefore not all of the Apostles were witness of this prodigy, but only some of them, who were present and watching at the sepulchre. The Saints and Angels entered Heaven in the order in which they had started; and in the last place came Christ Our Savior and at His right hand the Queen, clothed in the gold of variety (as David says Ps. 44, 10), and so beautiful that She was the admiration of the Heavenly Court. All of them turned toward Her to look upon Her and bless Her with new jubilee and songs of praise. Thus were heard those mysterious eulogies recorded by Solomon: Come, daughters of Sion, to see your Queen, who is praised by the morning stars and celebrated by the sons of the Most High. Who is She that comes from the desert, like a column of all the aromatic perfumes? Who is She, that rises like the aurora, more beautiful than the moon, elect as the sun, terrible as many serried armies? Who is She that comes up from the desert resting upon Her Beloved and spreading forth abundant delights? (Cant. 3, 6-9; 8, 5). Who is She in whom the Deity itself finds so much pleasure and delight above all other creatures and whom He exalts above them all in the heavens! O novelty worthy of the Infinite Wisdom! O prodigy of His Omnipotence, which so magnifies and exalts Her!

Amid this glory the Most Blessed Mary arrived body and soul at the throne of the Most Blessed Trinity. And the three Divine Persons received Her on it with an embrace eternally undissoluble. The Eternal Father said to Her: "Ascend higher, My Daughter and My Dove." The Incarnate Word spoke: "My Mother, of whom I have received human being and full return of My work in Thy perfect imitation, receive now from My hand the reward Thou hast merited." The Holy Ghost said: "My Most Beloved Spouse, enter into the eternal joy, which corresponds to the most faithful love; do Thou now enjoy Thy love without solicitude; for past is the winter of suffering for Thou hast arrived at our Eternal embraces." There the Most Blessed Mary was absorbed in the contemplation of the three Divine Persons and as it were overwhelmed in the boundless ocean and abyss of the Divinity, while the Saints were filled with wonder and new accidental delight. Since, at the occasion of this work of the Omnipotent happened other wonders, I shall speak of them as far as possible in the following chapter.

My Daughter, lamentable and inexcusable is the ignorance of men in so knowingly forgetting the Eternal Glory, which God has prepared for those who dispose themselves to merit it. I wish that Thou bitterly bewail and deplore this pernicious forgetfulness; for there is no doubt, that whoever wilfully forgets the Eternal Glory and happiness is in evident danger of losing it. No one is free from this guilt, not only because men do not apply much labor or effort in seeking and retaining the remembrance of this happiness; but they labor with all their powers in things that make them forget the end for which they were created. Undoubtedly this forgetfulness arises from their entangling themselves in the pride of life, the covetousness of the eyes, and the desires of the flesh (John 2, 16); for employing therein all the forces and faculties of their soul during the whole time of their life, they have no leisure, care or attention for the thoughts of Eternal Felicity. Let men acknowledge and confess, whether this recollection costs them more labor than to follow their blind passions, seeking after honors, possessions or the transitory pleasures, all of which have an end with this life, and which, after much striving and labor, many men do not, and can never attain.

This is a sorrow beyond all sorrows, and a misfortune without equal and without remedy. Afflict Thyself, lament and grieve without consolation over this ruin of so many souls bought by the Blood of My Divine Son. I assure Thee, My dearest, that, if men would not make themselves so unworthy of it, my charity would urge me, in the Celestial Glory where Thou knowest Me to be, to send forth a voice through the whole world exclaiming: "Mortal and deceived men, what are you doing? For what purpose are you living? Do you realize what it is to see God face to face, and to participate in His Eternal Glory and share His company? Of what are you thinking? Who has thus disturbed and fascinated your judgment? What will you seek, if once you have lost this true blessing and happiness, since there is no other? The labor is short, the reward is Infinite Glory, and the punishment is Eternal."

THE CROWNING
OF THE BLESSED VIRGIN MARY
AS QUEEN OF HEAVEN AND EARTH

THE CORONATION OF THE MOTHER OF GOD.

When Christ Jesus the Savior took leave of His Disciples in order to enter upon His suffering, He told them not to be disturbed in their hearts on account of the things He had told them; because in the house of His Father, which is Eternal Happiness, there are many mansions. He further assured them, that there was room and reward for all, although the merits and their good works be diverse and that no one should be disturbed in his peace and hope, though he should see others more favored or advanced; because in the house of God there are many grades and many dwellings, in which each one shall be content with what shall belong to him without envy. I have said that Most Blessed Mary was assigned to the supreme position and state on the Throne of the Most Blessed Trinity.

We call that the Throne of the Divinity, from which God manifests Himself to the Saints as the principal cause of Their Glory and as the Infinite, Eternal God, independent of all things and on whose will all creatures depend, from which He manifests Himself as the Lord, as the King, as the Judge and Master of all that is in existence. This dignity Christ the Redeemer possesses, in as far as He is God, essentially, and as far as He is man, through the hypostatic union, by which He communicates his Godhead to the humanity. Hence in Heaven He is the King, the Lord and Supreme Judge; and the Saints, though their glory exceeds all human calculation, are as servants and inferiors of this inaccessible Majesty. In this the Most Holy Mary participates in a degree next inferior and in a manner otherwise ineffable and proportionate to a mere creature so closely related to the Godman; and therefore She assists forever at the right hand of Her Son as Queen (Ps. 44, 10), Lady and Mistress of all Creation, Her dominion extending as far as that of Her Divine Son, although in a different manner.

After placing the Most Blessed Mary on this exalted and supereminent Throne, The Lord declared to the Courtiers of Heaven all the privileges She should enjoy in virtue of this participation in His Majesty. The Person of the Eternal Father, as the first principle of all things, speaking to the Angels and Saints, said to them: "Our Daughter Mary was chosen according to Our pleasure from amongst all creatures, the first one to delight Us, and who never fell from the title and position of a True Daughter, such as We had given Her in Our Divine Mind; She has a claim on Our dominion, which We shall recognize by crowning Her as the legitimate and peerless Lady and Sovereign." The Incarnate Word said: "To My True and Natural Mother belong all the creatures which were created and redeemed by Me; and of all things over which I am King, She too shall be the legitimate and Supreme Queen." The Holy Ghost said: "Since She is called My Beloved and Chosen Spouse, She deserves to be crowned as Queen for all eternity."

Having thus spoken the Three Divine Persons placed upon the head of the Most Blessed Mary a crown of such new splendor and value, that the like has been seen neither before nor after by any mere creature. At the same time a voice sounded from the throne saying: "My Beloved, chosen among the creatures, Our Kingdom is Thine; Thou shalt be the Lady and the Sovereign of the Seraphim, of all the Ministering Spirits, the Angels and of the entire universe of creatures. Attend, proceed and govern prosperously over them, for in Our Supreme Consistory We give Thee power, majesty and sovereignty. Being filled with grace beyond all the rest, Thou hast humiliated Thyself in Thy Own estimation to the lowest place; receive now the Supreme Dignity deserved by Thee and, as a participation in Our Divinity, the dominion over all the creatures of Our Omnipotence. From Thy Royal Throne to the centre of the earth Thou shalt reign; and by the power We now give Thee, Thou shalt subject hell with its demons and inhabitants. Let all of them

238

fear Thee as the Supreme Empress and Mistress of those caverns and dwelling-places of our enemies. In Thy hands and at Thy pleasure We place the influences and forces of the Heavens, the moisture of the clouds, the growths of the earth; and of all of them do Thou distribute according to Thy Will, and Our own Will shall be at Thy disposal for the execution of Thy wishes. Thou shalt be the Empress and Mistress of the Militant Church, its Protectress, its Advocate, its Mother and Teacher. Thou shalt be the special Patroness of the Catholic countries; and whenever they, or the faithful, or any of the children of Adam call upon Thee from their heart, serve or oblige Thee, Thou shalt relieve and help them in their labors and necessities. Thou shalt be the Friend, the Defender and the Chieftainess of all the just and of Our Friends; all of them Thou shalt comfort, console and fill with blessings according to their devotion to Thee. In view of all this We make Thee the Depositary of Our riches, the Treasurer of Our goods; we place into Thy hands the helps and blessings of Our grace for distribution; nothing do We wish to be given to the world, which does not pass through Thy hands; and nothing do We deny, which Thou wishest to concede to men. Grace shall be diffused in Thy lips ·for obtaining all that Thou wishest and ordainest in Heaven and on Earth, and everywhere shall Angels and men obey Thee; because whatever is Ours shall be Thine, just as Thou hast always been Ours; and Thou shalt reign with Us forever."

In the execution of this decree and privilege conceded to the Mistress of the World, the Almighty commanded all the Courtiers of Heaven, Angels and men, to show Her obedience and recognize Her as their Queen and Lady. There was another mystery concealed in this wonder, namely, it was a recompense for the worship and veneration, which, as is clear from this history, the Most Blessed Mary, notwithstanding that She was the Mother of God, full of grace and holiness above the Angels and Saints, had bestowed upon the Saints during Her mortal pilgrimage. Although during the time when They were comprehensors and She yet a pilgrim, it was for Her greater merit, that She should humble Herself beneath them all according to the ordainment of the Lord; yet now, when She was in possession of the Kingdom, it was just, that She should be venerated, worshipped and extolled by them as Her inferiors and vassals. This they also did in

239

that most blessed state, in which all things are reduced to their proper proportion and order. Both the Angelic Spirits and the Blessed Souls, while rendering Their adoration to the Lord with fear and worshipful reverence, rendered a like homage in its proportion to His Most Blessed Mother; and the Saints who were there in Their bodies prostrated themselves and gave bodily signs of Their worship. All these demonstrations at the Coronation of the Empress of Heaven redounded wonderfully to Her Glory, to the new joy and jubilee of the Saints and to the pleasure of the Most Blessed Trinity. Altogether festive was this day, and it produced new accidental glory in all the Heavens. Those that partook more especially therein were Her most fortunate spouse Saint Joseph, Saint Joachim and Anne and all the other relatives of the Queen, together with the thousand Angels of Her guard.

Within the glorious body of the Queen, over Her Heart, was visible to the saints a small globe or monstrance of singular beauty and splendor, which particularly roused and rouses Their admiration and joy. It was there in testimony and reward of Her having afforded to the Sacramental Word an acceptable restingplace and sanctuary, and of Her having received Holy Communion so worthily, purely and holily, without any defect or imperfection, and with a devotion, love and reverence attained by none other of the Saints. In regard to the other rewards and crowns corresponding to Her peerless works and virtues, nothing that can be said could give any idea; and therefore I refer it to the beatific vision, where each one shall perceive them in proportion as his doings and his devotion shall have merited. In the foregoing chapter I mentioned that the Transition of Our Queen happened on the thirteenth of August, while Her Ressurection, Assumption and Coronation happened on Sunday the fifteenth, on the day in which it is celebrated in the Church. Her Sacred Body remained in the sepulchre thirty-six hours, just as the body of Her Divine Son; for Her Transition and Her Ressurection took place in the same hours of the day. According to the computation given above, I advert that this miracle happened in the year of Our Lord fifty-five, which had advanced as many days as intervene between the Nativity of The Lord and the fifteenth of August. We have left the Great Lady at the right hand of Her Divine Son, reigning through all the Ages of Eternity.

My Daughter, if anything could lessen the enjoyment of the Highest Felicity and Glory which I possess, and if, in it, I could be capable of any sorrow, without a doubt I would be grieved to see The Holy Church and the rest of the World in its present state of labor, notwithstanding that men know Me to be Their Mother, Advocate and Protectress in Heaven, ready to guide and assist them to Eternal Life. In this state of affairs, when The Almighty has granted Me so many privileges as His Mother and when there are so many sources of help placed in My hands solely for the benefit of mortals and belonging to me as the Mother of clemency, it is a great cause of sorrow to Me to see mortals force Me to remain idle, and that, for want of calling upon me, so many souls should be lost. But if I cannot experience grief now, I may justly complain of men, that they load themselves with Eternal damnation and refuse Me the Glory of saving their souls.

How much My intercession and the power I have in Heaven is worth has never been hidden in the Church, for I have demonstrated My ability to save all by so many thousands of miracles, prodigies and favors operated in behalf of those devoted to Me. With those who have called upon Me in their needs I have always shown Myself liberal, and the Lord has shown Himself liberal to them on My account. The Most High still wishes to give liberally of His Infinite Treasures and resolves to favor those who know how to gain My intercession before God. This is the secure way and the powerful means of advancing the Church, of improving the Catholic reigns, of spreading the Faith, of furthering the welfare of families and of states, of bringing the Souls to Grace and to the Friendship of God.

PRAY THE ROSARY
FOR PEACE

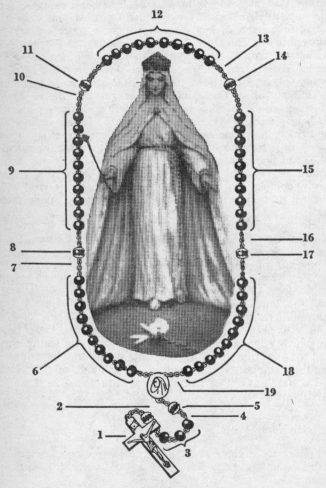

Our Hope

MARY IMMACULATE QUEEN
OF THE UNIVERSE

How to Say the Rosary

1. Kiss the Cross
   Make the Sign of the Cross
   Say the Apostles Creed
2. Recite the Our Father
3. Say three Hail Marys
4. † Glory be to the Father...
   * O My Jesus forgive us our sins . . .
   Announce first Mystery
   Annunciation or Agony or Resurrection
5. Recite the Our Father
6. Say 10 Hail Marys
7. Glory be to the Father . . .
   * O My Jesus forgive us our sins . . .
   Announce second Mystery
   Visitation or Scourging or Ascension
8. Recite the Our Father
9. Say 10 Hail Marys
10. Glory be to the Father...
    * O My Jesus forgive us our sins . . .
    Announce third Mystery
    Nativity or Crowning with Thorns or Descent of Holy Ghost
11. Recite the Our Father
12. Say 10 Hail Marys
13. Glory be to the Father...
    * O My Jesus forgive us our sins . . .
    Announce fourth Mystery
    Presentation or Carrying Cross or Assumption.
14. Recite the Our Father
15. Say 10 Hail Marys
16. Glory be to the Father...
    * O My Jesus forgive us our sins . . .
    Announce fifth Mystery
    Finding in Temple or Crucifixion or Coronation.
17. Recite the Our Father
18. Say 10 Hail Marys
19. Glory be to the Father...
    * O My Jesus forgive us our sins . . .

Mysteries above are listed in order of Joyful, Sorrowful, Glorious.

† Glory be to the Father, Son and Holy Ghost, as it was in the beginning, is now and ever shall be, world without end, Amen.

* O My Jesus, forgive us our sins, save us from the fires of Hell; lead all souls to Heaven especially those who have most need of Thy mercy.

Prayers of the Rosary

The Sign of the Cross

IN the name of the Father, † and of the Son, and of the Holy Ghost. Amen.

THE APOSTLES' CREED

I BELIEVE in God, the Father Almighty, Creator of heaven and earth; and in Jesus Christ, His only Son, our Lord; who was conceived by the Holy Ghost, born of the Virgin Mary, suffered under Pontius Pilate, was crucified; died, and was buried. He descended into hell; the third day He arose again from the dead; He ascended into heaven, sitteth at the right hand of God the Father Almighty; from thence He shall come to judge the living and the dead. I believe in the Holy Ghost, the Holy Catholic Church, the communion of Saints, the forgiveness of sins, the resurrection of the body, and life everlasting. Amen.

THE OUR FATHER

OUR FATHER, who art in heaven, hallowed be Thy name, Thy kingdom come, Thy will be done on earth as it is in heaven. Give us this day our daily bread, and forgive us our trespasses as we forgive those who trespass against us, and lead us not into temptation but deliver us from evil Amen.

THE HAIL MARY

HAIL MARY, full of grace, the Lord is with thee, blessed art thou among women, and blessed is the fruit of thy womb, Jesus. HOLY MARY, Mother of God, pray for us sinners, now and at the hour of our death. Amen.

GLORY BE TO THE FATHER

Glory be to the Father, and to the Son, and to the Holy Ghost; as it was in the beginning, is now, and ever shall be, world without end. Amen.

THE HAIL, HOLY QUEEN

Hail, holy Queen, Mother of Mercy! our life, our sweetness, and our hope! To thee do we cry, poor banished children of Eve; to thee do we send up our sighs, mourning and weeping in this valley of tears. Turn then, most gracious Advocate, thine eyes of mercy toward us; and after this our exile show unto us the blessed fruit of thy womb, Jesus; O clement, O loving, O sweet Virgin Mary.

V. Pray for us, O holy Mother of God.

R. That we may be made worthy of the promises of Christ.

LET US PRAY

O God, whose only begotten Son, by His life, death, and resurrection has purchased for us the rewards of eternal life, grant, we beseech Thee, that meditating upon these mysteries of the most Holy Rosary of the Blessed Virgin Mary, we may imitate what they contain, and obtain what they promise, through the same Christ our lord. Amen.

FATIMA EJACULATION

After each decade may be said the Fatima ejaculation: "O My Jesus, forgive us our sins, save us from the fires of Hell; lead all souls to Heaven especially those who have most need of Thy mercy."

INDULGENCES

The faithful, whenever they recite a third part of the Rosary with devotion, may gain:

An indulgence of five years.

If they recite a third part of the Rosary in company with others, whether in public or private, they may gain:

An indulgence of 10 years, once a day;

A plenary indulgence on the last Sunday of each month, with addition of Confession, Communion, visit a church or public oratory, if they recite the Rosary at least three times in any of the preceding weeks.

If, they recite this together in a FAMILY group besides the partial indulgence of 10 years, they are granted:

A plenary indulgence twice a month, if Rosary is recited daily for a month, go to Confession, receive Holy Communion, visit a church or public oratory.

Those who recite a third part of the Rosary in the presence of the Blessed Sacrament, exposed or even reserved in the Tabernacle, as often as they do this, may gain:

A plenary indulgence of going to Confession and receiving Holy Communion.

Note 1. The decades may be separated, if the entire chaplet is completed on the same day.

Note 2. If, as is the custom during recitation of the Rosary, the faithful make use of a chaplet, they may gain other indulgences in addition to those above, if the chaplet is blessed by a religious of the Order of Preachers or another priest having special faculties.   (Rac. #395)

Nihil Obstat: Joseph A. M. Quigley, Censor Librorum
Imprimatur: ✠ John J. Krol, D.D., J.C.D., Archbishop of Philadelphia

Feast of the Visitation B. V. M., July, 1961

PRAYER TO OUR LADY OF MT. CARMEL,
OR OF THE SCAPULAR

O ALL BLESSED, Immaculate Virgin, ornament and glory of Mount Carmel, Thou Who dost look with most gracious countenance on those who have been clothed with Thy venerable livery, look kindly also on me and take me under the mantle of Thy maternal protection. Strengthen my weakness with Thy Might; enlighten the darkness of my heart with Thy Wisdom; increase in me Faith, Hope, and Charity. So adorn my soul with graces and virtues that it may be always dear to Thy Divine Son and Thee. Assist me during life, comfort me in death with Thy most sweet presence, and present me as Thy child and faithful servant to the Most Holy Trinity, that I may be enabled to praise and extol Thee in Heaven forever. Amen. Hail Mary (three times), Glory be to the Father, etc. (once). Ind. of 200 days, once a day.—Leo XIII. Jan. 16, 1886.)

A PRAYER TO THE BLESSED VIRGIN
(Never Known to Fail)

O Most beautiful Flower of Mount Carmel, Fruitful Vine, Splendour of Heaven, Blessed Mother of the Son of God, Immaculate Virgin, assist me in this my necessity. O Star of the Sea, help me and show me herein You are my Mother.

O Holy Mary, Mother of God, Queen of Heaven and Earth, I humbly beseech You from the bottom of my heart, to succour me in this necessity; there are none that can withstand Your power.

O, show me herein you are my Mother. O Mary, conceived without sin, pray for us who have recourse to Thee. (3 times)

Sweet Mother, I place this cause in Your hands. (3 times)

247

PRAYER TO THE HOLY SPIRIT

Most Holy Spirit, Through the Sorrowful and Immaculate
Heart of Mary,
Make me Thine Instrument in Spreading the Reign of
Jesus on Earth.

PRAYER TO THE INFANT JESUS

Come to me, O Divine Savior, vouchsafe to be born in my
heart. Grant that, taught by Thine example, and assisted by
Thy grace, I may be poor in spirit and humble of heart. Keep
me chaste and obedient. I wish to live but for Thee, and to do
all things purely for love of Thee. O Mary, my Advocate and
Mother, obtain by Thy prayers forgiveness of my past offences
and holy perseverance unto death. St. Joseph, do Thou also
pray for me, that I may become daily more pleasing to Jesus.
Amen.

(WITH ECCLESIASTICAL APPROBATION)

ACT OF CONSECRATION
TO THE IMMACULATE HEART OF MARY
(St. Louis de Montfort's Consecration)

"I. N., a faithless sinner—renew and ratify today in Thy
hands, O Immaculate Mother, the vows of my Baptism; I
renounce forever Satan, his pomps and, works; and I give
myself entirely to Jesus Christ, the Incarnate Wisdom, to
carry my cross after Him all the days of my life, and to be
more faithful to Him than I have ever been before.

"In the presence of all the heavenly court I choose Thee this
day for my Mother and Mistress. I deliver and consecrate to
Thee, as Thy slave, my body and soul, my goods, both interior and exterior, and even the value of all my good actions,
past, present and future; leaving to Thee the entire and full
right of disposing of me, and all that belongs to me, without
exception, according to Thy good pleasure, for the greater
glory of God, in time and in eternity. Amen."

Nihil Obstat: Thomas W. Smiddy, S.T.D., Censor Librorum
Imprimatur: ✠ THOMAS EDMUNDUS MOLLOY, Bishop of Brooklyn

THE SCAPULAR IS A PRAYER

Our Lord taught us to say the "Our Father." Mary taught us the value of the scapular. When we use it as a prayer, Our Lady draws us to the Sacred Heart of her Divine Son. It is well, therefore, to *hold* the *scapular in the* hand, while addressing Our Lady.

A Prayer uttered thus while holding the Mystical Scapular is as perfect as a prayer can be.

It is especially in TIME OF TEMPTATION that we need the powerful intercession of God's Mother. The evil spirit is utterly powerless when a Scapular-wearer, besides his silent devotion, faces temptation calling upon Mary.

"If thou hadst recommended thyself to Me, thou wouldst not have run into such danger," was Our Lady's gentle reproach to Blessed Alan.

MORNING OFFERING

Oh my God, in union with the Immaculate Heart of Mary, I offer Thee the Precious Blood of Jesus from all the Altars throughout the World, joining with it the offering of my every thought, word, and action of this day. Oh my Jesus, I desire to gain every indulgence and merit I can and I offer them together with myself to Mary Immaculate that She may best apply them to the interests of Thy Most Sacred Heart. Precious Blood of Jesus, Save us; Immaculate Heart of Mary, Pray for us; Sacred Heart of Jesus, Have Mercy on us.

DAILY OFFERING TO THE
INFANT JESUS

I offer Thee, dear Jesus,
   Each action of today,
My prayers, my work, my sufferings,
   Accept them now, I pray.

I offer Thee, dear Jesus,
   The moments as they pass;
I join my feeble heart's desire,
   With Thine in Holy Mass.

And while Thy heart, Dear Jesus
    For sinners ever pleads;
I offer Thee, through Mary,
    Five decades of Her beads.

I offer Thee, dear Jesus,
    Oh, who could offer more?
Thyself, in sweet Communion,
    Thy Heart which I adore.

And to Thine Own, Dear Jesus,
    My poor heart closely bind;
In love and reparation
    For sins of all mankind.

Then take my gift, Dear Jesus,
    Take all I have to give;
Oh! would that I could give my life,
    Within Thy Heart to live.

THE MAGNIFICAT

My soul doth magnify the Lord.

And my spirit hath rejoiced in God my Saviour.

Because He hath regarded the humility of His handmaid;

For behold from henceforth all generations shall call Me blessed.

Because He that is mighty hath done great things to Me; and holy is His name.

And His mercy is from generation unto generations, to them that fear Him.

He hath shown might in His arm; and hath scattered the proud in the conceit of their heart.

He hath put down the mighty from their seat; and hath exalted the humble.

He hath filled the hungry with good things; and the rich He hath sent away empty.

He hath received Israel His servant, being mindful of His mercy;

As He spoke to our fathers, to Abraham, and to His seed forever. Amen.

(Luke 1: 46-55)

THE MEMORARE

Remember, O most gracious Virgin Mary, that never was it known that anyone who fled to Thy protection, implored Thy help, or sought Thy intercession, was left unaided. Inspired with this confidence, I fly unto Thee, O Virgin of virgins, my Mother. To Thee I come, before Thee I stand, sinful and sorrowful. O Mother of the Word Incarnate, despise not my petitions, but in Thy Mercy hear and answer me. Amen.

ASPIRATIONS

O Mary, conceived without sin, pray for us who have recourse to Thee. (3 times)

Immaculate Heart of Mary, pray for us.

Sorrowful and Immaculate Heart of Mary, pray for us and intercede for us.

Sweet Heart of Jesus be my love. Sweet Heart of Mary be my salvation.

Jesus, Mary, Joseph, I love you, save souls!

Mother of Mercy, pray for us!

To Jesus through Mary!

Seat of Wisdom, pray for us!

Queen of the Most Holy Rosary, pray for us. —300 days (394)

PRAYER TO THE QUEEN OF THE HOLY ROSARY

Queen of the Most Holy Rosary, in these times of such brazen impiety, show your power with the signs of your former victories, and from your throne, from which you bestow pardon and graces, mercifully look upon the Church of your Son, His Vicar on earth, and every order of clergy and laity, who are sorely oppressed in this mighty conflict.

Powerful Vanquisher of all heresies, hasten the hour of mercy, even though the hour of God's justice is every day provoked by the countless sins of men.

For me who am the least of men, kneeling before you in prayer, obtain the grace I need to live a holy life upon earth and to reign among the just in heaven. Meanwhile, together with all faithful Christians throughout the world, I greet you and acclaim you as Queen of the Most Holy Rosary. Queen of the Most Holy Rosary, pray for us.—500 days (399)

VIRGIN MOST POWERFUL

Virgin most powerful, loving helper of the Christian people, how great is the thanks we owe You for the assistance You have given our fathers who invoked Your maternal help by the devout recitation of Your Rosary when they were threatened by the Turkish infidels? From heaven You saw their deadly peril. You heard their voices imploring Your compassion. Their humble prayers, enjoined by the great Pope, Saint Pius V, were acceptable to You, and You came quickly to deliver them.

Grant, Dear Mother, that in like manner the prolonged sighs of the Holy Bride of Christ in these our days may reach Your Throne and win Your Pity. Be moved to compassion and rise once again to deliver Her from the many foes who surround Her on every side.

Even now from the four quarters of the earth there arises to Your throne the prayer of the Rosary, to beg Your Mercy in these troubled times. Unfortunately our sins hinder, or at least retard their effect. Wherefore, Dear Mother, obtain for us true sorrow for our sins and a firm resolution to face death itself rather than return to our former sins. It grieves us that through our own fault, Your help which we need so desperately, should be denied or come too late.

Turn to us, O Mary, and graciously listen to the prayers of the whole Catholic World: conquer the pride of those wicked men, who in their insolence blaspheme Almighty God and would destroy His Church, against which, according to the infallible words of Christ, the gates of hell shall never prevail. Let it be seen once more that when You arise to protect the Church, Her victory is sure. Amen.

—500 days (412)

LITANY OF THE BLESSED VIRGIN MARY

(Indulgence of seven years. Plenary indulgence, under the usual conditions, if recited with the versicle ond oration daily for a month.—Preces et Pia Opera, 290.)

Lord, have mercy.
Christ, have mercy.
Lord, have mercy.
Christ, hear us.
Christ, graciously hear us.
God the Father of Heaven, *have mercy on us.*
God the Son, Redeemer of the world, *have mercy on us.*
God the Holy Spirit, *have mercy on us.*
Holy Trinity, One God, *have mercy on us.*
Pray for us, is the response after each of the following,
Holy Mary,
Holy Mother of God,
Holy Virgin of virgins,
Mother of Christ,
Mother of divine grace,
Mother most pure,
Mother most chaste,
Mother inviolate,
Mother undefiled,
Mother most amiable,
Mother most admirable,
Mother of good counsel,
Mother of our Creator,
Mother of our Savior,
Virgin most prudent,
Virgin most venerable,
Virgin most renowned,
Virgin most powerful,
Virgin most merciful,
Virgin most faithful,
Mirror of justice,
Seat of wisdom,
Cause of our joy,
Spiritual vessel,
Vessel of honor,
Singular vessel of devotion,

Mystical rose,
Tower of David,
Tower of ivory,
House of gold,
Ark of the covenant,
Gate of heaven,
Morning star,
Health of the sick,
Refuge of sinners,
Comforter of the afflicted,
Help of Christians,
Queen of Angels,
Queen of Patriarchs,
Queen of Prophets,
Queen of Apostles,
Queen of Martyrs,
Queen of Confessors,
Queen of Virgins,
Queen of all Saints,
Queen conceived without original sin,
Queen assumed into heaven,
Queen of the most holy Rosary,
Queen of Peace,
Lamb of God, Who takest away the sins of the world, *spare us, O Lord!*
Lamb of God, Who takest away the sins of the world, *graciously hear us, O Lord!*
Lamb of God, Who takest away the sins of the world, *have mercy on us.*
V. Pray for us, O holy Mother of God.
R. *That we may be made worthy of the promises of Christ.*

Let us pray

Grant unto us, Thy servants, we beseech Thee, O Lord God, at all times to enjoy health of soul and body; and by the glorious intercession of Blessed Mary, ever Virgin, when freed from the sorrows of this present life, to enter into that joy which hath no end. Through Christ Our Lord. Amen.

THE ANGELUS

The Angel of the Lord declared unto Mary,
And She conceived of the Holy Ghost. Hail Mary . . . .
Behold the handmaid of the Lord.
Be it done to me according to Thy word. Hail Mary . . . .
And the Word was made flesh,
And dwelt amongst us.
  Hail Mary . . . .
Pray for us, O Holy Mother of God.
That we may be made worthy of the promises of Christ.

  (*Indulgence*: Ten years for each recitation; a plenary
  under the usual conditions, if the prayers are recited daily
  for one month.)

LET US PRAY: Pour forth, we beseech Thee, O Lord, Thy
grace into our hearts, that we, to whom the Incarnation of
Christ Thy Son was made known by the message of an Angel,
may, by His Passion and Cross, be brought to the glory of His
Resurrection; through the same Christ Our Lord. Amen.

REGINA COELI

(To be said from Holy Saturday to Trinity Sunday)
  V. Queen of heaven, rejoice.
      Alleluja.
  R. For He whom thou wast made worthy to bear.
      Alleluja.
  V. Hast risen as He said.
      Alleluja.
  R. Pray for us, to God.
      Alleluja.
  V. Rejoice and be glad, O Virgin Mary.
      Alleluja.
  R. For the Lord hath risen indeed.
      Alleluja.

LET US PRAY

  O God, who through the resurrection of Thy Son, Our Lord
Jesus Christ, hast vouchsafed to make glad the world, grant
us we beseech Thee, that, through the intercession of the
Virgin Mary, His Mother, we may attain unto the joys of
eternal life. Through the same Christ our Lord. Amen.
  Pray the Angelus Daily for Peace.
  Ask God, Through Mary, To Bless Your Family.

PRAYER FOR THE POPE

(Indulgence 3 years. Raccolta 654)

May the Lord preserve our *Holy Father Pope Paul VI,* give him life, and make him blessed upon earth, and deliver him not to the will of his enemies.

LET US PRAY: O God, the Shepherd and Ruler of all the faithful, in Thy mercy look down upon Thy servant, Paul, whom Thou has appointed to preside over Thy Church, and grant we beseech Thee that both by word and example he may edify those who are under his charge; so that, with the flock entrusted to him, he may attain life everlasting. Through Christ Our Lord. Amen.

PRAYER TO ST. JOSEPH

Oh, St. Joseph, whose protection is so great, so strong, so prompt before the throne of God, I place in You all my interest and desires. Oh, St. Joseph, do assist me by Your powerful intercession, and obtain for me from Your divine Son all spiritual blessings, through Jesus Christ, Our Lord. So that, having engaged here below Your heavenly power, I may offer my thanksgiving and homage to the most loving of Fathers. Oh, St. Joseph, I never weary contemplating you, and Jesus asleep in your arms; I dare not approach while He reposes near Your heart. Press Him in my name and kiss His fine head for me and ask Him to return the kiss when I draw my dying breath. St. Joseph, Patron of departing souls—Pray for me.

This prayer was found in the fiftieth year of Our Lord and Saviour Jesus Christ. In 1505 is was sent from the Pope to Emperor Charles, when he was going into battle. Whoever shall read this prayer or hear it, or keep it about themselves, shall never die a sudden death or be drowned, nor shall poison take effect on them; neither shall they fall into the hands of the enemy, or shall he be burned in any fire or shall be over-powered in battle.

Say for nine mornings for anything you may desire. It has never been known to fail.

PRAYER OF SAINT FRANCIS OF ASSISI
FOR PEACE

Lord, make me an instrument of Your peace. Where there is hatred, let me sow love; where there is injury, pardon; where there is doubt, faith; where there is despair, hope; where there is darkness, light; and where there is sadness, joy. O divine Master, grant that I may not so much seek to be consoled as to console; to be understood as to understand; to be loved as to love; for it is in giving that we receive; it is in pardoning that we are pardoned; and it is in dying that we are born to eternal life.

A VISIT TO OUR LADY

AFTER HOLY COMMUNION

Mother, upon my lips today
   Christ's Precious Blood was laid,
That Blood which centuries ago
   Was for my ransom paid;
And half in love and half in fear
   I seek for aid from Thee,
Lest what I worship, rapt in awe,
   Should be profaned by me.

Wilt Thou vouchsafe as Portress Dear
   To guard these lips today
Lessen my words of idle mirth,
   And govern all I say;
Keep back the sharp and quick retorts
   That rise so easily,
Soften my speech with gentle art
   To sweetest Charity.

O Mother! Thou art mine today,
   By more than double right!
A Soul where Christ reposed must be
   Most precious in Thy sight;
And Thou canst hardly think of me
   From Thy Dear Son apart,
So give me, from myself and sin,
   A refuge in Thy heart.

TAKE TIME

Take Time to THINK . . .
It is the source of power.
Take Time to PLAY . . .
It is the secret of perpetual youth.
Take Time to READ . . .
It is the fountain of wisdom.
Take Time to PRAY . . .
It is the greatest power on earth.
Take Time to LOVE and
      BE LOVED . . .
It is a God-given privilege.
Take Time to BE FRIENDLY . . .
It is the road to happiness.
Take Time to LAUGH . . .
It is the music of the soul.
Take Time to GIVE . . .
It is too short a day to be selfish.
Take Time to WORK . . .
It is the price of success.
Take time to DO CHARITY . . .
It is the Key to Heaven.

PRAYER TO SAVE AMERICA

O merciful God, we cry to you for pardon and for mercy. We are an unbelieving and perverse generation. We are disobedient, disloyal and ungrateful to you. We have excluded you from our homes, our schools, our places of business. We are no longer worthy to be called your children. Merciful Father, spare America! Forgive us! Save us from the scourge we deserve. Teach us your law, and move our wills to serve you today and everyday. Merciful God, please spare America!

PRAYER TO THE HOLY SPIRIT

Lord Jesus Christ, Son of the Father, send forth now your Spirit over all the earth. Let the Holy Spirit live in the hearts of all peoples, that they may be preserved from moral decline, disasters and war. May the Queen of the Holy Rosary, Queen of Peace be our advocate. Amen.

Visit, we beseech Thee, O Lord, this house, and drive far from it all the snares of the enemy; let Thy holy Angels dwell herein, who may keep us in peace; and let Thy blessing be always upon us. Through Christ, Our Lord. Amen.

Make Way for Mary

Make way for Mary and Her beautiful promise, and though over 700 years old, it is as new and vibrant with hope as when given. It all came about like this. An elderly man, the Prophet Elias, saw a "cloud" that rose up out of the sea. You may remember him as your Bible History called him "The Man of Fire". Yes, he called on Heaven for justice and fire came down from the clouds. The crops were drying up but when he prayed, the rain fell. At his command even the dead came back to life, and last but not least, he was taken up to Heaven in a fiery chariot and will come again to help us in our fight against the Antichrist.

This little cloud, when Elias first saw it, was about the size and shape of a man's foot, but gradually it seemed to cover most of the heavens. In it Elias saw the heal of a foot which to him was most symbolic, as he recalled the words of the Bible, "The heal of the Woman shall crush the head of the serpent". It was especially significant to him as the cloud became the image of the Immaculate Conception.

The vision inspired such a deep love in the heart of Elias, such a burning love, that he conceived the idea of founding a Religious Order of Men who would imitate the Virtues of Mary. As a group of hermits, they lived on Mount Carmel. Here they erected a chapel in Mary's honor and from this small group of men a huge Carmelite Order of Priests has spread throughout the World. Apparently the Blessed Virgin was so pleased that She visited them many times.

The Order continued to grow and in time a most saintly man, Simon Stock, joined them. It was during his time, the twelfth century, that the good Carmelite priests were having many difficulties. They were now branching out all over the world, and when coming from their home in the East, they were not always well received in the West. Some people even accusing them of being imposters and not the true followers of the Virgin Mary.

It was then Simon Stock, who was now General of the Order, and much concerned for them, knelt down and humbly asked the Queen of Carmel to give him a sign from Heaven to prove their identity as true descendants of the Order of Carmel as founded by the Prophet Elias.

Our Lady heard his prayer, appeared to him holding the Infant Jesus in Her arms and with the Scapular of their Order in Her hand said, "Receive My beloved son, the Scapular of Thy Order, as the Distinctive Sign of My Confraternity. Whoever dies invested with this Scapular shall be preserved from the Eternal Flames. It is a sign of Salvation, a sure safeguard in danger, a pledge of Peace and of My special protection until the end of the ages." She also told St. Simon to go to the Pope and he would end the persecution of the Order.

Fortunately for us, this outstanding promise from the Queen of Heaven and Earth was meant not just for them but for all people, everywhere. In other words, those who wear Her scapular are assured of Her solicitude and protection from harm in this life, and fulfilling Her requests, their salvation for all eternity.

Actually the wearing of the Scapular is a Mystical Prayer made possible by Our Lady's Sign. She has placed the Scapular about our necks to remind us that we have a Mother in Heaven waiting, and watching, and loving us more than our earthly mothers could love us. And when we make that Sign of Hers an incentive to virtue, a means of intensifying our oral prayers or those of affection, Her heart goes out to us and union with Her is deepened immeasurably.

Often, on our journey to Heaven, we may mystically embrace our Mother even though too far off to see Her, too far away to be ravished by Her actual presence and made exceptionally glorious, as the Little Flower says, by the radiance of such a Queen. Moreover, our wordless Scapular Prayer can take many forms. It may lead to any other kind of prayer such as ejaculatory prayer or the fervent recitation of the "Hail Mary" or "Our Father," even though it is in itself, according to the authorities on the spiritual life, a practice of the highest form of prayer. And who will measure the value of this prayer with the Mother who has promised: "Whosoever dies clothed in this (i.e., practicing the very minimum of the prayer) shall not suffer eternal fire"?

260

The Sabbatine Privilege

As beautiful as the promise of the Scapular was and is, Our Holy Mother in Her most generous and loving Heart added later still another. In a vision to Pope John XXII She said: "Those who have been invested with this Holy Habit will be delivered from Purgatory the first Saturday after their death."

What a promise, what concern from this Most *Wonderful* Mother, the Mother above all mothers, who tells us She will protect us, comfort us in our sorrows, assist us in our last agony, and deliver us the First Saturday after our death from the sufferings of Purgatory. Knowing this naturally most people lose no time in Consecrating themselves to Her by wearing Her Scapular, and fulfilling the other obligations She required.

1. Wear the Scapular faithfully after valid enrollment;
2. Keep chastity according to one's state;
3. Daily recite the Little Office of the Blessed Virgin (If one cannot read in place of reciting the Office, to abstain from meat on Wednesday and Saturdays (except Christmas) or when very difficult, to arrange with a priest with the proper faculty to substitute, 7 Our Fathers, Hail Mary's and Glory Be's, or if so desired 5 decades of Our Lady's powerful Rosary.

The first two however cannot be changed, but with so great and beautiful a promise it surely is worth any effort to comply with them.

TRULY IT IS SO MUCH FOR SO LITTLE.

Pope Benedict XV, the celebrated "World-War Pontiff"—granted five hundred days indulgence for the kissing of the Scapular, meaning everytime that it is kissed; and there are only one hundred days indulgence for making the Sign of the Cross with Holy Water!

Six Reasons Why The Cloth Is Preferred

In 1946, a Scapular Medal Crusade was begun here in America. In answer to this the Carmelite Curia in Rome issued special orders to all Carmelite houses throughout the world, making it mandatory to teach that the Scapular is preferred to the medal. The letter from the Carmelite Curia drew a parallel between the stations of the cross said on a single crucifix rather than by actual use of 14 stations, and the medal used in place of the cloth. Although it is *permissible* at times to use a single crucifix to make the stations of the cross, it is not preferred, nor can it be said to be equal to making the stations of the cross in the traditional manner. The concession was originally made for those who found it physically impossible to make the stations in church, even as the scapular medal was originally granted for those who found it almost impossible to wear a cloth scapular in some parts of the world.

SIX REASONS

1. Those who wear the medal rarely persevere in wearing it, or they wear it only from time to time . . . This fact is confirmed by experience and by actual tests conducted in Catholic schools and colleges. It is probably the one greatest reason why—

PREFERENCE OF THE CHURCH

2.—the church prefers that we use the cloth. The original decree which granted permission to substitute a medal for the cloth Scapular (in answer to requests from missionaries in tropical lands) states: "But the Holy Father vehemently desires that the Scapular be worn in its accustomed form."

Later, when the Scapular medal was being used promiscuously in Europe and America, without any care to reasons sufficient for the substitution, Pope Pius X (who granted the medal) said: "I never intended that the medal be used at all in Europe and America." Then the Holy Father opened his own cassock, took out his cloth Scapular, and said to his audience: "I wear the cloth Scapular of Carmel . . . Let us never take it off." All of his successors Pius XI and Pius XII, and especially his immediate successor, Pope Benedict XV, have expressed this preference with more or less vehemence. It was to xpress this preference that Pope Benedict XV provided that:

SPECIAL INDULGENCE

3. The cloth scapular bears a great indulgence not attached to the medal, namely, five hundred days each time the scapular is kissed. This is the largest indulgence ever attached to so small an act. It was deliberately excluded from the medal (by Pope Benedict XV) to emphasize ecclesiastical preference for use of the Brown Scapular over the medal.

SEVEN HUNDRED YEAR TRADITION

4. The cloth scapular has a tradition which is lost in the medal. Here is a sign which was used for seven hundred years . . . dear to such saints as Peter Claver, John of the Cross, Alphonsus Ligouri, Francis Xavier, the Little Flower, Grignon de Montfort, Claude de la Colombiere, and so many countless other holy souls who linked the Scapular with the Rosary in their devotion to the Blessed Virgin. As part of this tradition there are the hundreds upon hundreds of miracles, recorded in some three hundred books on the Scapular, some of which miracles are peculiar to a garment . . . such as being preserved in tombs (as in the case of St. Alphonsus), stopping a would-be suicide's dagger, flattening bullets, etc. To change the Scapular for a medal without good reason is to forfeit all this tradition . . . which, as in the case of anything spiritual, is not mere sentiment.

IMPORTANCE OF SACRIFICE

5. Sacrifice is a part of devotion . . . and Our Lady promises so much for the use of the Scapular . . . and the sacrifice of

wearing it is so little that to make the substitution of a medal for any but good reasons is to betray even the very little sacrifice Our Lady asks for such great rewards as Her Promise of Salvation, Her constant protection, and the Sabbatine Privilege. She has asked so little, and would we take advantage of a concession made to natives in Africa (or other tropical lands) to make that little she has asked even less?

SCAPULAR IS A GARMENT

6. The Scapular is a habit . . . Our Lady's habit. She appeared in it to Saint Simon Stock, holding the Scapular in Her hand even as she was wearing it (full size) on Her person. She appeared thus again, in 1917, at Fatima, where She promised the Conversion of Russia. And we recall the words of Saint Dominic spoken over seven hundred years ago in prophecy: "One day, by the Rosary and the Scapular, I will save the world." When we wear the Scapular, we are wearing a garment which was woven on the looms of Heaven and brought to earth by Our Lady Herself, in Her own hands. In wearing the Scapular we wear what Our Lady Herself was wearing when She made the promise . . . and when She appeared in the final vision of Fatima. It may be that in this Habit She will come to us at the hour of death to keep Her Scapular Promise. *The Scapular is essentially a religious habit.*

In commenting on the above cogent reasons for using the cloth scapular, we repeat the use of the medal is PERMISSIBLE. But we feel that anyone who knows the above reasons will follow the advice of Father Vermeerch, S.J., one of the greatest canonists of all time, who expressed the opinion that: "The medal may be used in place of all Scapulars, so that one may not have to wear many; but it *should* not be used in place of the cloth Scapular of Mount Carmel without a serious reason."

In other words, you MAY use a medal, but you lose much by doing it without a very good reason. Therefore the substitution for us in America is not at all advisable.

IMPRIMATUR: Geo. W. Ahr, Bishop of Trenton, New Jersey.

The Vicars of Christ Speak

Pope Pius XI, in his letter on the Sabbatine Privilege in 1922, designated it as "one of the greatest of our privileges from the Mother of God, She has promised the 'Whoever dies clothed in this Scapular shall not suffer eternal fire.' "

Pope John XXIII, in a broadcast to Lourdes on February 18th, 1959, in closing the Lourdes Marian Year said, "Like our Predecessor, we ardently wish for the renovation of Christianity with a unanimous impulse of Marian piety. When understood according to the doctrine of the Church this Marian piety cannot help but bring souls more rapidly and securely to Jesus Christ, Our Only Savior."

Pope Paul VI in the Papal Documents said, "We can see nothing more appropriate or efficacious than for the whole Christian family to raise its voice amid its many stresses and difficulties to pray the Mother of God, Whom we also address as Queen of Peace, to be generous, as a Good Mother, with Her gifts. During the Second Vatican Council we gave our confirmation to a point of traditional doctrine when we gave Her the Title of Mother of the Church, a Title acclaimed by The Council Fathers and the Catholic World."

"The Second Vatican Ecumenical Council clearly referred to the Rosary though not in express terms, when it reminded all the faithful that 'practices and exercises of devotion towards Her (Mary), recommended by the teaching authority of the Church in the course of the centuries, are to be held in high esteem.' "

The Recitation of the Rosary

Our Lady at all of Her apparitions in over one hundred years has repeatedly asked for everyone to pray the Rosary.

She has given Herself titles such as "Lady of the Rosary", "Queen of the Rosary", etc.

At Fatima, Portugal She added a tremendous promise referred to as THE FIVE FIRST SATURDAYS. She said: "I promise to help at the hour of death, with the graces needed for salvation, whoever on the First Saturday of five consecutive months shall: (1) Confess and receive Communion; (2) Recite five decades of the Rosary; (3) And keep me company for fifteen minutes while meditating on the fifteen mysteries of the Rosary, with the intention of making reparation to me."

The Fatima revelations have not only been repeatedly approved by our recent Popes Pius XII, John XXIII and Paul VI, but each of them has earnestly recommended our belief in, and our adherence to, the message of Fatima. Pope Pius XII stating, "The time for doubting Fatima is past, the time for action is now." Added to this, is the obvious approval of God as indicated by the authenticated miracles that take place at the Fatima shrine, many of which occur at the time when the sick are blessed by Our Lord in His Eucharistic Presence.

Pope Paul VI in March 1965 in his message to the Marian Congress at Santo Domingo in the Dominican Republic stated, "It is our conviction that the Rosary of Mary and the Scapular of Carmel are among these recommended practices." This was in reference to Vatican II documents, the Constitution on the Church, Article 67, "LET THE FAITHFUL HOLD IN HIGH ESTEEM THE PRACTICES AND DEVOTIONS TO THE BLESSED VIRGIN APPROVED BY THE TEACHING AUTHORITY OF THE CHURCH IN THE COURSE OF THE CENTURIES."

In September 1966 Pope Paul VI issued his inspiring Encyclical, CHRISTI MATRI ROSARII (Rosaries to the Mother of Christ) pleading for world-wide Rosary prayers, especially to be offered for peace.

In closing he stated: "It will be your task, venerable brothers, in keeping with your commendable religious zeal and your realization of the importance of this appeal, to prescribe the observances through which priests, Religious and laity and especially the innocent in the flower of youth and the sick in the midst of their sufferings, may be joined together in generous prayer to Her who is the Mother of God and of the Church."

"On the same day, in St. Peter's basilica, at the tomb of the Apostle, we also will hold a special ceremony of supplication in honor of the Virgin Mother of God, the protector of Christians and Our Intercessor for Peace. In this way, the one voice of the Church will resound on all the continents of the earth and reach the very gates of heaven. For as St. Augustine states, 'amid the various languages of men, the faith of the heart speaks one tongue.'

"Look upon all your sons with motherly love, O Blessed Virgin, Consider the anxieties of the bishops who fear the assaults of evil on their flocks; consider the anguish of so many men, fathers and mothers of families who are worried about their lot and that of their families and who are assailed with agonizing responsibilities. Calm the hearts of men at war and inspire them with "thoughts of peace." Through Your intercession may the demands of God's justice, which have been caused by sin, be turned into mercy; may He bring mankind back to the peace it longs for; may He lead men to true and lasting prosperity."

"Encouraged by the firm hope that the most high Mother of God will in Her kindness grant our humble prayer, we lovingly grant to you, venerable brothers. to the clergy and to the people entrusted to the care of each of you, the apostolic blessing."

LA SALETTE

Everyone knows of Our Lady's appearances at Lourdes and at Fatima. Many books have been written about these marvels, and a popular motion picture has dramatized each, thus bringing it forcefully to the attention of most people.

Several years before the happenings at Lourdes, and Fatima, Our Lady appeared to two children in the French Alps, giving them a message for the world. This apparition, pronounced authentic by Church authorities, is "The Story of La Salette."

In the United States, it is little known because of meagre publicity. The subject is of historical interest, also of practical importance. When Our Lady spoke to the astonished country boy and girl at La Salette, she asked that her words be brought to the attention of all the people. This meant those living in 1846, and the people of future generations. The message tells us, above all, of the power of God. It tells, further, of the divine displeasure because of irreligion, indifference, blasphemy, over-emphasis of materialism and sensuality, and the neglect of the spiritual in our daily life. It states the harsh consequences from neglecting God, the disorder and disaster in human affairs, the acute sufferings for everyone and lists the remedies—PRAYER and PENANCE.

La Salette is meant to rouse your mind and move your heart. One is personally drawn to it and personally involved in it because conditions in the U.S.A. today are even worse spiritually speaking than in France at that time.

What the Mother of God said:

"Come near, my children, be not afraid; I am here to tell you great news."

"If my people will not submit," she began, "I shall be forced to let fall the arm of My Son. It is so strong, so heavy, that I can no longer withhold it."

"For how long a time do I suffer for you! If I would not have My Son abandon you, I am compelled to pray to Him without ceasing; and as to you, you take no heed of it. However much you pray, however much you do, you will never recompense the pains I have taken for you."

"Six days have I given you to labor, the seventh I have kept for Myself; and they will not give it to me. It is this which makes the arm of My Son so heavy.

Those who drive the carts cannot swear without introducing the Name of My Son. These are the two things which make the arm of My Son so heavy.

If the harvest is spoilt, it is all on your account. I gave you warning last year with the potatoes, but you did not heed it. On the contrary, when you found the potatoes spoilt, you swore, you took the Name of My Son in vain. They will continue to decay, so that by Christmas there will be none left."

"Ah! My children, you do not understand. Well, wait, I will say it otherwise."

Resuming her discourse from the words, "If the harvest is spoilt," she continued:

"If you have wheat, it is no good to sow it; all that you sow the beasts will eat, and what comes up will fall into dust when you thrash it.

There will come a great famine. Before the famine comes, the children under seven years of age will be seized with trembling, and will die in the hands of those who hold them; the others will do penance by the famine.

The walnuts will become bad, and the grapes will rot."

"If they are converted, the stones and rocks will change into mounds of wheat, and the potatoes will be self-sown in the land."

"Do you say your prayers well, My children?"

"Ah! My children," She exhorted them, "you must be sure to say them well, morning and evening. When you cannot do better, say at least an Our Father and a Hail Mary; but when you have time say more.

There are none who go to Mass but a few aged women, the rest work on Sunday all summer; and in the winter, when they know not what to do, they go to Mass only to mock at religion. During Lent, they go to the meat-market like dogs."

"Have you never seen wheat that is spoilt, my children?"

269

"But you, my child," she insisted, addressing the little boy, "you must surely have seen some once when you were near the farm of Coin with your father. The master of the field told your father to go and see his ruined wheat. You went both together. You took two or three kernels of wheat into your hands and rubbed them, and they fell all into dust. Then you returned home. When you were still half an hour's distance from Corps, your father gave you a piece of bread and said to you: 'Here, my child, eat some bread this year at least; I don't know who will eat any next year, if the wheat goes on like that.'"

"Well, my children, you will make this known to all my people."

THE POPE RECEIVES THE SECRETS

"These are scourges," he said, "with which France is threatened, but she is not alone guilty. Germany, Italy, all Europe is guilty and deserves punishment. I have less to fear from open impiety, than from indifference and human respect. It is not without reason that the Church is called Militant, and here," pointing to his breast, "you behold its Captain. I must read these letters more at leisure."

THE BISHOP GIVES APPROVAL

We declare as follows:
"We judge that the Apparition of the Blessed Virgin to two cowherds, on the 19th of September, 1846, on a mountain of the chain of the Alps, situated in the parish of La Salette, in the arch-presbytery of Corps, bears within itself all the characteristics of truth, and the faithful have grounds for believing it indubitable and certain."

"We believe that this fact acquires a new degree of certitude from the immense and spontaneous concourse of the faithful on the place of the Apparition, as well as from the multitude of prodigies which have been the consequence of the said event, a very great number of which it is impossible to call in doubt without violating the rules of human testimony."

"Wherefore, to testify our lively gratitude to God and to the glorious Virgin Mary, we authorize the Cultus of Our Lady of

La Salette. We permit it to be preached, and that practical and moral conclusions may be drawn from this great event."

"In fine, as the principal end of the Apparition is to recall Christians to the fulfillment of their religious duties, to frequenting the divine worship, His Church, to a horror of blasphemy, and to the sanctification of the Sunday; we conjure you, our very dear brethren, with a view of your heavenly, and even of your earthly interests, to enter seriously into yourselves, to do penance for your sins, and especially for those against the second and third commandments of God. We conjure you, our well-beloved brethren, be docile under the voice of Mary who calls you to penance, and who, on the part of Her Son, threatens you with spiritual and temporal evils, if remaining insensible to Her Maternal admonitions, you harden your hearts."

(Signed)

"PHILIBERT, Bishop of Grenoble."

THE TWO SECRETS OF LA SALETTE AS GIVEN TO POPE PIUS IX

The La Salette apparition preceded the Lourdes apparition to St. Bernadette by 12 years. The Blessed Virgin appeared on the now famous La Salette Mount in France to two children. One was a little shepherd boy, 11 years af age, and the other a poor, timid girl, 14 years of age. These two children suddenly became famous in France, Italy, and throughout Europe. The name of the boy is: Peter Maximin Giraud; and that of the girl: Frances Melanie Mathieu. On Saturday, September 19, 1846, between 2 and 3 o'clock in the afternoon, they both beheld the apparition. It was recognized as worthy of credence by Pope Pius IX on August 24, 1852, and has been known throughout the Catholic World as Our Lady of La Salette. The following are the Secret Messages:

SECRET OF MAXIMIN GIRAUD

"On the 19th of September, 1846, I saw a lady brilliant like the sun, whom I believe to be the Holy Virgin. However, I have never said it was the Holy Virgin. I have always said that

271

I saw a lady, but never ventured to affirm that it was the Holy Virgin."

"From what I am going to state here, it appertains to the Church to judge whether it was truly the Holy Virgin or some other person. She gave me my secret about the middle of Her conversation with me, after these words: 'The grapes shall rot, and the chestnuts shall be bad.' The Lady began by saying to me:

"1. 'Three fourths of France shall lose the faith, and the other fourth, that will preserve it, will practice it with tepidity.

"2. 'Peace shall not be given to the world until men will be converted.

"3. 'A Protestant nation in the North shall be converted to the faith, and through the means of that nation, the others shall return to the Holy Catholic Church.

"4. 'The next Pope shall not be a Roman.

"5. 'When men shall be converted, God will give peace to the world.

"6. 'Afterwards this peace shall be disturbed by the monster.

"7. 'The monster shall arrive at the end of this nineteenth century or, at latest, at the commencement of the twentieth.

"8. 'In this time the Antichrist will be born of a nun of Hebraic descent, a false virgin, who will have intercourse with the ancient serpent, with the master of impurity and putrefaction. His father will be a bishop. He will perform false miracles and subsist only on vitiating faith. He will have his brethren, who will be children of evil but not incarnate devils like himself. Soon they will be at the head of armies, supported by the Legions of Hell.

"9. 'Up, ye children of light, and fight! For behold, the age of ages, the end, the extremity is at hand! The Church passes into darkness. The world will be in a state of consternation, perplexity and confusion.

"10. 'Enoch and Elias, they will suddenly appear on earth full of the Spirit of God, when the Church becomes darkened and the world in terrible agony. They will convert those of good will and comfort the oppressed Christians. With the help of the Holy Ghost, they will have great success against the heresies of the Antichrist. But in the end they will be delivered unto death.' "

Melanie's secret message, which follows, was published in its entirety in a brochure which she had printed in 1879 at Lecce, Italy, with the approval of the Bishop of Lecce.

"The Lady said to me:

" 'What I shall tell you now will not always remain a secret. You are allowed to publish it after the year 1858.

" 'There will be a kind of false peace before the advent of Antichrist. Man's only thought will be upon diversions and amusements. The wicked will indulge in all sorts of sin, but the children of the Holy Church, the children of the Faith, my sincere followers, will wax strong in the love of God and in the virtues that are dear to Me. Happy the humble souls that are guided by the Holy Ghost. I will fight with them until they shall have reached the completion of age.

" 'Italy will be severely punished for her efforts to shake off the yoke of the Most High Lord. She will become the play-ball of war. On every side blood will flow. The temples will either be closed or desecrated. Priests and members of Religious Orders will be put to flight. They will be beaten to death and otherwise die cruel deaths.

" 'The Vicar of My Son will be compelled to suffer much because for a time the Church will be delivered to great persecutions. That will be the hour of darkness, and the Church will experience a frightful crisis. The powerful officials of the State and the Church will be suppressed and done away with, and all law and order as well as justice. There will be murder, hate, envy and deceit, with no love or regard for one's country or family.

" 'God is going to punish in a manner without example. Woe to the inhabitants of the earth! God is going to exhaust His wrath, and nobody shall be able to evade so many combined evils. At the first stroke of His fulminating sword the mountains and the whole of nature shall shake with terror, because the disorders and crimes of men pierce the very Vaults of the Heavens. The earth shall be stricken with every kind of plagues. (Besides the pestilence and famine, which shall be general.) There shall be wars until the last war, which shall be waged by the ten kings of Antichrist. All these kings shall have a common design, and they only shall govern the world. Priests and Religious shall be hunted; they shall be butchered in a cruel manner. Many shall abandon the Faith, and great shall be the number of Priests and Religious who shall separate themselves from the True Religion; among these there will be found likewise several bishops. Let the Pope be upon his guard against miracle-workers, for the time is arrived when the most astounding prodigies will take place on the earth and in the air.

" 'Lucifer, with a very great number of demons will be unchained from hell. By degrees they shall abolish the Faith, even among persons consecrated to God. They shall blind them in such a manner that, without very special graces, these persons shall imbibe the spirit of those wicked angels. Many religious houses will entirely lose the Faith, and shall be the cause of the loss of many persons. The Superiors of Religious Communities should be alert regarding the ones they take into the community, for the devil will use all malice, to bring persons into the Orders who are addicted to sin.

" 'Bad people will abound upon the earth; and the spirit of darkness shall spread over the earth a universal relaxation about everything relating to the Service of God. Satan shall have very great power over nature (God's punishment for the crimes of men); temples will be erected for the worship of these demons. Some persons shall be transported from one place to another by these wicked spirits, even some priests, because these will not be animated by the Holy Spirit of the Gospel, which is a spirit of humility, charity, and zeal for the Glory of God.

" 'Some will make the dead rise and appear as holy persons. The souls of the damned shall also be summoned, and shall appear as united to their bodies. Such persons, resurrected through the agency of demons, shall assume the figure of holy persons, who are known to have been upon earth, in order more easily to deceive them. These self-styled resuscitated persons shall be nothing but demons under their forms. In this way they shall preach a Gospel contrary to that of Jesus Christ, denying the existence of Heaven.

" 'In every place there shall be seen extraordinary prodigies, because the True Faith has been extinguished, and a pale light shines in the world.

" 'My Son's Vicar shall have much to suffer, because for a

time the Church shall be exposed to very great persecutions. This shall be the time of darkness. The Church shall have to pass through an awful crisis. France, Italy, Spain, and England shall have Civil War. Blood shall flow through the streets. French shall fight French. Italians against Italians. After this there will be a frightful general war. For a time God shall not remember France, nor Italy (for two years or for one?), because the Gospel of Jesus Christ is no more understood. The Holy Father will suffer much. I will be with him to the end to receive his sacrifice. The wicked shall many times attempt his life.

" 'Nature demands vengeance against men, and she trembles with fright in expectation of what will befall the earth sullied with crimes. Tremble, O earth! And tremble you also who make profession of serving Jesus Christ, but inwardly worship yourselves, because God has delivered you to his enemies, because corruption is in holy places.

" 'In the year 1865 the abomination shall be seen in Holy Places, in Convents, and then the demon shall make himself as the king of hearts. It will be about that time that Antichrist shall be born. At his birth he shall vomit blasphemies. He shall have teeth; in a word, he shall be like an incarnate demon; he shall utter frightful screams; he shall work prodigies; and he shall feed on impure things. He shall have brothers, who, though not incarnate demons like him, shall nevertheless be children of iniquity. At the age of twelve years they shall have become remarkable for valiant victories, which they shall achieve; very soon each of them will be at the head of armies. Paris shall be burned, and Marseilles shall be submerged; many great cities shall be shattered and swallowed up by earthquakes. The populace will believe that everything is lost, will see nothing but murder, and will hear only the clang of arms and sacrilegious blasphemies.

" 'I address a pressing appeal to the Earth. I call upon the True Disciples of the Living God, Who reigns in the Heavens; I call upon the True Imitators of Christ made Man, the Only True Savior of mankind; I call upon My children, those who are truly devoted to Me, those who have offered themselves to Me that I may lead them to My Son, those whom I carry as it were in My arms, those who have been animated by My Spirit.

275

Finally, I call on the Apostles of these Last Days, these faithful Disciples of Jesus Christ, who have lived despising the world and themselves, in poverty and humility, in contempt and in silence, in prayer and mortification, in chastity and union with God, in suffering and unknown to the world. It is time for them to come out and enlighten the World. Go ye forth and manifest yourselves as My darling children; I am with you and within you, so that your Faith may be light which illumines you in these unhappy days, and that your zeal may make you long for the Glory and Honor of the Most High. Fight, ye children of light; combat, ye small band that can see, for this is the time of times, the end of ends.

" 'The seasons of the year will change, the earth will produce only bad fruits, the stars will depart from their regular course, the moon will give only a weak, reddish light. Water and fire in the interior of the earth will rage violently and cause terrible earthquakes, whereby mountains and cities will sink into the depths. Earthquakes will also devour whole countries. Together with the Antichrist the demons will work great false miracles on earth and in the air. Voices will be heard in the air. Then men will desert Religion and become worse and worse. Men will let themselves be deceived because they refused to adore the real Christ Who lives bodily amongst them. Woe to the inhabitants of the earth! Bloody wars, famines, pestilence and contagious diseases will develop. Terrible rain and hail will come with animals falling from the Heavens, thunder and lightning burning down entire cities. The whole universe will be gripped by fear. Finally the sun will be darkened and Faith alone will give light.

" 'A certain precursor of Antichrist, together with his followers from many nations, will fight the real Christ, the only Saviour of the World. He will endeavor to eliminate the adoration of God in order to be considered as God himself. Much blood will flow. Then the earth will be visited by all kinds of blows, from constant wars until the last war which finally will be made by the ten kings of the Antichrist.

" 'During the time of the arrival of Antichrist, the gospel will be preached everywhere, and all Peoples and Nations will then recognize the Truth.

" 'Rome will lose the Faith and become the seat of Antichrist. Yet the Heathen Rome will disappear. See, here is the

Beast with its subjects that claims to be the Saviour of the world. Proudly it rises in the air to go straight to Heaven, but it will be strangled by the Archangel Michael and cast down. And the earth, which for the past three days was in continuous convulsions, opens her fiery jaws and swallows him with all his cohorts forever into its hellish abyss. Eventually will water and fire cleanse the earth and the works of human pride will be destroyed and all will be renewed. Then will all serve God and glorify Him.

" 'The just will have much to suffer; their prayers, works of penance and tears will ascend to heaven. All of God's people will cry for forgiveness and grace and beg My help and intercession. Then Jesus Christ will command His Angels, by a special act of His Justice and Mercy, to deliver all His enemies to death. Then suddenly all persecutors of the Church of Jesus Christ and all evil doers will perish, and rest and peace between God and man will appear. Jesus Christ will be served, adored and glorified. Love of neighbor will begin to flourish all over. The new kings will be on the right hand of the Church which will grow strong, and which will be humble, pious, poor, zealous and followers of the virtues. All over, the Gospel will now be preached, people will make great progress in faith; there will be unity amongst the laborers of Jesus Christ, and people will live in the fear of God.

" 'Behold the reign of the ten Kings! Woe to the inhabitants of the earth; there shall be sanguinary wars, and famine, and plagues, and contagious maladies; there shall be showers of a frightful hail of animals; thunder shall shake entire cities; earthquakes which shall swallow up some countries; voices shall be heard in the air; men (in despair) shall knock their heads against the walls; they shall call on death; and death shall be their torment; blood shall flow from every side. Who shall be able to overcome (all these evils)? Fire shall rain from heaven, and shall destroy three cities. The whole world shall be struck with terror, and many will allow themselves to be seduced, because they have not believed the True Christ living among them. The sun becomes dark. Faith only shall survive. So the time! The abyss opens. Behold the king of kings of darkness! Behold the beast with his subjects!' "

277

HOLD FAST, LEGIONARIES—
THE CHURCH NEEDS YOU

In Bishop Thomas W. Muldoon's talk to his Legion of Mary at Sidney, Australia in 1970, he stressed two things that are appropriate today for all Christians as well as Legionaries.

THE ROSARY

There is one thing I would advocate very strongly. It is this—hold firm to the Rosary of the Mother of God; resist all temptation to remove it from the Legion system, the Legion structure. Hold firm to the Rosary of the Mother of God. I would not have wanted to have been anywhere else today than to have been with you just to say that Rosary. It proves once again, of course, that the Rosary should be said in a group, if possible. It gives one a real feeling of emotions, a real feeling of joy to hear a family like ours reciting the Rosary with devotion and fervour.

DEVOTION TO THE MOTHER OF GOD

My second point is this. Apart from your apostolic work which we cherish, the Church needs you today because there is a malignancy in the air. Not so much here in Australia, though I shall be surprised if we do not experience it within another 2 or 3 years. But throughout the whole of the Catholic World, almost, there is a malignancy in the air; there is a spirit of pride and self-assertion, of rebellion against authority, there is a questioning of even our most Sacred Truths. There are falsehoods, there are errors, there are near-heresies which are being written and spoken.

Amongst these aberrations, there is this aberration of the down-grading of devotion to the Mother of God; and indeed in some cases not only a down-grading and a denigration but a complete abolition of devotion to the Mother of God; and that is one of the worst aspects of this malignancy that is in the air because once you forego devotion, real genuine devotion to the Mother of God, you set yourself upon the path of error that ends in denying the very roots of Christianity.

Through the Christian Ages the word has been spoken: "She is the rock upon which all heresy is broken." Mary is the Mother of God—and history shows us that those who give up devotion to the Mother of God are quick to give up dogmas of the Christian revelation and practices of Christian conduct and morals that have been held sacred from the beginning. History has shown that a forsaking of genuine devotion to the Mother of God leads to corruption in the Church.

And that is another reason why we need the Legion of Mary. The reason why we need the women, young and old, who look to Her and declare Her before the world for Who She is, and what She is, the Mother of God, the Co-Redemptress with Her Son, Jesus Christ, and the Mediatrix of all Graces to mankind.

CONSTANT VIGIL OF PRAYER

Dear Reader,

This nation in which we live contains two million mothers who have destroyed their children. Two million abortions are only part of the symptoms of a society which is sick to the brink of death by a disease called sin. Among the noticeable symptoms we see anti-Christian forces working to destroy our Country and all that we hold dear—including our Faith in God.

How long will our Heavenly Father hold back His punishment of this nation for demoralizing its youth through drugs, pornography and X-rated movies? The latest destructive fad is devil worship of one form or another.

These evils which we see in our society are not something to be lamented. Rather, we must consider them a warning and a challenge; either this trend must be averted or we will face the wrath of God!

We have been given a solution for today's ills by an invitation issued by Our Lord in the Garden of Gethsemane; "Could you not then watch one hour with Me?" With these words as the guide and call to action, the Constant Vigil of Prayer movement began several years ago in the midwest. It has been tremendously successful wherever it has been introduced. The program is easy to understand. Dedicated workers visit churches and obtain promises of people to pray one extra hour per week in addition to Sunday worship. Praying can be done in the home, the car or wherever you happen to be at the chosen hour.

Our competent lecturers have been very successful in setting up new Constant Vigil of Prayer organizations in various cities in the country. There is no charge for most of the materials and no fee for a lecturer. We believe that only a massive crusade of prayer can save this country from impending disaster. We are appealing to you and people like you because we think that you would be willing to join us in prayer and help motivate others to pray.

The Constant Vigil of Prayer is now established in more than forty states. Wherever it is, that town, city or area becomes a better place to live. As we believe that you would want the same for *your town*, please let us hear from you soon.
R.R. 1, Box 808 Timber Lane, Necedah, Wis., 54646.

OUR LORD

CHRIST'S APPEAL FOR LOVE, by Sr. Josefa Menendez. Condensed version of "THE WAY OF DIVINE LOVE." Reprinted at request of many devotees of complete book. No interpretation of the Sacred Heart message equals in popularity this one given by Our Lord Himself to Sr. Josefa. Excellent for gifts to introduce the message and for those whose time is limited to read the full version. 176 pages. Paper. $2.50, 5 @ $2.00 ea.

DOCTOR AT CALVARY, by Pierre Barbet, M.D. The passion of our Lord Jesus Christ as described by a surgeon. Dr. Barbet feels that doctors should give relief from pain, but should also know the great spiritual value and purpose of suffering and help their patients to understand this great mystery of God's love. Science, the Shroud, and 15 years of study and research makes this a solid contribution to Christian piety, love, and respect for Our Lord who made the Supreme Sacrifice that the Gates of Heaven could once more be opened to all mankind. 213 pp. Paper. $1.45 ea.; 5—$1.25 ea.

ENTHRONEMENT OF THE SACRED HEART, by Rev. Larkin, SS.CC. Excellent explanation of devotion to the Sacred Heart and the enthronement ceremony. 416 pages, Paper. $2.00, 5 @ $1.75 ea.

FAITH OF MILLIONS, by Rev. John A. O'Brien, Ph.D. A splendid exposition of the doctrines and practices of the Catholic religion. The clarity, thoroughness and friendliness with which these have been presented have won for it millions of readers of all faiths and have caused it to be translated into French, German, Italian, Spanish, Chinese, Japanese, Hungarian, Korean, Malayalam, and British. 430 pp. Paper. $4.95 ea.

HE REIGNS FROM THE CROSS, by Rev. Gonzales, S.J. "The richness of these meditations of the Passion of Our Savior, should lead many to a more profound realization of the mystery of salvation, and the meaning of suffering." Cardinal McIntyre. 120 pp. Paper, $2.00 ea.; 5—$1.75 ea.

IMITATION OF CHRIST, by Thomas A. Kempis. An easy to read version of the immortal spiritual classic. Preserves all the spirit and beauty of the magnificent meditations of the original. Second only to the Scriptures. 477 pp. Paper. $2.25 ea.; 5—$2.00 ea., 10—$1.90 ea.

JESUS APPEALS TO THE WORLD, by Sr. Consolata Betrone. Taken from the diary of this 20th Century nun who had visions of Christ and who imparts to the world His words about the mystery of God's Love. The powerful ejaculation "Jesus, Mary, I love you, save souls" was given to us through her. 224 pp. Hard cover. $3.95 ea.; 5—$3.50 ea.

JESUS KING OF LOVE, by Fr. Mateo, SS.CC. As the enemy is working day and night to destroy the family, the main unit of strength in our society, Fr. Mateo comes through with a divinely inspired defense, the "Enthronement of the Sacred Heart in the Home." As there is no way to shield the children from many of the spiritual and moral dangers they face, enthronement of the home and consecration of its members to the Sacred Heart is one sure way to give them the graces and strength to stand firm and loyal to God, family and country. This, the family rosary, wearing of the scapular and a crucifix are vitally important for the very crucial period just ahead. 319 pages. Paper. 1—$2.50, 3 or more, $2.00 ea.

MEDITATIONS ON THE LITANY OF THE SACRED HEART, by Rev. Anthony Wolf. The Litany contains 33 invocations, one for each year of Our Lord's life. In each our attention is called to some attribute or virtue of Our Savior. You will surely pray the Litany with a new interest and fervor, receiving many more graces from it after reading Fr. Wolf's scholarly, yet easy to read explanation of each invocation. 87 pages, Paper, 1—$1.00, 5 or more 85¢ ea.

SELF-PORTRAIT OF CHRIST, by Rev. E. A. Wuenschel. Here is the wonderful account of the Shroud of Turin, its history and its defense, its authentic and beautiful image of Our Savior, Jesus Christ. Twelve clear sharp photos verify accuracy of story. 128 pages, Paper, $2.50 ea., 5 or more $2.00 ea.

SPIRITUAL CANTICLE, by E. Allison Peers. This book is a gift of God to man, and has become one of the richest sources of meditation in the treasury of Catholic literature. Its poetry is some of the loveliest that the human heart has ever conceived, or the human mind expressed. Few have ever known more of the meaning of true love of God than this humble Carmelite friar. Nowhere outside of Holy Scripture is such knowledge expressed so profoundly. 520 pages, Paper. $2.95, 5 @ $2.50 ea.

THE IMITATION OF THE SACRED HEART OF JESUS, by Rev. P. J. Arnoudt, S.J. A spiritual classic often compared to the "Imitation of Christ." The reader will have the Sacred Heart of Our Lord to guide him. There could be no safer or surer way to eternal happiness. 734 pp. Paper. $5.50 ea.; 5—$4.50 ea.

THE WAY OF DIVINE LOVE, by Sr. Josefa Menendez. Revelations of Our Lord to a Spanish nun about the mysteries of the Sacred Heart and the value He places on each soul. Explains the role of victim souls and how their suffering wins the graces for saving many other souls. A spiritual classic, once read means never to be forgotten. Placed by some as close if not next to Holy Scripture. 532 pages, Paper. $5.00, 5 @ $4.00 ea., 10 @ $3.50 ea., 25 @ $3.00 ea.

TRUSTFUL SURRENDER TO DIVINE PROVIDENCE, by Fr. Jean Baptiste Sainte-Jure, S.J. and Blessed Claude de la Colombiere, S.J. An outstanding treatise on doing God's will at all times and in all things. Authors explain how in this way we are led on our way to happiness and peace of mind in this life, along with a foretaste of the everlasting happiness we have been promised. Parts were used by the Cure of Ars as regular spiritual reading. 139 pp. Paper. 80¢ ea.; 5—70¢ ea.

WORDS FROM THE CROSS, by Rev. Christopher Rengers, O.F.M., CAP. Inspirational thoughts and meditations from the seven last words spoken by Our Lord from the Cross. (See records and tapes for outstanding cassette on subject.) Ideal for Lent or regular meditation. 66 pp. Paper. $1.25 ea.; 5—$1.00 ea.; 10—90¢ ea.

MASS AND HOLY EUCHARIST

BLESSED EUCHARIST—Our Greatest Treasure, by Fr. Michael Muller, C.SS.R. Our Lord in the Blessed Sacrament is an abundant source of continuous grace, comfort and inspiration. For how long do we fail to recognize and appreciate what Our Lord could and would do if only the Christian people would give Him one hour each week to kneel and pray in His presence. How many problems would be corrected, how many homes would find the love and peace they seek and what leaders would come forth to stop the evil, anti-Christian forces from continually promoting war, persecution and destruction. A spiritual classic for over 100 years. 360 pages, Paper, $3.50 ea., 3 or more $3.00 ea.

CHAMPION OF THE BLESSED SACRAMENT—Rev. M. Dempsey. A great saint, Peter J. Eymard, helps us recognize and appreciate the wonderful privilege to have Our Lord come down on our altars each day at Mass. Also the beautiful privilege to receive Him into our very hearts and souls in Communion.

As for daily Mass and Communion, Our Lord said to St. Gertrude, "They shall be more glorious in heaven who have received Me oftener on earth." What a reward both here and for all eternity.

A sincere devotee of Our Lady who helped many souls to attain their eternal reward. 286 pages. Hard cover. $3.95 ea., 2 or more $3.50 ea.

HOLY COMMUNION, by St. P. J. Eymard. Filled with the spirit of God thru Communion, devotion to Our Lord in the Blessed Sacrament became a dominant theme in the life of St. Peter Eymard. Shows the effects of grace on and in one's soul through proper preparation and the actual reception of Our Lord in Holy Communion. Explains Its life giving power, reconciliation between the Soul and God and lasting spiritual benefits that will go with us to our eternal reward. 330 pages, Paper, $1.95 ea., 3 or more, $1.65 ea.

THE HIDDEN TREASURE—Holy Mass, by St. Leonard. When a saint writes, one senses a true fervor and spiritual penetration in the words, especially when the subject is as sublime and eternal as the Holy Sacrifice of the Mass. This the perfect prayer and best possible way to thank, praise and adore God, given to us by Our Divine Savior Himself, could and should be our main interest here and for all eternity. True at every Mass Angels surround the priest, Jesus and Mary, the Apostles, Martyrs, Saints and Poor Souls in Purgatory are present and then at the Consecration Our Lord Himself comes down on our altars. What greater opportunity in any one day could one have than to share in all the merits and graces won by Our Lord on Calvary with the beautiful privilege of even sharing His divinity when receiving Him in Holy Communion. St. Leonard here uncovers for many this beautiful spiritual jewel, truly for too many, too long a "Hidden Treasure." 125 pages. Paper. 1 @ $1.50, 5 or more $1.25 ea.

THE WORLD'S GREATEST SECRET, by J. M. Haffert. An unusual, great book on the Mass. Convincing, inspiring treatment of the happy truth of Christ's abiding with us in the Holy Eucharist. Many pictures of the ancient catacombs that confirm Catholic Eucharistic doctrine. Padre Pio said, "It will succeed while the author is living but will have its greatest success after his death." Several years of preparation resulted in a gem that may take its place among the spiritual classics. Has special appeal for Catholics and non-Catholics. 310 pages, Paper, 1—95¢, 5 or more 75¢ ea.

THE BLESSED MOTHER

A WOMAN CLOTHED WITH THE SUN, by Delaney. Highlights eight important appearances of Our Lady. Shows God's hand in the affairs of men and nations. Also that unless God's plan is followed there cannot be peace. 274 pp. Paper. $1.75 ea.; 5—$1.55 ea.

BY THE QUEEN'S COMMAND, by Lawrence Harvey. The Irish Catholic says of it, "By the Queen's Command is a thousand times a book to be read, as there can be no possible doubt about the authenticity of the book's message . . . Trust Mary, Say the Rosary, Pray, Sanctify your work. Every lover of Mary will profit from this book. The stories of the reported apparitions are all delightfully told." 90 pp. Paper. $1.00 ea.; 10—75¢ ea.

GUADALUPE: For All Americans—A Pledge of Hope. People from all over the world come to Tepeyac Hill, Mexico City to see the famous picture of Our Lady introduced instantaneously on the rough tilma of Juan Diego in 1531. Scientists, photographers and artists have studied it all recognizing that after 450 years the colors are just as clear as originally.

This heaven sent portrait of Christ's Most Holy Mother came at a crucial time in history, dissolving the enmities between the Spaniards and Mexicans, and converting the whole Mexican Nation to God. How consoling Her words then and how true today. "I am a merciful Mother to all who love Me and trust Me, and invoke My help." 159 pages, Paper. 1—$1.75, 5—$1.50 ea.

MARY, HOPE OF THE WORLD, by Fr. J. Alberione, S.S.P., S.T.D. A brilliant consideration of Mary under various aspects; in the mind of God, prophecies, the longing of humanity; Her earthly life as Co-redemptrix of mankind; and Her life of Glory in Heaven, in the Church, and in the hearts of the faithful. A real addition to any Marian library. 222 pp. Hard Cover. $3.00 ea.; 5—$2.75 ea.

MARY WAS HER LIFE, by Sr. M. Pierre, R.S.M. The story of a Spanish nun, Sr. Mary Teresa Quevedo, who died in 1950. Her attitude is best expressed by her motto "May all who look at me see you, O Mary." A spiritual inspiration and a happy biography. 199 pp. Paper. 95¢ ea.; 5—75¢ ea.

MORE ABOUT FATIMA, by Rev. Montes de Oca, C.S.Sp. Complete and authentic account of God's peace plan given in 1917. Its purpose, to give directives to the Christian world to prevent World War II that was to happen in the reign of the next Pope, about 20 years. God's hand in world affairs and the destiny of man can be clearly understood through the prophecy given and the fulfillment by the war, etc. that followed. This was the cause of the war then so the answer to preventing WW III now will also be basically the same. 144 pp. Paper. $1.00 ea.; 5—85¢ ea.

OUR LADY OF FATIMA, by Thomas Walsh. "Beyond doubt the finest book on Our Lady of Fatima." Catholic Messenger. 223 pp. Paper. $1.45 ea.; 5—$1.20 ea.

OUR LADY'S KNIGHT, by Rev. Lovasik, S.V.D. Heartwarming story of T. Sgt. Leo E. Lovasik (1921-1943), who with undaunted courage and joy, gave his heart to Mary Queen of the Skies, and his life to his country. An inspiration for young and old. 232 pp. Hard cover. $3.00 ea.; 5—$2.50 ea.

SIGN OF HER HEART by John Haffert. A great spiritual book on the Brown Scapular, that ever important sacramental for our salvation. Includes interesting stories of very special graces and protection received through it. Sixth printing, acclaimed by many, one of the great spiritual books of our time. 270 pages. Paper. 85¢, 5 @ 75¢ ea., 10 @ 70¢ ea.

SORROWFUL AND IMMACULATE HEART OF MARY, Message of Berthe Petit, Franciscan Tertiary. 17 pictures. 20th Century revelations about the Blessed Mother's role in Christ's plan for redemption. 110 pp. Paper. $1.95 ea.; 5—$1.75 ea.; 10—$1.60 ea.

THAT MOTHERLY MOTHER OF GUADALUPE. The Mother of all the Americas shows Her power through the Rosary and the beautiful graces that She is privileged to grant. Again Her Divine Son's Church expands to embrace millions of souls who otherwise would be lost by the wayside. 74 pp. Hard cover. $1.50 ea.; 10—$1.25 ea.

THE FATIMA SECRET, by Emmett Culligan. Contains the revealed secret message of Fatima opened by Pope John XXIII in 1960. Also gives the secret message of LaSalette, France an apparition that happened in 1846. As LaSalette is to be repeated in America today it is vitally important that everyone understands it. 13 pictures. 38 pages. Paper. $1.50, 5 @ $1.25 ea.

THE GLORIES OF CZESTOCHOWA AND JASNA GORA. Our lady of Czestochowa is to the Polish people what Lourdes is to the French. The history, traditions, and miracles of the so called "Black Madonna make up a proud heritage of the Polish people. Most parish churches in Poland have a beautiful shrine dedicated to Our Lady under this title. Other countries whose churches have many Polish members are starting now to honor Her in this way. 155 pp. Paper. $2.00 ea.; 5—$1.75 ea.

THE HEART OF MARY, by Heinrich Keller, S.J. The object of this book is to introduce to the reader the reality of devotion to the Immaculate Heart of Mary, its mysteries and its meaning for our salvation. Higher moral standards and World Peace could follow if enough Christians sincerely practiced a devotion to Mary's Immaculate and Her Son's Divine Heart. 80 pp. Paper. $1.25 ea., 5 or more $1.10 ea.

THE LIFE OF THE BLESSED VIRGIN MARY. As visioned by Anna Catherine Emmerich. Gives intimate and unusual aspects of Our Lady's, St. Anne's, and St. Joachim's lives and others who figured in the Divine picture of the coming of Our Lord, also the last days on earth of the Blessed Mother. Many interesting items not contained even in the Scriptures. 400 pp. Paper. $3.50 ea.; 5—$3.00 ea.; 10—$2.75 ea.; 25—$2.50 ea.; 50—$2.25 ea.

THE QUEEN'S SECRET, by Sister Amatora, O.S.F. Simplified version of the Secret of Mary. Excellent for students in the upper grades or in high school who are interested to make the "Perfect Consecration." 83 pp. Paper. 90¢ ea.; 10— 80¢ ea.; 25—75¢ ea.

THE QUEEN'S WAY, by Sr. M. Amatora, O.S.F. An easy to read version of St. Louis De Montfort's great book TRUE DEVOTION. Adapted for reading by upper grade students or adults. 196 pages, Paper. 1—$2.00, 5 or more $1.75 ea.

THE WOMAN SHALL CONQUER, by Don Sharkey. Gives details of Our Lady's role of influence in the affairs of Nations and the World going back to 1830. God's emissary of Peace and good will has been making repeated visits to His children always as a concerned and loving Mother, warning when dangers threatened, comforting and consoling the sick and weary, reprimanding the wayward and bringing hope when catastrophy happened. If history should have taught mankind one clear and important lesson it should have been "Listen to the Mother of God so as to prevent floods, tornadoes, war, destruction, food shortages and now a Divine Chastisement that will make many of the living envy the dead." Covers 20 apparitions 1930-1954. 258 pages. Paper, 4 color cover, $2.25; 5 or more $2.00 ea.

TREASURE WRAPPED IN CLOTH, by Rev. Stephen Breen. As St. Pius X stated, "There is no easier or surer way of uniting men to Christ than Mary." For the first time the author of the above book has succeeded to give a composite picture of the privilege afforded so many Christians through the knowledge and use of the 18 various Scapulars. 162 pp. Paper. $2.00 ea.; 10—$1.75 ea.

TRUE DEVOTION TO MARY, by St. Louis De Montfort. Special treatise on the "Perfect Consecration." Other books required for making the perfect consecration: Secret of Mary, The New Testament, and Imitation of Christ. Outline of the 33 days of spiritual reading and prayers necessary for making the De Montfort Consecration available upon request. 226 pp. Hard cover: No charge. $3.00 ea.; 10—$2.50 ea. Paper: $2.00 ea.; 10—$1.50 ea.

CITY OF GOD, by Sister Mary of Agreda. The only complete history of the Blessed Mother's life here on earth, as revealed by Mary Herself to Venerable Mother Mary of Jesus, a Franciscan nun living in the seventeenth century in Spain. Pope Innocent XI in 1686 was the first Holy Father to give his approval. On April 29, 1929, Pope Pius XI granted a private audience to the publisher of CITY OF GOD. His Holiness said: "You have done a great work in honor of the Mother of God. She will never permit Herself to be outdone in generosity and will know how to reward a thousand fold. We grant the apostolic benediction to all readers and promoters of THE CITY OF GOD." Four volumes. Hard cover. $35.00.

WORDS OF WISDOM, by Venerable Mary of Agreda. Taken from every chapter of the 4 vols. in THE MYSTICAL CITY OF GOD, it reproduces in full the Words of Counsel given by the Blessed Virgin Mary to Sr. Mary for encouragement and guidance of souls. The weak or strong, the unlearned or the wise, all will find these words of wisdom and spiritual direction a real blessing. 577 pages. Hard Cover. $12.00, 2 or more $10.00 ea.

ROSARY AND SCAPULAR

HOW TO SAY THE ROSARY. Attractive colorful folder. Includes prayers and diagram how to say it. All fifteen Mysteries pictured in color. 5¢ ea.; 22/$1.00; 100/$4.00.

MY ROSARY, by Rev. Lelen. Excellent for Rosary Novenas, family Rosary, five first Saturdays, and private recitation. Includes explanation, indulgences, prayers. A beautiful full color picture 2½" x 3" of each Mystery. Also Litany of the Blessed Virgin Mary. 23 pp. Paper. 25¢ ea.; 10—20¢ ea.

NOVENA OF OUR LADY'S ROSARY by McCaffrey, C.S.C. Lithographed, full color, all fifteen Mysteries of the Rosary. Also St. Dominic receiving the Rosary from the Blessed Virgin Mary. Mysteries are reproductions of the original mosaics at Lourdes in France. Includes 54 Day Novena prayers and chart. Also brief history, some victories through the Rosary, and indulgences. 64 pages, Paper. 75¢ ea., 10 @ 65¢ ea.

THE GREEN SCAPULAR AND ITS FAVORS, by Father Mott, C.M. The information in this book is precious. First Fr. Mott introduces the recipient to the powerful instrument for cures, conversions, reversions, and protection during these evil times. Next he gives the historic and accurate origin of Mary's Badge of Mercy and how to use it with full trust and confidence to obtain the tremendous and unusual favors it is noted for. Closes with 23 pages of various cases who received these favors. 56 pp. Paper. 50¢ ea.; 10—40¢ ea.

THE ROSARY, by Father Lord, S.J. Excellent booklet for all. Explains how St. Dominic received the Rosary, and why it is the greatest string of beads. Has a full color picture of every Mystery, 3½"x5". Meditations are simple, yet sublime. 40 pp. Paper. 25¢ ea.; 10—20¢ ea.

THE SECRET OF THE ROSARY, by St. Louis De Montfort. Second best book on the Rosary. A real spiritual treat, inspired by Heaven, with a Saint for its author. Each bead is a rose and a short chapter is devoted to each bead. He warns us against both the ignorant and scholars who regard the Rosary as something of little importance . . . "The Rosary is a priceless treasure inspired by God." First Printing 1965. Close to a million copies sold. 126 pages, Paper. 50¢, 10 @ 40¢ ea., 25 @ 35¢ ea., 100 @ 30¢ ea., 500 @ 25¢ ea., 1000 @ 20¢ ea.

BROWN SCAPULARS. Chain, plastic covered 85¢ ea.; 5—75¢ ea.
Plastic covered, brown or white cord, 25¢ ea.; $2.50 per doz.
Washable brown scapular, White cord only, 50¢ ea.; 5—45¢ ea.
Regular brown scapular, White cord only, 10¢ ea.; $1.00 per doz.
Explanatory leaflets, 2/5¢; 100/$2.00.

GREEN SCAPULARS. With explanatory leaflet. 5¢ ea.; 25/$1.00.
RED SCAPULARS (Passion). With explanatory leaflet. 25¢ ea.; $2.50/doz.

LIVES OF THE SAINTS

CHAMPION OF THE BLESSED SACRAMENT, by Rev. Martin Dempsey. Pope Pius XII stated: "The life of Peter Julian Eymard, the standard-bearer, herald and champion of Christ's presence, in the Sacred Tabernacle, is, like that of the Baptist, a shining and burning light . . . through which the ancient Secret of the Eucharist was revealed to the world." The author, Fr. Dempsey, presents in an orderly, accurate and readable manner, as far as possible through Fr. Eymard's letters, notes, and writings, both the greatness of his destiny and the way he accomplished it. 286 pp. Hard cover. $3.95 ea.; 5—$3.50 ea.

DOMINIC SAVIO, by Lappin. A human and true-to-life inspiration to thousands of the youth in his time. A real spiritual hero, rapidly gaining popularity among many teens of today. 191 pp. Paper. 50¢ ea.; 5—45¢ ea.

57 STORIES OF SAINTS FOR BOYS AND GIRLS. These all stars on Christ's team were chosen because their lives and work apply to conditions and times today. When adverse winds from all directions tend to chill the fervor of our Faith, causing many to possibly lose their soul, this book gives a new direction and spiritual depth to help especially our young people hold the line for God, family and country. 580 pages. Hard cover. 1 copy $5.95, 2 or more $5.50 ea.; Paper $4.95, 2 or more $4.50 ea.

ST. JOAN OF ARC, by John Beevers. A girl of 19, inspired by God, convinces the King of France to let her lead the Army. In 15 months she defeats the British, saves Country and Church and changes history of Western Europe. Burned as a heretic, later canonized and now Patron Saint of France. Great story of a great Saint. 190 pages. Paper cover. $3.00 ea.; 5 or more $2.50 ea.

JOSEPH THE JUST MAN, by Rosalie Levy. Complete biography with beautiful stories of favors he has granted. Given titles as "Protector of the Church," "Patron of the Dying." "A powerful Saint for all times," etc., one can feel sure that he will come to the aid of those who are devoted to him. Many special prayers, novenas, litanies, chaplet, etc. are included. 285 pages. Paper. $3.00, 5 @ $2.50 ea.

LEO XIII, by Brother W. Kiefer, S.M. An adequate biography of one of our great pontifs, one whose reign of 15 years was one of the longest in the history of the Papacy. An outstanding spiritual leader, an astute political realist capable of determined action, and a great devotee of Our Lady and Her powerful Rosary. His accomplishments, his spirituality will surely inspire all, clergy and laity alike, to live for, defend, and promote Christ's One, True, Catholic, and Apostolic Church. A real addition to any home or school library. 222 pp. Hard cover. $3.95 ea.; 5—$3.25 ea.

LIFE OF VENERABLE SR. MARY OF AGREDA, by James A. Carrico. Biography of the author of MYSTICAL CITY OF GOD, depicting her mystical gifts, especially bilocation to America, and her writings of the MYSTICAL CITY OF GOD. 100 pages. Paper. 32 illus., $2.00.

LITTLE FLOWERS OF ST. FRANCIS, by Raphael Brown. A great book on one of our greatest spiritual men gives the true Franciscan way of life, considerations on the Holy Stigmata, the life and sayings of brother Giles, and the life of Brother Juniper. Includes 19 chapters that never before appeared in English. 357 pp. Paper. $1.95 ea.; 5—$1.50 ea.

LIVES OF THE SAINTS, revised from original by Fr. H. Hoever, S.O.Cist. Lists one saint for each day of the year, includes pictures of some with interesting highlights of the lives of each. 520 pp. Hard cover. $4.25 ea.; 5—$3.75 ea.

MOTHER SETON, based on "Elizabeth Seton" by Msgr. Joseph Bardi. A story of a living wife and mother, a courageous widow, a fervent convert, and foundress of the first native American religious community. Through prayer and faith she overcame all of the many trials and crosses permitted by God. Contains some of the spiritual gems of her own writings. A real heroine for the youth of today and an inspiration to all religious and lay activists. 140 pp. Paper. $2.45 ea.; 5—$2.00 ea.

SAINT ANTHONY THE WONDER WORKER OF PADUA, by Stoddard. "He possessed the science of the angels, the faith of the patriarchs, the foreknowledge of the prophets, the zeal of the apostles, the purity of a virgin, the austerities of confessors, and the heroism of martyrs," so declared St. Bonaventure. A most inspiring life of a great saint. 108 pp. Paper. $1.50 ea.; 5—$1.10 ea.; 25—90¢ ea.; 50—80¢ ea.

SAINT CATHERINE OF SIENA, by I. Giordan. The 14th century was about as turbulent in the history of Christianity as conditions are today. St. Catherine as torch bearer of truth, charity and justice, advised Popes, comforted the poor, gave direction to Bishops and Abbots, priests, religious, theologians and soldiers of her time. On a natural level she was one of the most virile and vigorous women in history, 259 pages, Hard Cover. $5.95 ea., 2 or more $5.50 ea.

ST. JOHN BOSCO, by Forbes. St. John Bosco's life is full of color and drama. His outstanding work to help the youth of his day can and should be an inspiration to all who want to help the youth today. 190 pp. Paper. 75¢ ea.; 5—65¢ ea.

ST. LOUIS DE MONTFORT, by G. Rigault. Full life story of this great saint and devotee of Our Blessed Mother. 178 pages, Hard Cover. $2.50 ea.; 5—$2.00 ea.

ST. LOUIS DE MONTFORT, by E. J. Moynihan, S.M.M. A brief story of the Life of St. Louis including his canonization in 1947. 38 pages, Paper, 41 pictures, colored cover. 1 @ 75¢ ea., 5 @ 65¢ ea., 10 @ 60¢ ea.

SAINT PETER JULIAN EYMARD, by Rev. Tesniere, S.S.S. The priest of the Eucharist who had a beautiful devotion to Our Lord in the Tabernacle and through it became a Saint. By always staying close to Our Lord on the Altar, Christ became his one and constant inspiration and guide. A saint of our time to bring many to the foot of the Altar. His writings are some of the best to renew the respect, understanding, and appreciation we should have as Catholics of the great privilege that is ours to attend daily the Sacrifice of the Mass, as well as the great opportunity to share in Christ's Divinity each time we receive Him in Holy Communion. 251 pp. Paper. $1.50 ea.; 5—$1.25 ea.

ST. THERESE THE LITTLE FLOWER, by Sr. Gesualda of the Holy Spirit. Another heart warming story of our great modern day Saint. Her fascinating life continues to inspire many to imitate the simple way of love and affection that gained for her a very high place in Heaven. Known as the "Patroness of the Mission," thousands of souls have and will continue to receive spiritual and physical help through her powerful intercession. Though she died when 24 years of age and never left the convent, she is now world renowned and famous. 270 pp. Paper: $3.00 ea.; 5—$2.50 ea. Hard cover: $4.00 ea.; 5—$3.50 ea.

THE LIFE OF BENEDICT XV, by H. Peters. Story of a man who worked quietly and competently, shedding spiritual light on many subtle, complicated issues with which he dealt during his reign. One of these was modernism, the same spiritual plague characteristic of our times. 274 pp. Hard cover. $4.50 ea.; 5—$4.00 ea.

THE MAN GOD CALLED FATHER (Life of St. Joseph). Various unusually interesting stories, taken from the autobiography of the Blessed Virgin Mary by Ven. Mary of Agreda in the MYSTICAL CITY OF GOD. Will take you back in spirit to the days when the world's greatest family, "The Holy Family" lived here on earth. 47 pages. Illustrated. Paper. 50¢ ea., 10 @ 40¢ ea.

THE PERFECT JOY OF ST. FRANCIS, by Felix Timmermans. The author reveals a knowledge and insight into the deep spiritual experiences of St. Francis and the ideals that enabled him to move and shake the whole world. Here, through many unusual and interesting personal stories, the reader sees St. Francis as the great spiritual man he was, imbued with a burning zeal and love for God, that inspired not only the people in his day, but world-wide now in our day. Shows what one man can accomplish during his life and especially after he has passed on when he is moved by and cooperates with the strongest force in the world, the grace of God. 276 pp. Paper. $1.95 ea.; 5—$1.50 ea.

SAINT OF THE IMPOSSIBLE. The story of St. Rita. A true model for wives and mothers, of small children who still spent 42 years as a devout religious. Because of the many miracles attributed to her intercession she is often called "The Saint of the Impossible." 138 pp. Hard cover. $3.95 ea.; 3 @ $3.50 ea.

WRITINGS OF THE SAINTS

ASCENT OF MOUNT CARMEL, by St. John of the Cross. A masterpiece in the literature of mysticism by St. John of the Cross. With a depth of spirituality, based on the philosophy of St. Thomas, this and the author's other main spiritual writings have a granite like spiritual solidity seldom achieved in his time or the present. 478 pp. Paper. $1.95 ea.; 5—$1.75 ea.

CITY OF GOD, by St. Augustine. The work which St. Augustine considered his masterpiece. He devoted a good part of fourteen years to its composition. An all time spiritual classic. 545 pp. Paper. $2.95 ea.; 5—$2.50 ea.

DARK NIGHT OF THE SOUL, by St. John of the Cross. A wonderful illustration of the divine truth that grace dignifies and ennobles the agreement always found between the natural and supernatural, between sound reason, common sense, and Divine Grace. Truly one of, if not the greatest of all Spanish mystics. 193 pp. Paper. $1.45 ea.; 5—$1.25 ea.

DIALOGUE OF ST. CATHERINE OF SIENA, translated by Algar Thorold. Dictated by St. Catherine while in ecstasy and speaking with Our Lord. One of the spiritual treasures of the Church. For this work and her letters, St. Catherine was named a Doctor of the Church. 344 pp. Paper. $3.50 ea.; 5—$3.00 ea.; 10—$2.75 ea.

FAITHFUL SERVANT—Spiritual Retreats and Letters of Blessed Claude La Colombiere, S.J. As spiritual director of St. Margaret Mary, he was largely responsible for spreading the Sacred Heart devotion and was famous and saintly in his own right. 450 pages. Hard Cover. $6.50 ea., 2 or more $6.00 ea.

FRIENDS OF THE CROSS, by St. Louis De Montfort. A saint who gives us some wise, prudent counsel that teaches us how to suffer and bear our crosses patiently, willingly and joyfully in the footsteps of Our Lord and Crucified Savior. 36 pages, 25¢ ea.

INTERIOR CASTLE, by St. Teresa of Avila. Probably no other books by a Spanish author have received such wide popular acclaim as the "Life" and "Interior Castle" of St. Teresa of Avila. A continuous source for all who seek true spiritual guidance and direction. 235 pp. Paper. $1.75 ea.; 5—$1.50 ea.

INTRODUCTION TO THE DEVOUT LIFE, by St. Francis de Sales. Recognized for over 3½ centuries as a masterpiece of mystical and devotional literature. Its greatness lies in its originality, completeness, sincerity, balance, penetration, and style. 291 pp. Paper. $1.95 ea.; 5—$1.75 ea.

LIVING FLAME OF LOVE, by St. John of the Cross. A most profound exposition of the spiritual life. 272 pp. Paper. $1.45 ea.; 5—$1.25 ea.

SECRET OF MARY, by St. Louis De Montfort. An introduction with prayers necessary for the "Perfect Consecration." Includes excellent description of the interior practices and the wonderful effects that the Consecration brings to all who make it. 90 pp. Paper. 35¢ ea.; 5—30¢ ea.

SPIRITUAL EXERCISES OF ST. IGNATIUS. A new translation of St. Ignatius' profound precepts regarding mental and vocal prayer and mysticism. A complete guide and framework to help all on the road to more complete spiritual perfection. 200 pp. Paper. $1.45 ea.; 5—$1.25 ea.

THE AUTOBIOGRAPHY OF ST. THERESE OF LISIEUX, by Beevers. "The greatest Saint of modern times" so stated Pope St. Pius X. She wanted to spend her heaven doing good on earth. Commonly known as St. Therese the Little Flower, she continues to win many and very special graces for all who sincerely seek her intercession. 159 pp. Paper. $1.45 ea.; 5—$1.25 ea.

THE AUTOBIOGRAPHY OF ST. TERESA OF AVILA, by Allison Peers. A Saint and first woman Doctor of the Church. Contributed much to correct the heresies of her day that were much like our own today. Persecuted greatly in her time, now admired and respected world-wide. A Saint for then, now, and all times. 400 pp. Paper. $2.45 ea.; 5—$2.00 ea.

THE CONFESSION OF SAINT AUGUSTINE. Called the greatest spiritual autobiography. A remarkable spiritual book for all by a man whose mother prayed for many years for his conversion. A hope and inspiration to many whose spiritual life in their youth or later life was not always up to par. 429 pp. Paper. $1.95 ea.; 5—$1.75 ea.

THE LOVE OF ETERNAL WISDOM, by St. Louis De Montfort. De Montfort outlines how one can find the Wisdom of Christ through true and sincere devotion to Mary His Mother, that it is the easiest and most perfect way to the Wisdom that is the Cross, and the Cross that is Wisdom. 139 pp. Hard cover. $2.00 ea.

THE RULE OF ST. BENEDICT. Marked by common sense, the spirit and prayer exercises followed by St. Benedict are explained here to strengthen all who ask and seek his help. True spiritual depth is surely available to all who sincerely follow this great saint in his approach to living close to God every day. 120 pages, Paper, 1—$1.45, 3 or more $1.25 ea.

THE WAY OF PERFECTION—St. Teresa of Avila. St. Teresa's superb classic on the practice of prayer. Almost 4 centuries have passed, yet her thoughts are as fresh and inspiring as when she first wrote them. With prayer so needed at this time to obtain God's help and protection this perfect form is most welcome to many striving to follow the Blessed Mother's requests and do God's will. 280 pages, Paper, 1—$1.75 ea., 3 or more $1.50 ea.

THE WRITINGS OF SAINT FRANCIS OF ASSISI. Includes all the saint's authenticated writings. St. Francis' life was founded on humility and this virtue is predominant in his inspired writing. Much has been written about St. Francis, here St. Francis himself shares with you his profound insight into the true spiritual meaning of life. 200 pp. Hard cover. $4.95 ea.; 5—$4.50 ea.

TREATISE ON THE LOVE OF GOD, by St. Francis de Sales. One of the greatest spiritual works since St. Thomas. Covers the soul's relationship to God in the most immediate and thorough manner. St. Francis here has spiritual wisdom coupled with divine inspiration that naturally gives much to all who seek more depth to their spiritual life. 670 pp. 2 Volumes. Paper. Sold in set of two only. $7.00 per set; 2—$6.00 per set.

GENERAL RELIGIOUS

A CANADIAN MYSTIC OF OUR DAY (ST. CECILE OF ROME). A reader's digest version of CANTICLE OF LOVE. One of God's chosen victim souls who had the unusual privilege of attending Mass in Heaven. 158 pages, Paper. $1.25 ea., 5 @ $1.00 ea.

AA 1025—THE MEMOIRS OF AN ANTI-APOSTLE, by Marie Carre. A true story of an Anti-Apostle who became a priest to work from within the Church to cause confusion and misdirect the efforts of true clergy and laity in doing God's work to save souls. Fills in the answers to many questions of how and why the destructive changes came about in our church. 109 pages. Paper. $1.50 ea., 10 @ $1.25 ea.

THE ANTI-PRIESTS. Adapted from the French by Yves Dupont. Digest version of AA 1025. 22 pages, Paper. 35¢ ea., 10 or more 25¢ ea.

CANTICLE OF LOVE. The autobiography of Marie Sainte-Cecile of Rome, a young nun from Sillery, in Quebec, Canada. A victim soul privileged to attend Mass in Heaven. The description inspires one to a deeper love and appreciation of this tremendous gift of receiving Our Lord Himself in Communion and the Mass at Calvary. 350 pages, Paper, $5.95 ea., 3 @ $5.00 ea.

CARDINAL MINDSZENTY—MEMOIRS. The full story of this God loving heroic priest, appointed Cardinal and Primate of Hungary in 1945 by Pope Pius XII. One of the most courageous and out-spoken foes of atheistic materialistic communism in our times. Arrested, tortured, brainwashed, and imprisoned for 8 years in solitary confinement, yet he spoke out to the very last, strong, clear, and unyielding. Through his timely book he continues to speak to us today. Everything as far as decency permits is stated so the world may see what fate communism has in store for us and all mankind. Illustrated, indexed. 391 pages, Hard Cover. $10.00, 2 @ $8.00 ea.

MINDSZENTY THE MAN, Vecsey as told to Phyllis Schlafly. Gives a good insight into the remarkable character of Cardinal Mindszenty and how his great spiritual strength enabled him to oppose his enemies and inspire his people. 241 pp. Paper. $3.25 ea.

FAITH—RESPONSE TO THE DIALOGUE OF GOD, by Pope Paul VI. What Pope Paul said and truly meant when speaking about the Ecumenical Council and the Church. 139 pages. Hard Cover. $2.00 ea., 5 @ $1.75 ea.

MAMA, WHY DID YOU KILL US?, by Rev. Mondrone. True story of abortion told to a priest by a mother haunted by her unborn child. Powerful deterrent for anyone thinking about an abortion without knowing the mental anguish, worry and remorse of conscience that follows. 47 pages, Paper. 75¢ ea., 5 @ 65¢ ea.

PADRE PIO THE STIGMATIST, by Rev. C. Carty. 26th Edition. 130 pictures. The author spent several months living in Padre Pio's monastery, gathering information for this great book. Describes miraculous cures, remarkable conversions, divine inspirations in the confessional, celestial perfume, bi-location, stigmata, prophetic insight, and suffering as a victim soul. A great spiritual man of our day who helped many find their way back from a materialistic, sinful life to a balanced and even noble, heroic, spiritual one. His life, writings, and intercession in Heaven will continue to help save all who sincerely seek guidance and direction from him. 310 pp. Paper. $3.50 ea.; 5—$3.00 ea.; 10—$2.75 ea.; 25—$2.50 ea.; 50—$2.25 ea.; 100—$2.00 ea.

PERE LAMY 1855-1931, by C. P. Biver. A saintly biography full of surprises. Considered another Cure of Ars, he had visions of Our Lord, the Blessed Mother, St. Joseph, the Angels, and even Lucifer. His writings are most enlightening and profound. Had the gift of prophecy, performed many miracles, and conversed regularly with his guardian angel. 224 pages, Paper. $3.00 ea., 5 @ $2.50 ea., 10 @ $2.25 ea., 25 @ $2.00 ea., 50 @ $1.75 ea.

SHE WEARS A CROWN OF THORNS, by Rev. Boyer. The life story of Marie Rose Ferron, known as "Little Rose," the stigmatized ecstatic of Woonsocket, Rhode Island. The tenth child, named for the Crucifixion or 10th Mystery of the Rosary. She had all the wounds of Christ, died at 33 years of age. Helps all to understand what happens when a victim soul suffers the Passion of Our Lord. 241 pages, Paper. $2.00 ea., 5 @ $1.75 ea., 25 @ $1.50 ea.

SOUL AFIRE, by H. A. Reinhold. Revelations by various reliable mystics. Interesting and informative. 466 pp. Paper. $2.45 ea.; 2—$2.25 ea.

SOUL OF THE APOSTOLATE, by D. Chautard, O.C.S.O. Bedside companion of St. Pius X. He said, "I can offer you no better guide than Soul of the Apostolate. Helps keep the proper balance between one's prayer, spiritual, and work life. 300 pages, paper—$3.50 ea., 3 or more $3.00 ea.

THE CATHOLIC ENCYCLOPEDIA, by R. C. Broderick, M.A. A combination dictionary and reference book. An ideal book for young or old who wish to grow in knowledge and love of their Faith. An excellent addition to a home or school library. 330 pp. Hard cover. $6.00 ea.; 2—$5.50 ea.

THE DEATH CAMP PROVED HIM REAL, by Maria Winowska. (Life story of Maximilian Kolbe.) A living example of a man who loved God more than life itself. A modern day inspiration for youth and adults. Heroic to the last, giving his life to save that of another caused his executioners to say in amazement, "The likes of this we have never seen." 190 pp. Paper. $1.25 ea.; 5—$1.00 ea.

THE FIFTEEN PROMISES OF THE ROSARY. Serves as a constant reminder of all that the Blessed Mother will do for those who will pray it daily and/or promote Her powerful weapon for peace. Minimum order of 100 copies. $1.00 per 100; $6.00 per 1000. **(Book Mark)**

THE PORTER OF ST. BONAVENTURE'S, by J. P. Derum. The life of Fr. Solanus Casey, Capuchin, is one of a typical American boy. Ball player, lumberjack, prison guard, street car motorman, and violinist formed his background before going to the seminary at age 21. Limited in theology, his priesthood for 60 years was mainly as a spiritual counselor to tens of thousands. Hundreds attributed to his intercession outstanding spiritual and physical cures. Over the years he became known and loved in practically every part of the U.S.A. and by many in Canada. His deep spirituality and warm personality won many souls for Christ. 280 pp. Hard cover. $5.95 ea.; 3—$5.00 ea.

THE STORY OF THE TRAPP FAMILY SINGERS, by Maria Trapp. Told in her own warm and friendly way. A beautiful family life success story. The spirit and closeness of their activities comes as a timely help for many today who see their family being pulled apart by outside influences. The story and inspiration for the all time great movie, "Sound of Music." 312 pp. Paper. $1.45 ea.; 5—$1.35 ea.

THE TWELVE PROMISES OF THE SACRED HEART TO ST. MARGARET MARY. Shows Our Lord's great desire to be loved by all men. Each promise is an inspiration. Every Christian deserves to have a copy as a ready reference. Minimum order 100 copies. $1.50 per 100; $13.00 per 1000. **(Book Mark)**

THERESE NEUMANN, by J. Steiner. A new book on this famous German mystic and stigmatist of our day. Complete story of her unusual life and spiritual gifts. 61 pictures. 278 pp. Hard cover. $4.50 ea.; 5—$4.00 ea.

THOU ART THE ROCK, by Rev. Richard Ginder. Explains the true Church of Christ and why the liberal movement in the Church is responsible for the many problems today and the deterioration of the best in music, art, and liturgy. 125 pp. Paper. $1.00 ea.; 5—75¢ ea.

THE TRUTH ABOUT TEILHARD, by Msgr. Leo Schumacher. A critical study of the works of Fr. Teilhard de Chardin, S.J., against which the Holy Office in Rome issued a monitum on June 30, 1963. It covered all of his works with no exception. The monitum is still in effect! Msgr. Schumacher's incisive analysis shows why they were condemned. All Catholics need to be informed about this matter, especially priests, teachers, and booksellers because he is very persuasive as a writer, to yes, even, if possible, deceive the elect. 46 pages. Paper. 50¢ ea.

VERONICA'S VEIL, New Edition translated by Rev. Scallan, S.T.B. Autobiography of a Carmelite nun, Sr. Mary of St. Peter. As the humble servant of God advanced along the true spiritual path, so too will the reader by following the simple but beautiful approach to spiritual perfection as practiced by Sr. Mary. Pope Paul said, "Let us appreciate the efforts of those who through these portraits on 'Veronica's Veil' help us advance in Faith toward the Visible Christ, Whose Face reflects the Invisible Divinity." 232 pp. Paper. $4.00 ea.; 5 at $3.25 ea.

WHO IS PADRE PIO?, by L. White; THE AGONY OF JESUS and MEDITATION PRAYER ON MARY IMMACULATE, by Padre Pio. Padre Pio is no doubt one of the greatest spiritual sons of St. Francis of Assisi. "Who is Padre Pio" is a brief story of a true man of God who has been sent to help us in this critical moment of world history. "The Agony of Jesus" will surely give everyone a greater devotion to the most sacred Humanity of Christ, Our Lord. The "Meditation on Mary Immaculate" shows the depth of love Padre Pio had for the greatest of all masterpieces created by God, the Immaculate Virgin Mary. Set of 3, Paper. Single set $1.65; 5—$1.45 ea.; 10—$1.30 ea.; 25—$1.15 ea.

HEAVEN HELL PURGATORY

A NOTEBOOK ON THE DEVIL AND EXORCISM, Series of articles from Immaculata Magazine. This collection of articles on Satan and how to cope with him helps meet an urgent need. Popular fascination with the occult is now entrapping many of our youth and adults. It is actually being taught in some schools. Satanic priests are being ordained. Evidence of the devil's tremendous influence in our society today is explained. How he is the archenemy of mankind and why it is necessary to pray, wear a crucifix and/or scapular and to reieve the sacraments as often as possible. Father Dominic, O.F.M. Conv. was an exorcist and at least two articles are in part from his work. 111 pp. Paper. $1.25 ea.; 5—$1.00 ea.

AN UNPUBLISHED MANUSCRIPT ON PURGATORY. Apparition of a Poor Soul to a nun, describes types of suffering and stages of Purgatory. Will surely help you avoid or shorten your time there. 69 pages. Paper. $1.25 ea., 5 @ $1.00 ea.

ANGELS OF GOD, by D.D.C. Pochin Mould. Dr. Mould shares years of his study, discusses them in scripture, philosophy, theology and human experience. Gives up-to-date summary of what the Church Fathers, from Augustine to Pius XI, have to say about Angels. One of best any single volume on subject. 177 pages. Hard Cover, $4.95.

BEYOND SPACE—A BOOK ABOUT THE ANGELS, by Rev. P. Parente. A wonderful explanation of the angels: their nature and purpose, the nine choirs, guardian angels, devotion to, saints who conversed with, etc. A real good book XI, have to say about Angels. One of best available on subject. 177 pages. Hard Cover, $4.95.

BEGONE SATAN, by Rev. Carl Vogl. A soul-stirring account of diabolical possession in Iowa. After 23 days' battle in December, 1928, the devil was forced to leave. The devil is real and it's best to understand it. Also what must be done in certain cases. 48 pp. Paper. 75¢ ea.; 5—60¢ ea.; 10—55¢ ea.; 25—50¢ ea.

EVIDENCE OF SATAN IN THE MODERN WORLD, by Rev. Leon Crisitani. Written in 1959, this is one of the best books on the devil, possession, and exorcism. Many cases thoroughly documented, including some from the Cure of Ars. Diabolical antics are very much in evidence today and everyone should wear a crucifix, say the exorcism and St. Michael's prayer each day. You will not need an explanation why after reading this timely and important book. 210 pages, Paper. $3.50 ea., 5 @ $3.00 ea., 10 @ $2.75 ea.

MARY CRUSHES THE SERPENT. Thirty years experience of an exorcist told in his own words. Sequel to "Begone Satan." 56 pp. Paper. 75¢ ea.; 5—65¢ ea.

PURGATORY, by F. F. X. Shouppe, S.J. Explained by the lives of individuals and Saints. Considered the best book on this important subject. Will dispose all who read it to work hard and pray that their period will be as short as possible or eliminated completely. Explains types of suffering in lower, intermediate, and upper parts. 312 pp. Paper. $3.50 ea.; 5 —$3.00 ea.; 10—$2.50 ea.

PURGATORY AND HEAVEN, by J. P. Arendzen, D.D. The nature, joys, and sorrows of Purgatory, plus the nature and happiness of Heaven. Short but good treatment. 96 pages. Paper. $1.00 ea., 5 @ 75¢ ea.

SO HIGH THE PRICE, by P. J. Kelley, S.T.L. Opens before your eyes the gates of hell, quoting Scripture and the Fathers of the Church. Has testimony of actual cases of condemned souls. A reading of this book will inspire all to work hard and persevere to gain Heaven. 85 pages, Paper. $2.00 ea., 5 @ $1.75 ea.

BIBLE HISTORY CATECHISMS HOLY BIBLE

AN ILLUSTRATED CATHOLIC FAMILY CATECHISM, by Msgr. Arthur Durand. Outstanding for home and school, accurate, inspiring. Total spectrum of Catholic Doctrine in three books, based on Council of Trent, Vatican II, and official directives. All lessons give doctrine in depth. Each beautiful picture is worth a 1000 words. Paper.

BOOK ONE Grades 1-4. Preparation for First Communion, Confession, Confirmation. $1.50 ea.; 10—$1.40 ea.

BOOK TWO Grades 5-7. Advanced, covers Creed, Sacraments, Commandments. $1.75 ea.; 10—$1.65 ea.

BOOK THREE Grades 8-10. Advanced instructions on the origin of man, the Creed, Sacraments, and Commandments. $1.75 ea.; 10—$1.65 ea.

BALTIMORE CATECHISM No. 3, by Rev. Thomas Kinkead. This is the original Baltimore Catechism Number 3, first issued in 1885. Still very excellent today. Amazing in its thoroughness and clarity. 314 pp. Paper. $3.00 ea.; 5—$2.50 ea.; 10—$2.25 ea.; 25—$2.00 ea.; 50—$1.75 ea.

BASIC TEACHING FOR CATHOLIC RELIGIOUS EDUCATION, by National Conference of Catholic Bishops. A guide to correct basic teaching for Catholic religious education. Prepared in consultation with the Catechetical Office of the Holy See. Indexed. 36 pp. Paper. 60¢ ea.

BIBLE HISTORY, by Schuster. Paper bound edition of old and new Testaments. A reliable famous Bible History used in Catholic grade schools for years. 6th-8th grades. 394 pp. Paper. $3.00 ea.; 5—$2.50 ea.; 10—$2.25 ea.; 25—$2.00 ea.; 50—$1.75 ea.

CATECHISM FOR ADULTS, by Rev. William Cogan. Orthodox, traditional. Includes prayers, Rosary, and Stations of the Cross. Excellent for adult convert classes. Bible quotes show correlation of Scripture with true catechetics. 143 pp. Paper. $1.50 ea.; 10—$1.35 ea.; 25—$1.25 ea.

CATECHISM IN STORIES, by Rev. Lawrence Lovasik, S.V.D. For all Priests, Sisters, and catechetical instructors. Adds meaning and depth to truths explained. Interesting stories from lives of various saints illustrate practical application in our lives. A source and aid for fruitful spiritual instruction for students, adults, or converts. 290 pp. Hard cover. $3.95 ea.; 5—$3.60 ea.

CATECHISM OF CHRISTIAN DOCTRINE. Published by order of St. Pius X. Called "Defender of the Faith" when canonized. Outstanding catechist of the 20th Century. 116 pp. Paper. $2.00 ea.; 10—$1.75 ea.

CHILD'S BIBLE HISTORY, by Msgr. Knecht, D.D. Old and New Testament. A favorite of teachers and parents. Brief review of main essentials of the True Faith as practiced during time of Old Testament with clear introduction of true Christian Faith by Christ in New Testament. Story book form, questions and answers after each topic. 86 pp. Paper. $1.00 ea.; 5—60¢ ea.; 10—50¢ ea.; 25—45¢ ea.; 100—40¢ ea.

FUNDAMENTALS OF CATHOLIC DOGMA, by Ludwig Ott. A very special book for students of the basic doctrines and dogmas of the "One, Holy, Catholic, and Apostolic Church." 544 pp. Paper. $6.00 ea.; 5—$5.00 ea.

NEW TESTAMENT—Confraternity Edition. A 1941 revision of the Challoner-Rheims Version (Douay-Rheims). In our opinion this is the best New Testament after the Douay-Rheims. 480 pages, Paper, Imprimatur. $2.00.

OUR CATHOLIC FAITH, by Bishop L. L. Morrow. Two outstanding and informative books on our Faith. Book I gives the History of Our Faith, Christ's Church and Sacraments. Book II covers the main aspects of the organization, function and missionary work of Christ's living True Church today. Complete with diagrams, illustrations and maps. 260 pages, Paper, sold in set only, $4.25.

ROMES ANSWER. General Catechetical Directory. Official Vatican instruction on teaching of Catholic Faith. Helps solve crisis in our Faith. Brings back stability and true catechetics. 45 pp. Paper. $1.25 ea.

THE CATECHISM OF THE COUNCIL OF TRENT. Published by command of Pope Pius V, and that all bishops were to see that it was faithfully translated into the vernacular and explained to all the people by all pastors. The purpose —so the faithful could approach the Sacraments with greater reverence and devotion.

First Printing 1829. Bound in blue and gold, gold edges, Hard Cover. 609 pages, complete. Best available anywhere.

Paper: 1—$5, 5—$4.50, 10 or more $4.00.

Hard cover: 1—$10.00, 5—$9.00, 10 or more $8.00.

THE CATHOLIC PICTURE BIBLE, by Rev. Lovasik, S.V.D. A most beautiful and inspiring book. Over 100 popular stories from the Old and New Testaments.

121 pictures in full color by some of the greatest artists past and present. A Holy Land map for Old Testament times in front and New Testament times in back. A family book, a treasure for anyone's library. 208 pp. Hard cover. $4.50 ea.; 5—$4.00 ea.

THE HOLY BIBLE, Douay-Rheims. Reprint of the original, Old Testament 1609, New Testament 1582. Complete with eight maps of the Holy Lands. Family record section, readable type, gold embossed cover. Best available today. Hard cover. $15.00 ea.

THE NEW SAINT JOSEPH BALTIMORE CATECHISM, by Fr. Bennet Kelley, C.P. Official text by Fr. Bennet, Imprimatur by Cardinal Spellman. Far more than just questions and answers, these texts include all important Catholic Prayers, excellent illustrations on points of doctrine and morality, numerous class projects, and pertinent references to Sacred Scripture. Complete, no Teacher's Manual required. Paper.

FIRST COMMUNION CATECHISM Grades 1 and 2. Complete, beautiful full color art. $1.25 ea.; 5—$1.15 ea.; 10—$1.05 ea.; 25—$1.00 ea.

BOOK NUMBER ONE Grades 3-5. Straight doctrinal answers. Excellent illustrations. $1.50 ea.; 5—$1.40 ea.; 10—$1.30 ea.; 25—$1.25 ea.

BOOK NUMBER TWO Grades 6-8. Concise, complete. 499 questions and answers. $1.60 ea.; 5—$1.50 ea.; 10—$1.40 ea.; 25—$1.35 ea.

THE PENNY CATECHISM, by Prow Books. 370 of the most important questions and answers on the Catholic Faith. Extensively used in Ireland and England. Clear and exact in answers, helps form a right conscience on difficult questions. Catholic prayers and mysteries of the Rosary. High school, college, and adult level. 74 pp. Paper. 75¢ ea.; 10—65¢ ea.; 25—60¢ ea.

VOCATIONS—FAMILY LIFE AND MARRIAGE

CHOOSE YOUR TOMORROW, by The Daughters of St. Paul. Helps one to choose the vocation best suited according to the will of God, giving to each peace of mind, happiness, and eternal salvation. 235 pp. Paper. $1.25 ea.; 5—$1.00 ea.

DARE TO DISCIPLINE, by Dr. James Dobson. A sound, straight forward, plainly written discussion of the ways in which order can be maintained, responsibility developed, and character built. Love alone is not enough. Discipline is not just punishment. One chapter is applied to behavior in schools, another for general good conduct and one entirely to drugs. Parents, teachers, clergy, and youth will profit from it. 228 pages, Paper. $1.95, 5 @ $1.65 ea.

THE HEAD OF THE FAMILY, by C. C. Barbeau. To be a successful husband and father in a true spiritual as well as economic way, always keeping the Love of God and doing His Will first in the heart and mind is the real essence of this well written book. Yes, many marriages would be happier and more beautiful if the author's application of a Christian outlook according to Scripture and God's plan for pro-creation was followed. Their success then will be here and in Heaven for all eternity. 144 pages, Hard Cover. $3.75 ea., 5 @ $3.25 ea.

THE MAN FOR HER, by Leo J. Kinsella. Over 500,000 copies sold. Spells out characteristics of the ideal husband. A help to a correct and better understanding of meeting the spiritual, emotional, and other problems basic to a happy marriage. 175 pp. Paper. $1.95 ea.; 5—$1.75 ea.

THE WIFE DESIRED, by Leo J. Kinsella. A real help to any girl who decides to marry. Many suggestions to keep the partnership and home interesting and enjoyable. Helps prevent rather than find an answer later to serious problems. 158 pages, Paper. $1.95 ea., 5 @ $1.75 ea.

PROPHECY

CATHOLIC PROPHECY, by Yves Dupont. Tells of coming Divine Chastisement and that U.S.A. and Western democracies are going to bear the full brunt of God's wrath. Draws the logical and reasonable conclusion that only God's peace plan will bring peace, all others only lead to destruction. 117 pages. Paper. $1.50 ea., 5 @ $1.25 ea., 25 @ $1.00 ea.

PROPHECY FOR TODAY, by Edward Connor. Traces prophecy back to Malachy, up through La Salette and Fatima with the partial fulfillment of the Apocalypse today. Explains also the "Last Judgment" and, these the times of Anti-Christ. 110 pages, Paper. 1 copy $2.00, 3 or more $1.75 ea.

THIS APOCALYPTIC AGE, by Robert Bergin. A commentary on prophecies relating to our times. Important signs that point up these times as the latter days. Prophetic warnings and direction from Heaven are contained. A book for all who recognize the crisis we face but find it difficult to see God's hand in the testing of individuals as well as nations. 159 pp. Paper. $1.00 ea.; 5—75¢ ea.; 10—65¢ ea.; 25—60¢ ea.

TRIUMPHANT PEACE, by Emmett Culligan. Explains the Apocalypse and parts to be fulfilled now, the anti-Christ and Heaven's warnings, punishments, and Christian action necessary for victory. 39 pictures. 132 pages, Paper. $3.00 ea., 5 @ $2.50 ea.

THE BOOK OF DESTINY, by Rev. Herman Kramer. A thorough, intelligent interpretation of the Apocalypse of Saint John. Proceeds by verse and chapter showing that we are in the ninth chapter. Father Kramer spent thirty years in preparation and unlocks much of the mystery contained in this oldest of our prophetic books. Providential for our times. 520 pp. Paper. $6.00 ea.; 2—$5.00 ea.

THE LAST WORLD WAR AND THE END OF TIME, by Emmett Culligan. Quotes apparitions, private prophecy, and Bible regarding severe crisis ahead and era of glorious living to follow. 210 pp. Paper. $3.50 ea.; 5—$3.00 ea.

THE PROPHETS AND OUR TIMES, by Rev. R. Gerald Culleton. Prophecies about the Great Monarch, the Angelic Pastor (a Pope), and the times in general which precede Antichrist. Lists those from Old and New Testament and other reliable sources. Essential reading for today's troubled world. 251 pp. Paper. $3.50 ea.; 5—$3.00 ea.

CHILDREN'S—
PRE-SCHOOL, LOWER AND UPPER GRADES

BLESSED MOTHER'S LAST CHRISTMAS, by Sr. M. Cleophus, S.C.L. The Blessed Mother tells St. John She would like to visit the Cave once more while here on earth. They follow the same road and in the Cave meet an old man who was one of the young shepherds to whom the Angel spoke when he announced Our Lord's Birth. You will relive in spirit the beautiful true story of that first wonderful night as Mary and the Shepherd recall the many intimate details of it. Hard Cover, colored illustrations, $1.00 ea., 5 or more 85¢ ea. (Lower Grade)

FLAME IN THE NIGHT (St. Francis Xavier). An ordinary boy whose prayerful dedication and zeal put him on the all-star team for Christ. A real hero for our youth today. 108 pp. Hard cover. $1.95 ea.; 10—$1.75 ea. (Upper Grade)

HER DREAM CAME TRUE (Bl. Imelda Lambertini). Learned to love Our Lord in the Blessed Sacrament at a very early age as well as to understand and appreciate the beauty and wonder of this greatest of gifts. She received great graces through Holy Communion because of her ardent love and great respect for Jesus in the Blessed Sacrament. 68 pages. Hard cover. $1.95 ea.; 10—$1.75 ea.

HEROES OF GOD and HEROINES OF GOD, by Father Lord. Set of two books. Full color pictures of 24 men and 24 women saints with story of each. Sold in sets only. Paper, 90¢ per set, 5 @ 75¢ per set. (Lower & Upper Grade)

IN GARMENTS ALL RED, by G. Poage, C.P. An inspiring true story of St. Maria Goretti, a heroic young girl of our times, who defended her purity with her life. For upper grades and high school. 79 pages, 1—60¢, 5 or more 50¢ ea.

JESUS AND I, by A. J. Heeg, S.J. Thirty-four black and white fine art sketches plus copy, forms wonderful explanation of our Faith for all preparing for First Communion. Includes examination of conscience, 17 prayers for before and after Communion, and 54 review questions. 138 pp. Paper. 75¢ ea.; 5—65¢ ea.

LIGHT IN THE GROTTO (St. Bernadette). Bernadette, a real spiritual heroine, who remained humble even though famous after having the great privilege of conversing with and bringing an important message to the world from the Mother of God. 88 pages. Hard cover. $1.95 ea.; 10—$1.75 ea. (Lower & Upper Grade)

LOVE AS STRONG AS DEATH (St. Thecla). One of our first Christian women martyrs who valued the love of God more than all the luxuries and pleasures available to her as part of the nobility of her times. One of God's great heroines. A true story how Christ can protect his own from wild animals, poisonous snakes, and fire. 77 pp. Hard cover. $1.95 ea.; 10—$1.75 ea. (Low. & Up. Gr.)

MARY'S PILGRIM (St. Peregrine). A story of a rough and rowdy boy who became a priest and is now considered "the cancer saint." A true life story from sinner to saint. 92 pp. Hard cover. $1.95 ea.; 10—$1.75 ea. (Low. & Up. Gr.)

MINIATURE STORIES OF THE SAINTS. Set of 4 booklets—includes over 70 All-stars on Christ's team. 35 men, 35 women. Full color picture is next to each 250 word story. High quality traditional art. Ideal for 4th grade and up. 40 pages each. Sold in set only. $1.00 per set. 5 @ 90¢ per set. (Low. & Up. Gr.)

MINITATIONS FOR TEENS. A practical discussion of 100 questions that require thoughtful and serious consideration. 28 line drawings. Helps mold a true Christian attitude and outlook for students, teachers, and parents. 135 pages. Paper. $2.00 ea., 5 @ $1.75 ea., 10 @ $1.60 ea. (Lower & Upper Grade)

MY FIRST COMMUNION, by Bishop Morrow, S.T.D. Excellent presentation of our true faith in simple story form, from Creation to the birth, death, and

Resurrection of Christ, along with the Mass, child's examination of conscience, basic prayers, and the meaning of the beautiful privilege to share in Christ's Divinity when receiving Him in Holy Communion. Fourteen regular prayers, 3 special before and 3 after Communion. 71 colored illustrations. 114 pp. Paper. 50¢ ea.; 5—40¢ ea. (Lower Grade)

MY JESUS AND I, by Most Rev. L. Morrow, D.D. The best by far for the pre-school child. 40 beautiful pictures with reading to give him basic prayers, Our Father, Hail Mary, Glory Be, etc. Also illustrations and explanations of right Christian attitudes and behavior in the home, school, and church. 40 pp. Paper. 50¢ ea.; 10—40¢ ea. (Pre-School)

MY ROSARY—Coloring Book. Excellent for the younger child to help him learn the prayers and how to pray the Rosary. By coloring the pictures they soon learn the meaning of each Mystery. Includes brief story of St. Dominic receiving the Rosary, and Our Lady's appearances at Lourdes and Fatima. 32 pp. Paper. 40¢ ea.; 10—35¢ ea.; 25—30¢ ea. (Lower Grade)

NO PLACE FOR DEFEAT (St. Pius V). Started out as a very ordinary but deeply spiritual boy. In time he became head of all Christendom and through the Rosary and processions in honor of the Blessed Sacrament, obtained God's help for victory by the Christians over the much greater forces of the Turks'. A real inspiration for any or all who wish to dedicate their life to help save souls. 96 pp. Hard cover. $1.95 ea.; 10—$1.75 ea. (Lower & Upper Grade)

NOBLE LADY (St. Helen). Laid aside her jewels and beautiful clothes and journeyed to Calvary and through inspiration led the excavation whereby the True Cross of Christ was found. A story to be cherished for an entire lifetime. 70 pages. Hard cover. $1.95 ea.; 10—$1.75 ea. (Lower & Upper Grade)

OUR FRIENDS, THE SAINTS. Eighty of the best known saints with full color picture and story of each. Four color cover, beautiful traditional art. 80 pp. Paper. $1.30 ea.; 5—$1.00 ea. (Upper Grade)

OUR LADY AND THE AZTEC, by J. M. O'Neil. This colorful story of Guadalupe will fascinate any child. Juan Diego, to whom Our Lady appears is a child at heart with a child's unspoiled faith. The miraculous blooming of the roses, the beautiful picture of Our Lady on Juan's coarse cloak and other miracles makes this true story of the "Queen of All America's" even more beautiful as time goes by. 72 pp. Hard cover. $1.00 ea.; 5—85¢ ea. (Upper Grade)

PICTURE BOOK OF SAINTS, by Rev. Lawrence Lovasik, S.V.D. Printed in full color with the highest quality art, each of the more than 100 saints is given a full page with picture, story, feast day and prayer. A most welcome addition to any school or home library. 116 pages. Hard Cover. $3.95 ea., 5 or more $3.50 ea. (Lower & Upper Grade)

SACRED HEART—Color and Learn Book, by Sr. John Vianney, S.S.N.D. Educational and inspirational for children, teachers, and parents. 24 excellent sketches by one of our most talented artists. Copy covers Life of Christ, His appearance to St. Margaret Mary, First Fridays and Enthronement in the home. Paper. 85¢ ea., 10 @ 75¢ ea. (Lower Grade)

ST. AGNES. A short story of a heroic young girl who loved God more than life itself. Outstanding colorful art work will lead the child to read and re-read this beautiful inspiring story. 19 pages. Hard Cover. $1.00 ea., 5 @ 85¢ ea. (Upper Grade)

SAINT BERNADETTE. An unlearned peasant girl chosen to speak for the Mother of God. She obediently followed instructions from the Queen of Heaven and now each year millions visit the world famous grotto, "Lourdes." Her body is still incorrupt after more than 100 years. 25 pages. Hard Cover. $1.00 ea., 10 @ 85¢ ea. (Lower & Upper Grade)

SAINT DYMPHNA, by Rev. Lawrence Lovasik, S.V.D. For more than a 1000 years St. Dymphna has brought light and contentment to victims of the saddest of human afflictions—nervous and mental disease. This book is an inspiring story of the virgin-martyr and an answer to many who want to know more about her and the help she has to offer. Illustrated. 116 pp. Paper. $3.95 ea.; 5—$3.50 ea. (Upper Grade)

ST. GERMAINE AND HER GUARDIAN ANGEL. An inspiring story that will help all children understand the noble and meritorious part that sacrifice and suffering plays in living a true spiritual life. God's reward to this brave little girl is the same he gives to all who dedicate themselves with true love to Him. Illustrated. 25 pp. Paper. 85¢ ea.; 5—75¢ ea. (Lower & Upper Grade)

ST. MARIA GORETTI, by her Mother. A detailed life story as told by her mother. Includes her testimony given during her stay at the Vatican, in the hospice of St. Martha for the solemn beatification of her daughter. Approved by ecclesiastical authority. 70 pp. Paper. 75¢ ea.; 10—65¢ ea.; 25—55¢ ea. (Upper Grade)

ST. MARTIN DE PORRES, by R. Cardinal Cushing. A perfect example of how to live the will of God and to accomplish it through consideration and help for the unfortunate. A real inspiration for the youth. 74 pp. Hard cover. $1.00 ea.; 10—85¢ ea. (Lower & Upper Grade)

ST. PANCRATIUS. Though only a young lad during the very severe persecution of the Christians under the Roman Emperors, yet his dedication to Christ will give courage to many of our youth today who will have to face persecution and in some cases even martyrdom. Full color art work. 28 pp. Paper. 60¢ ea.; 5—50¢ ea. (Lower & Upper Grade)

THAT WONDERFUL NIGHT. The story of the very first Christmas. Excellent for the pre-school or lower grades. Full color pictures. 32 pp. Paper. 65¢ ea.; 5—50¢ ea. (Lower & Upper Grade)

THE COUNTRY ROAD HOME (St. John Vianney, Cure of Ars). A peasant boy who had difficulty in his studies, but through prayers and deep love for God attracted thousands to his Church and became the model for all parish priests. A real spiritual inspiration for any student. 82 pp. Hard cover. $1.95 ea.; 10—$1.75 ea. (Lower & Upper Grade)

THE GIRL IN THE STABLE (St. Germaine). Orphan, mistreated, sickly, yet of great wealth spiritually. She not only shared her riches then, but because of her great love of God will continue to inspire and enrich the lives of many for all times. 55 pp. Hard cover. $1.95 ea.; 10—$1.75 ea. (Lower & Upper Grade)

THE SEVEN SACRAMENTS—Coloring Book. Each are pictured in a traditional line drawing with a simple explanation beneath them. Informative, instructive. Paper. 35¢ ea., 10 @ 30¢ ea. (Lower Grade)

WIND AND SHADOWS (Joan of Arc). One of the great heroines of God whose life will never fade as one generation after another review the valor and heroism of one dedicated completely to the will of God. A real saint for our times. 112 pp. Hard cover. $1.95 ea.; 10—$1.75 ea. (Lower & Upper Grade)

KATERI OF THE MOHAWKS—Coloring Book, by Fabyan Windeatt. A most interesting story about this heroic Indian Maiden who died a Martyr for her Faith. Declared Venerable by Pope Pius XII. 24 pp. Paper. 25¢ ea.; 5 or more 20¢ ea. (Lower Grade)

SAVE OUR SCHOOLS

CLASSROOM SEX EDUCATION, CANCEL IT—FOR KEEPS, by Rev. Msgr. Cleary, M.A. Finally a comprehensive and critical analysis showing the complete failure of the program. Documents and cases show increase in venereal disease and teenage pregnancies due to using this approach. Secular humanism replaces moral standards and a complete breakdown in moral and spiritual values takes place. This is to the detriment of the student, family, and community. 218 pp. Paper. $2.50 ea.; 5—$2.00 ea.

HOW TO SURVIVE IN YOUR LIBERAL SCHOOL, by J. K. Fitzpatrick. This book is a Godsend for thinking teachers, parents, clergy, and students. Each chapter fits into their survival kit. They are: Patriotism is not "mindless jingoism," Capital punishment is not "institutionalized murder," Pornography is not "just a matter of taste," Traditions are not "shackles of the past," Liberalism: a disease of the heart, Education does not mean learning "how wrong your parents are," Anti-Communism has not become obsolete, Conservatives are not "racist pigs," The New Left does not have all the answers, You don't have to be a "gun nut" to oppose gun control laws, Joseph McCarthy: he was not America's "great threat," God is not dead, Sex education: doing your thing is not the right thing, and Is there an answer? 224 pp. Hard cover. $7.95 ea.; 2—$7.00 ea.

OUR SCHOOLS AND THE FUTURE, by Dr. Max Rafferty. Dr. Rafferty explains the weaknesses and failings of our present day school system and gives practical suggestions to bring it back to standards that made it respected and admired the world over. Pamphlet. 25¢ ea.; 5—20¢ ea.

YOUTH

HIPPIES, HINDUS, AND ROCK AND ROLL, by Bob Larson. Firsthand account after a personal visit to India of this pagan, anti-Christian music characteristic of Hindu life. Explains how and why it is destroying Christian values in our youth. 90 pp. Paper. 95¢ ea.; 5— 85¢ ea.

THE DAY MUSIC DIED, by Bob Larson. Updated, more complete than his previous best seller, "Rock and Roll, The Devil's Diversion." Explains paganistic origin of rock, and why it is anti-Christian, satanic. Could prevent much moral and spiritual harm to our youth. Deserves a place in every home and school library. 213 pages. Paper. $2.95, 5 @ $2.50 ea., 10 @ $2.25 ea.

WHAT'S WRONG WITH ROCK AND ROLL, by Bob Larson. Brief highlights of harm to our youth through the devil's beat music of today. Once head of a rock band, Mr. Larson saw the destruction of minds and bodies, became a minister and is now America's No. 1 speaker and writer against it. 15 pages. Pamphlet. 25¢, 10 @ 20¢ ea., 25 @ 15¢ ea.

HEALTH

BACK TO EDEN, by Jethro Kloss. The author states: "I am sending forth the book for the purpose of helping humanity and giving courage to those who may have thought their cases hopeless. My prayer is that God may make this book a blessing to many." It contains tried, safe, and inexpensive remedies for the prevention of disease and sickness, remedies which are the result of his own practical experience of nearly forty years. There has been a growing demand for many years of practical knowledge of non-poisonous herbs. This is possibly the most complete book on the subject ever published. 684 pp. Paper. $2.95 ea; 5—$2.50 ea.

BODY, MIND, AND SUGAR, by Abrahamson and Pezet. This is the story of a highly prevalent but easily curable illness—hyper-insulinism—"sugar starvation." Symptoms, effects, and case histories of low blood sugar are given. Most important, the very effective means of prevention and cure are given—a simple, tasty, easy-to-follow diet. 240 pp. Paper. $1.25 ea; 5—$1.10 ea.

BREADS YOU WOULDN'T BELIEVE, by Anne Lerner. Some of the most intriguing yeast bread recipes you'll ever taste—individually developed for full flavor and quick and easy preparation. 119 fantastic recipes from Organic Corn Bread to Sour Dough. 128 pp. Paper. $1.95, 5 @ $1.75 ea.

CIDER VINEGAR, by Cyril Scott. In this book, the author reveals the therapeutic powers of cider vinegar, with special reference to its success in reducing overweight. Also the beneficial effects of this versatile beverage for eye strain, sore throat, tickling cough, diarrhea, hiccough, etc. 48 pp. Paper. $1.25 ea.; 5—$1.00 ea.

CRUDE BLACK MOLASSES, by Cyril Scott. The author describes how ordinary crude black molasses has been used in the successful treatment of anemia, arthritis, colitis, constipation, dermatitis, gall-stones, growths, and many other ills. This wonderful substance is a rich source of most of the vitamin B group, plus iron, copper and magnesium. 48 pp. Paper. $1.25 ea; 5—$1.00 ea.

DICTIONARY OF FOODS by Hauser & Berg. Here you have a list of foods and whether they are acid or alkaline-forming. Divided also into vitamin classifications with medicinal value of each. Digestive time and properties are also covered. A very useful book where diet problems cause difficulties. 136 pp. Paper. $1.95, 5 @ $1.65 ea.

THE HEART AND VITAMIN E, by Dr. Evan Shute. This is an answer in good part to one of our most pressing medical problems. The therapy discussed could benefit many and help establish a successful treatment for cardiac patients. Also information on beneficial effects of Vitamin E on high blood pressure. 132 pp. Paper. $4.00, 5 @ $3.50 ea.

THE HERB BOOK, by John Lust. Called "The Natural Remedy Bible" . . . complete with case histories, herbal formulas, full, yet concise description of herbs, their properties and uses. Many pictures. Explains in easy-to-understand way how you may use Nature's gentle medicines for a livelier, healthier and happier life! 660 pp. Paper. $2.50, 5 @ $2.25 ea.

THE HERBALIST, by Joseph Meyer. Herb medicines and teas have been used for years. Modern science is now re-evaluating them. Outstanding results are obtained in many cases. Being natural, there are no side effects as with chemical drugs. 10th printing, shows pictures of over 300 herbs. 50 pages in color. Indexed. 304 pp. Hard Cover. $5.95 ea.

HONEY AND YOUR HEALTH, by Bodog Beck, M.D. and Dores Smedley. A standard work on a most interesting subject. Considered nature's "miracle" health food. Included are many facts that science has discovered about its uses as a staple in one's daily diet as well as a remedy for various illnesses. A natural sweetening superior in almost every way to sugar. A recipe section is included. 210 pp. Paper. 95¢, 5 @ 85¢ ea.

HOW TO GROW YOUR OWN GROCERIES FOR $100 A YEAR, by C. Ridley. With a shortage of food imminent in the near future, it is well to consider the many methods as described and illustrated here. In a matter of days plants spring up and in less than a month you can be eating fresh foods daily out of your garden. You will have quantity, quality, and enough to freeze or preserve for the winter months. 128 pp. Paper. $2.95 ea.; 5—$2.75 ea.

LAETRILE—CONTROL FOR CANCER, by Glenn Kittler. Here is the story of B17—Laetrile itself and how it works, destroying cancer cells without harm to other tissues; actual case histories, medical records, reports and explanations from scientists and from doctors who have treated patients with Laetrile. This book is the result of 10 years of work. 255 pp. Paper. $1.95 ea; 5—$1.75 ea.

LET'S COOK IT RIGHT, by Adelle Davis. The best ways to prepare the foods that are best for you. The famous cookbook by America's #1 nutritionist. First time in paperback. Newly revised and updated. 571 pp. Paper. $1.95 ea; 5—$1.75 ea.

LET'S EAT RIGHT TO KEEP FIT, by Adelle Davis. A world famous nutritionist's bestselling guide to physical and emotional well-being through proper diet. Over 3 million copies in print. Newly revised, updated. 334 pp. Paper. $1.95 ea; 5—$1.75 ea.

LET'S GET WELL, by Adelle Davis. America's most celebrated nutritionist shows how the proper selection of foods and supplements can hasten recovery from illness. 476 pp. Paper. $1.95 ea; 5—$1.75 ea.

LET'S HAVE HEALTHY CHILDREN, by Adelle Davis. America's most famous food expert gives the vital nutritional do's and don'ts for expectant mothers, babies, and growing children. 381 pp. Paper. $1.75 ea; 5—$1.50 ea.

LIVE FOOD JUICES, by H. E. Kirschner, M.D. Try this natural way and find out for yourself how natural foods and good daily habits of living can bring you to positive health, extra energy, vitality, as well as a longer life. 120 pp. Paper. $3.00 ea; 5—$2.50 ea.

MAKE YOUR JUICER YOUR DRUG STORE, by Dr. L. Newman. To revitalize the chemistry of your body, you must consume natural and perfect food. Cooking and chemical interference change the natural properties of food, in some cases destroying the food value. As natural juices are a rich source of vitamins, minerals, enzymes, proteins, and amino acids, you are naturally fortifying your body against disease. 192 pp. Paper. $1.95 ea; 5—$1.75 ea.

MY WATER CURE, by Rev. Kneipp. This is in good part a photo copy of the original first published in Germany in 1886. Sixty-two editions printed to date. A rare method of improving health and curing some illnesses. Tested for more than 40 years. Also lists many herbs and their use in correcting certain conditions in a natural way. 450 pp. Paper. $6.00 ea.; 5—$5.50 ea.

NATURE'S MIRACLE MEDICINE CHEST, by C. Edwards Burtis. How to achieve abundant good health through everyday foods—pure natural foods, our gifts from the land and sea. 170 pp. Paper. $1.45 ea.; 5—$1.25 ea.

OUR DAILY BREAD, by Stella Standard. 366 recipes for a rich new world of wholesome breads—the natural organic way to better taste and better health. 280 pp. Paper. $2.00 ea.; 5—$1.75 ea.

RAW VEGETABLE JUICES, by N. W. Walker, D.Sci. Here are Nature's own drugless blood pressure regulators, anti-cavity enzymes, and aids to promote general good health. Lists a host of drugless organic healing substances for your every need. 175 pp. Paper. $1.25 ea.; 5—$1.00 ea.

SILENT SPRING, by Rachel Carson. The world-famous bestseller about our ravaged environment and the man-made pollution that is imperiling all life on earth. This is a factual explanation to help you better understand why in some areas there are strange diseases, poor vegetation, almost no birds, listless livestock, fruit trees with minimum yields, with wild game almost extinct. Answers to the problems are suggested. Basically it means stop using poison chemicals and return to the natural, God's way. 304 pp. Paper. $1.25 ea.; 5—$1.00 ea.

STOCKING UP, by Staff of "Organic Gardening." A real help in every way to all phases of growing and preserving fruits and vegetables. Covers harvesting, freezing, canning, drying, underground storage, juicing, smoking, curing, etc. 350 pp. Hard cover. $8.95 ea.; 3—$8.00 ea.

ZONE THERAPY, by Bergson and Tuchak. A step-by-step guide to applied pressure therapy. The first book to bring together and collate the best of various materials involving therapy by means of direct applied pressure on certain key parts especially of the hands and feet. Acupuncture, foot and hand reflexology and finger massage according to zones, gives relief to many illnesses. Diagrams illustrate both method and area of nerve sensitive areas. 152 pp. Paper. $1.25 ea.

PATRIOTISM AND AMERICANISM

LIBERTY ISSUE, Ideals Magazine. Truly a great tribute to our nation in this its 200th Birthday. The best of art, prose, and poetry by some of our nation's best writers and artists. Line drawings, sketches, and full color paintings combine to make this one of the best for home or school libraries or history class use. Ideal also for waiting or reception rooms in offices, etc. It will fill your heart with a justified joy in our heritage and accomplishments and why in a rather short time we became one of the greatest nations on the face of the earth. 80 pp. Paper. $2.50, 5 @ $2.25 ea.

A NATION BUILT ON GOD, by E. J. Melvin, C.M. A true evaluation of solid Christian and moral principles in the lives of the men and in the documents of our Constitutional Free Enterprise System of government set up by them. The author explains how a secular philosophy (humanistic) is replacing these very principles of life, liberty, and the pursuit of happiness. Also that the Supreme Court in their decision favorable to abortion undermines the basic Constitutional inalienable right to life. A book for all educators, congressmen, lawyers, and judges who wish to see our U.S.A. continue as a free nation under God. 223 pp. Hard cover. $4.95 ea.; 5—$4.00 ea.

DISCOVERING HEROES OF THE AMERICAN REVOLUTION. A punch out sticker history book. 70 figures in color. Map with stars where 26 major battles were fought is on outside back cover. Front cover is the Fife and Drum Corps in full color. Ideal for lower grades. Paper. 10¼ " x 12". $1.00 ea.; 10—85¢ ea.

GOD BLESS AMERICA, Ideals Magazine. Companion to the Liberty issue. Captures the true spirit of '76 in colorful photography, artwork, prose, and poetry spanning 200 years of our history. Here's America—with its traditions, people, history, noble achievements. A perfect hallmark of our Bi-Centennial year. 64 pages. Paper. $1.95, 5 @ $1.75 ea.

OUR FIFTY STATES, by Eugene and Katherine Sharp Rachlis. Facts about the history, industry, agriculture, and natural resources of our fifty states. Included is a full-color picture map of each state, showing major cities, important products, and famous landmarks. Ideal for history, geography, or social science classes. Grades 1-8. 50 pp. Paper. $1.00 ea.; 10—85¢ ea.

THE AMERICAN MIRACLE, BICENTENNIAL REVIEW OF AMERICA'S PAST, by G. Longarini. An excellent outline of the principles and deeds responsible for our nation's great achievements in the past 200 years; with ideas and thoughts on which to build a secure future with freedom and prosperity. Ideal for history or civic classes, or general essay contest on Americanism and patriotism. 21 line drawings. 60 pp. Paper. $1.00 ea.; 5—85¢ ea.

THE REPUBLIC: DECLINE AND FUTURE PROMISE, by A. E. Roberts, Lt. Col., AUS, Ret. A blue print for Freedom, a documented and detailed explanation of the socialistic, dictatorial programs that will set up a One World Atheistic Government to replace our Constitutional Free Enterprise System. We will no longer have inalienable God given rights to own our homes, businesses, a choice in employment or education, and worshiping God according to our conscience. In other words, all that our forefathers worked, saved, suffered, and died to give us will be taken away through government control. This book takes you through Regional Planning; The C.F.R.; Rockefeller Foundation; Land, Water, Transportation, and Economic Developments; a National Police Force; etc. All part of a one world government promotion that would take away all of our liberties and freedoms. The last part is also very important as it outlines how and why we must fight these unconstitutional laws that they are introducing and passing in both state and national legislatures. 102 pp. Paper. $2.95 ea.; 5—$2.50 ea.

BOOKLETS

ST. MICHAEL, by Rev. L Lovasik, S.V.D. Explains the nature, ranks and devotion to the angels along with St. Michael's chaplet to the nine choirs, includes prayers, litany, etc. to St. Michael. 1—25¢, 20 or more 20¢ ea.

ST. GERTRUDE, Herald of Divine Love. Our Lord explains to her about His Mass, frequent or daily attendance, the advantages of Holy Communion, value of suffering when united to those of His Life and Passion. 1—25¢, 20 or more 20¢ ea.

MERCY OF GOD DEVOTION, by Rev. Zarembo, O.F.M. Tells of Sr. M. Faustina through whom the devotion came, the meaning of the picture, Chaplet of Mercy, and the powerful Novena that starts on Good Friday finishing on first Sunday after Easter. Each 15¢, 25 or more 12¢ ea.

MY IDEAL, by E. Neubert according to the spirit of William J. Chaminade. Part 1 and 2, Our Lord tells you why and how you should love His Blessed Mother. In Part 3, Our Holy Mother tells you the right and better way to love Her Son and Part 4, Living the Ideal Christian way according to the above. 158 pp. 1—75¢, 5 or more 65¢ ea.

ST. ANTHONY MARY CLARET, by J. Mahoney. A brief interesting biography of this talented and dedicated servant of God. 48 pp. 1—35¢, 5 or more 30¢ ea.

ST. ANTHONY MARY CLARET NOVENA. Includes general prayers, exposition of the Blessed Sacrament, Novena prayers and very brief life story. 1—35¢, 5 or more 30¢ ea.

KATERI TEKAKWITHA, Venerable, by T. J. Coffey, S.J. America's marvelous maiden whose cause is now up for Canonization. A brief but interesting story of this young lady of our times. 32 pp. 1—25¢, 10 or more 20¢ ea.

CONSECRATION TO THE IMMACULATE HEART OF MARY, by Rev. N. A. Norman. Gives reasons why conditions today call for consecrating oneself to the Immaculate Heart of Mary, also the ways and means of making the perfect consecration according to St. Louis De Montfort. 1—25¢, 10 or more 20¢ ea.

LIFE & MIRACLES OF ST. BENEDICT, by Pope St. Gregory the Great. The St. Benedict Medal is considered one of the most powerful. This little book will tell you why St. Benedict is also one of our most powerful saints. The author Pope St. Gregory the Great. Indexed for reference. 87 pp. 1—75¢, 5 @ 65¢ ea.; 25 or more 55¢ ea.

MENTAL PRAYER, by B. Wilberforce, O.P. Describes what it is, importance and necessity of it, how to practice it, the better time for it and why it helps banish distractions and temptations. 48 pp. 1—25¢, 10 or more 20¢ ea.

INDULGENCED PRAYERS. Covers explanation of indulgences and their application. Also many prayers with attached indulgence and the value of ejaculatory prayers. 64 pp. 1—35¢, 10 or more 30¢ ea.

DEVOTION TO THE INFANT OF PRAGUE. Tells of origin, meaning of the devotion, regular and novena prayers with the powerful nine hour novena for urgency needs. 32 pp. 1—30¢, 10 or more 25¢ ea.

HEAVENLY COURT OF ST. LUTGARDE. The Heavenly Court prayer idea goes back to the year 1246. Time tested, powerful. 40 pp. 1—45¢, 10 or more 40¢ ea.

CONFORMITY TO THE WILL OF GOD. Drawn chiefly from the writings of St. Alphonsus Liguori. 64 pp. 1—25¢, 10 or more 20¢ ea.

TWO DIVINE PROMISES, by Rev. R. Hoppe. Covers the realization of God's Mercy. A private revelation from Poland 1954. Devotion is now practiced in 12 foreign countries and the U.S.A. 68 pp. 1—45¢, 10 or more 40¢ ea.

BROTHER SAVE YOURSELF, by Very Rev. J. Alberione. Moments for consideration of our eternal reward or loss of soul. Excellent prayers and reflections. 77 pp. 1—25¢, 10 or more 20¢ ea.

ENTHRONEMENT OF THE SACRED HEART IN THE HOME. Brief story of life of Fr. Mateo, founder of idea for Enthronement of the Sacred Heart in the home. Also object, spirit and need of it, with preparation for and ceremony of, in the home. 64 pp. 25¢.

HOLY HOUR OF REPARATION. This booklet is ideal for church or private use. Possibly the best available anywhere. Used in several foreign countries as well as U.S.A. 32 pp. 1—50¢, 10 or more 40¢ ea.

OUR LADY OF PROMPT SUCCOR, Manual of Devotion. Story of miraculous statue in Ursuline Convent, New Orleans, La. Novena prayers with Litany, Hymns and Mass of O. L. of Prompt Succor. 36 pp. 1—30¢, 10 or more 25¢ ea.

MY HEART SPEAKS TO THEE (Little Rose). Story of Mary Rose Ferron, an ordinary girl with an extraordinary life. Tenth child in the family named after the 10th mystery of the Rosary—Crucifixion. Had all the wounds of the Crucifixion, lived to be 33 years of age. A true victim soul that offered her life to suffer to save others. Noble, heroic. 38 pp. 1—25¢, 10 or more 20¢ ea.

MANUAL OF ST. JOSEPH. Includes Novena prayers, "Thirty Days" prayer, special intention prayers, Benediction of the Blessed Sacrament and list of indulgences. 48 pp. 1—30¢, 10 or more 25¢ ea.

ST. GERARD MAJELLA, C.SS.R. The Mothers Saint. Includes story of his life, with special Novena prayers. 72 pp. 1—50¢, 10 or more 45¢ ea.

WHO IS TERESA NEUMANN?, by Rev. C. M. Carty. Story of one of the great Stigmatists of our time. Lived an active vigorous life for over 30 years without earthly food, nourished only by the Blessed Sacrament. Suffered the Passion of Our Lord for many years. Had the thorn, nail and side wounds. 62 pp. 1—75¢, 5 or more 65¢ ea.

SECRET OF HAPPINESS. Gives the magnificent promises with the 15 Prayers revealed by St. Bridget of Sweden. Imprimatur. 20¢ per copy.

LITTLE WAY OF LOVE—Excerpts from full length book. Sr. M. Consolata Betrone, through whom the ejaculation "Jesus, Mary I Love You Save Souls" came through has some most interesting comments from Our Lord on making the perpetual "Act of Love," how Our Lord will save the world through His Most Merciful Love, and that war, misery, want are part of it and through this souls come back and save themselves, whereas in prosperity they forget Him and could easily be lost. 1—15¢, 10 or more 10¢ ea.

NOVENA TO THE HOLY SPIRIT. Oldest of all Novenas. First made by the Apostles at the direction of Our Lord. Includes Act of Consecration, Prayer for the 7 Gifts and information on the Archconfraternity. 25¢ ea., 10 or more 20¢ ea.

NOVENA TO OUR SORROWFUL MOTHER, by Rev. J. Keane, O.S.M. Complete with Prayers, Hymns, Benediction, Indulgences, etc. Close to 7 million copies sold. For congregation or private use. 1—40¢, 10 or more 35¢ ea.

NOVENA FOR RELIEF OF THE POOR SOULS IN PURGATORY, by Rev. J. F. Durin. A beautiful book with much more than Novena Prayers. Includes Meditations, examples, practices and Chaplet for the Poor Souls. 1—25¢, 10 or more 20¢ ea.

NOVENA IN HONOR OF ST. ANTHONY. Includes short story of Life of St. Anthony. Tuesday Devotion to him, Prayers for all occasions, Novena Prayers, Litany, etc. 20¢ ea.

NOVENA TO ST. PETER J. EYMARD. Along with special prayers a short biography is included of this great "Apostle of the Holy Eucharist." 1—25¢, 10 or more 20¢ ea.

WAY OF THE CROSS—St. Alphonsus Liguori. Arranged for congregational or private use. The traditional long-time favorite of the clergy, religious and laity. A complete Way of the Cross with Stabat Mater, Lenten Hymns, Benediction, etc. 30¢, 10 or more @ 25¢ ea.

NOVENA booklets, by Rev. L. G. Lovasik, S.V.D. 1—Pope Pius X. 1—St. Alphonsus—The Arthritis Saint. 1—St. Peregrine—The Cancer Saint. 1—St. Dymphna—Patron of Nervous and Emotionally Disturbed. 1—St. Raphael—Angel of Joy, Healing, Love. Cost 35¢ ea., 10 or more assorted or single title 30¢ ea.

PRAYER BOOKS

QUEEN OF APOSTLES. Many basic prayers to the Sacred and Immaculate Heart, the Mass, Rosary, Stations, Special favors and needs. Plastic cover. 445 pp. $3.00 ea.

MY DAILY PRAYER. Includes prayers for every day, meditative thoughts for various church seasons and a brief sketch of a saint for each day of the year. Black imitation leather. 512 pp. $2.00, 5 or more $1.75 ea.

MY DAILY BREAD, by A. J. Paone, S.J. A summary of the spiritual life simplified and arranged for daily reading, reflection and prayer. Maroon Imitation Leather. 448 pp. Duro finish. $2.00, 5 or more $1.75 ea. Duro DeLuxe Finish. $3.00, 5 or more $2.75 ea.

MY WAY OF LIFE. Pocket edition of the Summa of St. Thomas Acquinas, simplified so all can understand it. 630 pp. Hard Cover. Imitation Leather. $3.00, 5 or more @ $2.75 ea.

MY DAILY PSALM BOOK, by Fr. Frey. Inspired prayers and hymns arranged for each day of the week. The beauty of the canticles and praises of Our Lord in the Old Testament are here with well over 100 excellent illustrations. 370 pp. Art Board cover. $1.75, 5 or more $1.50 ea.

THE WHOLE STORY. Presents the story of man in the light of revelation. It is really God's story of man with answers to the all important questions. Whence have I come? Why am I here? Whither am I going? 690 pp. Hard Cover. Maroon Duro Finish. $2.00, 5 or more $1.75 ea. Maroon Duro Deluxe Finish. $3.50, 5 or more $3.25 ea. Genuine Leather. $6.50; 5 or more $6.00 ea.

MY IMITATION OF CHRIST, by Thomas A. Kempis. Next to the Scriptures, one of the all-time great spiritual guides. 480 pp. Duro Finish. $2.25, 5 or more $2.00 ea.

JESUS, MARY, JOSEPH NOVENA MANUAL. Consists of Novenas, Way of the Cross, Devotion to the Blessed Sacrament and the Mass, Prayers before and after Communion with special emphasis on devotion to Our Lord's Precious Blood. 158 pp. Grained heavy paper cover. $1.00 ea., 5 or more 85¢ ea.

PEACE THROUGH THE BLOOD OF HIS CROSS. Meditations and Prayers to the Precious Blood—Fifth printing. Very readable. 179 pp. Duro paper cover. $2.50 ea., 5 or more $2.25 ea.

PRECIOUS BLOOD AND MOTHER. A compilation of excellent Prayers from approved sources by the Religious Adorers of the Precious Blood. 175 pp. Duro cover. 1—$2.00, 5 or more $1.75 ea.

QUEEN OF HEAVEN. A book to help everyone grow in their depth of knowledge and love of the most perfect woman Who ever lived. As the Mother of God, She now occupies the throne next to Our Lord, Her Divine Son. Therefore no one has more grace or power from the Most Sacred Heart of the Son of God and through Him, from the Heavenly Father. You will develop a complete trust and confidence in Her intercession from the knowledge and prayers set forth in this treatise on true devotion to Our Lady. 96 pp. Paper. $1.00, 5-24 @ 75¢ ea., 25 @ 65¢ ea.

ROSARIES FOR ADULTS AND CHILDREN

COCOA BEAD. Rich oval genuine cocoa beads on solid nickel silver chain. Carved Our Father bead. Solid metal crucifix. Scapular center medallion. Guard rings for each bead. Plastic pocket case. Specify color, black or brown. $3.50 ea., 2 or more $3.00 ea.

WOOD BEAD. Square cut oblong bead, silver plated, strong chain, solid metal crucifix, center medallion Madonna and Child on front with Sacred Heart on back. Specify color, black or brown. Plastic pocket case. $3.00 ea., 2 or more $2.50 ea.

AURORA BOREALIS (Young Girls). Top quality round cut crystal beads, solid nickel silver chain, cut-out Scapular medal centerpiece, Crucifix with cast corpus. Specify color, blue, aqua, crystal, garnet. Gold plastic velveteen lined case. $2.50 ea., 3 @ $2.00 ea., 5 or more $1.75 ea.

AURORA BOREALIS (Ladies). Excellent quality, large round cut crystal beads, with chain and cross nickel silver. Center medallion has Madonna and Child in front, Sacred Heart on back. Specify color, crystal, light blue, dark blue, deep purple, garnet, vitrolite. Gold plastic velveteen lined case. $4.25 ea., 3 @ $3.75 ea., 5 or more $3.25 ea.

PLASTIC (Boys). Oval average size beads, double wire chain, Miraculous center medallion, wood-metal bound crucifix. Specify color, black or brown. Plastic pocket case. $1.35 ea., 5 or more $1.00 ea.

PLASTIC (Girls). Oval average size beads, double wire chain, Miraculous center medallion, wood-metal bound crucifix. Specify color, luminous, pink, (multicolor: one decade of red, white, blue, green and yellow). Plastic pocket case. $1.35 ea., 5 or more $1.00 ea.

ROSARY BRACELET. Beautiful five-decade Rosary bracelet with metal crucifix and miraculous medal. Moonstone Hail Mary beads with aurora borealis Our Father bead. Specify color—white, light blue, or pink. Also pearl. $5.50 ea.

ROSARY BRACELET. Beautiful five-decade Rosary bracelet with sterling crucifix and miraculous medal. Aurora borealis crystal Hail Mary beads with contrasting color aurora borealis Our Father bead. Specify color—white crystal or light blue. $9.95 ea.

FAMILY ROSARY. Large oval beads, strong nickel chain, metal bound crucifix, Madonna and Sacred Heart centerpiece, length 31″. Specify black or brown wood bead or luminous plastic bead. $2.00 ea., 3 or more $1.75 ea.

RECORDS L.P. PATRIOTIC

AMERICA THE BEAUTIFUL, by The Disney Concert Band and Glee Club. The best of the best—your heart will thrill to 9 favorites—America the Beautiful, Stars and Stripes Forever (Sousa), Star Spangled Banner (Francis Scott Key), Battle Hymn of the Republic, Columbia—The Gem of the Ocean, Caissons Go Rolling Along and God Bless America (Irving Berlin). Also a Medley of the great "Theme Songs" of our Air Force, Navy, Marines and Army. Excellent for school, club or radio use. $5.50 ea., 3 or more $5.00 ea.

TO AMERICA WITH LOVE, by Lawrence Welk. The best in the spirit of yesterday, now and tomorrow. New and truly inspired to recapture the "Spirit of '76" with lyrics and words to help us re-dedicate ourselves to our priceless heritage, under our Constitution, with Liberty, Freedom and Justice for all. Great for young or old, all who love our country, its noble past and "under God" its great future. $5.95 ea., 3 or more $5.50 ea.

MINE EYES HAVE SEEN THE GLORY, by Anita Bryant. You too will stand up and cheer for "Old Glory" and the "Land You Love" when you hear Miss Oklahoma sing your favorite "America Now and Forever" songs. She is one of the greatest of our young and talented singers. Whether it was in Viet Nam before our servicemen or in the Capitol of our U.S.A., all gave her a standing ovation. She truly deserves to be featured on radio, in school, and at church or service club programs. Her spirit is what we need today. $5.95 ea., 3 or more $5.50 ea.

FAREWELL ADDRESS, by Gen. Douglas MacArthur. This epic address was given to the Cadets assembled at West Point May 12, 1962. He has distinguished himself in college (highest scholastic average) and in every phase of his outstanding military career under eight presidents.

In the trenches in W.W. I he was awarded the Silver Medal by Gen. Pershing on seven different occasions.

World War II, the victory in the Pacific and his work after the war could and should have earned for him the nomination of the highest office in our land. Denied this opportunity to be our president he will always remain one of our greatest Americans.

His talk here is noted for his eloquence, wisdom and from the hush over crowd, the spirit that made and could keep America great. $5.95 ea., 3 or more $5.50 ea.

RECORDS L.P. RELIGIOUS

THE LENNON SISTERS AND LAWRENCE WELK. Presents THE BEST LOVED CATHOLIC HYMNS. Fourteen all-time favorites in the perfect blend of voice with professional organ and other accompaniment. A hallmark favorite of the past, the present and destined for all times. $5.95 ea., 3 or more $5.50 ea.

JIM NABORS. THE LORD'S PRAYER—Eleven outstanding hymns, also the Battle Hymn of the Republic. One of today's outstanding spiritual and inspiring vocalists who offers his superb talent to the greater honor and glory of God. $5.95 ea., 3 or more $5.50 ea.

HOW GREAT THOU ART. Again, the incomparable Jim Nabors lends his God-given talents to twelve all-time never-to-be-forgotten songs such as Ave Maria, My Rosary, I Walk With God, etc. $5.95 ea., 3 or more $5.50 ea.

PERRY COMO—CHRISTMAS ALBUM. In his own inimitable way through voice and song another of America's greatest vocalists will help you and your loved ones to share the joy of that first "Holy Night" when Christ our Savior was born. He will help you recreate in your mind and heart the spirit of "History's Greatest Moment." Sixteen songs including the all-time Christmas favorites are brought to you to rekindle the joy and beauty of the Christmas Season. They include Silent Night, Hark the Herald Angels Sing, Oh Holy Night, The First Noel, Ave Maria, etc. $5.95 ea., 3 or more $5.50 ea.

TAPES

1. TRIBUTE TO THOSE WHO HAVE OR NOW SERVE—2. THE MEANING OF OUR FLAG. These two short talks on same tape are both a recognition and appreciation for our Servicemen and Star Spangled Banner. Our youth deserve and need to hear them. Ideal for both private and public use especially during this our 200th Birthday. Available on reel 7½ speed for radio or as a Cassette—8 min. $2.50 ea.

GIVE ME LIBERTY OR GIVE ME DEATH. Patrick Henry's stirring speech before the House of Burgess. The voice, tone and resolution are such that you would think it was given by Mr. Henry himself. A masterpiece of expression characteristic of the spirit and resolution of a truly dedicated patriot. Should inspire a similar sense of purpose and unity of action in our youth and people today. Reel—10 min.—7½ speed, $3.25 ea. Cassette—10 min. $3.25 ea.

WALK WITH ME—WAY OF THE CROSS. A practical and devotional Way of the Cross with an excellent meditation on the "7 Last Words." As the Mass is the Renewal of Calvary, these inspiring spiritual thoughts are fitting for all at any time. They are especially valuable for our youth today as there has been a lack of emphasis on Our Lord's suffering and death on the Cross in the past several years, as well as the Mass being considered a celebration or only a meal. Cassette—Way of the Cross—55 min.; 7 Last Words—22 min. $3.50.

FILMSTRIPS

THE ROSARY STORY—Sound filmstrip. Outstanding color, narration, music and sound effects. Includes history, meditations on mysteries, origin of prayers. 2 filmstrips, part I and part II with cassette tape. $30.00 postpaid.

THE GREEN SCAPULAR STORY—Sound filmstrip. Historic, colorful, inspiring music, sound effects, professionally done. Cassette. $15.00 postpaid.

THE MIRACULOUS MEDAL—Sound filmstrip. Story of the Great Medal, source of so many graces, hence termed "Miraculous." Cassette. $15.00 postpaid.

THE BROWN SCAPULAR—Sound filmstrip. Full color, excellent narration, music and sound effects. Inspires all who see it to appreciate, respect and love this, one of our Holy Mother's great gifts. Her promise is so wonderful that it bears repeating at every possible occasion to both young and old, sick and well, clergy and religious. "Whosoever dies clothed in this shall never suffer eternal hellfire." What a beautiful help and guarantee of reaching safely, our Heavenly home, happy with God, the Blessed Mother, Saints and our loved ones for all eternity. Cassette. $20.00 postpaid.

OUR AMERICAN HERITAGE—Sound filmstrip. Helps all renew their sense of appreciation for the many advantages the Constitutional Free Enterprise System offers, most of which we would not have under any other form of government. This is especially timely as it comes when some loud voices persist in pointing up deficiencies at the same time overlooking the many special advantages. Available on reel—7½ speed, cassette or L.P. record. $25.00 postpaid.

ORDER BLANK

No. of Ea. Title	OUR LORD	Total Amount

CHRIST'S APPEAL FOR LOVE $2.50, 5 @ $2.00 ea.
DOCTOR AT CALVARY $1.45, 5 @ $1.25 ea.
ENTHRONEMENT OF THE SACRED HEART $2.00, 5 @ $1.75 ea.
FAITH OF MILLIONS $4.95
HE REIGNS FROM THE CROSS $2.00, 5 @ $1.75 ea.
IMITATION OF CHRIST $1.75, 5 @ $1.50, 10 @ $1.40 ea.
JESUS APPEALS TO THE WORLD $3.95, 5 @ $3.50 ea.
JESUS KING OF LOVE $2.50, 3 or more $2.00 ea.
MEDITATIONS ON THE LITANY OF THE SACRED HEART $1.00, 5 or more 85¢ ea.
SELF-PORTRAIT OF CHRIST $2.50, 5 or more $2.00 ea.
SPIRITUAL CANTICLE $2.95, 5 @ $2.50 ea.
THE IMITATION OF THE SACRED HEART OF JESUS $5.50, 5 @ $4.50 ea.
THE WAY OF DIVINE LOVE $5.00, 5 @ $4.00 ea, 10 @ $3.50 ea, 25 @ $3.00 ea.
TRUSTFUL SURRENDER TO DIVINE PROVIDENCE 80¢, 5 @ 70¢ ea.
WORDS FROM THE CROSS $1.25, 5 @ $1.00 ea, 10 @ 90¢ ea.

MASS AND HOLY EUCHARIST

BLESSED EUCHARIST $3.50, 3 or more $3.00 ea.
CHAMPION OF THE BLESSED SACRAMENT $3.95, 2 or more $3.50 ea.
HOLY COMMUNION $1.95, 3 or more $1.65 ea.
THE HIDDEN TREASURE $1.50, 5 or more $1.25 ea.
THE WORLD'S GREATEST SECRET 95¢, 5 or more 75¢ ea.

THE BLESSED MOTHER

A WOMAN CLOTHED WITH THE SUN $1.75, 5 @ $1.55 ea.
BY THE QUEEN'S COMMAND $1.00, 10 @ 75¢ ea.
GUADALUPE $1.75, 5 @ $1.50 ea.
MARY HOPE OF THE WORLD $3.00, 5 @ $2.75 ea.
MARY WAS HER LIFE 95¢, 5 @ 75¢ ea.
MORE ABOUT FATIMA $1.00, 5 @ 85¢ ea.
OUR LADY OF FATIMA $1.45, 5 @ $1.20 ea.
OUR LADY'S KNIGHT $3.00, 5 @ $2.50 ea.
SIGN OF HER HEART 85¢, 5 @ 75¢ ea., 10 @ 70¢ ea.
SORROWFUL AND IMMACULATE HEART OF MARY $1.95, 5 @ $1.75 ea., 10 @ $1.60 ea.
THAT MOTHERLY MOTHER OF GUADALUPE $1.50, 10 @ $1.25 ea.
THE FATIMA SECRET $1.50, 5 @ $1.25 ea.
THE GLORIES OF CZESTOCHOWA AND JASNA GORA $2.00, 5 @ $1.75 ea.
THE HEART OF MARY $1.25, 5 or more $1.10 ea.
THE LIFE OF THE BLESSED VIRGIN MARY $3.50, 5 @ $3.00 ea., 10 @ $2.75 ea., 25 @ $2.50 ea., 50 @ $2.25 ea.
THE QUEEN'S SECRET 90¢, 10 @ 80¢ ea., 25 @ 75¢ ea.
THE QUEEN'S WAY $2.00, 5 or more $1.75 ea.

_____	THE WOMAN SHALL CONQUER $2.25, 5 or more $2.00 ea.
_____	TREASURE WRAPPED IN CLOTH $2.00, 10 @ $1.75 ea.
_____	TRUE DEVOTION TO MARY Hard Cover $3.00, 10 @ $2.50 ea.
	Paper $2.00, 10 @ $1.50 ea.
_____	MYSTICAL CITY OF GOD, 4 vols. Hard Cover. $35.00 per set
_____	WORDS OF WISDOM $12.00, 2 or more $10.00 ea.

ROSARY AND SCAPULAR

_____	HOW TO SAY THE ROSARY 5¢ ea., 22/$1.00, 100/$4.00
_____	MY ROSARY 25¢, 10 @ 20¢ ea.
_____	NOVENA OF OUR LADY'S ROSARY 75¢, 10 @ 65¢ ea.
_____	THE GREEN SCAPULAR AND ITS FAVORS 50¢, 10 @ 40¢ ea.
_____	THE ROSARY 25¢, 10 @ 20¢ ea.
_____	THE SECRET OF THE ROSARY 50¢, 10 @ 40¢ ea., 25 @ 35¢ ea., 100 @ 30¢ ea., 500 @ 25¢ ea., 1000 @ 20¢ ea.

BROWN SCAPULARS

_____	Chain, plastic covered 85¢, 5 @ 75¢ ea.
_____	Plastic covered, brown or white cord 25¢, $2.50/doz.
_____	Washable, white cord only 50¢, 5 @ 45¢ ea.
_____	Regular, white cord only 10¢, $1.00/doz.
_____	Explanatory leaflets 2/5¢, 100/$2.00
_____	GREEN SCAPULARS with explanatory leaflet 5¢, 25/$1.00
_____	RED SCAPULARS (Passion) with explanatory leaflet 25¢, $2.50/doz.

LIVES OF THE SAINTS

_____	CHAMPION OF THE BLESSED SACRAMENT $3.95, 5 @ $3.50 ea.
_____	DOMINIC SAVIO 50¢, 5 @ 45¢ ea.
_____	57 STORIES OF SAINTS FOR BOYS AND GIRLS Hard Cover $5.95, 2 or more $5.50 ea.
	Paper $4.95, 2 or more $4.50 ea.
_____	ST. JOAN OF ARC $3.00, 5 or more $2.50 ea.
_____	JOSEPH THE JUST MAN $3.00, 5 @ $2.50 ea.
_____	LEO XIII $3.95, 5 @ $3.25 ea.
_____	LIFE OF VENERABLE SR. MARY OF AGREDA $2.00
_____	LITTLE FLOWERS OF ST. FRANCIS $1.95, 5 @ $1.50 ea.
_____	LIVES OF THE SAINTS $4.25, 5 @ $3.75 ea.
_____	MOTHER SETON $2.45, 5 @ $2.00 ea.
_____	SAINT ANTHONY THE WONDER WORKER $1.50, 5 @ $1.10 ea., 25 @ 90¢ ea., 50 @ 80¢ ea.
_____	SAINT CATHERINE OF SIENA $5.95, 2 or more $5.50 ea.
_____	ST. JOHN BOSCO 75¢ ea., 5 @ 65¢ ea.
_____	ST. LOUIS DE MONTFORT Hard Cover $2.50, 5 @ $2.00 ea.
_____	ST. LOUIS DE MONTFORT Paper 75¢, 5 @ 65¢ ea., 10 @ 60¢ ea.
_____	SAINT PETER JULIAN EYMARD $1.50, 5 @ $1.25 ea.

No. of Ea. Title		Total Amount

_____ ST. THERESE THE LITTLE FLOWER Hard Cover $4.00, 5 @ $3.50 ea. _____

Paper $3.00, 5 @ $2.50 ea. _____

_____ THE LIFE OF BENEDICT XV $4.50, 5 @ $4.00 ea. _____

_____ THE MAN GOD CALLED FATHER 50¢, 10 @ 40¢ ea. _____

_____ THE PERFECT JOY OF ST. FRANCIS $1.95, 5 @ $1.50 ea. _____

_____ SAINT OF THE IMPOSSIBLE 1 @ $3.95, 3 @ $3.50 ea. _____

WRITINGS OF THE SAINTS

_____ ASCENT OF MOUNT CARMEL $1.95, 5 @ $1.75 ea. _____

_____ CITY OF GOD $2.95, 5 @ $2.50 ea. _____

_____ DARK NIGHT OF THE SOUL $1.45, 5 @ $1.25 _____

_____ DIALOGUE OF ST. CATHERINE OF SIENA $3.50, 5 @ $3.00 ea., 10 @ $2.75 ea. _____

_____ FAITHFUL SERVANT $6.50, 2 or more $6.00 ea. _____

_____ FRIENDS OF THE CROSS 25¢ _____

_____ INTERIOR CASTLE $1.75, 5 @ $1.50 ea. _____

_____ INTRODUCTION TO THE DEVOUT LIFE $1.95, 5 @ $1.75 ea. _____

_____ LIVING FLAME OF LOVE $1.45, 5 @ $1.25 ea. _____

_____ SECRET OF MARY 35¢, 5 @ 30¢ ea. _____

_____ SPIRITUAL EXERCISES OF ST. IGNATIUS $1.45, 5 @ $1.25 ea. _____

_____ THE AUTOBIOGRAPHY OF ST. THERESE OF LISIEUX $1.45, 5 @ $1.25 ea. _____

_____ THE AUTOBIOGRAPHY OF ST. TERESA OF AVILA $2.45, 5 @ $2.00 ea. _____

_____ THE CONFESSION OF SAINT AUGUSTINE $1.95, 5 @ $1.75 ea. _____

_____ THE LOVE OF ETERNAL WISDOM $2.00 _____

_____ THE RULE OF ST. BENEDICT $1.45, 3 or more $1.25 ea. _____

_____ THE WAY OF PERFECTION $1.75, 3 or more $1.50 ea. _____

_____ THE WRITINGS OF SAINT FRANCIS OF ASSISI $4.95, 5 @ $4.50 ea. _____

_____ TREATISE ON THE LOVE OF GOD—2 vols. $7.00 per set, 2 @ $6.00 per set. _____

GENERAL RELIGIOUS

_____ A CANADIAN MYSTIC OF OUR DAY (ST. CECILE OF ROME) $1.25, 5 @ $1.00 ea. _____

_____ AA 1025 THE MEMOIRS OF AN ANTI-APOSTLE $1.50, 10 @ $1.25 ea. _____

_____ THE ANTI-PRIESTS—Digest Version of AA 1025 35¢, 10 or more 25¢ ea. _____

_____ CANTICLE OF LOVE $5.95, 3 @ $5.00 ea. _____

_____ CARDINAL MINDSZENTY—MEMOIRS $10.00, 2 @ $8.00 ea. _____

_____ MINDSZENTY THE MAN $3.25 _____

_____ FAITH—RESPONSE TO THE DIALOGUE OF GOD $2.00, 5 @ $1.75 ea. _____

_____ MAMA, WHY DID YOU KILL US? 75¢, 5 @ 65¢ ea. _____

_____ PADRE PIO THE STIGMATIST $3.50, 5 @ $3.00 ea., 10 @ $2.75 ea., 25 @ $2.50 ea., 50 @ $2.25 ea., 100 @ $2.00 ea. _____

_____ PERE LAMY 1855-1931 $3.00, 5 @ $2.50, 10 @ $2.25, 25 @ $2.00 ea., 50 @ $1.75 ea. _____

_____ SHE WEARS A CROWN OF THORNS $2.00, 5 @ $1.75 ea., 25 @ $1.50 ea. _____

_____ SOUL AFIRE $2.45, 2 @ $2.25 ea.

_____ SOUL OF THE APOSTOLATE $3.50, 3 or more $3.00 ea.

_____ THE CATHOLIC ENCYCLOPEDIA $6.00, 2 @ $5.50 ea.

_____ THE DEATH CAMP PROVED HIM REAL $1.25, 5 @ $1.00 ea.

_____ THE PORTER OF ST. BONAVENTURE'S $5.95, 3 @ $5.00 ea.

_____ THE STORY OF THE TRAPP FAMILY SINGERS $1.45, 5 @ $1.35 ea.

_____ THERESE NEUMANN $4.50, 5 @ $4.00 ea.

_____ THOU ART THE ROCK $1.00, 5 @ 75¢ ea.

_____ THE TRUTH ABOUT TEILHARD 50¢ ea.

_____ VERONICA'S VEIL $4.00, 5 @ $3.25 ea.

_____ WHO IS PADRE PIO?, THE AGONY OF JESUS and MEDITATION PRAYER ON MARY IMMACU-LATE Set of 3. $1.65, 5 sets @ $1.45, ea., 10 sets @ $1.30 ea., 25 sets @ $1.15 ea.

_____ THE FIFTEEN PROMISES OF THE ROSARY (Book Mark) $1.00 per 100, $6.00 per 1000

_____ THE TWELVE PROMISES OF THE SACRED HEART TO ST. MARGARET MARY (Book Mark) $1.50 per 100, $13.00 per 1000 (Min. order 100)

HEAVEN—HELL—PURGATORY

_____ A NOTEBOOK ON THE DEVIL AND EXORCISM $1.25, 5 @ $1.00 ea.

_____ AN UNPUBLISHED MANUSCRIPT ON PURGA-TORY $1.25, 5 @ $1.00 ea.

_____ ANGELS OF GOD $4.95

_____ BEYOND SPACE—A BOOK ABOUT THE AN-GELS $3.00, 5 @ $2.50 ea., 10 @ $2.25 ea.

_____ BEGONE SATAN 75¢, 5 @ 60¢ ea., 10 @ 55¢ ea., 25 @ 50¢ ea.

_____ EVIDENCE OF SATAN IN THE MODERN WORLD $3.50, 5 @ $3.00 ea., 10 @ $2.75 ea.

_____ MARY CRUSHES THE SERPENT 75¢, 5 @ 65¢ ea.

_____ PURGATORY $3.50, 5 @ $3.00 ea., 10 @ $2.50 ea.

_____ PURGATORY AND HEAVEN $1.00, 5 @ 75¢ ea.

_____ SO HIGH THE PRICE $2.00, 5 @ $1.75 ea.

BIBLE HISTORY—CATECHISMS—HOLY BIBLE

_____ AN ILLUSTRATED CATHOLIC FAMILY CATE-CHISM
Book I $1.50, 10 @ $1.40 ea.
Book II $1.75, 10 @ $1.65 ea.
Book III $1.75, 10 @ $1.65 ea.

_____ BALTIMORE CATECHISM No. 3 $3.00, 5 @ $2.50 ea., 10 @ $2.25 ea., 25 @ $2.00, 50 @ $1.75 ea.

_____ BASIC TEACHING FOR CATHOLIC RELIGIOUS EDUCATION 60¢ ea.

_____ BIBLE HISTORY $3.00, 5 @ $2.50 ea., 10 @ $2.25 ea., 25 @ $2.00 ea., 50 @ $1.75 ea.

_____ CATECHISM FOR ADULTS $1.50, 10 @ $1.35 ea., 25 @ $1.25 ea.

_____ CATECHISM IN STORIES $3.95, 5 @ $3.60 ea.

_____ CATECHISM OF CHRISTIAN DOCTRINE $2.00, 10 @ $1.75 ea.

_____ CHILD'S BIBLE HISTORY $1.00, 5 @ 60¢ ea., 10 @ 50¢ ea., 25 @ 45¢ ea., 100 @ 40¢ ea., 500 @ 35¢ ea.

_____ FUNDAMENTALS OF CATHOLIC DOGMA $6.00
5 @ $5.00 ea. _____
_____ NEW TESTAMENT $2.00 _____
_____ OUR CATHOLIC FAITH set of 2 $4.25 _____
_____ ROME'S ANSWER $1.25 _____
_____ THE CATECHISM OF THE COUNCIL OF TRENT
Hard Cover $10.00, 5 @ $9.00, 10 or more $8.00
Paper $5.00, 5 @ $4.50, 10 or more $4.00 ea. _____
_____ THE CATHOLIC PICTURE BIBLE $4.50, 5 @
$4.00 ea. _____
_____ THE HOLY BIBLE $15.00 _____
_____ THE NEW SAINT JOSEPH BALTIMORE CATE-
CHISM
FIRST COMMUNION $1.25, 5 @ $1.15, 10 @ $1.05,
25 @ $1.00 _____
BOOK NUMBER ONE $1.50, 5 @ $1.40, 10 @ $1.30,
25 @ $1.25 _____
BOOK NUMBER TWO $1.60, 5 @ $1.50, 10 @ $1.40,
25 @ $1.35 _____
_____ THE PENNY CATECHISM 75¢, 10 @ 65¢ ea., 25 @
60¢ ea. _____

VOCATIONS—FAMILY LIFE AND MARRIAGE

_____ CHOOSE YOUR TOMORROW $1.25, 5 @ $1.00 ea. _____
_____ DARE TO DISCIPLINE $1.95, 5 @ $1.65 ea. _____
_____ THE HEAD OF THE FAMILY $3.75, 5 @ $3.25 ea. _____
_____ THE MAN FOR HER $1.95, 5 @ $1.75 ea. _____
_____ THE WIFE DESIRED $1.95, 5 @ $1.75 ea. _____

PROPHECY

_____ CATHOLIC PROPHECY $1.50, 5 @ $1.25 ea., 25 @
$1.00 ea. _____
_____ PROPHECY FOR TODAY $2.00, 3 or more $1.75 ea. _____
_____ THIS APOCALYPTIC AGE $1.00, 5 @ 75¢ ea., 10
@ 65¢ ea., 25 @ 60¢ ea. _____
_____ TRIMPHANT PEACE $3.00, 5 @ $2.50 ea. _____
_____ THE BOOK OF DESTINY $6.00, 2 @ $5.00 ea. _____
_____ THE LAST WORLD WAR AND THE END OF
TIME $3.50, 5 @ $3.00 ea. _____
_____ THE PROPHETS AND OUR TIMES $3.50, 5 @
$3.00 ea. _____

CHILDREN'S
PRE-SCHOOL—LOWER AND UPPER GRADES

_____ BLESSED MOTHER'S LAST CHRISTMAS $1.00,
5 or more 85¢ ea. _____
_____ FLAME IN THE NIGHT $1.95, 10 @ $1.75 ea. _____
_____ HER DREAM CAME TRUE $1.95, 10 @ $1.75 ea. _____
_____ HEROES OF GOD and HEROINES OF GOD 90¢ per
set, 5 @ 75¢ per set _____
_____ IN GARMENTS ALL RED 60¢, 5 or more 50¢ ea. _____
_____ JESUS AND I 75¢, 5 @ 65¢ ea. _____
_____ LIGHT IN THE GROTTO $1.95, 10 @ $1.75 ea. _____
_____ LOVE AS STRONG AS DEATH (ST. THECLA)
$1.95, 10 @ $1.75 ea. _____
_____ MARY'S PILGRIM $1.95, 10 @ $1.75 ea. _____
_____ MINIATURE STORIES OF THE SAINTS $1.00 per
set, 5 @ 90¢ per set. 4 booklets in set. _____
_____ MINITATIONS FOR TEENS $2.00, 5 @ $1.75 ea.,
10 @ $1.60 ea. _____
_____ MY FIRST COMMUNION 50¢, 5 @ 40¢ ea. _____

No. of Ea. Title		Total Amount
_____	MY JESUS AND I 50¢, 10 @ 40¢ ea.	_____
_____	MY ROSARY COLORING BOOK 40¢, 10 @ 35¢ ea., 25 @ 30¢ ea.	_____
_____	NO PLACE FOR DEFEAT (ST. PIUS V) $1.95, 10 @ $1.75 ea.	_____
_____	NOBLE LADY (ST. HELEN) $1.95, 10 @ $1.75 ea.	.
_____	OUR FRIENDS, THE SAINTS $1.30, 5 @ $1.00 ea.	_____
_____	OUR LADY AND THE AZTEC $1.00, 5 @ 85¢ ea.	_____
_____	PICTURE BOOK OF SAINTS $3.95, 5 or more $3.50 ea.	_____
_____	SACRED HEART—Color and Learn Book 85¢, 10 @ 75¢ ea.	_____
_____	ST. AGNES $1.00, 5 @ 85¢ ea.	_____
_____	SAINT BERNADETTE $1.00, 10 @ 85¢ ea.	_____
_____	SAINT DYMPHNA $3.95, 5 @ $3.50 ea.	_____
_____	ST. GERMAINE AND HER GUARDIAN ANGEL 85¢, 5 @ 75¢ ea.	_____
_____	ST. MARIA GORETTI 75¢ ea., 10 @ 65¢ ea., 25 @ 55¢ ea.	_____
_____	ST. MARTIN DE PORRES $1.00, 10 @ 85¢ ea.	_____
_____	ST. PANCRATIUS 60¢, 5 @ 50¢ ea.	_____
_____	THAT WONDERFUL NIGHT 65¢, 5 @ 50¢ ea.	_____
_____	THE COUNTRY ROAD HOME (ST. JOHN VIANNEY) $1.95, 10 @ $1.75 ea.	_____
_____	THE GIRL IN THE STABLE (ST. GERMAINE) $1.95, 10 @ $1.75 ea.	_____
_____	THE SEVEN SACRAMENTS—Coloring Book 35¢, 10 @ 30¢ ea.	_____
_____	WIND AND SHADOWS (JOAN OF ARC) $1.95, 10 @ $1.75 ea.	_____
_____	KATERI OF THE MOHAWKS COLORING BOOK 25¢ ea.; 5 or more 20¢ ea.	_____

SAVE OUR SCHOOLS

_____	CLASSROOM SEX EDUCATION—CANCEL IT—FOR KEEPS $2.50, 5 @ $2.00 ea.	_____
_____	HOW TO SURVIVE IN YOUR LIBERAL SCHOOL $7.95, 2 @ $7.00 ea.	_____
_____	OUR SCHOOLS AND THE FUTURE 25¢, 5 @ 20¢ ea.	_____

YOUTH

_____	HIPPIES, HINDUS, AND ROCK AND ROLL 95¢, 5 @ 85¢ ea.	_____
_____	THE DAY MUSIC DIED $2.95, 5 @ $2.50 ea., 10 @ $2.25 ea.	_____
_____	WHAT'S WRONG WITH ROCK AND ROLL 25¢, 10 @ 20¢ ea., 25 @ 15¢ ea.	_____

HEALTH

_____	BACK TO EDEN $2.95, 5 @ $2.50 ea.	_____
_____	BODY, MIND, AND SUGAR $1.25, 5 @ $1.10 ea.	_____
_____	BREADS YOU WOULDN'T BELIEVE $1.95, 5 @ $1.75 ea.	_____
_____	CIDER VINEGAR $1.25, 5 @ $1.00 ea.	_____
_____	CRUDE BLACK MOLASSES $1.25, 5 @ $1.00 ea.	_____
_____	DICTIONARY OF FOODS $1.95, 5 @ $1.65 ea.	_____
_____	THE HEART AND VITAMIN E $4.00, 5 @ $3.50 ea.	_____
_____	THE HERB BOOK $2.50, 5 @ $2.25 ea.	_____
_____	THE HERBALIST $5.95 ea.	_____
_____	HONEY AND YOUR HEALTH 95¢, 5 @ 85¢ ea.	_____
_____	HOW TO GROW YOUR OWN GROCERIES FOR $100 A YEAR $2.95, 5 @ $2.75 ea.	_____

_____	LAETRILE—CONTROL FOR CANCER $1.95, 5 @ $1.75 ea.	_____
_____	LET'S COOK IT RIGHT $1.95, 5 @ $1.75 ea.	_____
_____	LET'S EAT RIGHT TO KEEP FIT $1.95, 5 @ $1.75 ea.	_____
_____	LET'S GET WELL $1.95, 5 @ $1.75 ea.	_____
_____	LET'S HAVE HEALTHY CHILDREN $1.75, 5 @ $1.50 ea.	_____
_____	LIVE FOOD JUICES $3.00, 5 @ $2.50 ea.	_____
_____	MAKE YOUR JUICER YOUR DRUG STORE $1.95, 5 @ $1.75 ea.	_____
_____	MY WATER CURE $6.00, 5 @ $5.50 ea.	_____
_____	NATURE'S MIRACLE MEDICINE CHEST $1.45, 5 @ $1.25 ea.	_____
_____	OUR DAILY BREAD $2.00, 5 @ $1.75 ea.	_____
_____	RAW VEGETABLE JUICES $1.25, 5 @ $1.00 ea.	_____
_____	SILENT SPRING $1.25, 5 @ $1.00 ea.	_____
_____	STOCKING UP $8.95, 3 @ $8.00 ea.	_____
_____	ZONE THERAPY $1.25	_____

PATRIOTISM AND AMERICANISM

_____	LIBERTY ISSUE—Ideals Magazine $2.50, 5 @ $2.25 ea.	_____
_____	A NATION BUILT ON GOD $4.95, 5 @ $4.00 ea.	_____
_____	DISCOVERING HEROES OF THE AMERICAN REVOLUTION $1.00, 10 @ 85¢ ea.	_____
_____	GOD BLESS AMERICA—Ideals Magazine $1.95, 5 @ $1.75 ea.	_____
_____	OUR FIFTY STATES $1.00, 10 @ 85¢ ea.	_____
_____	THE AMERICAN MIRACLE, BICENTENNIAL REVIEW OF AMERICA'S PAST $1.00, 5 @ 85¢ ea.	_____
_____	THE REPUBLIC: DECLINE AND FUTURE PROMISE $2.95, 5 @ $2.50 ea.	_____

BOOKLETS

_____	ST. MICHAEL 25¢, 20 or more 20¢ ea.	_____
_____	ST. GERTRUDE, Herald of Divine Love 25¢, 20 or more 20¢ ea.	_____
_____	MERCY OF GOD DEVOTION 15¢, 25 or more 12¢ ea.	_____
_____	MY IDEAL 75¢, 5 or more 65¢ ea.	_____
_____	ST. ANTHONY MARY CLARET 35¢, 5 or more 30¢ ea.	_____
_____	ST. ANTHONY MARY CLARET NOVENA 35¢, 5 or more 30¢ ea.	_____
_____	KATERI TEKAKWITHA 25¢, 10 or more 20¢ ea.	_____
_____	CONSECRATION TO THE IMMACULATE HEART OF MARY 25¢, 10 or more 20¢ ea.	_____
_____	LIFE & MIRACLES OF ST. BENEDICT 75¢, 5 @ 65¢ ea., 25 or more 55¢ ea.	_____
_____	MENTAL PRAYER 25¢, 10 or more 20¢ ea.	_____
_____	INDULGENCED PRAYERS 35¢, 10 or more 30¢ ea.	_____
_____	DEVOTION TO THE INFANT OF PRAGUE 30¢, 10 or more 25¢ ea.	_____
_____	HEAVENLY COURT OF ST. LUTGARDE 45¢, 10 or more 40¢ ea.	_____
_____	CONFORMITY TO THE WILL OF GOD 25¢, 10 or more 20¢ ea.	_____
_____	TWO DIVINE PROMISES 45¢, 10 or more 40¢ ea.	_____
_____	BROTHER SAVE YOURSELF 25¢, 10 or more 20¢ ea.	_____
_____	ENTHRONEMENT OF THE SACRED HEART IN THE HOME 25¢	_____

_____ HOLY HOUR OF REPARATION 50¢, 10 or more 40¢ ea. _____

_____ OUR LADY OF PROMPT SUCCOR 30¢, 10 or more 25¢ ea. _____

_____ MY HEART SPEAKS TO THEE (LITTLE ROSE) 25¢, 10 or more 20¢ ea. _____

_____ MANUAL OF ST. JOSEPH 30¢, 10 or more 25¢ ea. _____

_____ ST. GERARD MAJELLA 50¢, 10 or more 45¢ ea. _____

_____ WHO IS TERESA NEUMANN? 75¢, 5 or more 65¢ ea. _____

_____ SECRET OF HAPPINESS 20¢ _____

_____ LITTLE WAY OF LOVE 15¢, 10 or more 10¢ ea. _____

_____ NOVENA TO THE HOLY SPIRIT 25¢, 10 or more 20¢ ea. _____

_____ NOVENA TO OUR SORROWFUL MOTHER 40¢, 10 or more 35¢ ea. _____

_____ NOVENA FOR RELIEF OF THE POOR SOULS IN PURGATORY 25¢, 10 or more 20¢ ea. _____

_____ NOVENA IN HONOR OF ST. ANTHONY 20¢ _____

_____ NOVENA TO ST. PETER J. EYMARD 25¢, 10 or more 20¢ ea. _____

_____ NOVENA BOOKLETS by Rev. L. G. Lovasik 10 or more assorted or single title 30¢ ea. _____

_____ POPE PIUS X 35¢ _____

_____ ST. ALPHONSUS—The Arthritis Saint 35¢ _____

_____ ST. PEREGRINE—The Cancer Saint 35¢ _____

_____ ST. DYMPHNA—Patron of Nervous & Emotionally Disturbed 35¢ _____

_____ ST. RAPHAEL 35¢ _____

_____ WAY OF THE CROSS 30¢, 10 or more 25¢ ea. _____

PRAYER BOOKS

_____ QUEEN OF APOSTLES $3.00 _____

_____ MY DAILY PRAYER $2.00, 5 or more $1.75 ea. _____

_____ MY DAILY BREAD
Duro Finish $2.00, 5 or more $1.75 ea.
Duro Deluxe Finish $3.00, 5 or more $2.75 ea. _____

_____ MY WAY OF LIFE, $3.00, 5 or more $2.75 ea. _____

_____ MY DAILY PSALM BOOK $1.75, 5 or more $1.50 ea. _____

_____ THE WHOLE STORY
Maroon Duro Finish $2.00, 5 or more $1.75 ea.
Maroon Duro Deluxe Finish $3.50, 5 or more $3.25 ea.
Genuine Leather $6.50, 5 or more $6.00 ea. _____

_____ MY IMITATION OF CHRIST $2.25, 5 or more $2.00 ea. _____

_____ JESUS, MARY, JOSEPH NOVENA MANUAL $1.00, 5 or more 85¢ ea. _____

_____ PEACE THROUGH THE BLOOD OF HIS CROSS $2.50, 5 or more $2.25 ea. _____

_____ PRECIOUS BLOOD AND MOTHER $2.00, 5 or more $1.75 ea. _____

_____ QUEEN OF HEAVEN $1.00, 5 - 24 @ 75¢ ea., 25 @ 65¢ ea. _____

ROSARIES FOR ADULTS & CHILDREN

_____ COCOA BEAD Black_____, Brown_____ $3.50, 2 or more $3.00 ea. _____

_____ WOOD BEAD Black_____, Brown_____ $3.00, 2 or more $2.50 ea. _____

_____ AURORA BOREALIS (Young Girls) Blue_____, Aqua_____, Crystal_____, Garnet_____ $2.50, 3 @ $2.00 ea., 5 or more $1.75 ea. _____

_____ AURORA BOREALIS (Ladies) Crystal_____, Light Blue_____, Dark Blue_____, Deep Purple_____, Garnet_____, Vitrolite_____ $4.25 ea., 3 @ $3.75 ea., 5 or more $3.25 ea. _____

_____ PLASTIC (Boys) Black_____, Brown_____ $1.35, 5 or more $1.00 ea. _____

_____ PLASTIC (Girls) Luminous_____, Pink_____, Multi-color_____ $1.35, 5 or more $1.00 ea. _____

_____ ROSARY BRACELET White_____, Light Blue _____, Pink_____, Pearl_____ $5.50 ea. _____

_____ ROSARY BRACELET Aurora Borealis, White Crystal_____, Light Blue Crystal_____ $9.95 ea. _____

_____ FAMILY ROSARY Black Wood_____, Brown Wood_____, Luminous Plastic_____ $2.00, 3 or more $1.75 ea. _____

RECORDS L.P. PATRIOTIC

_____ AMERICA THE BEAUTIFUL $5.50, 3 or more $5.00 ea. _____

_____ TO AMERICA WITH LOVE $5.95, 3 or more $5.50 ea. _____

_____ MINE EYES HAVE SEEN THE GLORY $5.95, 3 or more $5.50 ea. _____

_____ FAREWELL ADDRESS $5.95, 3 or more $5.50 ea. _____

RECORDS L.P. RELIGIOUS

_____ THE BEST LOVED CATHOLIC HYMNS $5.95, 3 or more $5.50 ea. _____

_____ THE LORD'S PRAYER $5.95, 3 or more $5.50 ea. _____

_____ HOW GREAT THOU ART $5.95, 3 or more $5.50 ea. _____

_____ CHRISTMAS ALBUM $5.95, 3 or more $5.50 ea. _____

TAPES

_____ TRIBUTE TO THOSE WHO HAVE OR NOW SERVE—THE MEANING OF OUR FLAG 7½ speed Reel_____, Cassette_____ $2.50 ea. _____

_____ GIVE ME LIBERTY OR GIVE ME DEATH 7½ speed Reel_____, Cassette $3.25 ea. _____

_____ WALK WITH ME—WAY OF THE CROSS Cassette $3.50 _____

FILMSTRIPS

_____ THE ROSARY STORY $30.00 postpaid _____
_____ THE GREEN SCAPULAR STORY $15.00 postpaid _____
_____ THE MIRACULOUS MEDAL $15.00 postpaid _____
_____ THE BROWN SCAPULAR $20.00 postpaid _____
_____ OUR AMERICAN HERITAGE $25.00 postpaid _____

Total_____

10% postage and handling_____

THE BIBLE AND THE PRESIDENTS—Professionally done, color, sound. Inquire about filmstrips. Includes one on Washington, Lincoln, Jefferson and Teddy Roosevelt. Ideal for the Bi-Centennial, all schools, clubs or Service Men groups. Descriptive folder sent on request, moderately priced. Available individually or as set of four.

Due to rising costs in printing and materials all prices are subject to change without notice.

Write for a list of assorted titles of slightly soiled books at ½ to ⅓ of regular price sent upon request.

GIVE THE
DIVINE MYSTERIES
OF THE
MOST HOLY ROSARY

To Friends, Neighbors, and Relatives. Ask Doctors, Nurses, and Clergy to give it to Patients at home or in the hospital. Also Parents to their children, students in college, high school or upper grades. Likewise to Clergymen, Religious Instructors, Editors and Writers of religious papers and magazines. Distribute it through your Church, Club or Society. Pass it out at meetings, when you travel, in motels, etc. Recommend it to your Book Stores and Library.

Do your part in this excellent spiritual effort. When you bring people closer to Christ, you bring our Country and World closer to Peace.

Help fulfill Our Lady's request so She can make good on Her Promise. "WHEN ENOUGH PEOPLE WILL PRAY THE ROSARY EVERY DAY, RUSSIA WILL BE CONVERTED AND AN ERA OF PEACE GRANTED TO THE WORLD."

For complete confidence in the Rosary, see back cover with the 15 promises of Mary to Christians who recite the Rosary.

QUANTITY PRICES

1 to 5 copies....	$1.00 ea.	100 copies.......	$.45 ea.
10 copies....	.75 ea.	500 copies.......	.35 ea.
25 copies....	.65 ea.	1000 copies.......	.25 ea.
50 copies....	.55 ea.		

Add 10% for postage and handling.
Wisconsin residents add 4% sales tax.
Postage on all foreign orders will be billed at exact amount.

J. M. J. BOOK CO.

P.O. Box 15   Necedah, Wisconsin 54646
Telephone (608) 565-2516